The Supreme Court and Religion in American Life

NEW FORUM BOOKS

Robert P. George, Series Editor

*A list of titles in the series appears at
the back of the book*

The Supreme Court and Religion in American Life

VOLUME II
FROM "HIGHER LAW" TO "SECTARIAN SCRUPLES"

James Hitchcock

PRINCETON UNIVERSITY PRESS

PRINCETON AND OXFORD

Copyright © 2004 by Princeton University Press
Published by Princeton University Press, 41 William Street,
Princeton, New Jersey 08540
In the United Kingdom: Princeton University Press, 3 Market Place,
Woodstock, Oxfordshire OX20 1SY

Library of Congress Cataloging-in-Publication Data
Hitchcock, James.
The Supreme Court and religion in American life / James Hitchcock.
p.   cm.
Includes bibliographical references and index.
ISBN: 0-691-11696-2 (v. 1 : alk. paper) —
ISBN: 0-691-11923-6 (v. 2 : alk. paper)
1. Church and state — United States — History.
2. Freedom of religion — United States — History. I. Title.
KF4865.H58 2004
342.7308'52—dc22   2004040722

British Library Cataloging-in-Publication Data is available

This book has been composed in Sabon
Printed on acid-free paper. ∞
pup.princeton.edu
Printed in the United States of America
1 3 5 7 9 10 8 6 4 2

CONTENTS

The Supreme Court and Religion in American Life

Introduction to Volume 2

THE FIRST VOLUME of this work sought to establish, by close attention to particular cases, that the Supreme Court's understanding of the Religion Clauses underwent substantial change over the years, especially after 1940. Volume Two seeks to understand those changes in the context of the continuing dialogue about the role of religion in public life.

While this volume identifies constitutional and legal issues, its purpose is just as much historical and sociological, less concerned with the technical aspects of Supreme Court jurisprudence than with the Court's view of the nature of religion and its role in society. The volume approaches the subject primarily within the context of the dominant liberalism of American public life, in terms of perennial themes such as the nature of personal freedom and the character of the nation at its founding.

Volume II presumes that readers are already familiar with the relevant cases, which are extensively summarized in Volume I. Thus in many instances in this volume particular cases are merely refered to, without precise citations, which can be found in the first volume.

As in Volume I, the terms "separationist" and "accommodationist" are used here in a commonsense way—separationists are people who believe that government should give as little support to religion as possible, accommodationists those who argue that it is proper for government to support religion provided it does not do so in ways that infringe religious liberties.

Chapter One

ORIGINAL INTENT

WHEN THE FIRST religion case came before the Court in 1815, the justices referred to the Founding Fathers not for constitutional guidance but merely on a legal point, finding that a postrevolutionary Virginia statute had revoked all colonial land grants made to the Anglican Church and placed them under the state, which had then properly and legally sold some of the land to particular congregations.[1] Throughout most of the nineteenth century the Court was far more likely to cite prerevolutionary English cases as precedents than the writings of the Founding Fathers.

Only in the first of the Mormon polygamy cases in 1878 were the intentions of the Founders finally deemed relevant to a case involving the Religion Clauses.

As many justices would later do, Chief Justice Waite recalled that in 1784 the state of Virginia had considered mandating official procedures for the teaching of Christianity but that this had been opposed by, among others, James Madison, and that not only had the bill been defeated but a proposal by Madison and Thomas Jefferson was adopted whereby religious liberty was guaranteed to Virginia citizens. Jefferson later expressed disappointment at the absence of an explicit guarantee of religious freedom in the new Federal Constitution, a provision that Madison was eventually able to obtain.[2]

In 1878, for the first time, the Court quoted the momentous phrase, "Wall of separation between Church and State," which Jefferson used in a letter to a group of Baptists, assuring them that the Constitution did not establish a state church. Waite, for the first time with reference to the Religion Clauses, treated the opinion of the Founders as normative: "Coming as this does from an acknowledged leader of the advocates of the measure, it may be accepted almost as an authoritative declaration of the scope and effect of the amendment thus secured."[3]

However, Jefferson had also written that man "has no natural rights in opposition to his social duties," Waite noted, and his conclusion from this was that "Congress was deprived of all legislative power over mere opinion, but was left free to reach actions which are in violation of social duties or subversive of good order."[4] He noted that, shortly after enacting its *Act Establishing Religious Freedom*, the Virginia legislature in 1789 had explicitly incorporated the English law against polygamy, including a provision for the death penalty, thus demonstrating that the Bill of Rights was not intended to protect polygamy.[5]

The Court's first appeal to the will of the Founders, ninety years after the adoption of the Constitution, was therefore dictated by the need to show that it was permissible under the Bill of Rights to restrict certain religious practices.

Returning to the issue in 1889, the Court in the person of Justice Bradley deemed it "sophistry" to argue that it had ever been the intention of the Founders that the Constitution should protect acts that were "abhorrent" and "uncivilized," asking sarcastically "what about thugee and human sacrifice?"[6]

Thus, besides their importance in establishing the principle that there were limits to religious liberty, the Mormon cases were significant in expressing for the first time the Court's view that in matters of religion the intention of the Founding Fathers was to be taken as an authoritative guide in interpreting the Religion Clauses.

In the *Holy Trinity* case (1892), holding that a federal law prohibiting bringing foreigners into the United States for purposes of employment did not apply to churches, Justice Brewer cast his net much wider than merely the Constitution, going back to the voyages of Christopher Columbus, which had been commissioned under an explicitly religious mandate, and to the establishment of the various English colonies. The Founders were invoked in connection with their reference to "the Creator" in the Declaration of Independence and in the fact that the Constitution (Article I, Section 7) exempted Sunday as a day of official government business. Various state constitutions contained explicitly religious expressions, and the official form of oaths ("so help me God"), legislative chaplains, sabbath laws, and other customs demonstrated the Christian character of the nation, Brewer argued.[7]

But for almost fifty years after the *Holy Trinity* case, the Court again virtually ignored the thought of the Founders as it sorted out the meaning of the Religion Clauses, failing to allude to the subject in dealing with, for example, public aid to religious institutions or conscientious objection to military service.

In the 1940 *Gobitis* case requiring Jehovah's Witnesses to salute the flag, Justice Frankfurter made merely a passing reference to the subject, observing that freedom of religion as guaranteed by the First Amendment had never been intended to imply an exemption from general laws binding all citizens.[8]

Three years later, in a case challenging licensing fees imposed on distributors of religious literature,[9] Justice Reed (albeit that his summary was only three paragraphs in length) made the fullest examination to date of the intentions of the Framers with respect to the Religion Clauses.

Several states, he recalled, had objected to the absence of a Bill of Rights from the proposed Constitution, whereupon a bill was drafted. Its chief drafter, Madison, was called upon at one point to explain the meaning of the Religion Clauses, and he stated that they meant that "no religion shall be established by law, nor shall the equal rights of conscience be infringed." Reed then found that there was no evidence Madison intended that this should grant an exemption from taxes. The Founders were well aware of the unpopular taxes that the royal government had imposed on the press, and they would have explicitly banned such fees had they intended to outlaw them.[10]

When, also in 1943, the Court reversed its position with respect to the flag salute, Justice Murphy quoted the *Virginia Statute for Religious Freedom* as an apt summary of the meaning of freedom of religion.[11]

On the opposite side of the same case, Frankfurter repeated his 1940 claim that the writings of the Founders provided no evidence whatever that religious freedom implied an exemption from generally applicable laws. Jefferson understood, Frankfurter insisted, that religious minorities could be disruptive forces in society and that it "never would have occurred to them [the Framers] to write into the Constitution the subordination of general civil authority to sectarian scruples."[12]

Frankfurter also made an argument with implications vastly wider than the Religion Clauses themselves, when he insisted that the Founders did not intend for the courts to have any role in the legislative process.[13]

In the 1944 case overturning the conviction of the leaders of the I Am Movement for mail fraud, Justice Douglas stated for the majority that the "Fathers of the Constitution" were aware of the variety of religious sects and their propensity for strife, and therefore they fashioned a document providing "the widest possible toleration of conflicting views." Each man was granted the right to worship as he chose and was to be answerable to no one for his beliefs.[14]

The 1947 *Everson* case laid down the principles of the modern jurisprudence of the Establishment Clause, and an integral part of that jurisprudence was a particular reading of the intention of the Founders. In their various opinions the justices made the most extensive summary of those intentions yet undertaken from the bench.

The Establishment Clause, Black reported in his majority opinion, reflected the determination by "early Americans" to prevent the recurrence of certain "evils, fears and political problems" that existed in colonial times. The immediate background to the colonization of America had been rampant religious persecution in Europe, the use of government power to enforce conformity. But, even though many people came to America to escape such persecution, such occurrences were often replicated in the New World, with Catholics, Quakers, and Baptists, among others, often being subject to discrimination or persecution.[15]

These practices eventually shocked the consciences of many Americans, and the Religion Clauses were enacted to prevent them, Black asserted, and he proceeded to summarize the events leading to Jefferson's and Madison's successful fight to defeat the proposed tax in support of religion, and their enactment of the *Statute for Religious Liberty.*[16]

The Court, according to Black, had previously recognized that these sentiments underlay the Religion Clauses. Some states at the time practiced religious discrimination, but the Fourteenth Amendment extended to them as well.[17]

In recent years, Black warned, the greatest threat to religious freedom had been attempts to offer some kind of public support to church schools and to introduce religious teachings into public schools. For the first time since 1878, the Court, through Black, now invoked Jefferson's metaphor of the "wall of separation of church and state" as defining the meaning of the Religion Clauses.[18]

Justice Jackson, in dissenting from the majority conclusion that the reimbursement of bus fares to students in religious schools was constitutional, did not find it necessary to refer to the intentions of the Founders.[19]

However, in his own dissent Justice Rutledge addressed an argument often made by critics of strict separationism, when he recalled that Madison intended to prohibit not merely an official state church but any form of public aid to religion. It was the Religion Clauses' aim "to create a complete and permanent separation of the spheres of religious activity and civil authority" by comprehensively forbidding every form of public aid or support for religion. Just as "religion," with respect to its free exercise, was to be understood in the broadest possible sense, so it was to be understood with respect to establishment as well.[20]

Rutledge became the first justice to refer explicitly to the personal views of Jefferson and Madison to explain the meaning of the Religion Clauses. Both, he noted, showed in their various writings that they intended to prohibit all forms of public aid to religion, such aid being subversive of liberty and good order, and Rutledge summarized in some detail the events culminating in Jefferson's *Statute for Religious Liberty.*[21]

Because of Madison's efforts in the Constitutional Convention, the Virginia struggle, according to Rutledge, became "part of the warp and woof of our constitutional tradition." Madison saw religion as "a wholly private matter" beyond the state's power to support or coerce, and "he sought to tear out the institution [establishment] not partially but root and branch, and to bar its return forever."[22]

Tithes had been the life blood of the colonial religious establishment, and thus it was crucial to the Founders' vision that all such financial support be prohibited. By the time the issue reached the Constitutional Con-

vention, it was so well understood, because of the Virginia debates, that it required little discussion and was readily enacted.[23]

The *Everson* decision was anomalous in that the majority and the minority agreed broadly on principles but disagreed sharply on their application. For Rutledge the use of tax money to support the busing of children to religious schools was precisely the kind of activity Jefferson and Madison opposed. Religion could not be free unless it was wholly independent of the state. Even indirect aid led to the kind of religious strife that the Founders above all sought to prevent.[24] Rutledge's dissent, even more than Black's majority opinion, laid out the broad arguments concerning the Founders that the later Court would come to accept as virtually self-evident.

In the *McCollum* case the following year, terminating a program of religious instruction in public schools,[25] Frankfurter, in a concurring opinion, noted that the "wall of separation" was a metaphor that could only be understood historically. Most colonial education had been religious in nature, but Madison's *Remonstrance*, "an event basic in the history of religious liberty," was called forth in part by a proposal for state support of such education in Virginia. Jefferson's wall was thus to be taken quite seriously, as a line that could not be breached.[26]

Jackson also concurred but found the issues troublesome, threatening as they did to flood the Court with various kinds of divisive questions. In conclusion he predicted that the Court's attempts to deal with these issues would lead to a "'wall of separation between church and state' as winding as the famous serpentine wall designed by Mr. Jefferson for the university [Virginia] he founded."[27]

In his dissent Reed proposed the argument often made by opponents of strict separation—that in referring to an "establishment of religion," the Founders may have meant merely an official state church, which Madison himself had indicated was his intention. Reed reviewed some of the evidence showing that Madison and Jefferson were not always strict separationists.[28]

But in nullifying a state law against sacrilege in 1953, Frankfurter dismissed the importance of the Founders' intentions:

> It would startle Madison, Jefferson, and George Mason, could they adjust themselves to our day, to be told that the freedom of speech which they espoused in the Bill of Rights authorizes a showing of the film 'The Miracle' from windows facing St. Patrick's Cathedral in the forenoon of Easter.

The principle of free expression, he insisted, "must be put in historical and legal contexts. The Constitution, we cannot recall too often, is an organism, not merely a literary composition."[29]

But, despite Frankfurter's prestige on the Court, his dismissal was largely ignored. When the Court again began to turn its attention to the Religion Clauses after 1960, it had already sketched out, at least embryonically, a view of the Founders' philosophy, and a reverence for their authority, that would serve as the foundation of the new jurisprudence.

In striking down in 1961 a Maryland law requiring all public officials to affirm the existence of God, Black, speaking for the Court, noted the prevalence of religious persecution in colonial times but also the fact that "wise and farseeing men" had spoken against it and had framed the Constitution to prevent all forms of discrimination.[30]

In upholding sabbath laws the same year, Chief Justice Warren found that the Establishment Clause was not merely designed to protect the free exercise of religion but also reflected Madison's fear that the establishment of religion would lead to tyranny and the subversion of civil authority.[31] However, Warren also argued that the prohibition of commerce on Sundays was not incompatible with the Bill of Rights, as shown by the fact that Madison himself approved a bill for punishing "sabbath-breakers," and at no time was it suggested that this was incompatible with Virginia's *Statute for Religious Liberty*.[32]

Frankfurter believed that the purpose of the Establishment Clause was to:

> assure that the national legislature would not exert its power in the service of any purely religious need; that it would not, as Virginia and virtually all of the Colonies had done, make religion, as religion, an object of legislation. The Establishment clause sought to withdraw the whole subject of religion from the competency of the legislature.[33]

However, Frankfurter too could acquiesce in the Court's judgment, because neither Jefferson nor Madison had regarded the sabbath laws as repugnant to religious freedom.[34]

Justice Douglas dissented in the case, without challenging the majority's reading of the Founders' intentions.[35]

The following year, in the *Engel* case prohibiting officially authorized prayers in public schools, Black recapitulated the majority's view of the Founders, recalling again that official establishments of religion, and even persecution, had existed in colonial times but had been vigorously and successfully opposed by, among others, Jefferson and Madison. The First Amendment was added to the Constitution to stand as a guarantee that neither the power nor the prestige of the federal government would be used to control, support, or influence the kind of prayers the American people could say. The people's religion should not be subjected to pressures of government each time a new political administration was elected to office.[36] The Founders knew that a prayer book officially prescribed in

England had provoked vigorous dissent, even persecution, and they were determined to prevent the same from happening in America.[37]

The fact that the prescribed New York prayer was brief and general made no difference, Black held, quoting Madison saying that it was "proper to take alarm at the first experiment on our liberties" and warning that the authority to establish Christianity in general as an official religion implied also the authority to establish a particular sect of Christianity.[38] In his concurring opinion Douglas warned that any form of public support for religion would lead to conflict, as Madison realized, and that such conflict would in time lead to the curtailment of religious liberties.[39]

Justice Stewart in dissenting offered a brief summary of what had become the minority argument. He found the Court's version of the religious history of the colonial period "unenlightening." The Founders wanted merely to disestablish an official state church, not ban religion from public life. "What is relevant," Stewart insisted, ". . . [is] the history of the religious traditions of our people, reflected in countless practices of the institutions and officials of our government," going on to cite practices such as the opening prayers of the Court itself and of Congress, the presidential oath of office, the National Anthem, the Pledge of Allegiance to the flag, and the phrase "In God We Trust" on coins. In the person of Douglas, the Court itself, in the *Zorach* case (1952), had affirmed that "We are a religious people whose institutions presuppose a Supreme Being." The authentic American tradition came from the Declaration of Independence, which avowed "a firm Reliance on the Protection of divine Providence," Stewart proclaimed.[40]

Stewart became the first justice to question the relevance of the "wall of separation," dismissing the Court's "uncritical" acceptance of what was a "mere metaphor" and reminding his fellow justices that it was a phrase not found in the Constitution.[41]

In the *Schempp* case the following year, prohibiting officially mandated readings from the Bible in public classrooms, Justice Clark acknowledged that the Founders believed in God and that religious influences were to be found in many aspects of early American public life. In his *Remonstrance* itself Madison had "earnestly" prayed for divine guidance. However, Madison and Jefferson also had views about religious freedom that came to be incorporated into the federal Constitution and those of most of the states, and concern for that freedom dictated that there be no officially sanctioned bible reading.[42]

In effect responding to Stewart's argument of the year before, Justice Brennan acknowledged that the Founders' first purpose was to prevent the establishment of an official church. Instead of merely using the word "church," however, they used the much broader term "religion." They intended to prohibit "interdependence" of government and religion, which would be detrimental to both.[43]

But Brennan also became the first justice to state candidly that the intentions of the Founders with respect to religion might not always be enlightening in a particular modern case. It was not clear whether Jefferson and Madison would have approved of devotional activities in the public schools, but even if they had, Brennan admitted, that would not be the final word. Of itself the Court had to determine whether the practices in question threatened the kind of danger against which the Founders had struggled. Their expressions were often vague, and evidence could be found on either side.[44]

Brennan was fairly certain that the Founders had not given specific thought to the question at hand, so preoccupied were they with opposing a formal establishment of religion, and public schools in the modern sense hardly existed in their day. The country had also become far more religiously diverse, to the point where practices that might have seemed unobjectionable at the time of the Founding were now offensive to many citizens, Brennan argued.[45]

He admitted that there was some plausibility in the argument that the Fourteenth Amendment did not make the Establishment Clause binding on the states, precisely because part of the Religion Clauses' purpose was to prevent Congress from disestablishing official churches in the various states. However, this was now irrelevant, since all state churches had been disestablished long before the adoption of the Fourteenth Amendment in 1868.[46]

Brennan also rejected the argument that the Fourteenth Amendment did not incorporate the Establishment Clause, because the 1868 amendment merely spoke of "rights," and the prohibition of the establishment of religion was not a right. The Founders, however, had intended the Establishment Clause to be a bulwark of protection for religious liberty, Brennan insisted, hence it was just as essential as the Free-Exercise Clause.[47]

In looking at the intentions of the Founders, it was necessary not only to scrutinize those, like Jefferson, who might be counted as secularists, but also, for example, the devout Baptist Roger Williams, founder of Rhode Island, who held similar views about the role of religion in public life, Brennan cautioned.[48] Despite uncertainties over the Founders' intentions on the question of religion in the public schools, Brennan thought that the Court's decision in the *Schempp* case was harmonious with what the Founders had intended to accomplish through the Religion Clauses.[49]

In dissenting, Stewart accepted the argument that the Fourteenth Amendment in some sense incorporated the Establishment Clause but thought the Court's interpretation of that clause was "insensitive." It was ironic, he noted, that a clause in part designed to prevent Congress from interfering with the religious arrangements of the various states was now used to the opposite effect.[50]

In broadening the concept of religious freedom in 1965, in order to include non-theists as conscientious objectors to military service, the Court did not make reference to the intentions of the Founders.[51]

In a 1968 case granting taxpayers standing to bring suit challenging the constitutionality of government grants,[52] Warren claimed that one of the fears of the Founders was that the taxing power would be used to favor one religion over another.[53]

In dissenting, Justice Harlan conceded that the use of taxation for any religious purpose was something to which some of the Founders might have objected. However, the precise purpose of the Establishment Clause was nonetheless obscure, and that purpose was not simply to enact the terms of Madison's *Remonstrance*. There was no evidence, Harlan argued, that the First Amendment was intended to impose specific limitations on government spending, beyond those stated elsewhere in the Constitution. Madison had supported a proposal for a Council of Revision that would oversee congressional actions, and the Framers had rejected that idea, but the Court now threatened to function precisely as such a body.[54]

In the *Walz* case (1970)[55] upholding tax exemptions for churches, Warren judged that the Court had so often rehearsed the history of the First Amendment that it was no longer necessary to do so, merely noting that in colonial times the term "establishment" included direct financial support for religious bodies. But in passing he went on to make a comment that seemed potentially subversive of the Court's prevailing jurisprudence of the Religion Clauses—that it was "not the most precisely drawn portion of the Constitution." This had led the Court to "internal inconsistencies," Burger thought, sometimes deriving from "too sweeping utterances on these clauses." To Burger and to the majority the Constitution permitted tax exemptions for religious bodies.[56]

Brennan, ordinarily a separationist, concurred, finding that the Founders had meant to prohibit involvements between religion and government that might be harmful to either, but that the tax exemption did not fit that category.[57] Brennan offered an extensive review of early policy on the issue. It did not arise during debates over the Bill of Rights, and this showed that the Framers could not have regarded it as an evil. The practice of the state of Virginia, immediately following the enactment of the Constitution, was instructive. While disestablishing the Anglican Church, it had also granted tax exemptions to churches. Beginning in 1802 the District of Columbia, under federal authority, had also begun granting such exemptions. Madison had sat in the Virginia legislature, and Jefferson was president when the District exemption was enacted, and neither protested. The absence of evidence as to their personal views on the subject seemed to show that they were not opposed.[58]

Brennan dismissed Madison's *Detached Memorandum* as possibly an "extreme view" that Madison may have reached only late in life and that did not reflect the intentions of the Founders when they drafted the Constitution. There was no evidence, Brennan said, that Madison held such opinions in the 1780s, and, if he did, they were not shared by others.[59]

In dissenting, Douglas argued that Madison's warning that not even three pence of the citizens' money should go to a church was obviously applicable to the case at hand, and the justice cited Madison's opposition to even indirect support for religious bodies. Madison had warned against the possibility that ecclesiastical wealth would swell to a dangerous level, which Douglas believed had by now occurred.[60]

In his concurring opinion in the *Lemon* case in 1971,[61] Douglas again cited the *Remonstrance* and recalled that Madison had warned that public support of religion would destroy the harmony that existed among the various sects.[62] Brennan, in his concurrence in the *Lemon* case, recalled that conflict over the religious nature of education had occurred even in colonial times and that Jefferson, among others, had tried unsuccessfully to establish a public system of education. But private religious education continued to be normal long after the Revolution. Brennan found any form of public funding for religious schools contrary to the Founders' intentions.[63]

On the same occasion the Court in the *Tilton* case found that various kinds of public aid to religiously affiliated colleges were permissible. Douglas dissented, and in conclusion exclaimed, "It is almost unbelievable that we have made the radical departure from Madison's Remonstrance memorialized in today's decision." Madison had warned against the expenditure of three pence, whereas the *Tilton* program involved millions of dollars.[64] The next year he expressed the same outrage in a minor case concerning school aid, where he asserted that "The rule of no subsidy has been dominant since the days of Madison."[65]

In the same year, in recognizing the right of the Amish not to send their children to high school, Burger recalled that in Jefferson's time there had been no system of universal compulsory education, and observed that the Amish community embodied many of the qualities that Jefferson thought made the ideal citizen.[66]

In 1973, in again invalidating certain kinds of public aid to religious schools, Justice Powell once more cited Madison's *Remonstrance*. Despite Madison's warning, and the concurrence of other of the Founding Fathers, it had never been possible to "sanitize" the relationship between church and state, Powell feared, but neither had Jefferson's wall ever been breached.[67] In partially concurring in a 1977 decision that allowed some forms of indirect public aid to religious schools, Powell observed that the modern situation was far removed from that at the time of the Founders, in that there was now little danger of any particular sect becoming established, or of its gaining control over the government.[68]

The next year, the Court struck down a Tennessee law prohibiting clergy from holding public office.[69] Burger, writing for a unanimous Court, noted that the exclusion had been a part of the Tennessee constitution when that state entered the Union in 1796, reflecting a common fear at the time that clergy might exercise undue influence in politics. Others of the original states had similar provisions. Jefferson urged such a provision for the Virginia constitution, but Madison dissuaded him, arguing that such would be a violation of religious liberty.[70]

In a concurring opinion, Brennan argued that the fact that some of the Founders favored such an exclusion did not give the provision constitutional warrant. Pointedly, the Framers had not placed a similar provision in the federal Constitution, and there were numerous state laws at the time which were not harmonious with the federal document.[71]

In a 1981 case involving the rights of a Jehovah's Witness who refused to work in an armaments factory, Justice Rehnquist charged that the Court viewed the Establishment Clause and the Free-Exercise Clause as in tension with each other but such tension did not exist at the time of the Framers. It had arisen because of the growth of the welfare state and because of the Court's ruling that the Fourteenth Amendment incorporated the Bill of Rights.[72]

The following year, in his minority opinion opposing the gift of an unused army hospital to a religiously affiliated college, Brennan found it desirable once again to rehearse the early history of the Establishment Clause—America was settled by people many of whom were fleeing religious persecution; nonetheless persecution was inflicted even in America; this shocked many people and led to the Bill of Rights; and one of the purposes of the Establishment Clause was to prohibit even the smallest payment of public money to religious groups. In upholding the hospital gift, the Court showed itself hostile to the Framers' intention, Brennan charged.[73]

In a case the same year disallowing a church from exercising veto power over the granting of a liquor license, Burger stated that it was the Founders' intention that religion and government be "insulated" from each other. Jefferson's "wall" was "a useful figurative illustration." While in modern times some involvement of religion and government would be unavoidable, the wall should nonetheless never be breached.[74]

The *Marsh* case of 1983, upholding the constitutionality of legislative chaplains turned closely on the intention of the Founders. Burger rehearsed the long history of prayers an chaplaincies in various legislatures dating back to the Continental Congress. The actions of the earliest Congress were a reliable guide to the Founders' intentions, he asserted.[75]

Responding to Brennan's point in *Schempp* (1963) that some of the Founders had opposed legislative prayer, Burger argued that this in fact strengthened the case by showing that the issue had been carefully considered. The argument against prayer was that the members of the Continental Congress were too religiously divided to agree on a form, but Samuel Adams had announced that it was possible for him to join in any prayer offered by "a friend to his country." This debate showed that prayer was not intended to be a government endorsement but rather an exercise that "harmonized with the tenets of some or all religions."[76]

In his dissent Brennan found it significant that the name of God was not invoked in either the Constitution or the Articles of Confederation that preceded it. As president, both Jefferson and Andrew Jackson had refused to proclaim national days of thanksgiving, citing the Establishment Clause as their guide. Madison, sometime after his own presidency, specifically questioned the constitutionality of legislative chaplains.[77]

Brennan did not find significant the fact that the Framers permitted legislative prayers, since under the pressures of the moment legislators often "do not pass sober constitutional judgment on every piece of legislation they enact." Madison voted for the legislative chaplains that he later regarded as unconstitutional, a change of position that Brennan thought was less a change of mind than of "position"—Madison had moved from being a legislator "engaged in the hurley-burley of legislative activity" to being a detached observer. The Bill of Rights was forced on Congress by the states, and it could not necessarily be assumed that everything Congress did was consistent with that Bill.[78]

But according to Brennan, the Court's majority was also treating the Constitution as a static document, when in fact its interpretation had to change in each age in order to be faithful to its original purpose. "[T]he members of the First Congress should be treated not as sacred figures whose every action must be emulated, but as the authors of a document meant to last for the ages," Brennan concluded.[79] Brennan's opinion was significant in that one of the justices counted as a separationist acknowledged that the intentions of the Founders were not necessarily authoritative and that other criteria of constitutionality needed to be invoked.

In the same year, Rehnquist, from the opposite side of the judicial spectrum, observed in a school-aid case that modern America was far removed from the situation that existed when the Constitution was adopted. There was no longer any danger of sectarian control over government, or even of deep divisions along religious lines.[80] His claim, made almost in passing, suggested that the Court, from both sides of the ideological divide, was moving away from the authority of the Founders as its chief warrant for interpreting the Religion Clauses.

The following year, in the first of two cases concerning Christmas displays on public property, Burger characterized the "wall" metaphor as "not a wholly accurate description of the relationship that in fact exists between church and state," then repeated the historical evidence from the *Marsh* case.[81]

In his dissent Brennan noted that at the time of the founding of the nation, the celebration of Christmas, either as a religious or a secular feast, was not common in America and was even religiously divisive because of Puritan opposition. Thus the Founders could not have discovered a generally acceptable view of how Christmas should be observed, and they must have regarded it as "at least a sensitive matter." Some of those groups that opposed the public celebration of Christmas, such as Baptists, were also strong opponents of any kind of established religion, while some of those who did celebrate it—Anglicans and Catholics—were associated with state churches. Christmas did not become a legal holiday until well into the nineteenth century.[82]

In the *Jaffree* case the following year, prohibiting an officially authorized "moment of silence" in the public schools, Justice O'Connor reminded the Court that public education did not exist at the time of the Founders, thus they could not have foreseen the question. That did not, however, excuse the Court from trying to discern the Founders' probable intentions on the basis of their general principles, which she thought supported the majority decision.[83]

In his dissent Rehnquist made the most extensive criticism of the majority's Religion Clauses jurisprudence that any justice had ever mounted.

Jefferson's "wall" metaphor had for almost forty years been used by the Court in a misleading manner, Rehnquist insisted. Jefferson was on a diplomatic mission to France when the Bill of Rights was drafted, and he used the "wall" image in a "short note of courtesy" written some years after the Bill was adopted. He was scarcely a reliable guide as to the Framers' intentions.[84]

Madison, on the other hand, did play a key role, but a role often misunderstood. The very idea of the Bill of Rights had been a concession to some of the states that were reluctant to ratify the Constitution because of their fear of the power of the federal government, and Madison, sought to allay those fears.[85]

Madison's first proposed text for the Religion Clauses was considerably different from that which was eventually adopted, and there had been some debate on the matter, although Rehnquist found the record of the debate unenlightening. Madison, in the debate, said that he sought to allay the fear that one religious group, or a combination of several groups, might succeed in establishing a religion and forcing others to conform. Although Madison played a key role, the final Religion Clauses were the result of extensive debate and of committee action. His role was essentially that of "an advocate of sensible legislative compromise." He did not seek to incorporate the *Virginia Statute for Religious Freedom* into the Bill of Rights, and originally had opposed even having such a bill.[86]

The history of the adoption of the Bill of Rights showed that Madison merely opposed what he called a "national church" and wanted to prevent discrimination among religions, Rehnquist insisted. Madison did not intend the government to be neutral between religion and irreligion, and the modern Court was "totally incorrect" in holding that Madison intended to incorporate the *Virginia Statute* into the Bill of Rights. The debates over the Religion Clauses showed that the other Framers shared Madison's view of its purpose.[87]

The adoption by Congress of the Northwest Ordinance and other early legislation demonstrated this fact, Rehnquist continued, since some of those laws explicitly made provision for the support of religion. The Northwest Ordinance was enacted at the very time Congress was debating the Religion Clauses and could hardly have been at odds with the intended effect of the latter.[88]

Even before the Religion Clauses had been adopted, Congress asked President Washington to proclaim a day of thanksgiving to God, which he did. The Congressmen proposing this proclamation were among those supporting the Religion Clauses, clearly showing that they saw no conflict between the two, Rehnquist argued. As presidents, Adams and Madison also issued thanksgiving proclamations, although Jefferson did not, holding such a practice to be entirely a matter of private piety. However, he and all subsequent presidents and congresses throughout the nineteenth century supported grants made to religious schools for the eduction of Indians.[89]

Rehnquist also noted that classical nineteenth-century commentators on the Constitution, such as Justice Story and Thomas Cooley, explicitly stated that it was not the Framers' intention to promote religious indifference, that in fact they wished to promote Christianity.[90]

The "wall" metaphor, Rehnquist charged, was useless and misleading, lacking both historical foundation and practical usefulness. He recalled Justice Cardozo's warning that "metaphors in law are to be narrowly watched, for starting as devices for liberating thought, they end often by enslaving it." The "wall" metaphor, Rehnquist insisted, had been crucially misleading and should be "frankly and explicitly abandoned."[91]

If earlier both Rehnquist and Brennan seemed to say that probing the intention of the Founders was a dubious exercise for the modern Court, Rehnquist now concluded that the Founders' principles were real and should "control" later decisions. "Any deviation from [the Framers'] intentions frustrates the permanence of that Charter and can can only lead to the kind of unprincipled decision-making that has plagued our Establishment Clause cases since *Everson*." Nothing in the Framers' intention required the government to be neutral between religion and irreligion, Rehnquist concluded, and they would have been shocked to learn that the Bill of Rights somehow prevented a state legislature from "endorsing" prayer.[92]

Rehnquist's dissent in the *Jaffree* case was the strongest frontal attack against the prevailing jurisprudence of the Religion Clauses ever mounted within the Court itself.

In 1989, when the Court forbade the display of a religious Christmas scene on public property, Justice Blackmun held for the majority that the Framers had enacted the Establishment Clause precisely because of the religious diversity of the American people. At one time the protection of the Religion Clauses may have been thought to apply only to Christians, but that was no longer true.[93]

The following year, in a case in effect decreeing that American Indians did not have a constitutional right to use a prohibited drug in their religious rituals, O'Connor dissented in part by arguing that the Founders' purpose for the Free-Exercise Clause was precisely to protect the rights of those whose religious beliefs were not shared by the majority.[94]

In the 1992 case prohibiting officially authorized prayers at a public high school graduation ceremony,[95] Kennedy noted that Madison opposed all forms of establishment not only because of its affects on religious dissenters but also because it weakened the "the purity and efficacy of religion."[96] In effect Kennedy argued that the Establishment Clause was designed by the Framers to protect the integrity of religion.

In a concurring opinion Justice Souter conceded that an argument had been made that the Establishment Clause merely demanded equality among all faiths, but he did not think the argument strong enough to require the Court to rethink its traditional position.[97]

Like Rehnquist before him, he offered a detailed account of the legislative history of the Religion Clauses. The reasons for the numerous textual changes were no longer clear, but Souter thought it significant that the indefinite article was used before the word "establishment"—if the Framers merely wanted to prohibit a state church, they would probably have said "the establishment." As it was, they seem to have intended the clause to have broad application.[98]

Souter responded to Rehnquist's extensive dissent in the *Jaffree* case. Thanksgiving proclamations he dismissed as rather "trivial," while the long practice of appropriating public money to Indian schools of a religious nature merely showed that public officials could sometimes turn "a blind eye" to the Constitution. Madison as president opposed official proclamations of thanksgiving and yielded only under political pressure during the War of 1812; he later admitted to "backsliding" on the issue.[99]

Souter concluded that at best the early practices of the Republic showed that the Framers did not all share the same view of the Religion Clauses and, at worst, that they were politicians who sometimes acted against their principles. It might no longer be possible to know exactly what the Framers intended, but there was a respectable body of opinion that understood the Establishment Clause to have broad application.[100]

Justice Scalia in dissenting noted that public prayer had a long history in the United States. Washington, Jefferson, and Madison all prayed at their presidential inaugurations, and Jefferson invited those in attendance to pray with him. Although the Founders had been concerned about religious dissension, they also knew, Scalia claimed, that nothing would generate tolerance better than citizens "voluntarily joining in prayer offered to the God whom they all worship and seek."[101]

The case was significant in that, even though it embodied the Court's now traditional separationist interpretation, a member of the majority acknowledged that the historical evidence as to the Founders' intentions was ambiguous, and admitted that the separationist majority's position could not be derived with complete certitude from those intentions.

The following year, in a case upholding the rights of a student religious group in a public high school, Scalia characterized as a "strange notion" the idea that the Religion Clauses, which he said endorsed "religion in general" through the Free-Exercise Clause, simultaneously also forbade religion through the Establishment Clause. The Founders valued religion as inculcating virtues supportive of the public good, Scalia declared.[102]

In the 1995 case dissolving a New York State school district that had been organized along religious lines, Scalia in his dissent exclaimed that the Founders would have been astounded that the Religion Clauses, which had been enacted to prevent religious oppression, were now actually being used by the Court to thwart religious liberty.[103]

In the *Rosenberger* case the same year, upholding the right of a student religious publication to receive funding from a state university, there occurred another long and sharp debate over the intention of the Founders.

Justice Thomas voted with the majority but wrote a lengthy concurring opinion of his own, specifically to refute the reading of history offered by the dissenters. The controversy in early Virginia over the proposal to impose a tax for support of the clergy, even if taken as indicative of the purpose of the Religion Clauses, did not show that the government must discriminate against religion, Thomas insisted. The Virginia proposal was rejected because it would not have benefited everyone equally but was specifically aimed at the support of the clergy and the dissemination of

Christian doctrine. In his *Remonstrance*, Madison focused specifically on the bill's discriminatory provisions.[104]

Madison never held that religious institutions must be excluded from benefits that are generally available, or that monetary benefits conferred by the government are somehow different from other kinds, Thomas argued. Madison objected to the disputed proposal because it singled out religion for benefits and was therefore not neutral.[105]

Noting the continuing dispute as to whether the Establishment Clause forbade the government to aid religion in any direct way, Thomas found more plausible the claim that it merely required neutrality among the various creeds. Madison's *Remonstrance*, once again, was aimed primarily at perceived inequalities.[106]

The dissenters on the Court were themselves acting contrary to Madison's *Remonstrance*, Thomas charged, in that religious students at the state university were being treated unequally. Even in his 1776 proposal to disestablish the Anglican Church in Virginia, which was not accepted, Madison merely proposed that no one should receive special privileges by virtue of religion.[107]

However, Thomas also thought that the views of only one man, Madison, were not determinative—the first time any justice had suggested that Madison's authority was less than absolute as to the meaning of the Religion Clauses.[108]

Madison's views aside, there had been direct public funding of religious activity from the beginning of the nation, Thomas noted, as in the hiring of legislative chaplains, a practice in which Madison acquiesced. In early Virginia, public money was sometimes used to support education that was religious in nature, and Jefferson recommended professorships of religion in the state university he founded (a university that was the defendant in the very *Rosenberger* case then being resolved).[109]

Souter's dissent restated the traditional separationist argument concerning the Religion Clause. To Souter, Madison's authority for interpreting the Religion Clauses was "well settled." The *Remonstrance* was written against a background in which practically every colony taxed its citizens for the support of religion, and Madison clearly opposed this custom. The proposed Virginia tax against which Madison fought was in fact "even-handed," in that it allowed citizens to choose to not have any of their taxes go to religious bodies, in which case the money would be used for education. Thus even secular schools would have benefited. Notwithstanding this provision, Madison still opposed the bill. While he did note certain features of it that he thought treated different groups unequally, this was by no means the only reason for his opposition.[110]

It was not relevant, Souter argued, that Madison, in fighting to disestablish the Anglican Church in Virginia in 1776, did not oppose all public

aid to religion, since that was not the issue at hand. As it was, his disestablishment proposal was considered too radical by most of his colleagues,
and he would hardly have pushed an even more radical idea at the time.
If Madison passively cooperated in the hiring of a congressional chaplain,
he later opposed the practice and said that it was done "not with my
approbation."[111] Citing early legislative acts was not relevant, Souter
thought, since Congress was capable of acting inconsistently, and not always in accord with the highest constitutional principles.[112]

Also in 1995, in dissenting in a case that upheld the right of the Ku
Klux Klan to erect a cross in a public square, Justice Stevens said the
issue showed the importance of "rebuilding Thomas Jefferson's Wall of
Separation." He also cited Black's opinion in the *Everson* case concerning
the Founders' fear of religious strife.[113]

The issue returned again with some force in a 1997 case—*City of
Boerne*—in which the Court overturned the Religious Freedom Restoration Act. In her dissent, O'Connor argued that the Founders had intended
the Free-Exercise Clause to have broad meaning. Despite the misgivings
of some of them, the Bill of Rights was enacted in order to allay the fears
of those who were suspicious of the federal government's power over
individuals. She acknowledged, however, that it was not immediately obvious what "the free exercise thereof" was supposed to mean.[114]

To clarify its meaning she surveyed colonial American history to show
that some colonies had at certain times guaranteed religious liberty to
their residents. Quite early in the history of the United States the Northwest Ordinance extended that right to the Western territories.[115]

The key issue, according to O'Connor, was the Founders' view that
religious liberty superseded ordinary legislation and was only to be
abridged in extreme cases. The fact that some state constitutions explicitly
excluded from religious liberty such things as "subversion" or "disturbing
the peace" showed that, aside from those exceptions, it was understood
to have a broad meaning.[116] In Virginia the debate between Madison and
George Mason over the text of a statute for religious freedom showed,
according to O'Connor, that both sides understood that such liberty included exemption from generally applicable laws, which was the general
view at the time the Constitution was ratified.[117]

Madison asserted that duties to God were superior to those to the state,
and Jefferson explicitly stated that religious freedom could be infringed
only when "principles break out in overt acts against peace and good
order." In writing to a group of Quaker conscientious objectors, George
Washington indicated that government should attempt to accommodate
itself to citizens' religious scruples.[118]

Scalia's concurring opinion in the case was largely an attempt to refute
O'Connor's reading of the Founding Fathers. To him the colonial record

went against her claim, in that none of the colonies recognized that religious freedom required an exemption from a general law. The remarks by Jefferson and others that freedom could be curtailed only when it endangered the social order were in harmony with the Court's disputed *Smith* decision of 1990 refusing to recognize a religious right to use illegal drugs in a religious ceremony, a decision that O'Connor was now trying to get reversed. In the early days of the country, terms such as "keeping peace and order" simply meant obeying the law.[119]

The Founders did not believe that individuals had to be violent or openly disruptive in order to exceed the limits of religious liberty,[120] and the fact that government sometimes chose to accommodate itself to religious scruples, as in the case of the Quakers, did not mean that it was obligated to do so by the Constitution. Madison did not claim that the proposed tax in Virginia would violate religious freedom but that it would establish religion, and in writing to the Quakers, Washington merely expressed a personal wish, not a constitutional mandate.[121]

If O'Connor's sweeping view of the Free-Exercise Clause had indeed been the view of the Founders, Scalia argued, there would have been a good deal of litigation over it in the early decades of the country's history, but in fact there was practically none.[122]

In dissenting in a 2000 case prohibiting student-led prayers at high school football games, Rehnquist invoked the authority of the Founders to the same effect as Scalia, reminding the Court of Washington's public prayers and his proclamation of a day of thanksgiving while president.[123]

But in the same year, Souter, dissenting in a case permitting the use of public money to provide private schools with computers and other equipment,[124] invoked the Founders' authority to the opposite purpose. The Establishment Clause, he argued, was to be understood in terms of Madison's insistence that "not even three pence" of public money should be used for religious purposes.

In voting against educational "vouchers" in 2002, Souter lamented "the enormity of the violation" of the Establishment Clause and again cited Madison as expressing the intention of the Framers.[125]

Chapter Two

PATTERNS OF ESTABLISHMENT

The separationist philosophy of church-state relations predated the Constitution itself by several years, having been forged in the battle to disestablish the Anglican Church in Virginia at the time of the Revolution.

The effort at disestablishment, at first unsuccessful, was eventually completed principally through the efforts of James Madison and Thomas Jefferson, during the years 1784–86. By that time the Anglican Church in Virginia was weak and demoralized, and disestablishment was effected through a coalition of "enlightened" Anglicans like Jefferson and Madison and "low-church" Protestants who had suffered at Anglican hands.[1]

But the formal disestablishment of Anglicanism was far less controversial than a subsequent proposal to continue supporting religion through taxation, the money to be distributed equitably among the various churches. The coalition that had achieved disestablishment now fell apart, as Madison and Jefferson vehemently opposed any kind of public support of religion, while their former Presbyterian allies endorsed the assessment bill. The bill was defeated largely through Madison's energy and skillful political maneuvering,[2] as most of the Dissenters who were the putative beneficiaries of disestablishment did not accept Madison and Jefferson's separationist position.[3]

Madison's objection to the assessment bill was ostensibly that it favored Christianity, but not its doctrines, over other religions (at a time when there were practically no non-Christians in Virginia), but he probably would not have supported a broader bill.[4] His insistence that even the smallest amount of public support for religion violated the liberty of the taxpayers became one of the pillars of the separationist position, and his *Memorial and Remonstrance*[5] became one of its sacred texts, a passionate declaration of the need for religion to remain wholly free of any kind of political involvement.

For eighteenth-century Americans, "establishment" meant the privileged legal status of a single church, and it is unlikely that many people had thought about the possibility of multiple establishments, that is, public support of all religious groups. Madison drew on the prevalent belief that tax support of religion was in itself a violation of religious liberty.[6]

After the defeat of the assessment bill, the legislature adopted the *Virginia Statute for Religious Freedom* (1786),[7] of which Jefferson was the

principal author, which became the model for the later American understanding of the free exercise of religion.[8] But Jefferson tended to limit
freedom of religion to "opinion" only, considering such liberty safe because abstract philosophical and theological ideas could not really moti-
vate human behavior.[9] (He may also have limited religious liberty to
"opinion" in order to mollify slaveowners' fears that untrammeled religion would inspire abolitionism.)[10]

But even before the Constitution was ratified, Jefferson and Madison
had provided the theoretical basis for separationism, which they saw as
the only philosophy appropriate to the new nation, and as public officials,
they attempted to implement that philosophy. For example, as president
(1809–17), Madison vetoed Congressional bills incorporating an Episcopal church in the District of Columbia and appropriating land for a Baptist church in the Territory of Mississippi.[11] He also vetoed a bill exempt-
ing from taxation the printing plates of Bible societies, although he signed
two similar bills.[12]

However, although their theoretical commitment to strict separationism was unambiguous, neither Jefferson nor Madison was entirely
consistent.

Thus in 1789, Madison was a member of a committee that recommended the appointment of a chaplain for the House of Representatives,
and unlike Jefferson, he did proclaim days of prayer and thanksgiving
while president.[13]

Jefferson's *Statute for Religious Freedom* was one of five bills concerning religion that he helped draft during the mid-1780s, none of which
manifested a separationist position. One of those bills preserved some of
the property of the Anglican Church, vesting it in the members of the
parish at large rather than in a committee. Another authorized the punishment of sabbath-breakers, a third provided for official days of fasting and
prayer, and yet another authorized the punishment of those entering into
marriages "contrary to Levitical law" (bigamy or polygamy).[14]

The official days of thanksgiving that Jefferson would refuse to proclaim while in the White House, he did proclaim while governor of Virginia,[15] and his strict separationism seems to have applied mainly to the
federal government, not to the states.[16] But even as president, Jefferson
habitually used religious language in his public statements.[17] In 1803 he
acquiesced in a proposal for federal support of a Catholic priest to work
among the Indians.[18] Beginning in 1787, Congress periodically granted
land to the Moravian Brethren for the same work, and Jefferson acquiesced in the renewal of those grants during his presidency,[19] as well as
in the continued support of military chaplaincies and an official policy
encouraging soldiers and sailors to attend religious services.[20]

One of his proudest achievements was the establishment of the University of Virginia, and from the beginning, he provided for religious instruction there, at a time when there was no concept of purely secular higher education. Christian morality was to be inculcated, and students were to be taught arguments for the existence of God. There were, however, to be no theological readings as such, and students were to be taught only those religious ideas about which all faiths could agree. Particular religious groups could establish houses "in the confines of the university" where students could worship and be instructed in their various faiths.[21]

There were in reality two different Jeffersonian positions with regard to religion, the distinction between them not always recognized. One was the high road of constitutional principle—full religious liberty and complete impartiality by government in its treatment of religious groups. But what might be called the Jeffersonian low road involved strong personal intolerance in religious matters, a tendency to invoke separationist principles to promote the kind of religion Jefferson himself favored and to inhibit that which he opposed.

Jefferson was raised an Anglican and remained a member of the Episcopal Church all his life. Occasionally, in an ecumenical spirit, he gave financial support to other churches. However, in some respects he was a kind of Deist, who believed that a supreme being governed the universe but that the will of the deity was discoverable only through reason and that claims of divine revelation were fraudulent.[22]

For a time inclined to a negative view of Christianity in general, in the 1790s he became persuaded of the truth of Unitarianism, in which Jesus was seen not as divine but as the world's greatest moral teacher. Jefferson concluded that Unitarianism was the appropriate religion for free Americans and hoped to see the day when a majority of the people would adhere to that creed.[23]

As a Unitarian, Jefferson described himself as a "real Christian," insisting that traditional claimants to that name had corrupted the message of Jesus, especially through the importation of Platonic philosophy, which had spawned the deformity of religious dogma. He was especially fierce in his condemnations of the Apostle Paul and of John Calvin, and he detested the Presbyterian clergy who had been his allies in the battle for disestablishment in Virginia.[24]

Since he considered Unitarianism appropriate for America largely because of its nondogmatic spirit, for Jefferson the embrace of liberal religion also required the condemnation of all that he considered illiberal. Dogma necessarily made Christians intolerant, he charged, and he did not even credit his religious opponents with sincerity. In 1783 he opposed allowing clergy to hold public office, although he was later persuaded otherwise by Madison.[25] For Jefferson an appropriate American religion should be based on the moral and intellectual capacity of the laity to judge the teachings of their clergy, parallel to the democratic system in which they held their political leaders to account.[26] He did not consider religion, except in the most general sense, as an important motive for human behavior, and his spirit of tolerance grew partly out of his lack of respect for most religious beliefs.[27]

Jefferson in fact could find no place for organized religion in the public sphere, and his resolution of the problem of religious diversity required all groups to accept their status as mere "sects," a condition, arguably, not of genuine religious freedom but "a means by which the diversity of strange and peculiar opinions could be shipped off into a non-public (if not foreign) backwater." He hoped that, by bringing these diverse groups together at his new state university, the power of each could be neutralized.[28]

Jefferson was greatly interested in the Dartmouth College dispute, where his sympathies lay entirely with the attempt to transform the college into a state university and to liberalize its curriculum.[29] Thus the Supreme Court's decision in the case (1819) in part thwarted his ambition of reforming the nation's religious beliefs through the power of education.

In a parallel to the Dartmouth dispute, Jefferson, after leaving the White House, tried to arrange for his alma mater, the College of William and Mary, to become a state institution where divinity professorships would be abolished.[30]

That plan having failed (partly, perhaps, because the *Dartmouth* decision made it legally difficult), his devotion to the establishment of a state university arose in part from his belief that the kind of instruction he envisioned would free students from the "shackles" of religious dogma. Religion was to be part of the curriculum only in the form of the rational, generalized religious ideas to which he himself subscribed. His candidate for the professorship of divinity turned out to be an open enemy of orthodox Calvinism, and Jefferson was outraged when Presbyterians helped block the appointment. Thereafter he opposed allowing any clergy to teach at the university,[31] and in helping plan a public academy below the university level, he proscribed the reading of the Bible on the grounds that young people "are not sufficiently mature for religious inquiries."[32]

Jeffersonian separationism, besides seeking to shield the state from religion, may also have intended to "protect" individuals from churches and has been characterized as "elevating anticlerical rhetoric to constitutional law."[33] Jefferson in effect came close to "establishing" Unitarianism as a state religion, believing as he did that Trinitarianism was inherently authoritarian and threatening to the democratic spirit to which Unitarianism was admirably suited.[34] In the words of one historian, his "critique of sectarianism in the name of universalism turned out to be another sectarianism."[35]

Madison's personal religious beliefs are uncertain, since he carefully guarded them from the public. He too had been raised an Anglican and retained some affiliation with Episcopalianism. Affected by Enlightenment ideas as deeply as Jefferson was, Madison nonetheless does not seem to have shared Jefferson's hope that traditional religion would fade away, nor did he attack orthodox Christianity, as Jefferson did.[36]

On the contrary, fearful that "factions" would corrupt the political process, he paradoxically sought to guard against this by encouraging a multiplicity of such factions. Thus in his mind, it was healthy for the Republic that many religious groups flourish, each serving as a bulwark against the excessive influence of the others.[37]

But he also warned, after his retirement from public life, that churches should not be allowed to accumulate large amounts of property and to hold it in perpetuity,[38] a recommendation that seems a departure from his belief in full religious liberty. (During the nineteenth century the Supreme Court generally upheld property claims by religious groups and allowed them to receive bequests so long as they were incorporated, thereby ignoring Madison's recommendation.)

Madison's separationism was radical to the extent of holding that legislatures should take no legal cognizance of religion at all, although he made an exception in the Bill of Rights.[39] Although a few Baptists agreed with his stand, even most "low church" Protestants did not. Quakers, for example, opposed separationism because of their status as conscientious objectors to military service, recognized as such by the government, and most Baptists did not want to silence their own preachers on public moral issues.[40]

In a subtle and paradoxical way Madison exalted religion over politics—by making religious liberty dependent on the Creator, thus making it also prior to civil society. But at the same time, he saw religion as entirely otherworldly, so that the duties owed to God could not in principle infringe on political life. Even less than Jefferson does he seem to have believed in the necessity of a divine sanction for the political order.[41]

Virtually all the Founding Fathers agreed that civic virtue required a religious foundation, Jefferson perhaps the most ambivalent on the matter. For some this involved the conviction that Christians shared a broad faith that transcended particular differences,[42] and the Founders have been credited with forging a common faith that brought together the "ethical religiosity" of the intellectuals and the "emotionalism" of the common people, not a new religion but a way of accommodating the old to the needs of the new Republic. The Founders simply assumed the reality of a Christian nation and thought that liberty was made possible through the discipline forged by religion.[43]

The *Virginia Statute for Religious Freedom* itself included references to God as the author of liberty, and Jefferson wrote in 1822 that it was essential for the people to realize that their liberties came from God.[44] Madison's *Memorial and Remonstrance* concluded with a prayer and had a theological basis,[45] and in 1825 Madison acknowledged that belief in an all-powerful God was necessary to the moral order.[46] Jefferson compiled, but did not publish, a version of the New Testament that omitted everything that seemed to hint at the divinity of Jesus but preserved what Jefferson considered the moral essence of the Gospel.[47]

Next to the Constitution itself, perhaps the most influential document in American history relative to religion and public life was the 1802 letter that Jefferson as president wrote to a group of Baptists who expressed fear that the federal government would practice religious discrimination. In giving the Baptists complete assurances to the contrary, Jefferson used the phrase "wall of separation" between church and state, which was later taken by many people as the definitive understanding of the Establishment Clause.[48]

However, before sending the letter, Jefferson showed it to two of his Cabinet members, both of whom warned that it would offend many New Englanders,[49] thus showing that his formulation of the issue was by no means universally shared. The recipients of the letter did not make it public, and most Baptists did not share Jefferson's idea of separation.[50]

Jefferson found himself under strong attack especially from New England clergy who condemned him as an "infidel" and cited his separationist position as proof of their charge. The Federalist Party then undertook to defend the role of religion in public life in opposition to Republican separationism, with Republicans contending that no institution, such as a church, should intervene between the citizens and the government, and Federalists strongly defending the right of the clergy to speak on political matters. (Some of those who opposed clerical involvement in politics were not Jeffersonian separationists but feared that the high clerical office would be contaminated by politics.)[51] Perhaps in reaction to Federalist criticism, Jefferson began making public gestures of faith, attending religious services on occasion and refraining from advocating separationism while he remained president.[52]

Sometime after he left office, Madison wrote a private memorandum (not discovered for over a century) in which he regretted having supported legislative chaplains and official days of thanksgiving, having come to regard them as violations of the Constitution. In retrospect he saw his acquiescence in these practices as lapses from principle, dictated by the particular circumstances of the time, such as the War of 1812, while he was president.[53]

Madison's explanation of his seemingly inconsistent behavior demonstrates that his separationist position, like Jefferson's, was not shared widely enough to make it politically safe to adhere to in all its fullness. In the words of one historian, "Madison did not carry the country along with Virginia's sweeping separation of churches from the state; indeed, the country to some extent carried him."[54] What was achieved in the state of Virginia was not necessarily adopted at the national level.[55] (In any case, Madison himself, no proponent of "original intent," wished that his own views of the Constitution not exert undue influence on the ways in which the document was understood.)[56]

The relevance of Jefferson's beliefs to the interpretation of the Religion Clauses is also questionable, because he had nothing directly to do with the drafting of the First Amendment, being on a diplomatic mission to France during most of the time it was being considered.[57]

Given the fact that Jefferson's and Madison's positions did not command a consensus in their own day, the original intent of the Founders, to the degree that it is relevant to modern issues, can only be determined with reference to the full range of opinions extant in their time.

Jefferson's and Madison's separationism was a relatively new development, emerging from the Enlightenment of the eighteenth century. An older and probably more widely held theory of separation originated with the seventeenth-century Baptist leader Roger Williams, who demanded separation of church and state not to protect the civil order from the strife of religion but to protect religion from worldly contamination. It was for this reason that evangelical Protestants sometimes supported separation.[58]

As noted, even in Virginia itself separationism was controversial. While Jefferson and Madison commanded great authority, there were figures of comparable iconic status—Patrick Henry, John Marshall, Richard Henry Lee—on the other side, and so formidable was Henry's opposition that the assessment bill was defeated only after Madison had engineered Henry's election as governor, in order to remove his influence from the legislature.[59] (George Washington also supported the assessment bill until its defeat seemed certain.)[60]

The Revolution itself claimed religious justification, the pulpit being a principal organ for raising patriotic fervor, and during the war the Continental Congress urged citizens to acknowledge the Creator who approved their cause. Clergy were invited to preach and pray before the assembly, which occasionally attended religious services in a body, taking care to visit various denominations, even including a Catholic church. The Congress's official documents were replete with biblical references,[61] and in their writings and speeches the Founders cited the Bible more than any secular book.[62]

The Declaration of Independence has been characterized as "straddling deism and biblical Christianity" in a conscious attempt to satisfy differing beliefs among its drafters. In rehearsing American grievances against the Crown, religious liberty was not mentioned, and, although the Declaration grounded human rights in the Creator, the assertion of "self-evident truths" has been called an essentially secular claim.[63]

During the Constitutional Convention, Benjamin Franklin, who was scarcely an orthodox Christian, at one point proposed that the delegates suspend work in order to participate in a day of prayer for divine guidance. His proposal was rejected, not on grounds of principle but because the convention had no money to pay a clergyman, and some delegates feared that asking for divine guidance would lead the public to think that they were failing in their task.[64]

The Founders held a variety of personal religious beliefs. Some, like the great Virginians (including Washington), were affiliated with a church but showed considerable influence of Deism. Some were orthodox Calvinists, others devout Episcopalians, one a Catholic.[65] Of the members of the state conventions which ratified the Constitution, two thirds were church members.[66]

The great enigma of the Religion Clauses of the Bill of Rights is the fact that they occasioned so little discussion during their enactment. Although the clauses are often credited to Madison, he was in fact initially not in favor of a bill of rights, which he considered unnecessary, and initiated it chiefly to remove an objection to the ratification of the Constitution as a whole. Madison's was the first version of the Religion Clauses, but they went through several emendations before final adoption,[67] the ultimate version being the work of Fisher Ames of Massachusetts, an active Congregationalist who later became an Episcopalian.[68]

Crucial to determining the intention of the Framers is the question of how those who ratified the Constitution themselves understood its provisions, but there is little record of the way in which the Religion Clauses were received in the states. No state proposed any kind of national religious establishment, which can be taken as the minimal condition on which they all agreed.[69]

The Framers' silence about "establishment" and "free exercise" is mysterious given the passionate debates engendered by those terms in later history. However, that silence is comprehensible on the assumption that the terms were largely devoid of positive content and were intended merely to ensure that the federal government did not interfere with the religious arrangements of the various states.[70]

Some of the prerevolutionary colonies had established churches, but several moved rapidly toward disestablishment following independence. A few retained their state churches as late as the 1830s, and the states differed among themselves in the degree of religious liberty they allowed, some imposing legal discrimination on non-Protestants,[71] a practice the Supreme Court upheld in principle in the *Permoli* case (1845).

Following independence, Congress continued to manifest its religious concerns in a variety of ways—appointing its own chaplains, to which a handful of members objected; commissioning military chaplains, a practice of which Jefferson disapproved but Washington considered important; and proclaiming official days of prayer and fasting.[72]

When a committee was appointed to design the Great Seal of the United States, two of its more secular members—Jefferson and Franklin—wanted to compare the new nation explicitly to ancient Israel in terms of divine favor.[73] Congress officially endorsed a project to publish an American edition of the Bible but stopped short of providing a subsidy for the project.[74]

The Northwest Ordinance of 1787, which governed the territories waiting to be fully admitted to the Union, was originally drafted by Jefferson without mention of religion. But in its final version it offered positive encouragement to religion in the West, including a provision that land in each township be set aside for religious or educational purposes. The Ordinance forbade any new state from establishing a religion and guaranteed religious liberty to the citizens of the territories.[75]

Washington, during his presidency (1789–97), set an example of public religiosity that has been part of the American system ever since. He attended divine services after his inauguration, added the phrase "so help me God" (not in the Constitution) in taking the oath of office, frequently invoked the deity in his public addresses, urged the necessity of religion for a virtuous people, and proclaimed official days of prayer, fasting, and thanksgiving. John Adams (1797–1801), although not an orthodox Christian, nonetheless offered prayers that were more overtly Christian than Washington's—and he suspected that his proclamation of days of prayer and thanksgiving contributed to his electoral defeat in 1800.[76] It was left to Jefferson (1801–1809) and Madison (1809–17), with only temporary success, to associate the presidency with the separationist philosophy.[77]

The overall result was the emergence of what has been called a "*de facto* establishment" of a generalized kind of Protestantism that manifested itself in numerous public and official ways,[78] a pattern present not only from the beginning of the Republic but already part of the processes by which that Republic was called into being.[79]

A CHRISTIAN NATION?

Jefferson's fond hope that Unitarianism would become the preferred religion of the United States was ironic in view of the fact that during his own presidency there occurred that major explosion of evangelical piety—the Second Great Awakening—which stamped the evangelical character so deeply on American society as to make it seem ineradicable.[80] With still further irony, this awakening seemed to be a massive release of religious energy liberated precisely by the disestablishment of state churches, the opposite of the effect Jefferson hoped disestablishment would achieve.[81] In old age, he and Adams, who had been political enemies but now agreed on many things, deplored the social affects of this new religiosity.[82]

Most people virtually took for granted that the new nation was Christian. Thus James Kent, a New York judge and influential explicator of the Constitution, in 1811 interpreted his state's blasphemy law by ruling that the nation gave a special protection to Christianity that it withheld from other religions.[83]

However, some ardent Christians were embarrassed by the "godless Constitution"—the fact that, while the Declaration of Independence invoked the Creator, the foundation document of the Republic ignored him.[84] Some considered this an almost fatal flaw, possibly attributable to Jeffersonian "infidelity,"[85] while others made the best of it by explaining that mention of the Deity was unnecessary precisely because the nation was Christian, hence implicitly acknowledged divine authority.[86] The most likely explanation for the omission, which was not even debated, is that the Framers, given their diversity of views concerning establishment, wished to avoid a potential source of conflict. (One delegate, Benjamin Rush of Pennsylvania, is known to have objected to this absence.)[87]

In 1833 an Episcopal clergyman, Jasper Adams (cousin of the great Massachusetts political family), preached a sermon declaring the United States a Christian nation and calling on the federal government to remedy the defect of the Constitution. He sent copies of the sermon to various prominent citizens for comment.[88]

Chief Justice Marshall regarded the question as delicate, because both freedom of conscience and respect for religion made valid claims on the nation. However, he thought that American institutions "presuppose Christianity" and that in the United States, Christianity and "religion" were virtually identical.[89]

Justice Story thought that government could not long exist "without an alliance with religion *to some extent.*" Christianity was indispensable to a free nation, and a distinction was to be made between the establishment of Christianity and the establishment of a particular sect, with the Constitution forbidding only the latter. Story deplored the tendency to discard "old principles" and warned that infidelity was progressing under cover of religious liberty.[90] (His apparent belief that Christianity in general was established in the United States was consistent with his future opinion in the *Girard* case [1844], which in principle held that there was no constitutional right to offer insult to the Christian religion.)

Madison of course politely disagreed with Adams's claim. While the "line of separation" between government and religion was not always easily traceable, he conceded, complete separation was beneficial and religion was in no need of government support.[91]

The status of the Mormon Church in the territory of Utah was understood by many people as a challenge to Christian political hegemony in the orthodox Protestant sense. Because the common law condemned polygamy, Utah declared that that law was not applicable in the territory, a stance that confirmed the conviction of many people that the common law was Christian.[92]

On the other hand some Mormons argued that the law was indeed rooted in Christianity but that Christianity was in turn rooted in the Old Testament, which had allowed polygamy. Thus in their view the anti-polygamy laws were evidence of how the Constitution had been corrupted.[93]

In 1863 an ecumenical group of Protestants organized the National Reform Association (NRA), whose bland title did not reveal the nature of the reform it sought, which was nothing less than an amendment to the Constitution officially recognizing that the United States was a Christian nation. A number of political figures endorsed the proposal, and President Abraham Lincoln at one point expressed general sympathy for its goals, without specifically endorsing the amendment. In 1870 the president of the group, William Strong, was named to the Supreme Court, while continuing to serve as president of the organization for several years. (The NRA attempted to enact an amendment as late as the 1970s.)[94] Some Jews protested Strong's appointment to the Court on the grounds that he was not committed to the principles of the Constitution and in 1872 even called for his impeachment.[95]

The move to acknowledge officially that America was a Christian nation won a formal victory in the Supreme Court's *Holy Trinity* decision (1892), proclaiming precisely that, although little of consequence followed directly from the affirmation. The *Holy Trinity* verdict might be read in the same minimalist way as has been suggested for the *Girard* decision, as merely recognizing a social reality. However, in 1905 Justice Brewer, the author of the *Holy Trinity* decision, affirmed publicly that the Court had "formally declared" the United States a Christian nation. Christianity deserved respect above all other religions, and the virtue of tolerance itself derived from Christian principles. A true American must be a true Christian, according to Brewer.[96]

Story's response to Jasper Adams was based in part on Story's conviction that the common law of England, adopted in the United States, itself embodied the principles of Christianity.[97] This conviction was in turn based on the claim of the influential eighteenth-century English legal commentator William Blackstone, who cited a medieval judicial decision stating that the law had been found in "sacred scripture." Jefferson often disputed Story's thesis, claiming that Blackstone had misread the medieval text, which Jefferson insisted actually cited "ancient scripture."[98]

A possible understanding of Story's position is that he believed that the general moral principles of Christianity, but not its doctrines, were officially established in common law. Thus the *Girard* decision merely recognized that Christianity was the common faith of the United States and that social peace would be endangered if it were attacked.[99] In this view, by rendering the *Girard* decision as he did, Story himself struck the fatal blow to the very position of Blackstone that he had championed.[100] However, the *Girard* finding was ambiguous and is reconcilable with Story's earlier affirmation of the preferred place of Christianity within the American polity.

Particular religious issues provoked a variety of responses in the century following the ratification of the Constitution.

In signing a treaty with Tripoli in 1797, the American representative Joel Barlow included a clause denying that the United States was "in any sense founded in the Christian religion." The phrase was omitted when the treaty was renewed in 1805, and in 1930 it was discovered that the phrase had not been part of the original Arabic text of the treaty and had probably been added by Barlow, a religious skeptic, to the English translation that he sent to the American government. However, no one challenged the phrase at the time.[101]

An American treaty with Switzerland in 1850 protected the religious rights of all Americans, a provision inserted partly at the request of American Jews, because Christians had a privileged place in some Swiss cantons. However, in 1858 the United States signed a treaty with China explicitly protecting the rights only of American Christians.[102]

Beginning during Jefferson's administration and continuing until the Civil War, religious services were regularly held in the Capitol building in Washington, well attended by public officials (reportedly even by Jefferson himself). Preachers of numerous Christian denominations were invited, including a Catholic bishop and several women. Typically the sermons were not merely decorous and bland but fiery exhortations to repent sin and accept Christ as one's personal savior.[103]

Sabbath laws were in effect all over the country during the nineteenth century, and around 1830 some Protestants noticed the apparent anomaly whereby the Post Office, under the aegis of the federal government, transported and even delivered mail on Sundays. Thus one of the major evangelical crusades of the decade was to persuade the Post Office to cease all operations on Sunday.[104] (The crusaders could point to the fact that the Constitution itself [Article I, Section 7] treated Sunday as a no-business day for the federal government.)

The House of Representatives approved suspending Sunday mail service, but Richard Johnson, chairman of the Senate Post Office Committee, became one of the few leading political figures of the nineteenth century to issue a ringing declaration of separationism. To favor the Christian sabbath over those of other faiths would violate the letter and spirit of the Constitution, Johnson proclaimed, and he charged that the real purpose of the campaign was to assault the consciences of minorities by forcing them to acknowledge the Christian sabbath.[105]

Johnson was not, however, an unwavering separationist. A somewhat desultory Baptist, he introduced a bill in Congress to charter a Baptist college in the District of Columbia and opposed an amendment, imposed as a condition of its approval, that prohibited religious discrimination among faculty and students.[106] He was more representative of the Williams than of the Jefferson tradition of separation and to some extent articulated the revolt against Calvinist orthodoxy and social control that was part of the Second Great Awakening. On the Sunday mail issue he was advised by the radical Baptist preacher John Leland, who opposed all forms of clericalism and wanted to protect Christianity from the corruptions of power.[107] Partisan politics also affected Johnson's separationism. He was a Jacksonian Democrat, therefore a political heir to Jefferson, while the strongest support for sabbatarianism came from the old bastions of Eastern Federalism.[108]

President Andrew Jackson was himself a separationist, who perhaps straddled the traditions of Williams and Jefferson. When asked to proclaim a national day of fasting and prayer, he repeated Jefferson's objections, and a Whig attempt to override his decision failed.[109] Evangelical Protestants were among Jackson's strongest opponents.[110]

The Democratic Party's strong Southern base may also have dictated the party's semi-separationist stance, in that some Southerners claimed that Northern abolitionist clergy were in violation of the spirit of the Establishment Clause.[111]

Despite Johnson's unyielding stand, the Post Office gradually ceased its Sunday operations over the remainder of the century,[112] as the Supreme Court upheld the legitimacy of sabbath laws in every nineteenth-century case that came before it.

Jews were the only notable non-Christian religious group in nineteenth-century America, and some Jews felt acutely the constant reminders that they were living in a Christian nation. They coped with the problem sometimes by denying that the United States was Christian in any legal or official sense and sometimes by protesting what they regarded as discriminatory practices or rhetoric, as when in 1841 President John Tyler referred to the "duties of a Christian people" in conjunction with the death of his predecessor, William Henry Harrison. Jews strongly opposed the movement to amend the Constitution to recognize Christianity and strongly criticized the *Holy Trinity* decision. Some Jews petitioned local and state governments for exemptions from the sabbath laws.[113]

THE INDIAN SCHOOLS

During the 1790s the task of educating and "civilizing" the Indians was placed under the War Department, which immediately commissioned Christian clergy for this purpose, an arrangement in which even Jefferson acquiesced. The missionary schools received irregular government support until 1819, when their finances were made permanent.[114]

Although the schools' task was supposed to be educational rather than explicitly religious, most people of the time probably did not think it was possible to have the former without the latter. The curricula of the mission schools had a heavy religious content, and there were direct proselytizing activities by the clergy.[115]

The resistance of some missionaries to the federal government's project of removing the Cherokee from Georgia in the 1830s provoked a kind of anticlerical reaction, including charges in Congress that the Constitution was being violated by clerical "interference." The removal of the Cherokee was ordered by the separationist Jackson, who sought to blunt charges that he was anticlerical by appointing a Dutch Reformed minister to negotiate the termination of the Cherokee missions.[116]

After numerous complaints about corruption and political favoritism among government Indians agents, the administration of President Ulysses S. Grant in 1869 announced a "peace policy" under which, among other things, missionaries were given authority to nominate agents for the various reservations. A Board of Indian Commissioners was established, with representation from the various Protestant churches engaged in missionary activities.[117]

When the Indian missions were first recognized by the government in the 1790s, most were Protestant. However, by the 1870s the number of Catholic missions was increasing, and there was growing friction among the churches over the division of territory, giving Grant's "peace policy" an ironic meaning. Catholics complained that they had responsibility for only a small minority of the agencies, while Protestants resented the fact that the Catholic missions were receiving the lion's share of federal funds, apportioned according to school enrollments. In 1882 the government terminated the missions' control over agency appointments, judging that the policy had been unsuccessful.[118]

In 1889 the government initiated a plan for a comprehensive system of public schools for Indians, according to which the mission schools would gradually be discontinued, a decision probably at least partly motivated by the continuing acrimony between Catholics and Protestants. Congress incrementally reduced the subsidies for the mission schools, eliminating them completely in 1900.[119]

Beginning in the 1880s some Protestants claimed that government subsidies to the missions were a violation of the Constitution and themselves began withdrawing from the program.[120] However, their claim seems to have originated mainly because of their suspicion of the Catholic schools, since Protestant schools had been accepting government subsidies for many decades. Inconsistency was apparently endemic to the issue.

In 1896 the Indian Commission announced a policy of not sending Indian children to religious schools if public schools were available and ruled that funds given to the Indian tribes could not be used to support religious schools, although both policies were later rescinded. In 1904, President Theodore Roosevelt personally approved using tribal funds for mission schools, which by then were mainly Catholic. Protestant protests went as far as the Supreme Court, which upheld the practice in the *Quick Bear* case (1908).[121]

Government regulations in 1890 required that students in Indian schools attend church on Sunday and receive religious instruction, and Catholics sometimes protested that such instruction was not "nonsectarian," as it was supposed to be. In 1902 a new set of regulations forbade the conversion of Indian children to Christianity without parental approval, and a few years later the chief of the Indian Bureau urged that the schools avoid religious doctrine of any kind. The Bureau in 1911 ruled that the principle of separation of church and state did not apply in situations where the schools existed in a "quasi-parental" relationship with their students, then the following year forbade all religious symbols in the schools and forbade teachers to wear any kind of distinctive religious garb, a ruling that was rescinded when Catholics appealed directly to President William Howard Taft.[122]

Nowhere in the nineteenth century are the vagaries of establishment issues more vividly represented than in the Indian-school wars, the bewilderingly frequent changes in policy themselves major indications of the nation's lack of any settled view of the meaning of the Establishment Clause.

THE COMMON SCHOOLS

Until almost the middle of the nineteenth century most schools were "private," in the sense of not being primarily supported by taxes, a fact that renders problematical all attempts to relate the philosophy of the Founders to modern educational issues.

The first systematic attempt to establish "common schools"—an experiment that served as a model for many other regions—was in Massachusetts in the 1840s, under the direction of the state Commissioner of Education, Horace Mann.

Although the public schools would eventually come to be seen as institutions that were supposed to be religiously neutral, Mann's agenda was essentially the Jeffersonian low road of using education to effect fundamental changes in religious belief. Mann fulfilled one of Jefferson's hopes in that he was a Unitarian, at a time when Congregationalism, disestablished in Massachusetts in 1833, was losing influence. He was also Jeffersonian in his view of Calvinism, the theological basis of Congregationalism, as "an unspeakable calamity," a religion that rendered its adherents "mentally limited" and dishonest.[123]

Mann's associates, many of them fellow Unitarians, managed to get control of the "normal" schools set up for the training of teachers, and the common schools themselves reflected Mann's liberal religious beliefs. Partly to disarm criticism that he was undermining religion, Mann insisted that the Bible be read in the schools, but it was to be the Protestant Bible, and its exegesis was to be in hands of teachers who would guide students away from religious orthodoxies, especially Calvinism.[124] He also detested Catholicism and doubted whether Catholics should be allowed to teach in the common schools.[125]

In a sense the *Girard* case recognized in principle the right to conduct schools that were religiously "neutral," even if Mann's schools were in fact sectarian. However, in another sense the Supreme Court avoided the issue. While allowing Steven Girard to exclude clergy from the school he founded, the Court also suggested that religious instruction could be imparted by lay people.

Both Catholics and more conservative Protestants opposed Mann's program and soon began founding schools of their own, which Mann denounced as undemocratic.[126] Thus from the beginning, the idea of a "common" school was itself problematic, often increasing social division instead of healing it.

Mann's model for public education was by no means universally followed, given the fact that schools in the United States were entirely controlled by state and local governments, so that the character of particular schools varied widely according to local cultures. The early public schools seem mainly to have had a Protestant character, sometimes liberal, sometimes orthodox. In many places, clergy played a major role, as a deliberate educational policy.[127] These schools were often also anti-Catholic, Mann and his associates promoting the common-school movement, in part to counter the affects of foreign immigration, and the public schools were often represented as essential bulwarks against a foreign religion.[128]

During much of the nineteenth century, separationism was not a respected constitutional idea so much as an accusation hurled at those who
were said to be hostile to religion, and it came to be respectible primarily
as a Protestant attack on the Catholic schools, although a secularist version of the theory developed later in the century.[129]

Catholics began criticizing the public schools with increasing frequency, and their dissatisfaction had a momentous affect on American
education, as they set about founding a school system of their own that
in some places rivaled in size the public system. These schools in turn
were often denounced by Protestants as un-American,[130] and their right
to exist remained in doubt until the Court's *Pierce* decision of 1925.

Jews manifested a somewhat ambivalent attitude toward the public
schools. With few schools of their own, they generally supported public
education. While opposing its frequently Protestant character, most Jews
were at the same time not comfortable with an education that was wholly
secular. In the end, however, most probably concluded that the latter op-
tion was preferable to the former.[131]

The most notable nineteenth-century effort to make the public schools
religiously neutral occurred in Cincinnati in 1870, when a loose coalition
of Catholics, Jews, and "free-thinkers" persuaded the school board to
eliminate all religious practices from the schools. The Ohio Superior Court
overturned the policy, over the dissent of one of its members, Alfonso Taft,
who strongly articulated the classic separationist position in the face of
the court's claim that the Ohio Constitution favored Christianity. (Taft's
dissent was significant in part because he was the father of the future president and chief justice William Howard Taft.) But the Ohio Supreme Court
upheld the school board, avoiding the constitutional issue simply by ruling
that the school board had final legal authority over curricula.[132]

The lawyer for the school board was Stanley Matthews, who had been
raised a strict Calvinist, fallen away from that faith, and then returned
to it once again. While Taft may have been a Jeffersonian separationist,
Matthews was in the tradition of Roger Williams, denouncing the religiosity of the public schools as "humbug," ridiculing the "common Christianity," which he found offensive to Gospel truth, and insisting that true
Christianity did not need state support.[133] In 1881 Matthews was named
to the United States Supreme Court.

During the late nineteenth century some school districts followed the
lead of Cincinnati in banning religious observances from the schools,
while others actually began requiring such observances.[134]

The most significant manifestation of separationism in the nineteenth
century began in 1875, when President Ulysses S. Grant delivered a speech
reminding his former troops of the Religion Clauses, extolling the public
schools as bulwarks of Americanism, and urging the veterans to defeat
all proposals to provide public funds for private religious schools.[135]

The following year, Congressman James G. Blaine of Maine introduced a constitutional amendment designed to achieve Grant's purpose. It passed the House of Representatives but was defeated in the Senate by a partisan vote, all Republicans supporting it, all Democrats opposed.[136] The Democrats then attempted to co-opt the issue by proposing a similar amendment weaker than Blaine's, but it also failed.[137]

This division was ironic in view of the history of the two parties, the Republicans as the heirs to the Federalists and Whigs who had tended toward accommodationism, the Democrats as the heirs to Jefferson and Jackson.

Grant's view of establishment scarcely seems to have been consistent. On the one hand, he expanded the role of the churches in Indian affairs and appointed Strong to the Supreme Court, ignoring Jewish protests (Strong was also anti-Catholic),[138] while on the other hand, not only did he decry public aid to religious schools, in the same speech, he made the radical proposal that the churches be subject to taxation.[139] The explanation of these apparent anomalies probably lies in the complex politics of post–Civil War Reconstruction.

Following the defeat of the Confederacy, Republicans hoped to achieve a kind of cultural unification of the nation through the public schools, attempting through those schools to bring an end to Southern separatism. However, not only was Reconstruction resisted in the South, heavy Republican losses in the election of 1874 seemed to show that it was not even supported in the North.[140]

Whether or not any particular Republican leader was anti-Catholic, party strategists in the mid-1870s decided that a new focus on the public schools, with a corresponding hostility to the growing system of Catholic schools, could be a way of recouping political losses and continuing to move toward national unity, a strategy reinforced by the fact that Northern Catholics were disproportionately Democratic. Anti-Catholicism was to serve as the new basis of a political consensus in danger of eroding.[141] In his 1875 speech, Grant drew a contrast between "patriotism and intelligence on the one side, and superstition, ambition, and ignorance on the other,"[142] which to his hearers must have been an obvious reference to immigrant Catholics.

The strategy backfired to some extent, as Democrats charged that Republicans were championing the public schools in order to promote racial desegregation. In 1884 Blaine's perceived anti-Catholicism helped cost him the presidency, when a Protestant minister dubbed the Democrats the party of "rum, Romanism, and rebellion," a remark that probably pushed pivotal New York State into the Democratic camp.[143]

Modern separationism is two-pronged, holding both that there should be no public support of religious institutions and that there should be no religious influences on public institutions. Republican separationism of the 1870s, however, had only the first prong. Thus Governor Rutherford B. Hayes of Ohio successfully campaigned for the presidency in 1876 upholding religious practices in the public schools, even though Stanley Matthews was helping to manage his campaign. Hayes and James A. Garfield, who became president in 1881, warned that the secularization of the Cincinnati schools amounted to a kind of anti-Protestant conspiracy.[144] In extolling the public schools in 1875, Grant urged that they remain "unmixed with sectarian, pagan, or atheistical dogma,"[145] which in the context of the time was probably understood to mean that their general Protestant character should be preserved.

Public aid to Catholic schools was a viable political possibility in New York, although it was ultimately rejected. During the 1876 election, Republicans attacked Governor Samuel Tilden of New York, the Democratic candidate for president, for not opposing this aid.[146] (Once again it was anti-Catholicism rather than principled separationism that motivated the campaign, as opponents of public aid also insisted that the Protestant Bible continue to be used in the public schools.)[147]

Although the Blaine Amendment failed nationally, it did have significant affects in various states. Somewhat anomalously, after defeating the amendment at the national level, Congress proceeded to require that new states admitted to the Union include a clause in their own constitutions forbidding public aid to religious schools, and some older states adopted this provision as well. State courts occasionally found such aid unconstitutional.[148]

During the nineteenth century the federal government sometimes made land grants to private colleges and universities, most of which were under religious auspices.[149]

The Supreme Court would eventually make the Bill of Rights applicable to the states by holding that the Fourteenth Amendment (1868), which was explicitly intended to bind the states, incorporated the Bill of Rights. However, during the debates of the immediate post–Civil War period there is no indication that anyone thought that the Fourteenth Amendment had anything to do with religion. Had they thought so, the Blaine Amendment would have been unnecessary, and no one at any point linked the two, although Congressman Jonathan Bingham, one of the leading sponsors of Reconstruction legislation, did remind Congress that the rights of religious abolitionists had been violated before the Civil War.[150]

CIVIL RELIGION

In the nineteenth century, Europeans seeking to interpret the United States to their fellow Europeans sometimes found it necessary to correct a common misimpression. Since the new nation was famous for having enacted separation of church and state, there was often an assumption in other countries that America was a secular society.

The French nobleman Alexis de Tocqueville, the first and most astute of these interpreters, was perhaps also the first person to notice how the disestablishment of religion, far from weakening the churches, had actually strengthened them by creating a freedom in which they could compete vigorously with one another, and he offered the paradox whereby the clergy, in surrendering the support of the government, greatly increased their actual influence in society.[151]

The German Protestant theologian Philip Schaff, who taught for many years in an American seminary, pointed out the various ways in which separation had not been fully effected—military and legislative chaplains, sabbath and blasphemy laws, and religious services in the Capitol building itself.[152]

Robert Baird, a Scottish Presbyterian, noticed the same features of the system, along with public land granted to religious schools, and regretted what he considered the mere oversight of not mentioning God in the Constitution. Baird praised the American system as a successful example of the "voluntary principle" in religion.[153]

James Bryce, an English nobleman who made a close study of American government, thought that

> Christianity is understood to be, though not the legally established religion, yet the national religion. So far from thinking of the the commonwealth as godless, the Americans conceive that the religious character of a government consists in nothing but the religious belief of the individual citizens. . . . They deem the general acceptance of Christianity to be one of the main sources of their national prosperity, and think their nation a special object of divine favor.[154]

Besides being one of the most important justices ever to sit on the Supreme Court, Story was, until after the Civil War, the most influential constitutional commentator in the United States, one of his tasks being to explain the apparent anomaly that these foreign observers noted.

Story insisted that there could be "no pretense of any alliance between church and state in the national government" and cited the history of religious intolerance in Europe as the justification for this.[155] But at the same time, making the argument that the Supreme Court would institutionalize in the Mormon polygamy cases, he asserted that

> Indeed, the right of a society or government to interfere in matters of religion will hardly be contested by any persons, who believe that piety, religion, and morality are intimately connected with the well being of the state, and indispensable to the administration of civil justice.[156]

However, the right of the state to "interfere" with religion in the name of morality also implied the duty of government to promote sound religious beliefs.

> And at all events, it is impossible for those, who believe in the truth of Christianity, as a divine revelation, to doubt that it is the especial duty of government to foster and encourage it among all the citizens and subjects. This is a point wholly distinct from that of the right of private judgment in matters of religion, and of the freedom of public worship according to the dictates of one's own conscience.

He enumerated, as the basic doctrines of Christianity: the existence and attributes of God, divine rule over human affairs, a future state of rewards and punishments, and the cultivation of virtues.[157]

Story's ideas have been called "aberrational,"[158] and from a modern standpoint they were. However, his task was not to expound the meaning of the Constitution as an abstract document but to explain how its provisions reflected the reality of American life since the founding of the Republic.

He thought that, at the time of adoption of the Constitution, Christianity was generally considered to deserve special encouragement by the state and that a policy of treating all religions equally would have met with general disapproval. The government in no way sought to encourage Islam, Judaism, or other non-Christian religions, but it would also not force consciences. As Story acknowledged, the history of Christianity showed many instances of religiously inspired persecution, even the history of his own native New England revealing "dark bigotry and intolerance, as any which could be found to grace the pages of foreign annals."[159]

Having formulated the paradox whereby the government would both encourage Christianity and respect individual consciences, Story resolved it in the only way open to him at the time, by concluding that finally all matters of religion had been left to the discretion of the states, although he noted with apparent satisfaction that Jews and infidels "may sit down at the common table of *national* councils without any inquisition into their faith and mode of worship."[160] His ruminations in the *Girard* case showed him struggling to resolve these paradoxes in a concrete situation—Christianity had official standing in the Republic, and state laws concerning religion were to be upheld, but they were to be applied in a tolerant manner.

Story's successor as the nation's most influential constitutional commentator was a law professor, Thomas Cooley, who arrived at a similar position. The First Amendment, according to Cooley, was intended to apply only to Congress, although he was also one of the first people to suggest that under some circumstances the Fourteenth Amendment "is perhaps broad enough to provide some securities if they should be needful."[161]

He endorsed Story's view that Christianity was part of the common law, since law was based on the moral sense of the citizens, which was in turn shaped by Christianity. Some of the most important provisions of the law had been inspired by Christianity, not because that religion was recognized as sacred but because it was a fundamental part of the tradition of the American people. No Christian teaching could be enforced unless it was enacted into positive law.[162]

Noting occasional objections to such things as legislative chaplains, Cooley merely replied that "the general sentiment of the country has approved it." There had never been an attempt to violate religious liberty, he asserted, the suppression of Mormon polygamy being abundantly justified by the evils of the practice.[163]

The blasphemy laws seem to have been a source of some unease to Cooley, since in the name of religion they clearly inhibited personal freedom. They had been enacted, he thought, because the prevailing religion of the American people was Christianity, thus certain things were offensive to Americans that might not be offensive in another culture, just as cultural and religious differences might, for example, affect the law of contract. Cooley argued that, realistically, questions of public policy must always be dependent on the prevailing system of public morals, which in turn was dependent on prevailing religious belief. Blasphemy was not punished because of any official claim as to the divine origins of Christianity but because it was offensive to most of the citizens.[164]

The blasphemy laws in no way inhibited freedom of expression, Cooley insisted, because objections could be raised against religion so long as they were couched in respectful and rational terms. Blasphemy, on the other hand, was a deliberate insult to Christianity, for which there could be no justification. Ridicule of God had the "evil effect of sapping the foundations of society and public order."[165]

He admitted that Jews suffered as a result of the sabbath laws but concluded that "such laws only require the proper deference and regard which those not accepting the common belief may justly be required to pay to the public conscience."[166]

Writing just a few years after Grant's 1875 separationist speech, Cooley noted that tax exemptions for churches were not unconstitutional but thought it an open question whether they were "wise and just."[167]

To some degree Cooley's theory of the Constitution could be read as a precocious expression of cultural relativism—what was valid for one society might not be for another, and no transcendent standard should be applied. However, he went on to affirm that:

> the American constitution contains no provisions which prohibit the authorities from such solemn recognition of a superintending Providence in public transactions and exercises as the general religious

sentiment of mankind inspires, and as seems meet and proper in finite
and dependant beings. Whatever may be the shades of religious belief, all must acknowledge the fitness of recognizing in important
human affairs the superintending care and control of the great Governor of the Universe, and of acknowledging with thanksgiving his
boundless favors, of bowing in contrition when visited with the pen-
alties of his broken laws.[168]

Just as the government could legitimately encourage institutions of
charity and learning, it could also attempt to foster religious worship:

> . . . as conservators of public morals and valuable, if not indispens-
> able, assistants in the preservation of public order. . . . Nor . . . are
> we always precluded from recognizing also, in the rules proscribed
> for the conduct of the citizen, the notorious fact that the prevailing
> religion in the State is Christian.[169]

The Founding Fathers, Cooley believed, wanted to enact complete religious freedom, "except so far as is necessary to protect the civil rights of
others and to preserve the public peace."[170]

Cooley employed two quite distinct arguments in support of the existing relationship between religion and society. Sometimes he seemed
merely to say that residents of a particular country had to live with the
beliefs of the majority, but sometimes he also seemed to affirm the essential truth of Christianity. According to either position, far from espousing
the modern libertarian view that the Bill of Rights especially protects the
rights of minorities, Cooley conceded to the majority the right, within
limits, to enact their beliefs and customs into law. In doing so he was
simply justifying the actual relationship between religion and society as
it had existed since the founding of the nation.

The term "civil religion" has been used by modern scholars to describe
this relationship, a religiosity that was never official but was present at
the highest levels of public life. Possessed of few formal doctrines, it was
enunciated primarily through biblical imagery, such as the United States
as the new Israel.[171] America was considered a primary means through
which the divine will was manifested, and a close relationship was
thought to exist between religious righteousness and good citizenship.[172]

Although present to some degree from the beginning, civil religion took
some decades to form itself completely and was perhaps not fully developed until after the Civil War. In certain ways it marked the coming together of two previously disparate, even antagonistic, Christian traditions—Calvinism and Wesleyan Methodism, the former pessimistic about
human possibilities and inclined toward authoritarian institutions, the
latter more optimistic and democratic. Civil religion was not a "third

way" between sectarianism and secularism but fit harmoniously with existing churches, a common Christianity (really Protestantism) that was thought to transcend sectarian differences without undermining them.[173]

Despite the Establishment Clause, the principal American tradition was one of alliance between religion and politics, since God, whose will was thought manifested through democratic processes, had anointed the nation as his agent in history. Church and state did not compete with each other, which allowed public officials to treat religion favorably and to draw inspiration from it. The chief support for this civil religion came not from political institutions but from the religious community itself, which in turn influenced politics.[174]

For most Americans of the nineteenth century, the distinction between "public" and private" religion would have been unintelligible, since religion was assumed to influence social and political life. What was originally called "public religion" has been characterized as Protestant in tone and congregationalist in form, inculcating virtue and republican principles.[175]

Later separationists came to regard the principal manifestations of this religiosity as violations of the Establishment Clause, but such practices were from the beginning part the fabric of American public life—official chaplaincies in the legislatures and the armed forces, public business sealed by religious oaths, religious references almost endemic to political discourse, fervent reiteration of the conviction that God rules over the nation, insistence that good citizenship rests on a religiously inspired moral foundation, religious practices and instruction in public schools.

As president, Lincoln became perhaps the most exalted icon of the civil religion, partly in very specific ways, such as greatly expanding the chaplain corps during the Civil War and making the day of thanksgiving a permanent institution in national life. Beyond that, however, he was, paradoxically, the most eloquent preacher of the national faith. Far from being an orthodox Christian, he was troubled by religious doubts yet also obsessed with the belief that human affairs were in the hands of a higher power, a conviction that made his Second Inaugural Address (1865) the greatest political sermon in the nation's history.[176]

This civil religion went against the intentions of Jefferson and Madison, and some organized opposition developed after the Civil War, especially through the National Liberal League, which was formed partly in reaction to the National Reform Association. Just as religious believers sometimes claimed that the Constitution was essentially religious despite its failure to acknowledge God, separationists insisted that the document was essentially secular even while advocating a constitutional amendment making that explicit.[177]

But these protests only occasionally succeeded in altering public practice. Thus a proposal in the 1850s to abolish chaplaincies brought forth in Congress a declaration of "the belief of our people in the doctrines and divine truth of the Gospel of Jesus Christ," a belief declared to be necessary "for our salvation."[178]

The Liberal League's failure was in part due to the vexed question of the relationship between public morality and religion. The organization split during the 1880s because some of the leadership opposed anti-pornography laws that other members thought were necessary.[179] (President Theodore Roosevelt, acting in the tradition of Roger Williams, wanted the inscription "In God We Trust" removed from coins, because he thought religion was demeaned by being associated with money.)[180]

Beginning in 1899 the Supreme Court decided a short series of cases involving religious establishment, in none of which it found any violation of the Constitution. This broad consensus about religion and public life, already more than a century old, would survive until after World War II.

PILLARS OF A WALL

FROM ITS FOUNDATIONAL statements in *Everson* (1947) and *McCollum* (1948), the modern Court's separationist jurisprudence rested on the assertion that strict separationism was the intention of the Framers of the Constitution. However, it also rested on a series of related assumptions—that religion has great potential for stirring up division and strife in society, that it is therefore intended to be a wholly "private" matter, that it has subjective and possibly irrational roots, and that it is often inculcated by means of "indoctrination."

RELIGION AS DIVISIVE

The *Girard* case (1844) turned precisely on the divisiveness issue. The exclusion of clergy from teaching in a school was attacked on the grounds that it was an insult to Christianity and thus a violation of a state blasphemy law. In his will setting up the school, the donor noted that there were many religious sects and that he did not want students in the school "subject to the excitement of religious controversy."[1]

In defending the terms of the will, Stephen Girard's executors asked:

> Does anyone desire that the old times in religion should return, when a man was allowed to do good in only a particular way, and in no other? What was the spirit which led to burning the convent near Boston? Precisely this. Religious animosity now destroys property if it does not doom to the stake.[2]

(Even as the case was being heard by the Supreme Court, anti-Catholic violence worse than that in Boston erupted in Philadelphia itself, where the case originated.)[3]

The plaintiffs argued that the idea of what would later be called "religious pluralism" was derived from the atheist Thomas Paine and was thus inimical to Christianity. The fact of division within Christianity was used as an excuse "to lay the axe to the tree," they charged, and Girard ignored agreement among Christians on some common beliefs.[4]

Writing for the Court, which upheld the terms of Girard's will, Justice Story recognized the religious diversity of the nation only in order to conclude that such diversity made any general discussion of the issue impossible and that the case was to be decided solely on the basis of the law and the Constitution.[5] (Story was of course aware of the religious strife alluded to in Girard's will and, in 1834, had presided over a public meeting in Boston protesting the burning of a convent by an anti-Catholic mob.)[6]

In the *Watson* case (1872), settling an internal Presbyterian dispute, Justice Miller at the conclusion of his decision expressed regret that a matter of religion should have become a legal dispute and confessed that the justices had waited a year before rendering a judgment, hoping that the conflict would be settled internally. Charity, he recalled, was held by Christianity to be the highest of the virtues, and it was regrettable that it had failed in this case.[7] The *Watson* case was paradigmatic of all those cases involving religious divisions, not between groups but within a single group, which the Court has encountered throughout its history.

The Mormon polygamy cases a few years later presented the single most divisive religious issue in American history, and they were settled by finding in effect that the division was not a genuine dilemma—there could be no tenable argument in favor of a practice that civilized people found abhorrent. Ironically, in one of those cases, Justice Field became the first justice in the history of the Court to allude to the history of religious strife and persecution in Europe, something that later courts would do with regularity, but he drew from that history the conclusion not that the Mormons were being persecuted but that they could not expect toleration for their practices.[8]

For the next sixty years the Court was called upon repeatedly to settle religious disputes, but while rendering judgments of various kinds it took little notice of the phenomenon of religious conflict as a social reality. Religion cases were decided on various grounds, but never was religiously generated strife treated as a relevant consideration.

However, the Jehovah's Witnesses cases, beginning in 1940, presented the reality of sectarian strife in a vivid way, and in the *Gobitis* case Justice Frankfurter noted that religious liberty had been guaranteed by the Constitution precisely because of such strife,[9] an observation that did not prevent him from ruling against the Witnesses who claimed to be persecuted in being required to salute the flag.

However, in the *Cantwell* case the same year, the Court ruled in favor of Witnesses who had been arrested for public proselytizing on behalf of their faith, and Justice Roberts pronounced for the Court that:

> In the realm of religious faith, and in that of political belief, sharp differences arise. In both fields the tenets of one man may seem the rankest error to his neighbor. To persuade others to his own point of view, the pleader, as we know, at times, resorts to exaggeration, to vilification of men who have been, or are, prominent in church or

state, even to false statements. But the people of the nation have ordained, in the light of history, that, in spite of the probability of excesses and abuses, those liberties are, in the long view, essential to enlightened opinion and right conduct on the part of the citizens of a democracy.[10]

The Witnesses cases brought before the Court the most religiously divisive issues since polygamy, and Roberts's unanimous opinion seemed to declare that such division was a sign of a healthy democracy.

When in the *Barnette* decision (1943), the Court reversed its ruling in *Gobitis*, Justice Jackson rehearsed the history of religious persecution and reached the opposite conclusion from Frankfurter: "Those who begin coercing elimination of dissent soon find themselves exterminating dissenters. Compulsory unification of opinion achieves only the unanimity of the graveyard."[11] Frankfurter stood by his 1940 opinion, finding in the dangers of religious conflict an argument for restraining religious expressions that threatened the public order.[12]

In another Witnesses case the following year, Justice Murphy acknowledged the danger of religious strife but warned that "in no area have men been so ingenious than in persecuting and restricting religious belief,"[13] and he too argued for the widest possible tolerance.

In shielding the leaders of the I Am movement from prosecution for mail fraud in the same year,[14] Justice Douglas also argued that the Founding Fathers, knowing the bitter reality of religious persecution, intended to ensure the widest possible toleration.[15] Jackson hinted at his belief that the I Am movement was fraudulent but thought the Court should not probe the question. Religious beliefs were inherently divisive, but Jackson's conclusion from this was that "I would dismiss the indictments and have done with this business of judicially examining other people's faiths."[16]

Thus when the modern Court first began to identify the phenomenon of religious strife as a social reality, the various justices who did so drew three quite different conclusions—that it mandated the widest possible freedom, that it required limits on potentially disorderly actions, or that the Court should refrain from becoming involved in religious disputes at all.

As with other elements of the modern jurisprudence of the Religion Clauses, the importance of religious strife, in the Court's understanding, was first explicitly stated in Justice Black's majority opinion in *Everson*, which permitted the reimbursement of parents for the cost of transporting their children to religious schools. Here for the first time the Court began to adopt the consistent view that religious strife was a danger to the nation and needed to be controlled.

The European background to American history was one of relentless religious persecution, Black recalled, with Christians persecuting Jews, and Catholics and Protestants persecuting each other and simultaneously persecuting deviant members of their own groups. Unfortunately these practices soon became common in America as well. Black traced not only the Free-Exercise Clause to these roots but the Establishment Clause as well—the Founders prescribed rigorous separation of church and state to prevent any group from gaining ascendancy over another.[17]

Jackson agreed with Black's theory but found his decision upholding the reimbursement to be illogical. To Jackson "the whole historic conflict in temporal policy between the Catholic Church and non-Catholics comes to a focus on their respective school policies," and he went on to assert that "Our public school, if not a product of Protestantism, at least is more consistent with it than with the Catholic culture and scheme of values." Jackson, therefore, thought the Court should disallow the reimbursement because the practice threatened to ignite ancient sectarian quarrels, which were best prevented by keeping every form of religion from gaining influence over public policy or the public purse.[18]

Likewise dissenting, Justice Rutledge argued that the price of religious liberty was double, in that to obtain its benefits believers had to forgo any kind of public support. Otherwise there would be sectarian conflict, with the largest group winning and the result being the destruction of religious liberty.[19] Children in religious schools chose to forgo the benefits of the "common" (public) school, Rutledge pointed out, and there was necessarily a price to be paid for that. Such believers would be the first to object if creeds other than their own were taught in the common schools, hence they had to accept the denial of all forms of public aid.[20]

The minority in the *Everson* case—to become the majority the following year—saw Catholic-Protestant conflict as lurking just beneath the surface of national life and saw the public schools as guarantors of national peace and unity, although possibly closer in spirit to Protestantism than to Catholicism. Thus the schools had to remain rigorously free of even a shadow of religious taint. Frankfurter insisted in the Jehovah's Witnesses cases that religious liberty could not be granted absolutely, because of the danger of religious strife, but could be enjoyed only in exchange for certain concessions by believers.

In the *McCollum* case the majority of the Court began applying the principles enunciated in *Everson*, and, in a concurring opinion prohibiting religious instruction in public schools, Frankfurter announced that the public schools were a product of the spirit of freedom enshrined in the First Amendment. They had long been nonsectarian in character, which reflected the experience of the American people with sectarian strife. The schools existed to educate citizens in an environment free of pressure and sharp conflict, and were the most powerful agencies of cohesion in an otherwise heterogeneous democracy. Thus they had to be "scrupulously free from entanglement in the strife of sects."[21]

Experiments in "released time" religious education had a long history, Frankfurter noted, but he judged that they had the affect of sharpening a sense of religious difference, especially when some children might choose not to attend the instructions. He referred to "destructive religious conflicts of which the history of even this country records some dark pages" and lauded the public schools as a necessary antidote, ending with the homey advice "Good fences make good neighbors."[22]

Reluctantly concurring in the decision, Jackson also focused on the reality of religious division but drew from it a different lesson, one he had already expressed in the *Ballard* case. Noting that there were 256 religious bodies in the United States (in fact a gross underestimate), he warned that: "If we choose to eliminate everything that is objectionable to these warring sects or inconsistent with any of their doctrines, we will leave public education in shreds."[23]

Jackson saw this task as extremely delicate, partly because religious influence was pervasive in the culture, and it was not possible that art or music, for example, could be taught without reference to it. However, certain historical subjects, such as the Reformation, were inherently divisive.[24]

In the *Zorach* case of 1952, when the Court allowed public-school students to leave the premises during school hours for religious instruction, Black expressed considerable exasperation at what he thought was the majority's inconsistency, exclaiming that: "It was precisely because eighteenth-century Americans were a religious people divided into many fighting sects that we were given the constitutional mandate to keep Church and State separate." He went on to remind the Court that "zealous sectaries would sometimes torture, maim, and kill those they branded 'atheists' or 'agnostics.'" Such things could be prevented only by ensuring that no group could gain enough power to punish dissenters.[25]

When, after a hiatus, the Court in 1961 again began to show interest in religious issues, Black again reminded his brethren that the threat of religious persecution lay behind the Religion Clauses.[26]

In a case that year upholding sabbath laws, Frankfurter, both concurring and dissenting, argued that in view of the endemic competition among sects, whatever "established" one necessarily disadvantaged others. This was something of which the Founders were quite aware, and memories of religious strife were strong among them.[27]

The following year, in the landmark *Engel* case prohibiting officially authorized prayers in public schools, Black recalled that history again, noting that even in America there had been much strife over the official adoption of the Anglican *Book of Common Prayer* in Virginia, for example. History showed that any form of establishment tended to increase

hatred and contempt by one religion against another.[28] Douglas concurred, adding that such prayers introduced a "divisive element" into the
schools.[29]

In his 1963 decision (*Shempp*) prohibiting officially mandated Bible
reading in the public schools, Justice Clark also affirmed that Americans'
strong commitment to religious liberty was due to their ancestors' experience of persecution. He counted eighty-three religious groups of more
than 50,000 members each in the United States, and it was necessary that
the Court guard against conflict among them.[30]

In his concurring opinion Justice Brennan approvingly recalled Douglas's assertion that "we are a religious people," but drew from it the conclusion that religious strife was therefore a real danger. He proposed again
the idea that the public schools were uniquely unifying, because they were
based on democratic values that fostered democracy, while private
schools might have different values. Brennan found the Bible inherently
sectarian, hence divisive, as the existence of various translations showed,
as did the long-standing controversies over which versions should be used
in the public schools.[31]

On the other hand, in the 1968 decision nullifying a state law that
prohibited the teaching of biological evolution, Justice Fortas held that
religious groups had no right to protection from views that were distaste-
ful to them.[32] Although offered almost in passing, it was an important
step in the development of the Court's principle that one of the purposes
of the Religion Clauses was to forestall credal conflict. Although overt
theological divisions were to be treated with suspicion, broader ideological conflicts were not.

In the same year, in a case where the Court permitted the lending of
textbooks to students in religious schools, Black and Douglas both entered vehement dissents, dismayed that the majority apparently did not
appreciate the full danger of religious strife.[33] Black urgently warned
against certain religious groups "which happen to be strong enough politically to write their own religious preferences and prejudices into law."
American society was composed of a myriad of such groups, he pointed
out, some of which were bitterly hostile to and completely intolerant of
the others.

> The same powerful sectarian propagandists who have succeeded in
> securing passage of the present law can and doubtlessly will continue
> their propaganda, looking toward complete domination and suprem-
> acy of their particular brand of religion.

Black warned that it was "nearly always by insidious approaches that the
citadels of liberty are successfully attacked."[34] (The decision upheld the loan

of textbooks to children in religious schools, and Black's warning was presumably against the Catholic, Church, which operated most such schools.)

The Constitution, Black insisted, was written on the assumption that any such aid "generates discord, disharmony, hatred, and strife among our people," and it was necessary for government to protect minorities from majority domination. Otherwise the government itself would become a tyranny.[35]

In his own dissent, Douglas pointed out a seemingly irresolvable dilemma—if the state "supinely" gave aid to religious schools when asked, it breached the wall of separation; if it resisted, religious conflict was ignited.[36] The lending of textbooks created specific conditions where religious conflict would occur, in that religious schools would tend to choose only books that were harmonious with their own creeds. Would they adopt a science book, for example, that, while recognizing the theory of evolution, also spoke of God as part of the process and of human beings as having souls? Douglas asked. History texts would present special problems in dealing with the Crusades, the Spanish conquest of Mexico, or the Franco government in Spain. These problems would give rise to battles within the educational system, attempts to force the state to provide textbooks that religious groups found acceptable.[37]

The *Walz* case (1970),[38] upholding the constitutionality of tax exemptions for churches, raised in an especially obvious way the question of the role of religion in American life. Here Chief Justice Burger found that churches deserved such exemptions because they were institutions that exist in "harmonious relationship with the community at large." They are "beneficial and stabilizing influences in community life."[39]

Concurring, Justice Blackmun thought that the existence of a plurality of religious groups was a positive benefit to society and that tax exemptions contributed to that diversity. In fact, denying such exemptions would itself cause strife.[40]

In his dissent, Douglas once more noted the long history of religious conflict in American life. Tax exemptions subsidized creeds that were repugnant to some of the citizens. Even if a church made its facilities available to everyone, "Its sectarian faith sets it apart from all others and makes it difficult to equate its constituency with the general public."[41]

The *Walz* case was one of the very few in which the Court took note of the unifying functions of religion, as opposed to its divisive potential, although Douglas still thought the latter far outweighed the former.

The following year, in dissenting from a decision allowing public aid to religiously affiliated colleges and universities, Douglas again raised specific issues that he thought would be divisive within the framework of such education—the Reformation, for example, or the government of Quebec under the premiership of Maurice Duplessis. He also warned that the wealth of the churches, which he claimed was considerable, could lead to violent revolution, as it had in various countries of eastern Europe.[42]

In formulating the Lemon Test the same year, Burger elevated the danger of religious conflict into a working constitutional principle, in that the third part of his triple test was that a public policy not engender "excessive entanglement" between church and state, meaning among other things that government must not be forced to scrutinize religious bodies, thereby risking such conflict.[43]

Programs of public aid were inherently dangerous, Burger argued, in that they could give rise to political divisions along religious lines. Here he became the first justice to make explicit the full implications of the fear of divisiveness:

> Ordinarily political debate and division, however, vigorous or even partisan, are normal and healthy manifestations of our democratic system of government, but political division along religious lines is one of the principal evils against which the First Amendment was intended to protect. The potential divisiveness of such conflict is a threat to the normal political process. To have State or communities divided on the issue presented by state aid to parochial schools would tend to confuse and obscure other issues of great urgency.[44]

In his concurring opinion, Douglas warned again that "the zeal of religious proselytizers promises to carry the day and make a shambles of the Establishment Clause." He reviewed the history of the public schools, recalling that Protestants had in some places taken control of them quite early and had introduced practices, such as required readings from the Protestant Bible, that were offensive to Catholics, thereby provoking the latter into founding their own schools. Now economic and other pressures were leading to demands on the public treasury on behalf of Catholic schools. Once again he raised the question of the divisive affect of what might be taught in religious schools—"I can imagine what a religious zealot, as contrasted to a civil libertarian, can do with the Reformation or with the Inquisition."[45]

Although the majority of the Court never gave the divisiveness issue the importance that Black and Douglas thought it should have, Burger's claim that the Religion Clauses were intended to dampen public debates of a religious nature went far toward recognizing divisiveness as a major principle of constitutional interpretation.

Also in 1971, the Court responded sympathetically to a religious group that was in some ways radically at odds with American society, when it permitted the Amish not to enroll their children in high school.[46] Burger, in writing the majority opinion, found that even such a stance of radical withdrawal might be beneficial to society, as with medieval monks.[47]

However, Douglas in dissenting feared that the Amish might harm their children in separating them from the culture.[48]

The following year, in a decision invalidating various kinds of public support of religious schools, Justice Powell acknowledged that such grants might be the cause of religious strife and held that while such a factor was not determinative, it was relevant,[49] seemingly an attempt by the majority of the Court to reach a compromise position on the issue.

In a similar case in 1975, Brennan again warned of the divisive potential of political battles over public assistance. This danger had been formally identified by the Court only in the *Lemon* case of 1971, and he therefore questioned the continuing applicability of the Court's decision in the 1968 *Allen* case, which upheld the loan of books, because it had failed to take account of the danger of divisiveness.[50] The next year, he repeated the warning in another dissent,[51] and in the year following, Justice Marshall also raised the issue in dissent.[52]

Also in 1977, Marshall lamented that the Court's failure to accommodate an employee with religious scruples concerning his work undermined "one of the Nation's pillars of strength—our hospitality to religious diversity,"[53] an opinion that brought into relief a paradoxical aspect of the strict separationist position—that, while strife among groups was deemed socially destructive, the multiplicity of such groups was deemed a positive good.

In the same year Brennan joined in striking down a state law barring clergy from holding public office, ruling that

> The mere fact that a purpose of the Establishment Clause is to reduce or eliminate religious divisiveness does not place religious discussion, association, or political participation in a status less preferred than rights of discussion, association, and political participation generally.

The antidote that the Constitution provided against zealots who would inject sectarianism into the political process, Brennan urged, was to subject their ideas to refutation in the marketplace of ideas and their platforms to rejection at the polls.[54]

Brennan's position was significant in that while he was ordinarily inclined to be more a separationist than was the chief justice, he seemed in this case to stop short of Burger's claim in the *Lemon* case that religiously based political controversy enjoyed less protection than did other kinds of disputes. However, Brennan obviously also believed that such controversy was unhealthy for the country.

In the 1982 case approving the gift of an unused army hospital to a religious college, the dissenters, led by Brennan, again argued the danger of religious divisiveness. Besides those restrictions explicitly imposed by the Constitution, the only limit on the government's taxing power was precisely in matters of religion.[55]

In his own dissent Justice Stevens held that taxpayers had a special interest in the church-state issue

> in terms of the structure and basic philosophy of our constitutional government, and it would be difficult to point to any issue that has a more intimate, pervasive, and fundamental impact upon the life of the taxpayers—and upon the life of all citizens.

Far from finding the gift defensible, he thought there were "urgent necessities" for disallowing it.[56]

In the same year, the Court nullified a state law giving churches the authority to veto liquor licenses in their vicinities, with Burger quoting from his own opinion in the *Lemon* case that such a law created the danger of "political fragmentation and divisiveness along religious lines."[57] In dissenting, Justice Rehnquist made a bold effort to exorcise the fear of division, arguing that the Court was reacting almost hysterically to a "sensible" state law, making it seem almost as though it threatened "another St. Bartholomew's Night."[58]

The following year, in approving the removal of a tax exemption from a religious college found to be following racist policies, Powell thought that religious tax exemptions encouraged divisive, even sharply conflicting, groups to compete for such benefits. Rather than forming a "common community conscience," exemptions tended to force conformity to government orthodoxy.[59]

The same year, in dissenting from a judgment allowing chaplains in state legislatures, Brennan found that such chaplaincies were inherently divisive, as the very fact that they were being challenged in court showed. Brennan now appeared to accept Burger's opinion in the *Lemon* case that the Constitution enjoined all political battles along religious lines, even while encouraging other kinds of political debate.[60] Stevens pointed out that by hiring a chaplain from one denomination, the legislature was by definition excluding others.[61]

But in permitting the public display of a religious Christmas scene in the *Lynch* case (1984), Burger denied that the custom was religiously divisive, pointing to its forty years of noncontroversial endurance. In so ruling he touched on an apparent anomaly concerning divisiveness—the mere filing of a suit itself revealed a dispute, hence plaintiffs would triumph automatically, which Burger pointed out was clearly not a tenable legal principle.[62]

Justice O'Connor flatly rejected the idea that religious divisiveness should be the test of constitutionality. The Court should inquire into the character of the government's actions themselves, not into their possible effects.[63]

exist in complete isolation from each other, and thus "various sects
their adherents will frequently intersect, conflict, and combine." But
voted with the majority on the grounds that the official silence
unted to an endorsement of particular religious views.[71]

Dissenting the same year in a case that nullified various forms of public
to religious schools, Burger observed tartly that the conditions that
d prevailed in the eighteenth century no longer existed, and charged
at the Court's preoccupation with possible religious conflict "borders
paranoia."[72]

In another such case the same year, Brennan made one of the strongest
atements ever on the issue:

> For just as religion throughout history has provided comfort, guid-
> ance, and inspiration to many, it can also serve powerfully to divide
> societies and to exclude those whose beliefs are not in accord with
> particular religions or sects that have from time to time achieved
> domination.[73]

In upholding in 1987 a program of sex education that emphasized chastity,
Rehnquist recognized that there were divisions of opinion along religious
lines about adolescent sexual behavior, but ruled that those did not constitute divisiveness.[74] The dissenters led by Blackmun thought otherwise.[75]

In a case the same year involving the inviolability of an American Indian
cemetery, O'Connor, citing the *Federalist* papers, said that the affects of
sectarianism could be dangerous but were restrained through the competition of many sects.[76]

In voting to invalidate official prayers at a public highschool graduation
in 1992, Justice Souter rejected the argument that by inviting clergy of
various denominations to lead prayers, the school was promoting diversity of religious views. As Madison warned, such pluralism would over
time narrow to an official orthodoxy, Souter predicted.[77] Concurring,
Blackmun observed that religion had not lost its power to engender divisiveness, citing death threats allegedly made against officers of the American Civil Liberties Union in certain cases.[78] The minority, led by Justice
Scalia, argued that the practice was not divisive—being present when
prayers were said was merely a sign of a tolerant society whose people
respected one another's beliefs.[79]

In the 1995 *Rosenberger* case requiring a state university to provide
funds to a student religious journal, the majority held that the encouragement of diverse viewpoints and vigorous debate on campus were part of
the school's purpose.[80]

In dissent in a 1995 case concerning the right of the Ku Klux Klan to
erect a cross in a public square, Stevens cited Black's opinion in the *Ever-*

In his dissent Brennan argued the opposite
symbols would stimulate a demand by other g
and the law suit had in fact unleashed power.
community. In the nineteenth century, when publ.
were first being introduced into the United States
troversial, with some Protestant groups oppos
grounds. Brennan suspected that the Founders wei
controversial nature of such celebrations and had t.
drafted the Establishment Clause. They wanted "a ι
disorder among all denominations, so that each sect v
the others for the allegiance of its followers, without ;

But when the issue returned to the Court in 1989, in
ent context, the majority disallowed such public sym
found for the majority that the display of Christian sy
violate a proper respect for religious diversity.[65]

O'Connor now also found religious division relevant t
displays conveyed to non-Christians the message that the
ers in the political community." She agreed with the majori
of their respective locations on public property, the Christi.
not tolerable, while the Jewish display was. She added that
was a minority religion, no one could mistake the Jewish ;
enjoying an official endorsement.[66]

In holding that both displays should be disallowed, Bren.
out that the "message of pluralism" conveyed by both Ch
Jewish symbols together might itself be offensive to some pe
some religions are hostile to others.[67] Stevens also disapprove
displays, holding that they had the affect of emphasizing "sii
deeply felt differences" and the government ought not to fom
disagreements.[68]

The dissenters led by Justice Kennedy accused the majority of m
ing an actual hostility to religion. By permitting only secular sym.
the holiday, the government was in fact excluding religious believers
nedy again reviewed the numerous ways in which religious faith w
firmed in public life, such as the official proclamation of Thanksg.
Day, and pointed out that such things excluded nonbelievers as muc
did the Christmas display.[69]

Calling the majority's reasoning "Orwellian," Kennedy warned that ι
Court was in danger of creating a new jurisprudence based on the numb
of adherents a particular religion had—"those religions enjoying th
largest following must be consigned to the status of least favored faiths sc
as to avoid any possible risk of offending members of minority religions."[70]

In the 1985 *Jaffree* case invalidating an officially mandated "moment
of silence" in public schools, O'Connor noted that church and state could

son case to the effect that the Founding Fathers above all feared religious strife and that this was the reason for the Establishment Clause.[81]

The case also manifested unique examples of divisiveness, in Stevens's judgment, in that a Jewish group had been allowed to erect a menorah, the Klan had reacted by erecting a cross, and other Christian groups then also erected crosses in order to undercut the Klan's symbolism. The Latin cross was not even acceptable to all Christians, Stevens pointed out, and overall, the incident demonstrated how religious symbolism in public places could be offensive even to members of the same religion.[82]

Postulating an "ordinary person" who might erroneously construe the cross as being endorsed by the state, Stevens urged that "a paramount purpose of the Establishment Clause is to protect such a person from being made to feel like an outsider in matters of faith, and a stranger in the political community."[83]

Evidence that the Court was retreating from a stern view of the dangers of divisiveness came in a 1997 case, when O'Connor admitted that a particular program of aid to religious schools had the potential for generating "political divisiveness" but ruled that this was not sufficient in itself to render the program unconstitutional.[84]

But in a 2000 decision forbidding school-endorsed prayer at high school football games, Stevens once more warned that the practice "encourages divisiveness along religious lines in a public school setting."[85]

Also in 2000, dissenting in a case permitting public funds to be used to provide computers and other equipment for private schools,[86] Souter insisted that the Framers were strongly motivated by fear of sectarian conflict. Programs such as the one being upheld would breed divisiveness, in the form of resentment on the part of those who objected to having their taxes used for such purposes and demands by others for what they regarded as their share.

Dissenting in the 2002 case upholding "vouchers" for private schools, Stevens warned of the potential for religious strife present in the program and cited the Balkans, Northern Ireland, and the Middle East as areas of the world plagued by religious conflict,[87] while Souter warned that the competition for public funds would itself lead to strife.[88] Justice Breyer too thought the program posed a special danger of social conflict.[89]

DEFINING RELIGION

The fundamental irony of the Court's jurisprudence of the Religion Clauses is the fact that despite the numerous cases it has been called upon to adjudicate, it has never attempted a final definition of the phenomenon it is called upon to judge. In the *Reynolds* polygamy case (1878), Chief

Justice Waite felt compelled to strive toward a definition. Noting that the Constitution itself did not define it, Waite found it necessary to look elsewhere, especially to the way in which the term was understood at the time of the Founders. Waite did not actually attempt to retrieve such a definition but merely held that the Founders had not intended to exempt polygamy from the criminal laws.[90]

In another polygamy case, in 1890, Justice Field again attempted the definition that Waite had promised: "The term 'religion' has reference to one's views of his relations to his Creator, and to the obligations they impose of reverence for his being and character, and of obedience to his will." "Religion," according to Field, was often confused with "*cultus*," which he defined as the "form of worship of a particular sect." Thus while the Constitution intended to guarantee full freedom of belief, it did not intend to protect actions inimical to good order.[91]

But Field too failed to deliver on his promise of a workable definition, since by most understandings its "mode of worship" would be considered part of a religion, and it could hardly be thought that the Free-Exercise Clause meant to protect beliefs only, not their practice. Waite and Field felt compelled to define religion because the Constitution guaranteed its free exercise and they had to show that in banning polygamy, they were not contravening that guarantee.

In a famous remark about obscenity, Justice Stewart said in 1963 that, "I shall not today attempt further to define [it] . . . and perhaps I could never succeed in intelligently doing so. But I know it when I see it,"[92] and in effect that has also been the Court's approach to religion through most of its history. In the vast majority of cases, "religion" has come before the Court in its conventional form—organized groups of people holding beliefs concerning supernatural powers in the universe. Thus throughout most of its history the Court could take the definition for granted, as when Chief Justice Marshall, in the *Dartmouth* case (1819), referred to Christianity, again almost in passing, as "our holy religion."[93]

Dissenting in a conscientious-objector case in 1931, Chief Justice Hughes, also almost in passing, defined religion as "belief in a relation to God involving duties superior to those arising from any human relation."[94] It was a late attempt at what might be called a classical definition and would have little force in the post–World War II era when the Court began once again to grapple with the question that had defeated the nineteenth-century justices.

The problem of definition inevitably kept arising. In a Jehovah's Witnesses case in 1940, Frankfurter referred, almost in passing, to "the affirmative pursuit of one's convictions about the ultimate mystery of the universe and man's relation to it."[95] But, in his lengthy dissent in another Witness case three years later,[96] he appeared to have repented this attempt and stated explicitly that the Court could not define religion, because to do so would be discriminatory, drawing the conclusion that the law could not accommodate everyone who made a claim of conscience in the name of religion.[97]

In dissenting from a ruling that Witnesses could not be made to pay a fee in order to distribute literature, Justice Reed held in 1943 that the distribution of literature was not a religious activity, hence was not protected by the First Amendment. Putting a price on the literature destroyed its sacred character, he believed, and in fact many church activities, such as running orphanages, were not religious in nature.[98]

In a related case the same year Roberts dissented with a similar argument. Many activities, such as nursing the sick or working for social improvement, could be called religious and thus demand special constitutional protection, he warned, but he did not think that the Court should allow such an elastic understanding.[99]

Reed and Roberts, in these two cases, were the last justices to think that the distinction between the religious and nonreligious activities of churches could be readily made. Both seemed to regard the definition of religion as virtually self-evident and as based on objective criteria.

In the *Everson* case, Rutledge seemed to expand the definition of religion beyond the conventional one, referring to "believers of all faiths, and others who do not express their feeling towards ultimate issues of existence in any credal form,"[100] his apparent definition of religion as "a feeling towards ultimate issues of existence" announcing the Court's new understanding of the phenomenon. As in so many other ways, the *Everson* case was truly seminal for the modern interpretation of the Religion Clauses. In the same decision Rutledge decreed that "The realm of religious training and belief remains, as the Amendment made it, the kingdom of the individual man and his God. It should be kept inviolately private."[101]

In the equally seminal *McCollum* case, Jackson pointed out that the Constitution itself was of no help in determining where the sacred ended and the secular began, nor was the law, and he went on to predict that the wall of separation would therefore have to be a very irregular one.[102]

In the 1952 case upholding "released time" religious instruction, Black warned against allowing the government "to steal into the sacred area of religious choice,"[103] and in the "sacrilege" case three years later, Frankfurter warned that the government could not "put within unascertainable bounds the varieties of religious experience."[104]

Jackson, the acerbity of whose opinions was legendary, in 1952 seemed to reject even the conventional view of religion as an organized body of people professing a particular creed, when he asserted with respect to the Russian Orthodox Church that "I do not think New York State must yield to the authority of a foreign and unfriendly state masquerading as a spiritual institution."[105] Jackson's opinion was a rare instance of a member of the Court attempting to deny the term "religion" to those who claim it. Another instance was a 1958 case in which Justice Clark thought that religious freedom did not protect church employees' refusal to take a loyalty oath, since the refusal could not be characterized as "religious in nature."[106]

In 1961, in upholding a state law prohibiting commerce on Sunday, Frankfurter attempted to broaden the constitutional understanding of religion:

> of its nature religion—in the comprehensive sense in which the Constitution uses the word—is an aspect of human thought and action which profoundly relates the life of man to the world in which he lives. Religious belief pervades, and religious institutions have traditionally regulated, virtually all human activities.[107]

Later he held that the Constitution had withdrawn from legitimate political concern "man's belief or disbelief in the unity of some transcendent idea and man's expression in action of that belief or disbelief."[108]

Although the issue at hand was the sacredness of the Christian sabbath, Frankfurter obviously intended to enlarge the definition of religion beyond the traditional one, and, in forbidding prayer in the public schools in 1963, Clark was already warning that the Court could not "establish a religion of secularism," which he assured the public it was not in fact doing.[109] His comment was of significance in seeming to acknowledge that possibility, implying that "secularism" and "religion" were not necessarily contradictory terms.

In the same year Black, in writing the unanimous opinion finding that atheists could not be excluded from public office, included a footnote with profound implications, often quoted: "Among religions in this country which do not teach what would generally be considered belief in the existence of God are Buddhism, Taoism, Ethical Culture, Secular Humanism, and others."[110] The inclusion of the term "Secular Humanism" in a list of recognized "religions," although at this point in history it did not necessarily represent more than Black's own view, nonetheless held great portent for the Court's future understanding of the phenomenon.

But it was the series of cases involving conscientious objection to military service, beginning in 1965, that directly confronted the Court with a problem of definition that could not be avoided.

In the *Seeger* case (1965)[111] the Court noted that the Selective Service Act defined religion as "an individual's belief in relation to a Supreme Being involving duties superior to those arising from any human relation," and excluding "merely" philosophical ideas or "a personal moral code."[112]

The appellant admitted "scepticism or disbelief" in the "existence of God" but affirmed "belief in and devotion to goodness and virtue for their own sakes, and a religious faith in a purely ethical creed." Another appellant believed in "goodness" defined as "the Ultimate Cause for the fact of the Being of the Universe," while a third defined religion as "the consciousness of some power manifest in nature which helps man in the ordering of his life in harmony with its demands,"[113] a collection of beliefs that on their face seemed to be precisely the kind Congress had intended to exclude.

Clark approached the issue by commenting that few people would deny that "in no field of human endeavor has the tool of language proved so inadequate in the communication of ideas as it has in dealing with the fundamental questions."[114] He acknowledged that Hughes's definition of 1931 seemed to govern the Selective Service Act, although pointing out that Congress had changed the word "God" to "Supreme Being" and that even Hughes had admitted that the word "God" had many meanings.[115]

Clark then attempted his own definition: "a sincere and meaningful belief which occupies in the life of its possessor a place parallel to that filled by God of those admittedly qualifying for exemption."[116] Clark thought the creed of the appellants resembled in certain ways the theology of the Protestant theologian Paul Tillich, who spoke of God as "the ground of Being," and he noted that the Anglican bishop John A. T. Robinson rejected traditional ideas of God as "up there" and placed God far beyond human comprehension.[117]

Clark also attempted to place religion in a larger cultural context:

Ever since primordial days numerous peoples have had a certain perception of that hidden power which hovers over the course of things and over the events which make up the lives of men. Some have even come to know of it as Supreme Being and Father.

Religions in "advanced cultures," he observed, made use of "more developed language."[118]

Besides Tillich and Robinson, Clark quoted at some length from the decrees of the Second Vatican Council of the Catholic Church, whose deliberations were then in their final stages, in order to show that there was broad agreement about the nature of religion. He quoted also from the leader of the Ethical Culture Society, a group disclaiming any belief in a personal deity.[119]

A lower court had ruled that a "religion" had to be based on "externally compelled belief," that is, beliefs that did not originate with the individual but were thought to emanate from a superior source. However, Clark thought that was not a tenable principle under the Constitution.[120]

For Douglas, in his concurrence, the term "Supreme Being" could embrace "the cosmos as well as another anthropomorphic entity." In the history of religion the term had no "narrow, technical meaning," as a perusal of Buddhist, Hindu, and other sources showed.[121]

The Court seemed obviously ill at ease in its efforts at definition, aware of the anomaly whereby too precise a definition would itself become an "establishment of religion." However, the broadening of the definition was essential if the benefits of conscientious objection were not to be restricted to believers in a personal God, and it was no doubt the intention of at least some of the justices, as it had been of Frankfurter a few years before, to extend the benefits of the Free-Exercise Clause to as many people as possible.

The *Welsh* case (1970) again presented an applicant for conscientious-objector status who belonged to no church and had deleted the phrase "my religious training" from his application, stating that his opinions had been formed by his study of history and sociology, although he later referred to his beliefs as "religious in the ethical sense." He explicitly denied that his pacifism was based on beliefs "arising from duties superior to those of a merely human relationship."[122]

For the most part the Court this time avoided the question of definition, merely holding that Welsh's beliefs were implicitly permitted under the Selective Service Act. Concurring, Justice Harlan nonetheless confessed misgivings, finding it necessary to accept the Court's dubious reading of the conscription law only in order to save the law from unconstitutionality. He thought there was a significant difference between religions that

> usually have an organized and formal structure and dogma and a cohesive group identity, even where nontheistic, and cults that represent schools of thought and in the usual case are without formal structure or are, at most, loose and informal associations of individuals who share common ethical, moral, or intellectual views.[123]

Here Harlan seemed to place the defining emphasis merely on a group's level of organization, recognizing that a religion could be "nontheistic," that is, without belief in a personal god.

The following year the Court denied the right of conscientious objection to appellants whose position was "selective," that is, did not extend to all wars. One of these appellants also acknowledged that he had no formal religious beliefs, and in his dissent, Douglas thought the Court should recognize the proffered definition of "humanism:" "respect and love for man, faith in his inherent goodness and perfectibility, and confidence in his capability to improve some of the pains of the human condition."[124] In this case, by focusing on the issue of "selective" conscientious objection, the Court did not have to decide whether the proposed definition fit the Constitution's understanding of religion.

In the *Yoder* case Burger observed that not every belief was entitled to protection under the Free-Exercise Clause and that, while it was a "delicate question" to ascertain what was or was not religion, the Court was obligated to attempt to do so. The Amish would not be entitled to an exemption if their objection to the public schools was based on "their subjective evaluation and rejection of contemporary secular values accepted by the majority." But their way of life was evidently religious, based as it was on their understanding of injunctions found in the New Testament.[125]

Douglas, expressing severe misgivings as to whether the Amish should receive such an exemption, also regretted what he saw as the Court's backward step in its definition of religion, recalling Clark's formulation in the *Seeger* case, which Douglas called "exalted views of religion."[126]

In fact Burger did not attempt a definition of religion; he merely found that the Amish community, in following biblical teachings, fit a conventional understanding.

In a 1972 case concerning whether the "political" activities of a religious group could cause it to lose its tax-exempt status, the group raised an issue that seemed to follow logically from the Court's wariness about definition on the one hand and its fear of "entanglement" on the other— was it not a violation of religious liberty even to inquire whether a particular group was a "religion"? The Court ignored the question.[127]

In a school aid case in 1977, Stevens held that there was a fundamental distinction between what was religious and what was secular, quoting the attorney Clarence Darrow saying that "the realm of religion . . . is where knowledge leaves off, and where faith begins."[128]

In a 1981 employment case, Burger again noted that a definition of religion was difficult and that courts were ill-equipped to adjudicate such definitions but could, as in the case at hand, determine that a particular individual had genuine religious beliefs. But Burger also foresaw the possibility of "an asserted claim so clearly nonreligious in motivation as not to be entitled to protection."[129]

Dissenting in a 1982 case nullifying the requirement that all charities register with a state government, Rehnquist thought that it was not evident that the Unification Church of the Rev. Sun Yung Moon was a religion and held that it should be required to prove the claim if it was entitled to the protection of law.[130] He did not indicate the criteria for such proof, whose necessity the majority of the Court did not acknowledge.

In the two cases during the 1980s concerning Christmas displays in public places, the justices debated among themselves the distinction be-

tween religion as a creed and religion as merely a cultural and social tradition, without reaching any firm conclusions concerning the difference.[131]

O'Connor, in 1983, attempted to formulate a secular definition of religion:

Those government acknowledgements of religion serve, in the only
ways reasonably possible in our culture, the legitimate secular purposes of solemnizing public occasions, expressing confidence in the
future, and encouraging the recognition of what is worth [sic] of
appreciation.[132]

Paradoxically, while the majority was attempting to secularize religious
symbols in order to permit their public display, a minority of the Court
who wanted to forbid their display were, led by Justice Brennan, offering
their own exalted spiritual definition: "[A] divine Savior was brought into
the world and the purpose of this miraculous birth was to illumine a
path to salvation and redemption, For Christians that path is exclusive,
precious, and holy." Citizens who went out merely to shop, seeing the
crèche scene, nonetheless experienced "awe and wonder that God sent
his son into the world as Messiah." To suggest otherwise, Brennan
charged, would be offensive to Christians.[133]

By contrast, Brennan argued, the kinds of public religious expressions
often cited as proof that the First Amendment did not mandate secularism—inscriptions on coins, for example—constituted "ceremonial
deism" without real religious significance. Such practices were intended
merely to "solemnize public occasions" or were "expressing inspiration,"
not affirming actual religious faith, hence could be permitted.[134]

In a 1987 case upholding the right of a church to require its employees
to belong to that church,[135] Justice White admitted that distinguishing
between the religious and nonreligious activities of churches was difficult,
the effect of his ruling being that, for purposes of law, all church activities
could be considered religious in nature.[136]

Concurring, Brennan thought that defining as religious the nonreligious
activities of churches was unnecessary to the churches' own "self-defini-
tion" but that for the Court to make such a distinction would require
"excessive entanglement."[137] Brennan's opinion here was the most direct
statement by any member of the Court that attempts to define religion
might themselves violate the Religion Clauses.

In the same year, the Court ruled against American Indians who sought
to prevent a road from being built on land they considered sacred. Dissenting from the majority, Brennan presented a disquisition on the nature
of Indian religion that, he said, in contrast to the Christian emphasis on
creeds and dogmas, depended primarily on the performance of rituals
closely tied to the land. He then offered a detailed account of Indian rituals and beliefs. Federal land regulations, Brennan found, were "inherently

ethnocentric," in that they "ascribed religious significance to land in a traditional Western hierarchical manner."[138] A 1990 case concerning Indian ritual use of peyote was decided in the same manner—the legitimacy of the belief was not questioned but it was found not to outweigh the state's interest in forbidding the use of drugs.[139]

In 1989 yet another employment case raised the question of definition, since the appellant refused to work on Sundays merely because of general religious principles, not because of the teachings of any particular church. White thought that it was difficult to distinguish religious from secular motives but held that general principles were sufficient, even if not tied to a particular creed.[140]

In the 1992 case prohibiting prayers at a public-school graduation, Blackmun made a distinction with potentially profound implications for the Court's understanding of religion: "Democracy requires the encouragement of dialogue and dissent, while religious faith puts its trust in ultimate divine authority above all human deliberations."[141]

The following year, in a case involving animal sacrifice, the Court confronted the most exotic religious practice ever brought to its attention, but did not find it necessary to inquire whether the practice was authentically religious. The appellants' claim to be a religion was accepted implicitly, and the Court found that they had been the victims of overt discrimination.[142]

The disposition of the case was typical of the Court's way of handling the problem of definition. It has never attempted in an authoritative way to state what the term means but, more significant still, has never attempted to state what it does not mean. In the history of the Court every appellant claiming to hold religious beliefs has been treated as genuine, and disputes have centered not on what is or is not a religion but on what rights and restrictions religion, however defined, is thought to have under the Constitution.

RELIGION AS PRIVATE

But, as the Court was disposing of an increasing number of religion cases without having to state definitively what religion was, its own understanding of the phenomenon was nevertheless undergoing significant development.

In a 1931 case involving conscientious objection,[143] Justice Sutherland proclaimed that: "We are a Christian people according to one another the equal right to religious freedom and acknowledging with reverence the duty of obedience to the will of God." He found the military conscription law not incompatible with the will of God, which he apparently understood as an objective reality, even suggesting that God willed national military preparedness.[144]

It was in the same case that Hughes offered his formula about "a relation to God involving duties superior to those arising from any human relationship." According to the Chief Justice, it was impossible even to speak of religious liberty without assuming "supreme allegiance to the will of God."[145]

Thus both Sutherland and Hughes, on opposite sides of the case, posited an authority superior to the individual believer in which faith had to be rooted. But Justice Cardozo, in a similar case three years later, raised the question of the subjectivity of belief: "One who is a martyr to principle—which may turn out in the end to be a delusion or error—does not prove by his martyrdom that he has kept within the law."[146]

In the *Gobitis* case in 1940, the first of the major Jehovah's Witnesses cases, Frankfurter radically relativized the basis of religious belief, going so far as to argue that religious freedom required the rejection of all absolutes, including the absolute of religious freedom itself, and the acceptance of beliefs as merely personal, the essence of the Court's position, as expounded by Frankfurter, being that beliefs as such could not justify an exemption from the general laws.[147]

When the Court reversed itself on the issue three years later,[148] Black once again referred to the authority of a higher law. He noticed that the appellants did not refuse to salute the flag simply out of personal principle but because they saw it as what the Bible condemned as a "graven image." Thus the *Gobitis* decision forced school children "to participate in a ceremony which ends in nothing for them but a fear of spiritual condemnation." Black added that, if their fears were thought groundless, the proper antidotes were "time and reason."[149] Black's concurring opinion was the last time the Court would define religious liberty as rooted in an obligation to a power higher than the self, in this case including the prospect of personal damnation.

In dissenting, Frankfurter insisted that such beliefs were "sectarian scruples" that of their very nature could not override the general law. Sincerity of belief was not sufficient to establish a right.[150]

The Court's view of religion as rooted in personal, subjective perceptions was solidified in the *Ballard* case of 1944, when the leaders of the I Am movement were prosecuted for mail fraud.[151] In his majority opinion, Douglas pointed out that, not only were Americans free to believe anything they chose, they were also not obligated to prove their beliefs, which of their nature might be utterly incomprehensible to other people, the miracles of the New Testament or belief in the power of prayer being examples.[152]

Dissenting, Chief Justice Stone seemed to want to salvage some sense that beliefs could be rooted in objective reality; specifically he held that the authenticity of alleged cures could be established.[153]

Jackson, who indicated that he considered the appellants frauds ("I see humbug"), thought that the test of sincerity was whether something was believable in terms of an individual's own experience. The issue at hand raised profound psychological questions, and Jackson referred to the philosopher William James's discussion of the ambiguities of the "will to believe." Courts would find it impossible to judge the quality of individual experiences, and the criteria of proof in matters of religion were quite different from those for secular questions.[154]

Jackson wondered whether, if certain beliefs gave people peace and comfort, believers did not thereby "get what they paid for," adding drily that he hoped there would not be many such people. The real damage of such beliefs, he warned, was in the possibility of later disillusionment and cynicism. In constitutional terms it was finally necessary to accept that "we must put up with, and even pay for, a good deal of rubbish."[155]

When in 1961 the Court began to apply systematically the jurisprudence it had first articulated in 1947–48, its view of religion as radically subjective was a key element in its reasoning. Thus in ruling against prayer in the public schools in 1961,[156] Black found that religion was "too personal, too sacred, too holy" to be imposed by magistrates.[157] Douglas in the same case recalled his earlier assertion that "we are a religious people" but explained that such religiosity was to be expressed only privately.[158] In 1963, while invalidating mandated Bible reading in the public schools, Clark saw the religious tradition of the nation embodied in the home, the church, and "the inviolable citadel of the individual heart and mind," which the government should not "invade."[159] In an employment case the same year, Douglas asserted that "religious scruples" were to be "fenced off" from government.[160]

Dissenting in the *Schempp* Bible-reading case, Stewart argued that the Court's jurisprudence placed at a disadvantage those who did not believe that religion should be practiced only in private.[161] His was by now a decidedly minority position, however, with the majority of the Court committed to the principle that the First Amendment envisioned religion as a private and personal matter.

In this as in other ways, the conscientious-objector cases of the 1960s were crucial. The Selective Service Act had explicitly embodied the older view of religion as based on submission to a higher power beyond the self, but the Court reinterpreted that to mean fidelity to one's own deepest beliefs.

This majority view supported the expansion of religious liberties, since virtually any proclaimed creed was now entitled to protection, while at the same time there was to be an increasingly strict surveillance of public life to guard against the "intrusion" of religion. Thus in 1970, Douglas questioned tax exemptions for churches, referring to "the relative emotional values they placed on their activities."[162] The following year, Burger held that "the Constitution decrees that religion must be a private matter for the individual, the family, and the institutions of private choice."[163] In the same case Douglas conceded that the public schools had a tendency to induce conformity and did not allow for "personal idiosyncracies," while regretting that religious schools permitted those idiosyncracies only in conformity with their own creeds.[164]

In the *Yoder* case Burger insisted that a mere "way of life," or personally held ideas, was not enough to override compulsory school attendance. Authentic religious commitment, such as the Amish possessed, was necessary.[165] This was an apparent attempt at treating religion as something more than personal belief, but Burger offered no guidance on the matter other than the fact that the Amish were a conventionally recognized religion. More characteristic of the Court's view was Douglas's dissent, in which he pronounced that "religion is an individual experience,"[166] in order to suggest that Amish children should not have to conform to the faith of their parents.

In the 1992 case forbidding prayer at a public-school graduation,[167] Kennedy held that the Constitution "mandates that the presentation and transmission of religious beliefs is committed to the private sphere."[168] In dissent Scalia directly contradicted this claim: "The Court apparently thinks it [religion] to be some purely personal avocation that can be indulged in secret, like pornography in the privacy of one's room. For most believers it is *not* and never has been."[169] Scalia's opinion was a late and unsuccessful attempt to persuade the Court to approach religion in terms other than those of personal preference.

RELIGION AS IRRATIONAL

The Court's finding in the *Ballard* case established the assumption that belief could be validated solely on the basis of individual subjective apprehensions, which were of such a nature as to be incredible, even incomprehensible, to others. Religion was seen as lacking objective foundation and resting on a purely personal view of reality.

Thus in a Jehovah's Witnesses case also in 1944, Rutledge pronounced that "Heart and mind are not the same thing. Intuitive faith and reasoned judgment are not the same. Spirit is not always thought."[170]

In the *Everson* case, he referred to "believers of all faiths, and those who do not express their feelings towards ultimate issues of existence in

any credal form," later adding "The realm of religious training and belief remains, as the Amendment made it, the kingdom of individual man and his God. It should be inviolately private."[171]

In 1952, Jackson, who sometimes allowed himself to speak of appellants with contempt even as he was voting to uphold their rights, dissented in a case involving a property dispute within the Russian Orthodox Church. His dissent stemmed in part from his insistence that the dispute should be treated simply as a property case, without religious significance, and he warned the Court that unlike the majority, he would not "wallow through the complex, obscure, and fragmentary details of secular and ecclesiastical history, theology, and canon law in which this case is smothered,"[172] which he apparently viewed as a morass beneath the notice of a rational man.

In adjudicating another Eastern Orthodox dispute in 1976, Brennan seemed to view church law and church history in a way similar to Jackson's fastidious distaste, but drew the opposite conclusion. He reviewed the law and history of the Serbian Orthodox Church in considerable detail and found that internal church procedures were the only permissible way by which such disputes could be settled. "Indeed, it is the essence of religious faith that ecclesiastical decisions are to be reached and are to be accepted as matters of faith whether or not rational or measurable by objective criteria." Secular criteria like "fundamental fairness" were not applicable, and Brennan warned against "intrusion into a religious thicket."[173]

Brennan's position, now that of the majority, seemed to be that religion rested on foundations that were not even comprehensible to people outside the faith and could not be governed by ordinary rationality. It was a view that Burger endorsed in an employment case in 1981, when he held that religious beliefs "need not be acceptable, logical, consistent, or comprehensible to others in order to merit First Amendment protection."[174]

The cases involving the public display of Christmas scenes led to a debate within the Court over the subjective affects of religious symbolism. In the *Lynch* case in 1984,[175] Burger found that "the display engenders a friendly community spirit of good will in keeping with the season." He thought the Nativity scene, like a religious painting in a museum, was "passive" and therefore subject to varying understandings on the part of those viewing it.[176]

O'Connor, concurring, pointed out that messages are not always received in the way they are intended. The city did not intend to convey a message of approval of Christianity, although the citizens might perceive it in that manner, but she did not find that this invalidated the practice.[177]

Dissenting, Brennan argued in effect that the symbolic meanings were not so ambiguous—the Nativity scene had an obvious religious meaning, which would be its primary affect on the public, although he also thought that certain venerable customs, such as religious inscriptions on coins, had lost their religious significance.[178] Also dissenting, Blackmun pointed out that the majority's argument trivialized religious symbolism, and he refused to participate in the "desacralization of symbol."[179]

The second such case, in 1989, renewed the argument in a more complex way, since it involved Jewish as well as Christian symbolism, and the justices debated the relative degree to which such symbols might in context have predominantly secular, as well as religious, meanings. Once again those upholding the displays argued that their meaning was equivocal, while those opposed thought the overt meaning was the dominant one.[180] In his dissent Justice Kennedy insisted that the Court did not have the competence to decide the meaning of every religious symbol and accused the majority of functioning as a "national theology board."[181]

The 1995 *Capitol Square* case, involving the right of the Ku Klux Klan to erect a cross in a public square, heavily involved the possible ways in which the public might perceive the symbol—as an affirmation of Christianity, as an anti-Jewish symbol, as a symbol of "white racist government," and other things—and whether members of the public might construe it as having official endorsement. The conflicting symbolism of the cross erected by the Klan and crosses erected as a counterweight by various Christian groups was also noted, as was the potentially controversial nature of the cross even among Christians. The majority of the Court postulated what a "reasonable person" might think about such a symbol, but its inherent ambiguity was recognized.[182]

These inconclusive debates raised a new kind of issue that the Court did not seem prepared to resolve—if religion is primarily a personal, subjective phenomenon, then its significance lies not only in how its adherents regard it but also in how it is perceived by others.

Beginning in the mid-1980s the Court found itself increasingly confronted by unfamiliar religious beliefs and practices—the fear that possessing a Social Security number would diminish a person's soul, the sacredness of an Indian burial ground, the ritual use of a prohibited drug, animal sacrifice. In one sense all these issues could be resolved with relative ease, given the Court's view, now firmly established, that religious belief is radically personal and cannot be evaluated by any "outside" criteria. Although appellants did not always obtain from the Court the relief they sought, even when they were rebuffed their professed faiths were accepted as authentic.

But the 1987 case concerning the Indian cemetery—the claim that sacred ground should be protected from a planned public road[183]—confronted the Court with a new kind of dilemma. While recognizing that many Indians considered the inviolability of the burial ground necessary for their "personal spiritual development," the majority led by O'Connor found that it was not possible to "satisfy every citizen's religious needs."[184] In his dissent Brennan sharpened the dilemma by expounding the difference between two conflicting views of land possession—the Indian versus the European.[185]

Religion as Indoctrination

The modern Court's view of religion as essentially subjective, even irrational, in turn dictated its view of religious instruction as not education at all, in the proper sense, but rather as a form of "indoctrination."

Thus dissenting in the *Everson* case, Jackson expounded what he thought was the essential character of Catholic education:

> The Roman Catholic Church, counselled by experience in many ages and many lands and with all sorts and conditions of men, takes what, from the viewpoint of its own progress and the success of its mission, is a wise estimate of the importance of education to religion. It does not leave it to the individual to pick up religion by chance. It relies on early and indelible indoctrination in the faith and order of the Church by the word and example of persons consecrated to the task.

He went on to suggest that the public schools were themselves more consistent with Protestantism than with Catholicism.[186]

In the *McCollum* case Frankfurter made a similar argument. Virtually all education prior to modern times had been based on the Bible, he recalled, and its chief aim was to inculcate religion. He affirmed an individual's "right of indoctrination in the faith of his choice," which could not be permitted in the public schools, whose existence was reflective of the spirit of democracy.[187]

In the *Zorach* case (1952), Black in dissent asserted that the purpose of the "released time" program was to "compel" reluctant children to attend religion classes and recalled in contrast that formerly people attended church "because they loved their God."[188]

Frankfurter reached a similar conclusion, asserting that the program showed "surprising want of confidence in the inherent power of the various faiths to draw children to outside sectarian classes—an attitude that hardly reflects the faith of the greatest religious spirits."[189] Jackson thought students were being deprived of freedom, in effect forced to attend church, while the school itself became "a temporary jail" for those not attending religion classes. He wondered why religious faith could not be held "with enough confidence" not to require governmental support.[190]

A shifting majority of the Court in the post-1947 era shared the suspicion that religious education was perhaps not education at all but "indoctrination." The Court did not define indoctrination, the formal meaning of which is "to instruct in doctrines, theories, principles," with the secondary meaning of "to imbue with a partisan or sectarian opinion,"[191] but implied the latter definition, with the connotation of coercive or manipulative methods designed to gain adherence to ideas that would not otherwise withstand scrutiny.

Thus dissenting in the *Allen* case (1968), allowing some forms of aid to religious schools, Black warned that even secular textbooks could be used for that purpose, while Douglas added that "textbooks may contain many, many more seeds of creed and dogma than do a prayer." He and Justice Abe Fortas both questioned whether teachers in religious schools could be trusted to teach objectively. In *Allen*, Black also questioned whether teachers in Catholic schools could deal properly with historical issues like the Inquisition, the Crusades, or Spain under Francisco Franco.

Thus in the majority's view, government aid to religious education, and religious expression in public life, were forbidden by the Establishment Clause in part because they might be dangerous and unfair, exposing people, especially children, to psychological manipulation that they were unequipped to resist.

In the *Lemon* case the majority of the Court accepted the gist of the argument about indoctrination, prohibiting various kinds of aid to religious schools, with Burger citing the danger of a sectarian bias always present so long as the schools were controlled by religious bodies. He also cited the "impressionable age" of students enrolled in religious schools.[192]

Douglas implied that religious schools taught secular subjects in an inferior manner, requiring close scrutiny to ensure that religion was not smuggled into, for example, classes on Shakespeare or mathematics, and suggesting that "we deal not with wicked teachers but with zealous ones." Thus he found it necessary to raise the question how such schools might teach about the Protestant Reformation. For Douglas, instruction in religious schools was "indivisible," so that it was impossible to separate secular from religious subjects.[193] (He offered an ingenious reconciliation of modern separationism with the *Bradfield* decision [1899]—religious persons could not use hospitals to indoctrinate, as they could use schools.) Dissenting, White argued that there was no proof that secular subjects were taught improperly in religious schools.[194]

In the same year, the Court upheld public aid to religiously affiliated colleges,[195] thereby refining the theory of indoctrination. The majority of the Court, led by Burger, found a formula for distinguishing higher from lower education—the contention that older students possessed a "skeptical" mentality and were therefore less susceptible to indoctrination than younger ones. Public money given to colleges would thus be used for genuine education, whereas at the lower level it might be used to indoctrinate.[196] Dissenting, Douglas warned of "slanted" college courses, even in ostensibly secular subjects.[197]

In 1976 the Court, on similar grounds, again upheld grants to religiously affiliated colleges.[198] In dissenting Stewart thought the record showed that theology was not taught in those colleges as an academic subject and that there was a religious bias in the hiring of faculty.[199]

In the *Yoder* case Douglas seemed do think that parents should also not be permitted to "indoctrinate" their children with their own religious beliefs, lest they inhibit the children's intellectual development.[200]

In disallowing some forms of public aid to religious schools in 1975,[201] Stewart noted for the majority that, while arithmetic might seem to provide less opportunity for religious indoctrination than did medieval history, and chemistry less than guidance counseling, such uses were not impossible.[202] In dissent Rehnquist complained that the majority did not require proof of such bias but merely assumed it,[203] a point he repeated in dissenting in two school-aid cases in 1985.[204]

In voting to uphold some forms of public aid in 1977, Blackmun concluded that "diagnostic and therapeutic" services were less likely than counseling to involve indoctrination, especially when they were provided on private-school premises. However, tax-financed field trips were illegitimate, because a teacher might use them for sectarian purposes.[205] Marshall offered a similar opinion.[206]

In banning the posting of the Ten Commandments in public-school classrooms in 1980, the Court noted the possibility that their mere presence, with the apparent endorsement of the school, could serve as a form of indoctrination of young students.[207] By contrast, in allowing an official chaplain in a state legislature in 1983, the majority made a particular point of the fact that, as mature adults, those attending legislative sessions would not be likely to regard this an official endorsement of religion.[208]

In a 1985 case concerning public-school classes held on private-school premises and taught by the latter's faculty, Brennan took the dangers of indoctrination a step further by pointing out that schoolchildren might be subject to such a process without realizing it. The "symbolic union of church and state" brought about by holding public-school classes on private-school premises was especially crucial for such children, who lacked the sophistication to distinguish public from private classes.[209]

Dissenting in a 1987 decision nullifying a state law requiring the teaching of "creation science," Scalia argued that, far from an infringement of academic freedom, the law safeguarded it, intending to protect students from "indoctrination" by their teachers in beliefs inimical to their own.[210] Here Scalia, speaking for a minority of the Court, in effect argued that religious belief was not itself uniquely likely to lead to indoctrination but that secular teaching might as well, the only time anyone on the Court explicitly confronted that possibility.

Dissenting in 1990 in a case upholding the meetings of a religious club in a public high school, Stevens worried that the Court was treating high school students as "too mature" and that the existence of the club would be perceived as an endorsement by the school.[211]

In the 1992 case disallowing prayers at a public high school gradua-tion,[212] the majority led by Kennedy placed much emphasis on the vulnera-bility of "impressionable" young people coerced by "peer pressure" into participating in a religious ceremony.[213] Scalia in dissent argued that high school students, "often thought to be in transition to maturity," were not so vulnerable, and he wondered sarcastically if "soon we will have a jurisprudence of mature and immature adults."[214]

Dissenting in a 1993 case permitting a deaf student in a religious school to be aided by a sign-language interpreter paid by the state, Blackmun objected that the interpreter was being required to participate directly in "religious indoctrination" and would be assisting in the conveyance of a religious message.[215]

Joining the majority in dissolving an all-Jewish public-school district the following year,[216] Stevens placed much weight on the fact that the purpose of the district was to assist parents in cementing their children's loyalty to their faith.[217] Scalia in dissent attacked this position as one of hostility to "any state action which helps parents to raise their chil-dren."[218]

In the 2002 "voucher" case, Stevens objected that giving students pub-lic money to attend private religious schools would result in "the indoctri-nation of thousands of grammar school children in particular religious faiths" and provide an inducement for parents to permit their children to be indoctrinated, something they might otherwise resist.[219]

Chapter Four

THE FAITHS OF THE JUSTICES

THE SUPREME COURT is the most elite political institution in American life, and what are considered elite religions have accounted for a disproportionate share of its membership. In the period prior to the Civil War, Episcopalians accounted for over half the members of the Court, and Presbyterians 21 percent, the two faiths between them making up almost two-thirds of the Court. By contrast, Baptists and Methodists, the country's fastest growing churches, achieved only one justice apiece,[1] at a time when the elite churches were rapidly losing ground to newer groups. (The greatest loss was by Congregationalists, who nonetheless placed three men on the Court.)[2]

Chief Justice John Marshall (1801–35) was perhaps the most important person ever to sit on the Court. His religious history was the familiar one of the Virginia elite of his time. Raised an Anglican, he maintained some affiliation with the Episcopal Church, although early in the century he thought that institution corrupt and doubted whether it would even survive. His public expressions of belief were tinged with Deism, although there are uncertain reports that later in life he embraced orthodox Christianity.[3]

Like most of the Founders, he regarded religion as essential to public morality and true patriotism. As he grew older he lamented what he saw as a moral and religious decline among the young, and he expressed somewhat cautious agreement with Jasper Adams's sermon about America as a Christian nation. As a Southerner, Marshall conceded that because of their Puritanism, New Englanders for a time were able to rise above material self-interest. However, their religion was based on "enthusiasm" and was hence unreliable and unstable, as well as inspiring the horrors of religious persecution, because the Puritans engaged too much in "abstract theological quarrels."[4] In Virginia, Marshall opposed Madison and Jefferson's successful effort to deny public funds to the churches.[5]

Marshall's most important decision involving religion was the *Dartmouth* case (1819), upholding the charter of a private religious college against an effort by the State of New Hampshire to take control of it. As a lawyer in Virginia, Marshall had acted in a rather similar case, involving the question whether the College of William and Mary could alter its curriculum by introducing modern languages. Marshall argued, successfully, that the college was required to remain faithful to its three chartered tasks—teaching divinity, philosophy, and languages—but that within those categories could make prudential innovations,[6] an argument that could have been used by either side in the *Dartmouth* dispute.

In another important case—*Worcester* (1837)—Marshall once again acted to protect religious liberty without citing it explicitly, in nullifying the prosecution of a Methodist minister by the State of Georgia because the clergyman defied state law by living and working among the Cherokee Indians. In the *Hart's Executors* case (1819), Marshall held that a Baptist missionary organization could not receive a bequest because it was not incorporated.

Next to Marshall, the most important member of the Court in the first half of the nineteenth century was Joseph Story (1811–45), who was also the leading constitutional authority of his day. Story's rise seemed part of the fulfillment of Jefferson's hope that Unitarianism would become the preferred American religion, but ironically he also gave Jefferson reasons to reexamine that hope.

Story was raised in Massachusetts in a Congregationalist household, although his father was somewhat liberal in his beliefs. As a student at Harvard in the 1790s, the future justice rejected Calvinism and embraced Unitarianism, at about the time Jefferson himself was embracing it. Unlike Jefferson, Story actually joined the Unitarian Church and remained active in it all his life, serving a term as its national president.[7]

A contemporary said of him that he espoused a "conservatively liberal theology," which was certainly more orthodox than Jefferson's. Thus, while rejecting claims about Jesus' divinity, Story referred to him as "our Savior," and to the Bible as "our holy book." Humanity's highest duty was "piety and devotion towards God," and Story believed that duty was to some degree imposed by the civil law itself, which incorporated much of Christian morality, a contention that brought him into sharp controversy with Jefferson. On the other hand Story excoriated the "Puritan theocracy" that had prevailed in New England in colonial times. Like Marshall, he responded with cautious agreement to Jasper Adams's sermon proclaiming the Christian character of the nation.[8]

Story thought the civil law to be based on natural law and thus discoverable by human reason, which ultimately emanated from God but did not require a specifically religious sanction. When the practice of Mormon polygamy was first becoming noticeable, Story condemned it. He believed that sexual offenses should remain crimes but that the state might occasionally permit divorce for reasons in addition to adultery, which was the sole basis that Protestant Christianity allowed.[9]

Harmonious with his personal opinions, some of Story's decisions on the Court were also at odds with the Jeffersonian view of religion in public life. In the *Terrett* case (1815) he partially reversed the process by which the Episcopal Church in Virginia had been stripped of its lands, but in the *Pawlet* case the same year, he reached the opposite conclusion concerning an Episcopal church in New Hampshire, because the latter, unlike the former, had no clear colonial antecedent. Then in an 1824 case, he validated the property claims of an Episcopal church in Vermont, claims that derived from an English group called the Society for the Propagation of the Gospel in Foreign Parts.

His concurring opinion in the *Dartmouth* decision said nothing about religion but supported the decision with a learned review of the law of contract. (Originally Story had been thought sympathetic to the proposal to bring the college under state control, and he was actually named to the Board of Overseers by the liberal Governor William Plumer.)[10]

His boldest decision on behalf of religion was the obscure *Beatty* case (1829), where he invoked the law of equity to protect a Lutheran congregation's ownership of its cemetery, despite a defective title, in order to "preserve the repose of the ashes of the dead, and the religious sensibilities of the living."

Perhaps the most important of his decisions involving religion was his last, the *Girard* case (1844), where his findings seemed to go in opposite directions. There he reaffirmed in principle his own long-settled conviction that Christianity enjoyed a privileged place in civil government but at the same time allowed clergy to be excluded from teaching in a semi-public school.

Daniel Webster's speech before the Court in opposing that provision was a passionate assertion of the necessity of Christianity to any true charity. Privately, Story ridiculed the speech and dismissed it as merely an appeal to the prejudices of the clergy.[11] The fact that his own Unitarianism de-emphasized the role of the clergy may have influenced his decision,[12] in which he pointed out that religious instruction could be imparted by laypeople.

Altogether Story epitomized the dominant nineteenth-century view of church and state. On the one hand his Unitarianism, like Jefferson's, inclined toward religious toleration. But in common with most people of the age he assumed that the moral teachings of Christianity were essential to society. Unlike Jefferson and Madison, he was therefore prepared to offer various kinds of legal support to Christianity, his Unitarian creed harmonizing with the prevailing "civil religion" in affirming Christianity in general while treating "sectarian" differences as unimportant or possibly divisive.

Justice John McLean (1829–61) was the first Methodist to serve on the Court. As a youth he had abandoned religion, until he was converted by a traveling Wesleyan preacher,[13] becoming perhaps the first product of the Second Great Awakening to achieve national political prominence.

He was postmaster general when the issue of the Sunday mails arose, and he attempted to compromise the dispute by ordering post offices to remain open on Sundays but to minimize their services. He was a strong opponent of the use of alcohol but did not favor prohibition by law. After leaving the Court he served as president of the American Sunday School Union.[14]

Ambitious for the presidency but apparently fated not to receive the Democratic nomination, McLean flirted at different times with seemingly opposite political movements—the Anti-Masons in 1832, the Know-Nothings during the following decade.[15]

As a devout and active Methodist, he attempted during the early 1850s to mediate a dispute over funds between the Northern and Southern branches of his church, stemming from their division over slavery.[16] When his mediation efforts failed, he abstained in the *Swormstedt* case (1853), which brought the issue before the Court. McLean's only opinion on a religious issue was in the *Goessele* case (1852), upholding the rules of a utopian religious community that forbade ownership of private property.

Chief Justice Roger Brooke Taney (1836–64) was the first Catholic to serve on the Court.[17] During his long tenure he voted with the majority in all religion cases but issued no opinion of his own. Justice John Catron (1837–65), a Presbyterian,[18] rendered the important *Permoli* decision (1845), ruling that the Free-Exercise Clause did not apply to the states. Justice Robert Grier (1846–70), also a Presbyterian,[19] wrote the decisions in the *Federal Street Meeting House* case (1861), where he ruled against claimants of his own faith in a dispute over possession of a church building, and in two cases (1859–60) upholding in principle that state sabbath laws applied to interstate commerce, while giving them a somewhat narrow interpretation.

Justice John A. Campbell (1853–61) was also raised a Presbyterian but became a devout Episcopalian.[20] He rendered the verdict in the *Henrici* case (1856), also involving a utopian religious community, and in 1860 decided the *Christ Hospital* case affirming in principle tax exemptions for churches but denying the particular claim, which was brought by an Episcopal institution.

During the period 1860–1900 the percentage of Episcopalians on the Court declined to about a third. Presbyterians occupied slightly fewer than a quarter of the Court's seats during the period, while Unitarians had three justices, far in excess of their number in the nation at large.[21]

Justice Stephen J. Field (1863–97) was probably the most important member of the Court in the second half of the nineteenth century, one of the chief architects of the doctrine of "substantive due process," which became the principal basis for the Court's vigilant protection of property rights. Field was born in Massachusetts to devout Congregationalist parents, his father a minister. Later in life the justice, who moved to California as a young man, passed through Presbyterianism into Episcopalianism, although he does not appear to have been particularly devout.[22]

Field rendered the majority opinion in the *Cummings* case (1866), overturning the prosecution of a Catholic priest for refusing to take an oath of loyalty to the Union. In 1889 he joined two other dissenters in the *Late Corporation* case, where they argued that Congress had no authority to punish the Mormon Church by seizing its property, but the next year he wrote the unanimous anti-polygamy decision in the *Beeson* case. In the *Soon Hing* case (1884) he upheld California's sabbath laws, but with a secular justification.

Next to Field, Justice Samuel Miller (1862–90) was probably the most important member of the Court during the second half of the nineteenth century. A Unitarian who abhorred "the tests and rituals of religious orthodoxy," Miller, like Story, served as president of the church's national body.[23]

During his long tenure on the Court he wrote only three opinions in religion cases, dissenting in the *Cummings* case and in the *Cannon* case (1884), a minor Mormon polygamy case. His most important opinion on a religious issue was in the *Watson* case (1872), where he laid down the principle that internal church disputes were to be settled solely by the courts' deferring to each religion's own governing system. Curiously, in terms of his Unitarianism, he added that while ordinarily the courts were not to judge doctrinal quarrels ("the law knows no heresy"), they could find that church property was being used for purposes for which it was not originally intended, such as a trinitarian church having been given over to unitarian worship. It was an invitation that the Court never chose to accept and that in the *Federal Street Meeting House* case it had already rejected.

Chief Justice Morrison R. Waite (1874–88) was born a New England Congregationalist, then became a devout "low church" Episcopalian.[24] He issued the Court's decision in the *Reynolds* case (1878), the first of the Mormon polygamy cases, during which he became the first member of the Court to recall Jefferson's metaphor of the "wall of separation" between church and state. He sent a copy of the decision to his minister, calling it "my sermon on polygamy."[25]

Justice William Strong (1870–80) was the son of a Congregationalist minister but he became a Presbyterian and president of both the American Tract Society and the American Sunday School Union.[26] As head of an organization (the National Reform Association) seeking to amend the Constitution to affirm officially the nation as Christian, he was the most religiously zealous of any justice in the Court's history. But during his decade on the bench he had opportunity to write an opinion in only one minor religion case—*Kain* (1879)—holding that a community of Catholic nuns could not receive a legacy because they were not incorporated.

In the mid-1870s Strong lectured on religion and the law at a Protestant divinity school. For the most part he restricted himself to explaining how the courts habitually dealt with religious issues, but he ventured a few significant remarks. As a participant in the unanimous *Watson* decision, he pointed to Miller's comments about a trinitarian church becoming unitarian and asserted that it was therefore necessary for the courts to understand religious doctrine in order to settle cases of disputed trusts. Curiously, in view of his decision in the *Kain* case a few years later, he assured his audience that the law of equity would allow a religious group to receive a bequest even if it was not incorporated. But he did not think the courts would uphold a bequest for the purpose of propagating "infidelity" or "irreligion."[27] Most significant was his assertion that the law would not countenance "vice under cover of religion," warning that "it would be idle" for Mormons to offer the sanction of religion to justify polygamy,[28] a judgment that which he rendered several years before the issue first came before the Court.

Justice Stanley Matthews (1881–89) was born into a staunch Presbyterian family, became a "rationalist," then a Unitarian, before returning to his boyhood faith with renewed commitment. In 1864 he was a delegate to the Presbyterian Church's General Assembly and was a member of the committee that introduced the antislavery resolution that led directly to the *Watson* case, where the Court in effect voted to uphold the Assembly's action.[29] Matthews was both a firm Calvinist and a separationist with regard to the public schools. His only written opinion on a religious issue was in the *Murphy* case (1884), involving a minor polygamy question.

Chief Justice Melville W. Fuller (1888–1910) was born into a Congregationalist family in Maine that was excommunicated when he was a boy for allowing dancing in their home. (His parents were later divorced, because of his father's infidelities.) The future Chief Justice became a devout "high church" Episcopalian and a lifelong foe of what he considered Calvinist rigor.[30]

As a lawyer in Chicago in 1869, Fuller represented a "low church" Episcopal clergyman, Charles Cheney, who had been suspended from office by his "high church" bishop for allegedly heterodox teachings and practices. Fuller persuaded a state court to reinstate Cheney, but the judgment was overturned by the Illinois Supreme Court.[31] Fuller's brief triumph in the case was based on a principle—theological disputes settled by the civil courts—that the United States Supreme Court would negate in the *Watson* case three years later, citing the Illinois Supreme Court's *Cheney* decision as a precedent.

Fuller issued the Court's ruling in only one religion case—*Municipality of Ponce* (1907)—affirming the validity of a colonial land grant to a Catholic church. As a Protestant he showed exquisite courtesy in his decision, where he referred to "His Holiness the Pope." Unusual for the times, the remainder of Fuller's contribution to religious issues was three dissents. He wrote the opinion signed by two other justices in the *Late Corporation* case, and in the *Hennington* case (1895) argued that the Interstate Commerce Clause of the Constitution precluded the State of Georgia from stopping interstate trains on Sundays. In the *Duss* case (1902), he was in the minority in thinking that a religious community had turned itself into a business and should be treated as such.

Justice Joseph P. Bradley (1870–92) was in some ways the most religiously interesting of the nineteenth-century justices. He was raised in the Dutch Reformed Church in New York State, but his personal faith evolved in a broadly liberal direction. Himself disdaining creed or dogma, he thought that the Apostle Paul had distorted Christianity by making Jesus into the Savior. Bradley considered the Bible worthy of respect ("a book of copious meditations and excertations on morality and religion") but also thought that divine revelation occurred in many other ways. Jesus was a great moral teacher, but only on a level with Confucius, Mahomet, and Socrates. (Somewhat paradoxically, while denying that the Bible was the unique source of religious truth, he opposed all efforts to modernize the authorized ["King James"] translation.)[32]

The essence of Christianity is belief in a loving father, the equality of all men, the "primacy of the spiritual," and the need for divine forgiveness, according to Bradley. The divine spirit manifests itself through human thoughts that inspire religious belief, and it would be impossible to believe in great principles like justice without also believing in "the subject in which they inhere—God." According to Bradley, all persons naturally have some notion of a divine being, hence religious dogmas are unnecessary.[33]

Since everything in life manifests progress, Bradley asked why the same could not occur in religion. The Old Testament was full of "crudities" that the New Testament overcame, but belief in the Bible as divine revelation would require believers to accept the former as well as the latter. Jesus marked the highest development of religion—an awareness of the fatherhood of God and the religion of righteousness and love. While the Bible ("golden sentences which address themselves to the universal consciousness") could be studied profitably, God manifested himself primarily in nature, and revelation was found "on every hillside and in every valley where wells of moral purity and freshness have sprung up."[34]

But after concluding in effect that organized Christianity was based on an outmoded understanding of reality, Bradley proceeded to justify the necessity of the churches for the welfare of society: "[W]e cannot without danger to society and its dearest interests turn our backs upon the religious institutions which play so important a part in humanizing and refining mankind." He came close to arguing in favor of organized religion as a kind of beneficial lie—for example, an enlightened individual might not believe in miracles but could appreciate the usefulness of miracle stories for inspiring good conduct. Religion could be safely dispensed with only as human beings became perfect.[35]

Even if the "guesses of science" were correct in positing that the world evolved rather than being created, Bradley warned that the human race was not ready for such an idea:

[T]he masses are too little developed in moral perception and principle to make it safe to abandon the artificial methods and sanctions by which order is maintained. Until the world is ready for the truth it is not safe to communicate it, except to a select few.

Thus, in Confucian fashion, Bradley thought the "wise man" would observe all "external customs," because to overthrow existing institutions would be to overthrow morality itself. It was necessary to maintain the "pretence" that morality was based on supernatural sanctions.[36]

Bradley opposed a constitutional amendment affirming Christianity, regarding it as antithetical to the intentions of the Founding Fathers, who had wanted complete religious liberty.[37] But he defended the sabbath laws as merely making it possible for people to enjoy a day of rest, noting that the ancient Jewish observance of the sabbath was not as strict as the Puritan practice.[38]

Bradley is considered one of the leading conservatives on the late nineteenth-century Court, along with Field an architect of the doctrine of "substantive due process." But his conservatism in religion took an unexpected, almost cynical turn, like that of an eighteenth-century French nobleman—enlightened people were to support an institution whose teachings were doubtful, since to do otherwise would threaten the stability of society. Bradley wrote only two opinions in religion cases—the majority rulings in the *Late Corporation* case and in the *Neilson* case (1882), a minor Mormon polygamy issue.

Justice Horace Grey (1882–1902), whose religion is uncertain,[39] rendered the opinions of the Court in the *Gibbons* case (1886), denying a Catholic claim for a tax exemption while upholding such exemptions in principle, and in the *Henrici* case the following year, one of the series of cases involving property claims on utopian religious communities.

Justice Lucius Q. C. Lamar (1888–93), one of the dissenters in the *Late Corporation* case, was a Methodist of a somewhat troubled personal spiritual history.[40]

Justice George Shiras (1892–1903) was raised in a staunch Presbyterian family but moved away from the church after reading theology and "finding myself none the wiser." Further inquiry, he admitted, brought him to the "agnostic stage." He then abandoned all hope of religious certainty and decided merely to attempt to live a good life, with some hope of immortality.[41] He voted with the majority in all the religion cases while he was on the Court but wrote no opinion of his own. His participation in the *Duss* case seems to have involved conflict of interest, since many years before, his parents had lived, apparently free of charge, in a residence operated by the successful appellants in the case.[42]

Justice David J. Brewer (1889–1910) was, along with Strong, the most religiously zealous person ever to sit on the Court. He was born in the Ottoman Empire to American missionary parents, his mother being the sister of Justice Field. Unlike his uncle and several others on the nineteenth-century Court, Brewer, who made his career in Kansas, remained faithful to his boyhood Congregationalism.[43]

His most famous opinion in a religion case was the *Holy Trinity* decision (1892), in which he found that, the United States being a "Christian nation," Congress could not have intended to prohibit the hiring of clergy from abroad. In reaching that highly controversial conclusion, Brewer did not merely cite the history of the thirteen English colonies but went back to "their Catholic Majesties, Ferdinand and Isabella" and to the voyages of Christopher Columbus, in order to show that from the beginning, America had been religious. Besides the Protestants of the East, he included the Catholic French and Spanish of the West in that same heritage, a recognition of Catholics as Christians that was probably unacceptable to many of his fellow Protestants.

However, having established that a Christian nation would not interfere with Christian liberty, Brewer seemed to reverse himself in the *Berea* case (1908), where he upheld a Kentucky law prohibiting a Protestant college from enrolling a racially mixed student body, the difference between the two cases presumably that Brewer did not believe that the Bill of Rights applied to the states.

The *Holy Trinity* decision might be read narrowly, as merely showing that the nation was historically Christian. However, in a later book Brewer made it clear that he considered the United States Christian in an official, legal sense.[44]

He rendered the Court's verdicts on two other religious issues—a minor Mormon polygamy case (*Barrett* [1890]) and the *Bishop of Nesqually* case (1894) concerning a Catholic land claim in Oregon. Presumably because of his parents' missionary activities, he abstained in the two *Lowery* cases (1907, 1910) involving a missionary college in Hawaii.

Justice John Marshall Harlan I (1877–1911) was a Kentucky Presbyterian who remained highly active in the church all his life, hoping eventually to see a Presbyterian "cathedral" built in Washington to manifest the denomination's strength. He was a theological conservative who thought the United States was especially an instrument of divine providence, and in 1905 urged that the nation use some of its great wealth "to spread the gospel of Christ all over the world."[45]

Although he smoked in defiance of a Presbyterian resolution against the practice, he advocated strict observance of the sabbath and opposed government subsidies for Chicago's Columbian Exposition in 1893 because there would be activity on Sunday. He told his son that the Bible warned of the danger of eternal punishment but advised him not to engage in theological speculation.[46] Although generally orthodox in his theology, the justice served on a Presbyterian committee that rescinded official doctrinal statements that unbaptized infants were damned to hell and that the pope was the Antichrist foretold in the Bible.[47]

Harlan was opposed to slavery and was one of the attorneys for the victorious Northern Presbyterians in the *Watson* case. He argued successfully against a court decision to place his alma mater, Centre College, under the jurisdiction of the Southern branch of the church, and he also opposed placing a black Presbyterian congregation under that jurisdiction.[48]

Harlan was apparently the only justice of his time who believed that the Free-Exercise Clause applied to the states. He dissented vehemently in the *Berea* case, warning that the decision threatened religious liberty in a basic way. He also dissented in the *Hennington* case, arguing that a state had the right to prohibit interstate trains from operating on Sundays. Sabbath laws had secular purposes but had also been found beneficial to the moral and religious life of the community. In two cases—*Yount* (1878) and *Gilmer* (1887)—he upheld the rights of religious organizations to purchase land.

Justice William R. Day (1903–22) also dissented in the *Berea* case but without written opinion. His religious affiliation is uncertain.[49]

Justice Rufus Peckham (1895–1909), an Episcopalian,[50] rendered two important decisions—*Bradfield* (1899) and *Speer* (1905)—committing the Court to an accommodationist position. In both cases he held that institutions under religious auspices were not "sectarian" in the legal sense so long as they provided beneficial services to society. In two other instances—the *Chicago Seminary* case (1902) and the *Missoula* case (1905)—he construed religious tax exemptions narrowly.

For the period 1900–40, Episcopalians continued to occupy the largest number of seats on the Court—slightly fewer than a third. Now, however,

Catholics had an equal number with Presbyterians—three each—while Unitarians and Jews were the only faiths with two.[51]

Following Taney's death in 1864, no Catholic sat on the Court for three decades, until Edward Douglass White (associate justice 1894–1910, chief justice 1910–21). White, the offspring of an old Louisiana family, was educated by the Jesuits and while on the Court communicated frequently with Cardinal James Gibbons of Baltimore.[52] Except for a dissent in the *Chicago Seminary* case, he voted with the majority on all religious issues and wrote only one decision—the *Select Draft Law* cases (1917), where he dismissed, as unworthy of serious consideration, the claim that it was discriminatory to grant conscientious-objector status only to members of certain denominations. The *Speer* case, in which he participated, involved his alma mater, Georgetown University.

A second Catholic, Joseph McKenna (1898–1925), was named to the Court only four years after White's appointment, a sign of Catholics' growing numerical and political significance, which inevitably provoked some anti-Catholic murmuring. McKenna was the son of Irish immigrant parents and was a practicing Catholic all his life. But while campaigning for office in California during the "school wars" of the 1870s he opposed public aid to private schools.[53]

McKenna's most significant decisions concerning religion were the two *Lowry* cases, in which he determined that, under the terms of an old contract, the Territory of Hawaii was obligated to teach Calvinist theology in a public college that had been founded by missionaries. He also wrote the majority decision in the *Duss* case and voted with the majority in all the religion cases during his tenure on the Court.

The first Jew named to the Court was Louis D. Brandeis (1916–39). He was born into a family that had ceased to observe Jewish practices and regarded their religion as a cultural tradition and a guide in moral matters. The future justice occasionally referred to "the Creator" but admitted that he had no sense of a divine presence in his life. He thought the idea of personal immortality had been rendered incredible by science and that its survival was evidence of the "deep darkness of the human mind." He served on the boards of Jewish organizations and became a leading American Zionist.[54]

William Howard Taft, then out of office and himself hoping to be appointed to the Court, strongly criticized Brandeis's appointment, insisting that his opposition had nothing to do with Judaism but was solely because of Brandeis's liberal judicial philosophy, and claiming that "intelligent Jews" agreed with him. Overt anti-Semitic opposition was relatively slight, and ironically, some of Brandeis's fellow Jews were cool to the appointment because he was not religious.[55]

Brandeis dissented in the *Schwimmer* and *MacIntosh* cases, voting to extend the rights of conscientious objectors to foreign applicants for citizenship and wrote only one opinion on a religious issue—the *Gonzalez* case (1929)—settling a dispute within the Catholic Church in the Philippines. In that decision he reaffirmed the *Watson* principle that such disputes were to be settled by reference to each church's own governing structure but added the important corollary that it was proper to have recourse to the civil courts to determine what those structures were. Brandeis abstained in the *Hygrade Provision* case (1924), involving the legal regulation of the sale of food that conformed to Jewish dietary law.

Justice James C. McReynolds (1914–41) was a pious lifelong member of the Disciples of Christ (Campbellites). Racist and anti-Semitic, he has been called the most bigoted person ever to sit on the Court,[56] and it was therefore surprising that the two decisions concerning religion that he wrote—*Meyer* (1923) and *Pierce* (1925)—became liberal landmarks. In the first case his upholding of the right to teach German in the schools went against his own bitter anti-German prejudice, dating from the First World War.[57] The second case guaranteed the freedom of private religious schools and, while McReynolds's views of Catholicism are not recorded, it is unlikely, in terms of his background and outlook, that he was favorable toward it. (Meyer's attorney thought McReynolds was won over to the plaintiff's cause by his repugnance at the suggestion, made during oral arguments, that all children might be required to attend public schools, which to McReynolds was a dangerous expansion of governmental power.)[58]

In 1922, with White deceased but McKenna still on the Court, President Warren G. Harding, in a show of bipartisanship, told his advisors that he wanted to appoint a conservative Democrat, preferably a Catholic, to the Court. Archbishop Patrick J. Hayes of New York was consulted and recommended a federal judge, Martin Manton.[59]

Taft, who had succeeded White as chief justice, considered Manton wholly unqualified, a judgment eventually borne out when Manton was sent to prison for bribery some years later. While insisting that religion ought not be a consideration in appointing judges, Taft bowed to political realities and advised Catholic associates to consult other bishops. Eventually this consultation produced the name of a Minneapolis lawyer, Pierce Butler, whom Taft then urged to get hierarchical support to offset Hayes's influence. After this support manifested itself, Butler was appointed,[60] an appointment that marked the first time there was open discussion of a "Catholic seat" on the Court.

Butler was the son of Irish immigrant parents. Although he never attended Catholic schools, he considered himself influenced by Catholic doctrine and was close to several bishops.[61] During his time on the Court

(1922–39), he voted with the majority in all the religion cases and wrote the Court's decisions in the *Schwimmer* case and the *Hamilton* case (1934), upholding the obligation of pacifist college students to participate in military training. In 1928 he was the sole dissenter in a case upholding the forcible sterilization of a woman alleged to be mentally deficient. Taft urged Justice Holmes, who wrote the decision, to try to satisfy Butler, who seemed troubled over the issue.[62] Butler gave no reasons for his dissent, which may have been motivated by his religious principles.[63]

The period 1905–37 is often considered the apex of the Court's conservatism, its sense of mission the defense of threatened values, especially the sanctity of property, a conservatism that beginning in 1937 provoked a reaction that soon transformed the entire character of the Court. But by the 1920s justices deeply committed to protecting the right of property were not necessarily committed to conservatism in religion, and to some extent the opposite was true. During the latter period McReynolds and Butler were perhaps the only members of the Court who held orthodox theological beliefs.

In some ways the most secular member of the Court was Oliver Wendell Holmes (1902–32). Raised in a Boston Unitarian family, he found that religion not oppressive but tedious, although he retained his affiliation. (His wife once explained, "In Boston you have to be something, and Unitarianism is the least you can be.") Almost corrosively skeptical toward both religious and rationalist claims to truth, he may have been an agnostic.[64]

He once said that he would rather see power in the hands of Jews than Catholics, but "I do not wish to be run by either."[65] His votes on the Court were somewhat unpredictable. For the first almost thirty years he voted with the majority in most religion cases, his only written opinion being in the *Santos* case (1907), upholding a colonial land grant to the Catholic Church in the Philippines. He dissented in the *Meyer* case, arguing that the banning of foreign languages was not unconstitutional, but joined in the unanimous *Pierce* decision, as well as the *Cochran* decision (1930), permitting a state to provide textbooks for students in religious schools.

He dissented in the *Schwimmer* case, using the occasion to praise the pacifist Quakers as model citizens and to lament, sarcastically, that the nation penalized people who followed Jesus' Sermon on the Mount "more than the rest of us." At the same time he admitted privately that he thought the appellant's beliefs bordered on atheism and that this had harmed her cause. He also dissented in the *MacIntosh* case. Paradoxically, while supporting pacifist principles, he expressed contempt, as himself a wounded veteran of the Civil War, for "religious squeamishness about the taking of human life."[66]

Justice George Sutherland (1922–38), a leading economic conservative, had an unusual religious history. He was born in England to parents who converted to Mormonism and moved to Utah. There they became disillusioned and left the Mormon Church, so that the future justice was raised without any formal religion, although he counted a Mormon teacher one of the great influences on his life. As a senator from Utah, he was helpful to the Mormons, especially in regaining some of their seized property, but only on the condition that they continue to forbid polygamy and that they not discriminate against "gentiles."[67]

Sutherland's personal beliefs were almost those of an eighteenth-century Deist:

> I am not religious in the customary acceptation of that term. . . . I have no patience with mere forms or mere creeds or mere ceremonies. . . . I believe in a power in the universe, not ourselves, which makes for righteousness.[68]

Sutherland dissented in the *Meyer* case. His most important contribution to religious issues was his majority opinion in the *MacIntosh* case, where he attracted some attention by repeating the claim that the United States was a Christian nation. But he drew the opposite conclusion from the one Brewer drew in the *Holy Trinity* case. Whereas Brewer concluded that the nation was Christian and Congress therefore could not have intended to place impediments in the way of church activity, Sutherland held that even though the nation was Christian, claims of Christian pacifism need not be honored.

Charles Evans Hughes (associate justice 1910–16, chief justice 1930–41) was the son of a Welshman who came to the United States to spread the Baptist faith. As early as age fifteen the future jurist began to chafe at the strict piety of his parents, which he said "ended by creating in me a distaste for religious formalities." While a college student, he gave up his parents' theological orthodoxy but remained active in the Baptist faith, eventually serving as president of the American (Northern) Baptist Convention, a relatively liberal group.[69]

Hughes told his Sunday-school class to ignore creeds and to concentrate on the Sermon on the Mount as the essence of Christianity, and his aversion to rituals was so complete that he and his family did not even recite prayers in their own home ("a wretched business"). Conceding that doctrinal statements might be of value to some people, he said he had been careful never to offend those who believed in them. He seemed often to choose a deliberately vague religious language, referring to "the Father of Spirits" and "the unseen world."[70]

Hughes helped lead the successful fight to eliminate all Baptist requirements at his alma mater, Brown University, and was one of the founders

of the National Conference of Christians and Jews. He saw little importance in traditional Baptist tenets but valued his inherited religion primarily for its tradition of religious liberty.[71]

Although his beliefs could scarcely have made him sympathetic to Catholicism, during his first term on the Court he rendered the obscure but
important *Steinhauser* decision (1912), holding that a Catholic monk's
vow of poverty did not impinge the liberties guaranteed by the Constitution, and during his term as chief justice he wrote the decision in the
Cochran case, also upholding Catholic interests.

His dissent in the *MacIntosh* case included an important statement
about the ultimate impossibility of reconciling the absolute demands of
religion with the requirements of civil law, a conflict he seemed inclined
to settle in favor of religion. However, in the *Gobitis* case (1940) he was
part of the majority that voted to require Jehovah's Witnesses to salute
the flag. When that decision was reversed in the *Barnette* case three years
later, Hughes, then in retirement, wrote to Justice Felix Frankfurter to
congratulate him on abiding by the earlier decision.[72]

Justice Owen J. Roberts (1930–45) was an Episcopalian[73] who was considered one of the Court's more conservative members. But he delivered
the opinion of the Court in the seminal *Cantwell* case (1940), upholding
the right of Jehovah's Witnesses to proselytize.

Justice Benjamin N. Cardozo (1932–38) was the second Jew named to
the Court. He was born into a devout Orthodox family but ceased attending the synagogue after the ceremony of his bar mitzvah, although
he retained formal membership and kept a kosher table in his home. Addressing a graduating class of rabbis, he apologized for being unable to
share much of their faith and urged that religion be understood as the
commitment to "spend oneself" on behalf of some great ideal. He was
active in Jewish civic organizations and became a reluctant Zionist.[74] Taft,
who was dead by the time of Cardozo's appointment, had considered
him unsuitable for the Court, again on the grounds of his liberal judicial
philosophy, warning that Cardozo would vote with Brandeis.[75]

During his relatively brief time on the Court, Cardozo's only contribution to religious issues was his concurring opinion in the *Hamilton* case,
where he was the first justice to affirm from the bench that the Fourteenth
Amendment incorporated the Free-Exercise Clause and applied to the
states. However, having opened this wide door to the expansion of religious liberty, he immediately moved to narrow it again, warning that government could not accommodate all the claims of religious conscience,
some of which might simply be erroneous.

Harlan Fiske Stone (associate justice 1925–41, chief justice 1941–46)
was an Episcopalian.[76] He dissented in the *MacIntosh* case, and his lone

dissent in the *Gobitis* case was the basis on which the Court reversed itself three years later.

For the period 1940–2000, Episcopalians continued to lead all other religions in membership on the Court, with slightly less than a fourth. Presbyterians, Catholics, and Jews each had 15 percent, Methodists 10 percent. Although Baptists were now the largest Protestant denomination in the country, only one Baptist served on the Court in the late twentieth century, while there were two Unitarians.[77]

President Franklin D. Roosevelt had the most important transforming influence in the history of the Court, as he set about appointing justices who would be sympathetic to the legislation of the New Deal.[78] There is no evidence that Roosevelt, an active Episcopalian, had the Religion Clauses in mind when he chose his nominees, but their liberalism on economic issues would prove to have a counterpart in religion.

Justice Hugo L. Black (1937–71) had been a very active Baptist, as well as a Mason, while living in his native Alabama.[79] However, in his son's recollections the elder Black, by the time he came to Washington as a senator, had already severed many of his connections with his youthful faith, sometimes poking fun at Baptist beliefs he considered harsh or incredible and finding few religious teachings he could accept. But the Bible continued to have "relevance to life," and he thought the Golden Rule ("Do unto others as you would have others do unto you") was the heart of every religion. In the early 1960s Black began attending a Unitarian church, where his funeral was held. "I cannot exactly believe and I can't exactly not believe" was his explanation of his religious state.[80]

Rather like Justice Bradley, Black seems to have regarded religion, even if based on doubtful beliefs, as necessary to society. His son recalled his father's saying:

> Some people got to be scared into doing the right thing. Others got to be given the blind hope you gonna find it better somewhere else by doing right on this earth. . . . I'm not talking about fellas like us who just do good for the sake of it, study ethics and the Bible and know in their minds you got to treat the other fella the way you want him to treat you to keep society together—it's the fella who's got to get it some other way. . . . Most of these people . . . are true hypocrites who never pray anywhere but in public for the credit of it. Prayers ought to be a private thing, just like religion for a truly religious person.[81]

Black's nomination to the Court was almost derailed when it was revealed that he had belonged to the Ku Klux Klan while in Alabama. He was able to overcome the scandal by a speech in which he disclaimed any sympathy for the Klan's ideology and said he had joined out of political expediency and because "all the preachers belonged."[82] But Black's son also said:

> The Ku Klux Klan and Daddy, so far as I could tell, had only one thing in common. He suspected the Catholic Church. He used to read all Paul Blanshard's books exposing power abuse in the Catholic Church. He thought popes and bishops had too much power and property. He resented the fact that rental property owned by the Church was not taxed. He felt they got most of their revenue from the poor and did not return enough of it.[83]

As a lawyer in Alabama, Black successfully defended a Methodist minister who shot and killed a Catholic priest in front of witnesses, because the priest had officiated at the marriage of the minister's daughter to a Puerto Rican. Black is described as having fought the case with unusual aggressiveness, including anti-Catholic comments and the tactic of darkening the courtroom while the groom was on the witness stand, so as to make him appear negroid.[84]

Black gave lectures before Ku Klux Klan groups, exposing what he considered to be the evils of the Catholic Church and, despite being a loyal Democrat, considered Governor Alfred E. Smith of New York unqualified for the presidency in 1928 because his Catholicism would lead him to abuse his office.[85]

In writing the majority *Everson* opinion, Black attracted considerable criticism from Protestants and secularists, because he allowed the government to reimburse parents for the cost of transporting their children to religious schools. Privately, however, Black assured his critics that he had rendered the decision for strategic purposes only and that he was fully committed to separationism,[86] a claim that was certainly borne out by his subsequent career.

Justice Stanley F. Reed (1938–57), the lone critic of separationism in 1947–48, was apparently not affiliated with any church.[87]

Justice Felix Frankfurter (1939–62) continued the tradition of the "Jewish seat" following the deaths of Cardozo and Brandeis. Frankfurter was born in Austria to "observant" (but not "Orthodox") Jewish parents who immigrated to the United States when he was a boy. Like Cardozo, he ceased attending the synagogue when he was an adolescent, embarrassed that the other men in attendance were so much more devout than he was. He was influenced by "Victorian agnosticism" and later described himself as "a believing unbeliever" and "a reverent agnostic."[88] As with the two previous Jewish justices, Frankfurter's nomination to the Court was attacked more because of his political liberalism than his religion.[89]

Justice William O. Douglas (1939–75) was the son of a conservative Presbyterian minister. When the elder Douglas died, his family was plunged into poverty, and the future justice grew up with a sense that respectable church-going people were "not only a thieving lot, but hypocrites, and above all else dull, pious and boring." He thus carried with him

> a residue of resentment of which I have never quite got rid—resentment against hypocrites in church clothes who raise their denunciations against petty criminals, while their own sins mount high. This feeling somehow aligned me emotionally with the miserable people who make up the chaff of society.[90]

Already as an adolescent he had doubts about Presbyterian doctrine and underlined those parts of the Creed that he could believe—God, the existence of Jesus Christ, the forgiveness of sin, life everlasting. He began to commune with nature in an almost mystical sense of union, which he considered his true religious experience.[91]

Like Black, Douglas discerned the essence of all religions as the obligation to love one's neighbor as oneself and to "heal the world's miseries." The American political system, he judged, was based more on the teachings of Jesus than on any other source. The Bible "promotes a diversity of views" and was a dangerously subversive document for authoritarian governments.[92]

Throughout his life Douglas, who left a fuller record of his beliefs than any other person who ever sat on the Court, judged religion exclusively in terms of whether it supported "progressive" social causes. Thus while he retained his Presbyterian ties, he was on one occasion outraged when offered communion by an usher who was "a right-wing Republican," and he claimed to have abandoned belief in heaven and hell because he could not stand the prospect of spending eternity with people like J. Edgar Hoover of the FBI, Secretary of State John Foster Dulles, or Cardinal Francis J. Spellman of New York, who Douglas thought "dishonored the American ideal" by his support for the Vietnam War. Religion, Douglas finally concluded, was essentially used to control people. As he traveled he identified pockets of religious progressivism amidst what he considered a sea of callousness and exploitation, with Catholic priests often both the villains and the heroes.[93]

During the 1960 elections, when Catholic bishops in Puerto Rico denounced one of the candidates for governor, Douglas pronounced their action a clear violation of the Establishment Clause,[94] and in 1967, when a priest-professor at a Catholic university publicly rejected church teaching on birth control, Douglas wrote to congratulate him "in the name of the First Amendment community."[95]

During his world travels he found himself drawn more and more to Eastern religions, which he thought promoted "brotherhood with nature" more than did Christianity, which had "turned men into vandals." He ceased to believe that Jesus was divine except in the sense that "he knew he could be god, as we all could."[96] Douglas was buried, however, in a Presbyterian ceremony.[97]

When Butler died in 1939, Roosevelt honored the tradition of a "Catholic seat" by appointing Francis P. Murphy (1940–49), a man whose personal religious history was also somewhat unusual. Murphy imbibed from his father a paradoxical relationship to Catholicism—strong, even ostentatious, piety on the one hand, suspicion of the Church as an institution on the other. (The elder Murphy had once been arrested in Canada for activity in the Fenian Brotherhood, an Irish independence organization.) As governor general of, then high commissioner to, the Philippines, Murphy by his conspicuous religiosity helped win trust for himself, even as he pursued certain policies opposed by the Catholic bishops. While in the Philippines he became formally affiliated, as a layman, with the Franciscan Order.[98]

Murphy then plunged into the politics of his native Michigan with the full zeal of a New Deal liberal, receiving the strong support of some members of the hierarchy, the disapproval of others. Murphy urged that the Church remain aloof from politics, but he regularly sought clerical support in his election campaigns. In the late 1930s he complained that rumors that he was a Communist sympathizer had cost him the support of most priests, "even though I say more prayers than any of them," and he reluctantly repudiated the Communist Party endorsement. Cardinal George J. Mundelein of Chicago, a strong supporter of the New Deal, called Murphy "a lay bishop."[99]

For a time, he was on good terms with the influential "radio priest" Charles Coughlin and at one point acted as Roosevelt's emissary in an unsuccessful attempt to reverse Coughlin's sudden opposition to the New Deal. In 1941, also at Roosevelt's request, Murphy appeared before a Catholic organization to defend the American policy of lend-lease to the Soviet Union, which the Vatican opposed.[100]

Having never attended a Catholic school at any level, Murphy read Catholic writers and claimed to have been particularly influenced by the French philosopher Jacques Maritain and the writings of several modern popes on social issues, as well as by the leading American Protestant theologian of the day, Reinhold Niebuhr, who praised Murphy effusively as possessed of "a certain wisdom and grace without reference to ecclesiastical connections."

Murphy thought American democracy reflected the divine will and that a "higher law" should govern the interpretation of the Constitution, characterizing this belief as a combination of "the Goddess of Reason and the Sermon on the Mount," to indicate that he had bridged the gulf between Christianity and Enlightenment secularism. He regarded his service as mayor of Detroit and governor of Michigan as an exercise in "practical Christianity," and in an address to a Jewish group in 1937 affirmed that both Christians and Jews shared a goal "which, in a sense, is larger, more vital, than religion itself . . . the fulfillment of the ideal of democracy in its every phase."[101]

Defeated for reelection as governor in 1938, Murphy entered the Justice Department where, ironically, one of his tasks was to investigate Martin Manton, the judge who had almost been given the "Catholic seat" on the Court in 1922. Murphy hoped to succeed Roosevelt as president in 1941, if Roosevelt observed the tradition of serving only two terms, but Roosevelt persuaded him that it was impossible for a Catholic to be elected. Murphy was restless on the Court and from time to time inquired about a position in the wartime Cabinet. In 1942, Frankfurter urged Murphy to deny publicly a rumor that there was a cabal in the White House preventing Catholics from gaining high positions in the war effort. Although usually inclined to discount anti-Catholicism, in this case Murphy believed the rumor was true and that he was himself a victim of the cabal. During the war he served as cochairman of the Christian Committee against the Persecution of Jews.[102]

Murphy had first been recommended to Roosevelt by the latter's brother-in-law, who lived in Michigan and told the president that Murphy was a Catholic "who will not let religion stand in his way," and the future justice himself assured a Roosevelt advisor that he kept religion and politics "in air-tight compartments." Following Murphy's death in 1949, a fellow Catholic, Attorney General J. Howard McGrath, eulogized him as "a devout Roman Catholic, who disregarded personal preferences which we all know were very dear to him, in favor of what his conscience told him to be his duty as justice of this Court."[103]

Justice Robert H. Jackson (1941–53) was raised in New York State in a community where various kinds of "enthusiastic" Christian groups flourished. His parents, however, disdained the religiosity of their neighbors, and the future justice imbibed a strong distaste for "silly emotional stuff" in religion[104] and became an Episcopalian.[105]

Justice Wiley Rutledge (1943–49) was the son of a "fundamentalist" Baptist minister, but the future jurist abandoned the Baptist faith, and his funeral was conducted by a Unitarian minister.[106] Rutledge thought that science often clashed with both religion and politics but that reason was an insufficient guide to truth. Faith had its legitimacy, but it was faith "more felt than thought," and Rutledge proclaimed that "law, freedom, and justice—this trinity is the object of my faith."[107]

By 1940 the New Deal justices formed a majority that was presumably inclined to liberal positions, with Hughes, Stone, and Roberts also willing to support, at last, some expansion of religious liberty. The *Cantwell* case that year was the first important manifestation of this liberalism, although Murphy, who would turn out to be the most committed of civil libertarians, was at first uneasy about the decision, wondering if it allowed the government enough authority to control religious strife.[108] (The case involved Jehovah's Witnesses who went into Catholic neighborhoods to spread inflammatory anti-Catholic propaganda.)

However, the *Gobitis* decision the same year seemed to move in the opposite direction. When the justices met in conference to consider the issue, Hughes remarked that "I come up to this case like a skittish horse to a brass band," indicating that he had misgivings.[109] But, although Murphy was at first inclined to support the Witnesses and actually drafted a dissent, no one took that position in conference, and the other members of the Court were surprised when Stone read his passionate dissent from the bench, a dissent that changed the minds of Black, Douglas, and Murphy and led to the reversal three years later. (Murphy later referred to his concurrence in the *Gobitis* case as a "Gethsemane," a reference to the garden where Jesus suffered anxiety the night before his death.)[110]

Stone's dissent seems to have galvanized three of the New Deal justices to a much broader view of religious liberty, so that the Witnesses proceeded to triumph in most of the cases that came before the Court in the 1940s. Frankfurter, on the other hand, wrote a dissent in the *Barnette* case as passionate as Stone's three years earlier, but to the opposite effect—upholding civil authority in the face of claims of religious liberty. To his brethren Frankfurter spoke of people, presumably including himself, "who had to shed the old loyalties and take on the loyalty of American citizenship."[111]

Jackson wrote the *Barnette* decision, and he, Black, Douglas, Murphy, and Rutledge formed the reliable nucleus in support of most (but not all) Witnesses appeals, with Stone and Frankfurter somewhat more cautious, Roberts and Reed the most likely to be opposed. (Both dissented in the *Barnette* case.)

Murphy became increasingly passionate in his defense of the Witnesses, dissenting in the *Prince* case (1944), for example, when even Rutledge reached a decision holding that taking children on evangelistic missions at night violated the child-labor laws. Privately Murphy said, "It comforts me that with eight hundred years of Catholic background I can speak in defense of a people opposed to my own faith." But even some liberals were troubled by what they considered his emotionalism unaccompanied by careful legal argument.[112]

Frankfurter said of him, rather condescendingly, "When I think of the many Catholics that have taken the life of dissenters, I'm not surprised that F. M. wants the undivided glory of being a dissenter."[113] Murphy's most antagonistic relationship on the Court was with Roberts, who derisively labeled Murphy "the Saint," leading Murphy to retaliate by dubbing Roberts "the Senior Warden," an Episcopalian office. Roberts claimed that Murphy told him he always voted in support of religion and found it "a new idea" when Roberts suggested that judges should rule impartially.[114]

Murphy's most surprising opinion, given his Catholicism, was his dissent in the *Cleveland* case (1946), reaffirming the ban on polygamy. The eventually thrice-married Douglas wrote a stinging condemnation of the practice, while the bachelor Murphy argued that polygamy might enjoy a legal status midway between marriage and fornication.

Another important religious-freedom case of the war years was *Ballard* (1944), where Douglas wrote a majority opinion finding that the leaders of the I Am Movement should not have been prosecuted for mail fraud, because inquiring into the sincerity of their beliefs already violated their liberty. Stone dissented.

Justice Harold H. Burton (1945–58) was a Unitarian who, like Story and Miller before him, served as national president of the church.[115] He proved to be a consistant liberal on all religious issues.

The *Everson* (1947) and *McCollum* (1948) cases were momentous, in that for the first time, the majority of the Court committed themselves to a separationist interpretation of the Establishment Clause. Black wrote both decisions, he, along with Douglas, Frankfurter, Murphy, Jackson, Rutledge, and Burton now forming the solid separationist nucleus, although the latter four dissented from Black's accommodationist conclusion in *Everson*. In the *McCollum* case Reed alone dissented, questioning the Court's reliance on Jefferson and Madison for its authoritative understanding of the Establishment Clause.

Murphy, although troubled, accepted the separationist position. The *Everson* case involved Catholic interests—reimbursing parents for the cost of transporting their children to religious schools—and Murphy considered abstaining. But in a sense, in supporting Black's majority opinion he had the best of both worlds, adopting the separationist position but also allowing the disputed practice. Frankfurter, who was outraged at what he deemed Black's inconsistency, strongly pressed Murphy to join him in dissent, an action that Frankfurter promised would redound to Murphy's reputation as a man of courage ("for the sake of history, for the sake of your inner peace, don't miss"). Prior to the decision Rutledge circulated a warning to his brethren that the Catholic Church was mount-

ing a major campaign for public support that would have a deleterious affect on the political climate.[116]

Black was stung by charges of inconsistency in the *Everson* case and defended himself in part by pointing out that his opinion had brought him a good deal of criticism from Catholics. In allowing reimbursement for bus fares, he said, he provided the appellants with a "pyrrhic victory." During the *McCollum* deliberations, he announced that he would not concur in any opinion that did not cite *Everson* as a precedent, something Frankfurter was unwilling to do.[117]

Murphy also experienced anguish over the *McCollum* decision, which forbade the practice of letting students in public schools attend religion classes on school premises. Prior to the vote he asked Frankfurter if he should expect Catholic criticism if he supported the decision, and afterward he was stung when that criticism materialized. Frankfurter responded that with one exception (presumably Frankfurter himself), every member of the Court was a religious believer. Rutledge said of Murphy, "He was in a very hard spot, but that didn't keep him from coming through one hundred percent."[118]

In the somewhat anomalous *Zorach* case (1952) the Court seemed to pull back from its separationist position, when Douglas rendered a majority opinion allowing public-school students to be released from classes to attend religious instruction off school premises, uttering the famous, "We are a religious people whose institutions presuppose a Supreme Being." Black, Frankfurter, and Jackson all strongly dissented.

During the 1950s, when the Court showed little interest in religious issues, its membership changed substantially, so that by 1961, when religion once again came into its purview, only Black, Frankfurter, and Douglas were left from the 1940s, with Frankfurter soon retiring.

The period 1949–56 was the only time since 1894 that no Catholic served on the Court. When Murphy retired in 1949, President Harry S. Truman declined to accept the claim of a "Catholic seat" on the Court, insisting that religion should not be a criterion. He passed over McGrath, who wanted the nomination, and named Tom C. Clark (1949–67), a Presbyterian, and later in the same year Sherman Minton (1949–56), also a Protestant.[119]

At first President Dwight D. Eisenhower took the same position, but by 1956 he was persuaded that a Catholic should be appointed. Taking a bipartisan stance like Harding's in 1922, he instructed his aides to find a Catholic who was also a conservative Democrat. This search proved difficult, but eventually it produced the name of William J. Brennan, a justice of the New Jersey Supreme Court. Cardinal Spellman was consulted and confirmed that Brennan was a practicing Catholic but said he knew little else about him.[120]

An acquaintance said of Brennan at the time, "Those who knew him realized that, although he was a decent person and God-fearing, he was not a zealously religious man. He was Catholic with a small 'c.' " During his confirmation hearings Brennan was asked whether his allegiance to the pope would outweigh his allegiance to his country and replied that nothing could take precedence over his patriotic duties. Some Catholics criticized his answers, but several bishops publicly endorsed him.[121]

Brennan proved to be one of the strictest of separationists, and his position seems to have been motivated in part by his liberal religious outlook and his estimate of the affects separation might have on his church. Thus during deliberations in the *Lemon* case, he told his brethren that: "If public funds are not given, parochial schools will not perish. Two winds are blowing: (a) in the United States, education is no business of Catholics; and (b) it won't be many years until Notre Dame is like Harvard, etc."[122] Apparently Brennan thought that the issue of public aid to Catholic schools would soon be irrelevant, because many of the schools would be closed, while the rest would cease to be identifiably religious.

Chief Justice Earl Warren was once the head of the Masonic Order in California. His son called him "the most religious man I ever knew," but Warren, who was described as a "quondam Methodist married to a devout Baptist" and whose children belonged to various churches, may not have been affiliated with any church. He considered religious belief essential to a good life and usually attended his wife's church, without much regard to denominational differences.[123]

Warren prided himself on his activities on behalf of religious toleration, and in one speech quoted "the Apostle's" (Paul's) definition of faith— "the substance of things hoped for, the evidence of things unseen"—and said that for Americans faith meant the hope that they could retain their liberties.[124]

Justice John Marshall Harlan III (1955–71), grandson of the first Justice Harlan, was a somewhat inactive Episcopalian,[125] and Justice Potter Stewart (1958–81) was a member of the same church.[126]

Justice Byron R. White (1962–93) was raised in a pious family that attended a nondenominational "Federated Church." The future justice was married in an Episcopal ceremony, but at the time of his appointment to the Court, his father said that the family read the Bible but were not regular church-goers.[127] The justice's funeral in 2002 was in an Episcopal church.[128]

When Frankfurter retired in 1962 the "Jewish seat" went to Arthur Goldberg (1962–65), and when he resigned it was given to Abe Fortas (1965–69), who came from a family "steeped more in the cultural than the religious traditions of Judaism."[129] But when Fortas resigned, President Richard M. Nixon rejected the idea that his successor should be

Jewish and appointed the Methodist Harry A. Blackmun.[130] No Jew then sat on the Court until Ruth Bader Ginsburg in 1993, the period 1969–93 being the only time since 1916 that this was the case.

Justice Thurgood Marshall (1967–91), the first black appointed to the Court, was an active Mason and Episcopalian who, as a delegate to his church's General Convention 1964, led a public protest when the Convention condemned acts of civil disobedience in connection with the Civil Rights Movement. His relationship to the Masons seems to have been ambivalent. Once, while pleading before the Court as a lawyer, and fearing that he was not making his case, he flashed a Masonic distress signal to Justice Jackson. However, he also told people that he had joined the Masons mainly to generate support for the National Association for the Advancement of Colored People, and he warned John F. Kennedy that Kennedy could not be elected president because the Masons "killed off Al Smith" and would do the same to him. Marshall was publicly critical of the Nation of Islam, a black religious group, which in turn issued threats against him.[131]

The Warren Court was solidly liberal in its judicial philosophy, and with regard to religion, this manifested itself in a willingness to expand the scope of religious liberty while at the same time taking an increasingly strict view of the Establishment Clause.

In the *Burstyn* case (1951), Frankfurter and Clark both wrote opinions, for a unanimous Court, overturning New York State's "sacrilege" law, marking the first time the Court formally ruled that freedom of expression included the right to give offense to Christianity, something the *Girard* decision had denied. In another unanimous decision (*Torcaso* [1961]) Black rendered a judgment that atheists could not be denied public office.

Black remained a major figure on religious issues, writing the majority decision in the *Engel* case (1962), which, in forbidding official prayer in public schools, began the process by which the modern Court systematically applied the principles Black had first laid down in *Everson*. He helped expand the scope of religious liberty further still in the *Welsh* decision (1970) extending the rights of conscientious objectors who were not conventionally religious, and he dissented in the *Allen* case (1968), which allowed some forms of public aid to religious schools. While contemplating the *Engel* case he recounted for his wife the history of religious persecution in Europe, and he once told his nephew that "all my religion decisions are influenced by what happened to our Toland ancestors in Ireland," a reference to relatives hanged for rebellion in the eighteenth century.[132]

Douglas too continued to be an important figure in the religion cases. His libertarianism manifested itself in dissent in the *Negre* case (1971), where he voted to extend the rights of pacifists in ways the rest of the

Court would not do. His dissent in the *Yoder* case (1972), where he was unwilling to exempt Amish children from attending high school, seemed to go against this libertarianism, but he cast his opinion in terms of the rights of children, not their parents, to determine their futures. He remained a strong separationist, dissenting in the *Allen* case and in the *Tilton* case (1971), which upheld public aid to religious colleges and universities, as well as from the *Walz* decision (1970), allowing tax exemptions for religious institutions.

Clark was also a consistent liberal. He wrote the majority opinion in the *Seeger* case (1965), involving pacifism, where, a few years before Black, he sought to define religion in the broadest possible terms. He was also the author of the *Schempp* decision (1968), disallowing prescribed Bible reading in the public schools.

Four Warren decisions in 1961 seemed to indicate that he was an accommodationist, as in the *McGowan, Braunfeld, Two Guys*, and *Gallagher* cases he upheld the sabbath laws, finding that they no longer had religious significance. However, he also rendered the important *Flast* decision (1968), extending "standing to sue" in Establishment Clause cases to taxpayers who did not have a personal stake in the dispute.

He was in fact a staunch separationist who, like Black, recalled the religious persecutions in Europe and believed that Jefferson's "wall" defined the meaning of the Establishment Clause, and he rejected the claim that banning prayers and Bible reading from the schools infringed religious liberty.[133] In order to make the *Schempp* decision more palatable to the public, he assigned the ruling to Clark, who, as a known church member, could not be accused of hostility to religion.[134] In his memoirs, recounting the landmark cases of his day, Warren paid little attention to religious issues.

Harlan was essentially conservative on such issues. He dissented in the *Sherbert* case (1963), which ruled that private employers could not require their employees to work on the latters' sabbaths, supported the *Allen* decision, dissented in the *Flast* case, and only reluctantly joined the majority in the *Seeger* decision, where he pointed out that the Court's ruling flatly contravened the words of the Selective Service Act.

Brennan proved to be the most liberal member of the Court over a period of three decades, in many ways Douglas's philosophical heir. In the *Gallagher* case he thought the Sunday laws imposed unlawful burdens on Jews, in the *Schempp* case he wrote a long concurring opinion that considerably elaborated separationist theory, and he wrote the seminal decision in the *Sherbert* case.

Stewart was an accommodationist with regard to the public schools, his most significant opinions being his lone dissents in the *Engel* and *Schempp* cases and his dissent from the *Stone* decision (1980), which forbade the posting of the Ten Commandments in public-school classrooms. But he was a separationist with regard to the Catholic schools, concurring in the *Flast* decision, and dissenting in the *Roemer* case, which upheld public aid to religious colleges and universities, although he also rendered the mixed verdict in the *Meek* case.

Goldberg had little opportunity to vote on religion cases during his brief term on the Court, but he was philosophically a strong separationist.[135] Fortas was as well. He wrote the decision in the *Epperson* case (1968), nullifying an Arkansas law that forbade the teaching of evolution in the public schools, and he dissented in the *Allen* case the same year.

The election of 1968 began a period in which Republicans would occupy the White House for most of the next quarter-century, and part of the Republican agenda was to move the Court in more conservative directions, including on religious issues. It was an agenda that was only partially realized, but by the end of the century, it did leave the Court's orientation considerably different from what it was when Richard M. Nixon became president.

Blackmun was a Methodist, Chief Justice Warren E. Burger (1969–86) a Presbyterian, Justice Lewis F. Powell (1971–87) a Presbyterian, William H. Rehnquist (associate justice 1972–86, chief justice 1986–) possibly the Court's first Lutheran, Justice John Paul Stevens (1975–) apparently without formal religious affiliation, Justice Sandra Day O'Connor (1981–) the first woman named to the Court and an Episcopalian, Justice David Souter (1990–) also an Episcopalian.[136] (President Gerald R. Ford in the mid-1970s rejected the possibility of a Mormon on the Court because he feared a Mormon might not be confirmed by the Senate.)[137]

Indicative of changing political alliances, the Republican ascendancy, for the first time in history, had by 1988 produced three Catholics sitting on the Court simultaneously. Brennan remained, Justice Antonin Scalia was appointed in 1986,[138] and Justice Anthony Kennedy in 1988.[139] When Brennan retired in 1990, he was succeeded by Souter, and when Marshall retired the following year, his replacement was another black Episcopalian, Clarence Thomas.

Born in North Carolina, Thomas was raised by grandparents who were Catholics. As a young man he studied for the priesthood at a seminary in Missouri but left in disillusionment when a classmate gloated over the assassination of Martin Luther King in 1968. Thomas then attended Holy Cross College, a Jesuit institution.[140]

He left the Catholic Church for many years and was for a time an Episcopalian. However, at a Holy Cross alumni reunion in 1996, he announced that he had once again become a practicing Catholic, and in a speech three years later, he said,

There are those who stayed the course of faith when I faltered and quit. There are those who remained steadfast when I doubted. A quarter century is a long absence from the church where I grew up. Absence instills a profound sense of humility, it makes one aware of one's own weaknesses.

He recalled that the nuns who taught him in elementary school looked forward to the day of racial equality "and prepared us in anticipation of the opportunities which were to come." His faith, he affirmed, rested on "the wonderful miracle of the Mass," and since returning to the Catholic Church, he had found peace.

Judging that "Our culture seems to have slipped and slouched. . . . I submit, so much that is wrong today can only be addressed by going to God first." Having once abandoned thoughts of the priesthood, he now found that "the Court is my new vocation. It is the vocation that I lost in 1968. I do it with reverence. I do it for God, at least I try."[141]

Brennan remained the staunchest liberal on the Court until his retirement, his Catholicism having no visible impact on his constitutional opinions. However, as the philosophical complexion of the Court changed, his contributions were as often as not in the nature of dissents.

Thus he dissented in the *Meek* case and *Roemer* cases and from the *Wolman* decision (1977), which again allowed some forms of aid to religious schools, Brennan arguing that all such aid was disallowed. He dissented in the *Valley Forge* case, which allowed the army to donate an unused hospital to a religious college, and in the *Marsh* case (1983), when the Court upheld the practice of legislative chaplains. He rendered the *Aguilar* decision (1985) prohibiting the use of religious schools and their faculties for "remedial" education, and the *Grand Rapids* decision the same year, disallowing similar arrangements in regular academic programs. He wrote the majority opinion in the *Edwards* case (1987) overturning a state law mandating that "creation science" be taught in the public schools. His only gesture of accommodation was in the *Walz* case (1970), where he wrote a concurring opinion.

On the side of religious liberty, Brennan's contributions were also often in the nature of dissents from the decisions of an increasingly conservative Court. He was in the minority in the *Goldman* case (1986), which found that a Jewish air force officer did not have the right to wear a ritual hat with his uniform; in the *Smith* case (1990), where the Court found that a state could dismiss drug counselors who used an illegal drug in an Indian ritual; and in the *Lyng* case the following year, where he offered a vigorous argument in favor of Indians who feared that their sacred lands would be violated by a government road.

White's opinions continued to be relatively conservative. He rendered the decision in the *Allen* case; in the *Regan* case (1980), allowing religious schools to be reimbursed by the state for mandatory testing programs; and in the *Hardison* case (1977), rejecting certain employment claims made on religious grounds. He dissented in the *Welsh* case and in the *Nyquist* case (1973), the first case that flatly disallowed public aid to religious schools. In the *Luetkemeier* case (1974), he was the only member of the Court to accept the plaintiff's claim that the *Everson* decision, by permitting states to reimburse parents for bus fares to religious schools, made such reimbursements a right. He dissented in the *Wolman* case, arguing that religious schools should be allowed to receive the entire package of subsidies that the Court reviewed.

In the *Wheeler* case (1975), the Court found that Kansas City was not obligated to include religious schools in a remedial-education program, a decision in which White concurred, praising the majority for recognizing that such inclusion was not constitutionally prohibited. His dissent in another case involving Kansas City—*Widmar* (1981)—seemed to depart from his usual accommodationism, in that he argued that a state university did not have to accommodate a student religious group on campus. However, White's approach to religious issues was probably less an overt friendliness to religion and more a conservative sense of judicial restraint—he was usually willing to defer to other branches of government on such matters.

Marshall was strongly liberal on religious issues. In the *Wolman* case he was among those dissenting because the decision was too accommodationist, and he dissented also in the *Mueller* case (1983), allowing tax deductions for certain kinds of private-school expenses. His libertarianism also manifested itself somewhat unexpectedly in the *Witters* decision, which he rendered in 1980, permitting a deaf student to use a state scholarship to enroll in a divinity school, and in the *Mergens* case (1989), where he voted with the majority to allow a student religious group to meet at a public high school. Marshall also dissented from White's judgment in the *Hardison* case, believing that the appellant's religious rights had been violated. The intensity of his separationist principles was expressed in his annual refusal to attend the Court's Christmas party, which he regarded as a violation of the Establishment Clause.[142]

Burger was generally an accommodationist, writing the *Yoder, Marsh, Tilton,* and *Walz* decisions, as well as the *Lynch* decision (1983), allowing a Nativity scene to be erected in a public park. He concurred in the *Meek* decision and dissented from the *Aguilar* decision and in the *Jaffree* case (1985), which disallowed an official "moment of silence" in the public schools.

But Burger's important *Lemon* decision (1971) was an exception, in which he laid down what came to be called the Lemon Test for evaluating public programs as they impinged on religion, a test that, as it turned out, few programs could pass. In the same decision he first articulated the "divisiveness" doctrine, whereby the Court had the duty to prevent religious issues from becoming matters of political dispute.

Whatever Nixon may have expected, Blackmun proved to be a consistant liberal on religious issues. During the 1980s, as the Court grew more conservative about religion, he dissented in the *Goldman* and *Smith* cases and, in 1989, rendered the *Allegheny* decision, which in effect overturned the *Lynch* ruling of a few years before. He wrote the *Wheeler* decision and the mixed-verdict *Wolman* decision. He dissented in the *Regan* case, and from the *Zobrest* decision (1987), which required a state to pay a sign-language interpreter to assist a blind child enrolled in a Catholic school. He did, however, write the *Roemer* decision.

Rehnquist was by far the most important conservative on the modern Court in terms of religious issues. He wrote the decisions in the *Goldman*, *Valley Forge*, *Mueller*, and *Zobrest* cases, and in the *Bowen* decision (1987), finding that a sex-education program urging premarital chastity was entitled to federal funds. He concurred in the *Meek* decision. His dissents were in the *Stone*, *Nyquist*, and *Aguilar* cases, and the *Santa Fe* decision (2000), which forbade "voluntary" prayer by students in a public high school. In the *Wolman* case, unlike Brennan and others, Rehnquist thought the flaw in the decision was that it went too far in disallowing certain kinds of aid to religious schools. Perhaps Rehnquist's most important opinion was his dissent in the *Jaffree* case, where he became the first justice to attempt a systematic refutation of the separationist philosophy that had prevailed since 1947.

Powell was a separationist who wrote the *Nyquist* decision, dissented from the *Wolman* decision because he regarded it as too accommodationist, and concurred in the *Aguilar* decision. However, he also wrote the *Widmar* decision.

Stevens was an unwavering Republican separationist who viewed the Religion Clauses as having been enacted because of the Founders' horror of religious persecution in Europe. He saw abortion as an essentially religious issue, which therefore precluded any restrictive regulation.[143]

Stevens wrote the majority opinion in the *Jaffree* case. He dissented in the *Roemer* case, from the separationist side in the *Wolman* case, in the *Mergens* case, and in the *Capitol Square* case (1995), which allowed the Ku Klux Klan to erect a cross on public property. In the *Thornburgh* case (1985) he formally argued the position that laws restricting abortion were unconstitutional because religiously motivated, a contention that White disputed. Stevens concurred in the *Kiryas Joel* decision (1995), dissolving a school district established to include only Orthodox Jews, and in 2000, he rendered the verdict in the *Santa Fe* case.

O'Connor was raised on a Texas ranch, and her family did not attend church regularly, both because there was none close by and because her father, who proclaimed that "nature is our church," had a low regard for preachers. She was married in an Episcopal ceremony and subsequently listed herself as an Episcopalian.[144]

Shortly after she was appointed, she received an inquiry from a citizen asking whether the Court considered the United States a Christian nation. The new justice responded affirmatively, citing the *Holy Trinity*, *Zorach*, and *McGowan* cases as evidence. But when her answer was made public she said that she had been misunderstood and that she regretted her reply.[145]

She was a highly influential "swing vote" in religion cases and often determined which side would prevail. On the accommodationist side she concurred in the *Lynch* and *Capitol Square* decisions, dissented in the *Aguilar* case, and wrote the *Agostini* decision, which in effect overturned *Aguilar*. She concurred in the *Mitchell* decision (2000), allowing a state to provide certain kinds of equipment to religious schools and, in rendering her opinion, made a significant departure from earlier Court rulings by judging that private schools could be trusted to obey the law and need not be monitored. She also wrote the *Mergens* and *Lyng* decisions. On the liberal side she concurred in the *Kiryas Joel* decision, dissented in the *Goldman* and *Smith* cases, and rendered the *Allegheny* verdict, which in effect overturned *Lynch*.

More than any other justice except Story and Douglas, Scalia left a public record of his judicial philosophy, which was a modified "original intent"—not the personal opinions of the Framers of the Constitution or later lawmakers but the "evident meaning" of the texts themselves as they would have been understood at the time they were drafted. On that basis Scalia was a severe critic of the modern Court's approach to constitutional issues.[146]

Along with Rehnquist, he was the strongest opponent of the prevailing liberal jurisprudence of the Religion Clauses and sometimes wrote opinions scathing in their contempt for the dominant position. He rendered the Court's verdict in the *Smith* and *Capitol Square* cases and dissented in the *Weisman* case (1992), which disallowed prayer at a public high-school graduation ceremony, and in the *Edwards* and *Kiryas Joel* cases.

In a public address in 2002, Scalia disagreed with Catholics, including Pope John Paul II, who opposed capital punishment and asserted that judges who did not support the death penalty should resign from the bench.[147] This brought him into debate with other Catholics, including Archbishop Charles Chaput of Denver, who argued that the Constitution should embody moral principles, with "the flexibility to speak to new circumstances and understandings." To this Scalia replied as before, asserting that judges who departed from the intended meaning of the constitutional text were irresponsible, and recalling that the constitutional "right" to abortion had been posited by justices who believed in a flexible Constitution embodying higher principles of justice.[148]

Kennedy, like O'Connor, tended to occupy the ideological middle of the bench. He dissented from the *Allegheny* decision and rendered the *Rosenberger* judgment (1995), holding that a state university could not exclude a student religious publication from sharing in university funds. But he also issued the *Weisman* decision, concurred in the *Kiryas Joel* case, and wrote for a rare unanimous Court in the *Boerne* case (1997), overturning the Religious Freedom Restoration Act, passed by Congress, which the Court found to have infringed the authority of the judiciary.

Souter was, like Stevens, a consistant Republican liberal, writing the Court's decision in the *Kiryas Joel* case, dissenting in the *Rosenberger*, *Agostini*, and *Mitchell* cases, concurring in the *Capitol Square* decision.

Thomas was often allied with Rehnquist and Scalia. His most important contribution in a religion case was the *Mitchell* decision, in which he went even further than O'Connor in holding that the Court's previous understanding of the Establishment Clause was fundamentally in error.

President William J. Clinton in 1993–94 became the first Democratic President in over a quarter of a century able to name a member of the Court, and he chose two Jewish justices—Ruth Bader Ginsburg and Stephen Breyer.[149] By 2002 Ginsburg had written no substantial opinion in a religion case, her votes showing her to be a separationist. Breyer reluctantly concurred in the *Good News* decision, allowing a Bible-study group to meet in a public high school, but dissented in the 2002 case permitting "voucher" payments to students in religious schools.

Thus by the beginning of the twenty-first century the religious complexion of the Court was vastly different from what would have been even imaginable a century before, much less at the beginning of the Republic. Through much of its history the Court had been an entirely Protestant body, but Protestants were now for the first time in the minority, with three Catholics and two Jews, although the two Episcopalians continued that historic ascendancy. Southern Baptists, America's largest Protestant denomination, continued to fare the worst, never having placed one of their active members on the Court, Black and Rutledge having abandoned that church before being elevated to the bench.

Chapter Five

A FRAGILE WALL

EARLY IN THE twenty-first century the future of the Court's jurisprudence of the Religion Clauses depended on the justices who might be nominated in the future. It was also a time when each of the pillars that had upheld that jurisprudence for over fifty years—that strict separationism was the intention of the Framers of the Constitution, that religion has great potential for stirring up division and strife in society, that it was intended by the Constitution to be a wholly "private" matter, that it has subjective and irrational roots, and that it is inculcated by means of "indoctrination"—were wearing away.

ORIGINAL INTENT

The debate over "original intent" has usually been seen as a conflict between "liberals" and "conservatives," the latter insisting that the Constitution must be interpreted and applied only as its Framers intended, the former holding it to be a "living" document that lays down broad principles capable of new and changing applications.[1]

But if the modern debate over original intent pits liberals against conservatives, the foundation of modern separationist theory, as set down by Black, Douglas, Rutledge, and Frankfurter in 1947–48, was the liberal claim that the original meaning of the Establishment Clause was plain, in terms of the intention of the Framers, and that the Court was obligated to follow that intent. With occasional dissents, which grew louder toward the end of the twentieth century, this remained the majority position. (For example, Warren himself, who presided over the extended application of the Establishment Clause during the 1960s, believed that the modern theory embodied Jefferson's "wall of separation.")[2]

The *Walz* and *Marsh* decisions were strongly criticized as inconsistent with the Court's understanding of the Establishment Clause, a criticism that overlooked the fact that the two decisions were fully consistent with the way the Establishment Clause had been understood throughout most of American history, the post–1947 interpretation itself a departure from earlier jurisprudence. The *Walz* decision had to be based on historical practice, which was admittedly of only limited constitutional relevance, because of the modern Court's assumption that the Establishment Clause intended to ban all public support of religion, even that which was non-discriminatory, the Court's dilemma in *Walz* stemming from its failure to comprehend the historical phenomenon of civil religion.[3]

The 1947 separationist claim concerning original intent was seriously flawed in that it assumed that the opinions of Jefferson and Madison alone determined that intent, prescinded from the views of virtually all other Framers, exaggerated Jefferson and Madison's own degree of separationism, and ignored the realities of the religious establishment as they existed in America from the beginning. The soundness of the new jurisprudence was criticized by, among others, the two leading constitutional scholars of the day,[4] but Justice Reed was the only member of the Court to question it, and he offered no sustained argument.

The fact that original intent was treated as fixed and certain was itself anomalous in view of the legal history of the nation during the first half of the twentieth century. The movement called "Legal Realism" rejected what was variously called "legal formalism," "legal conceptualism," or "legal classicism"—the belief that laws embody abstract principles to be applied in particular cases—in favor of an approach that takes into account social realities and the affects that court decisions are likely to have on such realities. The Roosevelt Court was thought to represent the triumph of that movement, with its determination to penetrate "high-sounding rationalizations" of power relationships, some Realists going so far as to hold that judges should base their decisions on "hunches" as to what was socially desirable, then look for legal arguments to support them.

Black remained adamant in his belief that the Court was merely engaged in disclosing the "plain meaning" of the Constitution,[5] but other justices disagreed. Douglas in particular held realist views, contrasting "the law in books" with "the law in action." Convinced that established institutions embodied prejudices in favor of the powerful, he believed that it was necessary to expose the courts' pretensions to objectivity, so that enlightened judges could render just decisions,[6] and he was fond of quoting the "wise remarks" made to him by Chief Justice Hughes: "At the constitutional level where we work, ninety per cent of any decision is emotional. The rational part of us supplies the reasons for supporting our predilections."[7]

Rutledge once said that, as cases came before him, he tried to decide "on which side justice lay," then "searched the law for legitimate means of rendering justice."[8] He believed that justice was "concrete, finite, ever-changing, imperfect and incomplete, alive."

> [O]nly the legislator or judge who can catch the vision of what has come or will come and sense the moment of its common acceptance, from out of the realm of abstract justice into the area of realizable application, is worthy to give his people their laws or judgments.[9]

As a liberal separationist has acknowledged,

> Felix Frankfurter . . . once explained that the words of the Constitu-
> tion are so unrestricted by their intrinsic meaning, or by history, or
> by tradition, or by prior decisions, "that they leave the individual
> justice free, if indeed they do not compel him, to gather meaning not
> from reading the Constitution but from reading life . . . the control-
> ling concepts of the justices are their "idealized political picture" of
> the existing social order . . . even the best and most impartial judges
> . . . cannot escape the currents that have tugged at them throughout
> their lives and inescapably color their judgment. Personality, the be-
> liefs that make the man, has always made the difference in the Su-
> preme Court's constitutional adjudication."[10]

Justice Goldberg also candidly admitted that in reaching decisions, the
Warren Court often disregarded legal formalities "in an attempt to take
hold and measure the real impact of the action being challenged." The
Court, he insisted, "must possess and convey an empathy for and understanding of the facts of life for those who come before it."[11]

In the words of another liberal separationist, conservatives claim that
the Constitution is to be interpreted within "a single community of meaning," whereas liberals hold that this community "is continually being
recreated by acts of the will."[12]

Thus, according to modern jurisprudence, the Court in the 1940s was
free to interpret the Establishment Clause in almost any way it chose. In
recovering original intent it could have cast its net much wider than Madison and Jefferson—recognizing the reality of de facto establishment
throughout American history, denying that original intent should govern,
questioning the assumptions on which Jefferson and Madison's separationism was based. Since public educational systems did not exist in 1787,
it could have concluded that the Constitution gave little guidance for dealing with these modern realities. Instead it concealed the extent of its revolution behind claims about original intent.

This inevitably led to difficulties in reconciling the Religion Clauses,
and the most common way of doing so was to claim that the prohibition
on establishment was intended to prevent violations of religious liberty.
But the separationists in *Everson* did not show that the alleged establishment of religion violated anyone's freedom[13] and instead claimed that acts
of establishment were intolerable in themselves, apart from any provable
harm they might do. After that, separationist plaintiffs have not necessarily been required to show that their freedom was violated by some government action, and separation is treated as a good in its own right,[14] an
assumption given unusual constitutional status in the *Flast* decision
(1968), which departed from precedent in granting separationists standing to sue solely in their capacity as taxpayers.

Perhaps the most basic constitutional question in 1947 was how the Establishment Clause could be understood to restrict state action, when its original purpose was precisely to guarantee the states wide latitude in the area of religion.[15] There are special difficulties with the theory that the Fourteenth Amendment incorporated the Establishment Clause and applied it to the states, which is the alleged reason the Court in 1947 found itself faced with new issues. The Framers of the Constitution obviously did not intend to outlaw state religious establishments, and the framers of the Fourteenth Amendment gave no indication that they intended to incorporate the Religion Clauses. For example, there was no citation of the Amendment in the *Watson* case (1872), where it would logically have been applicable.[16]

But if *Everson* and *McCollum* were in fact the first establishment issues brought before the Court after incorporation, the Establishment Clause should then have been applied to the states in the same way in which it was applied to the federal government, and in 1947 all federal precedents—*Holy Trinity, Bradfield, Speer, Lowery* I and II, *Quick Bear, Cochran*—were accomodationist. The Court ignored some of these precedents and misstated those that it did cite.[17]

This theory of the Establishment Clause necessarily opened a wide gulf between the modern understanding and the prevailing beliefs and practices of earlier American history, so that, for example, Justice Brennan in the *Lynch* case (1983) could only justify invoking God at the opening of the Court's own sessions by dismissing the practice as "ceremonial deism."

However, by the very enactment of the Free-Exercise Clause, the Framers in effect "established" religion by giving it special protection. The Lemon Test's fear of "entanglement" would, if applied consistently, require the repeal of the Free-Exercise Clause and render constitutionally suspect all exemptions that the modern Court has granted to religious believers.[18] (Douglas himself recognized religion's special place in the Constitution but did not explain how he reconciled it with his strict separationism.)[19]

The separationist position lost some of its influence on the Court during the 1970s, and in some ways the principal significance of the *Jaffree* case (1985) was that it marked the first time a member of the Court (Rehnquist) mounted a systematic critique of the dominant separationism, pointing out various ways in which accomodationism had been the prevailing American tradition.

But the question of original intent was still alive after 2000, as Scalia in *Santa Fe* invoked the Framers on behalf of prayer in public schools and in *Mitchell* and *Zelman* Souter cited them in opposition to public aid to religious schools, original intent an issue over which factions on the Court remained as divided as they were over other questions of jurisprudence.

RELIGION AS DIVISIVE

The modern Court is heir to a certain kind of liberalism that has always been suspicious of the "divisive" potential of religion and therefore seeks to exclude it from public life.[20] Civil religion itself, if it places some kind of piety at the center of national life, also tames the "fractiousness" of individual groups and promotes a love of country transcending differences.[21] Traditionally religion in America was thought of as something broader than individual "sects," indeed as broader than the political community itself.[22]

In the *Everson* case Justice Jackson referred disdainfully to "those warring sects," thereby beginning a tradition by which the Court often used the term "sect" to refer to any kind of organized religion, implying narrow and fractured groups, in contrast to the habit throughout most of American history of conceiving religion as transcending denominational differences.[23] Now, however, there is no common religion transcending specific faiths, thus "sects" are unavoidable.[24]

The Religion Clauses are in tension with one another only on the assumption that, rather than both protecting religious liberty, the Establishment Clause protects freedom from religion,[25] and the clauses are often treated as though they are in conflict with one another. Thus, for example, it becomes an issue whether student religious groups should have access to school facilities open to other groups or whether the Establishment Clause actually allows them fewer rights than their classmates.

Fear of religious divisiveness reached its peak in the *Lemon* case, which went much further than the Court had ever gone in that it seemed to require that even freedom of expression be restricted if it threatened to cause religious division. Some justices acknowledged that the danger of religious conflict was no longer as great as it once was, but the principle remained.

Although in the *Lemon* decision Chief Justice Burger raised divisiveness to the level of a constitutional doctrine, based on original intent, he later seemed to back away from it. However, for other justices it remained a potent principle. Stevens, for example, believed that the Framers were motivated by the fact that "English emigrants burned [*sic*] witches at the stake in Salem,"[26] and in school-aid cases separationist justices routinely warned that granting such aid would lead to destructive competition for funds among religious groups. Justice O'Connor's test in *Allegheny*— whether a particular arrangement made some citizens feel "excluded" from the community—was an application of the divisiveness doctrine. An anomaly was pointed out by Justice Thomas in the *Capitol Square* case— if a cross erected by the Ku Klux Klan were frankly acknowledged as "a symbol of hate," it would be protected as freedom of expression. Only the claim that it was the Christian symbol of love made it suspect.

Liberal pluralism, formulated already by Madison, holds that a multiplicity of religious groups is good for society, in that it prevents any particular group from becoming too powerful. But this presents the danger of conflict among such groups. At various times the same justices have expressed what seem like contradictory views—that competition among a multiplicity of religions is dangerous to the peace of society but that it is also a healthy expression of the democratic spirit. In a sense the modern Court treats religions as instances of Madison's "factions"—self-interested groups each pushing its own agenda and in need of restraint.[27] Ironically, despite the liberal insistence that the Constitution be a "living document" responsive to changing historical conditions, the separationist majority has continued to speak as though the social affects of religion have not changed since the eighteenth century.

Frankfurter in the flag-salute cases warned, with some logic, that tolerating certain religious practices weakened national unity, and implicitly he recognized the troubling fact that the establishment of religion has caused less civil strife than has religious liberty. Historically there had been a good deal of violent anti-Jewish and anti-Catholic activity in America, and Mormon polygamy was the single most divisive religious issue in the history of the nation. The Witnesses were hated by many people as unpatriotic, but their unpopularity also stemmed from their virulent attacks on other faiths, and Court decisions in their favor sometimes fomented new violence against them.[28] (In the *Kunz* case [1953] the Court upheld the liberties of a street preacher whose attacks on other religions were so offensive that they were thought likely to cause a riot.)

Thus when Burger in the *Lemon* case asserted that the Constitution intended to prevent religious controversy from erupting in the public square, and that it was the Court's duty to enforce this inhibition, the logic of his position seemed to demand not a stricter application of the Establishment Clause but less vigilance on behalf of religious liberty. Historically much religious strife would have been avoided if the nation had never tolerated Jews, Catholics, Mormons, or Jehovah's Witnesses. Disputes over public aid to private schools are likely to fall well within the boundaries of normal democratic debate over government programs, at worst provoking rancorous verbal exchanges. But religious liberty has often led to violent conflict.

Frankfurter was the member of the Court who best understood the full implications of this and did not shrink from accepting them. During deliberations in the *Zorach* case, for example, he exclaimed to his brethren that:

McCarthyism is a filthy, dirty, smearing technique, but there is another group who feels that they alone are *God's anointed* and who also smear others. Secularism in the schools is a fighting issue. I agree with Bryce who says that sectarianism has ruined Europe and secularism has saved America from exclusions, etc. The real issue in *McCollum* was whether the school was put behind sectarianism.[29]

During the *Engel* case deliberations, Frankfurter asserted that "We ought not to forget that the public schools are secular."[30]

Although separationists have usually denied that their philosophy enforces secularism, Frankfurter seemed to imply that it should do so, and the logic of his position was not only that religious influences should be excluded from the public schools but that the "smearing" tactics of religious groups should be excluded from public discourse.

But attempts to forestall religious conflict, as by excluding all religious expression from the public schools, may actually have the affect of increasing it.[31] Decades after the crucial cases of 1962–63, a large majority of Americans still strongly disagreed with the Court's position about religion in the schools, and it was periodically the focus of political agitation.[32] As Brennan pointed out in the *Allegheny* case, the "message of pluralism" might itself be offensive to some people.

The claim that historically the Court anticipates shifts in public opinion and that its controversial decisions are later ratified by the voters,[33] whatever other validity it may have, fails completely with respect to the Court's interpretation of the Establishment Clause. (Goldberg took satisfaction in the fact that controversial Court decisions are soon accepted by the public as legitimate, but in order to make that argument he too had to ignore the religion cases.)[34]

The misgivings that the majority of the Court had about the divisiveness of organized religion in general have been particularly focused on Catholicism, and, ironically, a Court proclaimedly fearful of divisiveness along religious lines has if anything exacerbated divisions between Protestants and Catholics. The strict separationist position, not consistently applied, was formulated in the 1870s primarily against Catholic schools,[35] and the chief *Everson* plaintiff was an organization called the Junior Order of United American Mechanics, a group with a long history of nativism and anti-Catholicism.[36] Some Protestants who denounced the *Everson* ruling, because it helped Catholic schools, a year later attacked the separationist philosophy as applied in *McCollum*.[37]

Black explained his seemingly illogical ruling in *Everson*—reimbursing bus fares while affirming a strict separationist philosophy—by saying that he wanted it to be a "pyrrhic victory" for the Catholic schools.[38] His son thought his father was anti-Catholic, and the senior Black studied the

works of Paul Blanshard, a polemicist who charged that the Catholic
Church was a threat to American democracy. Black, a Mason, was of-
fended by the fact that the Catholic Church condemned Masonry, whose
adherents he characterized as "free-thinkers."[39] He also disagreed with
the *Meyer* and *Pierce* decisions and persuaded Warren not to cite them as
precedents.[40]

As early as the *Everson* case Rutledge warned that "every religious
institution in the country will be reaching into the hopper if we sustain
this,"[41] and he particularly feared a Catholic raid on the treasury.[42] During
preliminary discussions he warned his brethren:

> Once this is done, the field is wide open and there is no telling where
> this ends. First it was textbooks, now buses and transportation, and
> next it will be lunches and teachers. . . . You can't draw the line be-
> tween a little and a lot of pregnancy. . . . Every religious institution
> in the country will be reaching into the hopper for help if you sustain
> this. . . . We must stop this thing right at the threshold of the public
> schools.[43]

Like Black, Douglas approved of Blanshard's anti-Catholic polemics[44]
and in 1959 wrote to Black, "I think if Catholics get public money to
finance their schools, we better insist on getting some good prayers in
public schools or we Protestants are out of business."[45] Some prominent
Protestants warned against government aid to private schools by reminding the public that it was Catholics who had by far the largest system
and would therefore reap the greatest benefits.[46]

Rutledge and Frankfurter seemed to think that Justice Murphy, as a
Catholic, had to prove his devotion to the Constitution. Frankfurter
pressed Murphy hard (and unsuccessfully) to dissent from Black's opinion
in *Everson*, urging Murphy to rise above "flattery," "false friends," and
"temporary fame" and to look to his place in history.[47] After Murphy
voted with the separationist majority in *McCollum*, Rutledge expressed
satisfaction that "he was in a very hard spot, but that didn't keep him
from coming through one hundred per cent."[48] (Ironically, it was the pious
Catholic Murphy who alone saw any redeeming social value in polygamy
at the end of World War II.) In his *Everson* dissent Jackson asserted that
"Our public school, if not a product of Protestantism, at least is more
consistent with it than with the Catholic culture and scheme of values,"
but he thought the Court should keep every form of religion from gaining
influence over public policy.

The fear that religious schools would undermine public education was
repeated by Blackmun during deliberations over the *Mueller* case, when
he warned his brethren that "An affirmance here goes a long way toward

killing off our public schools," adding that "I don't agree that parochial schools produce a superior product to public schools."[49]

The strong separationist position not only holds that religious schools should receive no direct government aid but that public policy should not in any way validate them. Thus in discussions during the *Aguilar* case, Brennan objected to state-supported remedial-education programs in Catholic schools on the grounds that "they serve the principal purpose of integrating the child, both socially and educationally, into the parochial school. Such services foster in the child a profound dependence on the religious school,"[50] something that might be considered a legitimate effect of public policy, if the parochial schools themselves have legitimate existence and serve a recognized public purpose.

Will Herberg, perhaps the best-known Jewish scholar of the 1950s, suggested that "fear of Catholicism" lay behind much of the separationist campaign,[51] and one of the leading separationist groups—Protestants and Other Americans United for Separation of Church and State (POAU)—was particularly anti-Catholic.[52] In the minds of some of the justices, the Catholic Church manifested with maximum intensity those dangerous tendencies of organized religion from which the Court had a duty to protect the nation. In the *Mitchell* case (2000), Thomas traced the separationist position to the Blaine Amendment of the 1870s, which he characterized as simply anti-Catholic and called "a shameful pedigree."

At one time there was an alliance, as in the *Everson* case, between secularists and certain kinds of Protestants, both of whom, for different reasons, supported separation. (After the *McCollum* decision the influential Protestant theologian Reinhold Niebuhr noted that the secular idea of religion as dangerous to the peace of society had merged with certain Protestant convictions that religion was purest when it was most private.)[53] Since about 1970, however, conservative Protestants have tended to see separationism as hostile to their faith, and the alliance has dissolved.[54] Prior to 1979 no conservative Protestant organization ever participated in a church-state case, but after that, they began to do so with increasing frequency,[55] separationism now understood by many Protestants as a threat to their religious liberties. Although Jews have generally been considered strongly separationist, there has been a tradition of Jewish accommodationism since 1947, to some extent correlated with religious orthodoxy.[56]

In making itself vigilant against religious divisiveness, the Court itself threatens religious liberty, in that it ignores or inhibits precisely the "prophetic" (alternatively, "antisocial") dimensions of religion—its opposition to prevailing social conditions and the underlying cultural consensus in the name of a higher truth.[57] Without offering a clear rationale for it, the Court treats such claims in contradictory ways, rewarding nonconformity in the *Yoder* case, punishing it in the *Bob Jones* case.

Some believers' claims that they benefit society rests, paradoxically, on their opposition to that society, just as others (Jehovah's Witnesses) justify their social utility precisely on the grounds that they promote true religious belief and oppose falsehood, exactly the stance that the Court considers divisive. When religion is "prophetic" and when it is merely "divisive" requires judgments that are themselves religiously based, and it may be naive to expect truly prophetic religions to be subsidized through tax exemptions. The unique "service" that religion offers society may be precisely something that neither the government nor a majority of the citizens want, for example, pacifism. Rules for tax exemptions inhibit the freedom of religious groups by forbidding them to engage in "political" activity, even if the churches themselves believe not that they are being political but that they are addressing serious moral and social issues.[58]

In the *Walz* case (1970) Burger partly justified tax exemptions for churches by positing a harmonious relationship between religion and society, religion embodying and promoting society's highest values. But in the *Yoder* case two years later, he found that a disharmonious relationship might also be tolerable, a finding made possible by the fact that the Amish merely sought to withdraw from society, not to oppose it. Douglas on the other hand feared religious divisiveness to the point where he questioned the right of any religion to "divide" its members from that society.

At the heart of this anomaly is the fundamental conundrum of democracy itself—that the state undertakes to guarantee the widest possible freedom for its citizens and at the same time to promote national unity. Prior to the modern era the Court had little difficulty in choosing the latter over the former, and in the flag-salute cases Frankfurter was the last justice to assert that position openly. The modern Court's preoccupation with religious, to the exclusion of other kinds, of divisiveness is an anachronistic expression of this outlook, one that hardly comports with the same Court's solicitude for liberty. While the government has an obvious interest in promoting civic unity, there is no constitutional mandate to do so,[59] and to posit obligatory unity is to deny the nature of democracy itself.

The Catholic refusal to be assimilated into the general Protestantism of the nineteenth century had the affect of greatly broadening the scope of religious freedom,[60] an expansion ratified by the *Pierce* decision, which in effect "disestablished" public education.[61] If there were a constitutional mandate to promote national unity, both the *Pierce* and *Barnette* cases were wrongly decided, as Frankfurter recognized.[62] The very existence of private religious schools is itself an important "division," and, as one separationist has put it, government has strong reasons for favoring public schools "to foster an integrated national (or state) polity," to break down barriers, and to promote good citizenship.[63] Indeed the logic of the position implies that even the existence of a variety of "sects" threatens national unity.[64] (In deliberations during the *Mueller* case, Stevens told his brethren: "I question whether the diversity of educational facilities helps states.")[65]

The claim that religion is divisive can be sustained with respect to some religions, or with respect to all religions some of the time. But this begs the question, since the Constitution does not address "divisiveness" and provides no basis for deciding which phenomena of this kind are to be excluded from the public square. The mere feeling of being excluded or dishonored is conceded no legal or constitutional significance in contexts other than religion,[66] and such alienation is perhaps merely a price democracy exacts from those who lose political battles.[67] Fear of religious division is especially anomalous in a democracy, which of its very nature encourages "division" among the citizens, insofar as they are encouraged to form and express their opinions. (Daniel Webster noted this anomaly as early as the *Girard* case.)[68]

To protect society from divisiveness would require examining not just religion but all other kinds of public activity, according to certain purported tests of harmony, tests that numerous secular ideologies would also fail. There is no basis for thinking that religious believers are more disruptive than the devotees of numerous other causes, or than the average citizen who makes political judgments.[69] The dangers ascribed to religion can easily be discerned in all areas of civic life, such as race, ethnicity, and gender.[70] Throughout American history there has been far more violence generated by those divisions than by religion, and the separationist fear of civil strife rests on the belief that despite all historical evidence to the contrary, religion is uniquely dangerous to civil peace.[71]

The Court's "alienation" test, first articulated by O'Connor in the *Allegheny* case, established a standard of judgment without constitutional warrant, among other things ignoring the fact that most public policies, including the Court's own decisions, have the affect of alienating some of the citizens. The policies of the liberal state itself tend over time to weaken the sense of community, which for some people is itself a major cause of alienation.[72]

For "divisiveness" is merely another name for aggressive public activity, which is presumably exactly what the Constitution protects, and the full exercise of religious freedom requires that believers not be required to bifurcate their private and public selves.[73] Yet religion has been excluded from the public square on the grounds that it is "something of a danger to democratic political life [that] is based on certain values and practices, which religion has the potential to undermine."[74] Besides government, there are also substantial social and cultural pressures in the liberal society for religious groups to mute any claims that might offend others,[75] and political activity by religious groups itself has a tendency to tame their prophetic character.[76]

The separationist argument has thus become perfectly circular: A rigid "wall of separation" is necessary because the Framers so decreed. Why did they do so? Because religion is divisive. Why should religion be held to a stricter standard in this regard than other kinds of activity? Because the Framers so decreed.

The various state churches in the early republic were disestablished without recourse to the courts,[77] and the modern Court has itself unintentionally encouraged religious divisiveness precisely by confirming the assumption, not common before 1947, that litigation is the appropriate way of resolving such differences. The result of its vigilant separationism has been to discourage "forbearance"—attempts by citizens to resolve these problems in good faith, through ordinary community channels. In a sense the Court, by its haste to settle such disagreements by judicial decree, has deprived citizens of the valuable experience of negotiating differences in a truly pluralistic way.[78] Ironically, by the end of the twentieth century, religious conflict, some of it (abortion, school prayer) the direct result of court decisions, was perhaps sharper than it had been a quarter century before.[79]

RELIGION AS PRIVATE

In developing its view of the Religion Clauses, the Court faced a dilemma—if religious liberty were to be expanded, how could the nation avoid the religious strife that the Establishment Clause supposedly sought to prevent? The solution was a new definition of religion as a purely private matter, a position foreshadowed in the traditional but increasingly problematic distinction between belief and action. The Religion Clauses were reconciled by in effect "establishing" a definition of religion as wholly private, meaning that it was a personal belief or preference only. The Court's duty was to protect such beliefs as far as possible but at the same time to rebuff any assertion that they had applicability beyond personal choice. (This position has been attributed to Madison and has been characterized as a particular kind of Protestant "low church" understanding of religion, opposed, for example, to Jewish and Catholic communitarianism.)[80]

Religion was not kept private in the sense that it could not express itself publicly, freedom to proselytize being precisely one of its major liberties, but in the sense that it could not ask for anything more than toleration from the larger society. The Witnesses could be as aggressive as they chose in preaching (Douglas referred rather admiringly to their "fanatic zeal"),[81] but public schools could offer no hospitality to religious instruction.

In the *Schempp* case, expanding on Rutledge's dictum in *Everson*, Clark described religion as "the inviolable citadel of the individual heart and mind," a phrase Warren later quoted as expressing the Court's consensual understanding.[82] As one historian of the Warren Court put it, "There was a dominant view shared by the well-educated—and therefore by the justices of the Court—that religion was a private matter, best left to the homes and the churches."[83] Religion, in the view of the separationist majority, must be kept private precisely because of its divisive potential,[84] Justice Stewart in *Schempp*, being a lone voice asking whether this was an adequate understanding.

Traditionally the Court understood religion to be based on claims of higher authority, although such claims, as with polygamy, did not necessarily require legal tolerance. In traditional religion, final authority does not lie with "conscience" but with God,[85] so that in the *Duss* case (1902), for example, Justice McKenna could praise the spirit of "self-abnegation" that a utopian religious group instilled in its members. But in the *Hamilton* case (1934), Justice Cardozo bluntly warned that government need not and could not accommodate all claims of religious duty, some of which might simply be mistaken. As late as the flag-salute cases, the Court treated religion as based less on personal choice than on transcendent divine commands, with Jackson warning against requiring children to do things they feared would damn them to hell.

In *Yoder*, somewhat anachronistically, Burger placed great emphasis on the Amish sense of the divine will and explicitly insisted that generalized claims of conscience were not sufficient for religious exemptions. But granting exemptions from general laws itself has the effect of making religion a purely private commitment and is probably permitted only because those who receive such exemptions are relatively few in number and regarded as marginal to the larger society.[86]

The personalist definition of religion was in effect "established" in the *Seeger* decision (1962), which, together with *Welsh* (1970), accomplished the purposes that a majority of the Court probably intended—giving relief to young men with conscientious scruples about war, ratifying the definition of religion as broader than theism, making that definition essentially personal and subjective, and ratifying the equality of theists and nontheists before the law.[87] In these two cases religion ceased definitively to be treated as a sense of duty or obedience to higher powers and came to mean something emanating solely from the individual conscience. (Daniel Seeger, who later described his position as "kind of agnostic," was himself

dissatisfied with the Court's formulation, which he considered "artificial
. . . geometric, and forced.")[88]

In a sense the Court has almost eliminated religion altogether as a category of freedom and has substituted "conscience," with a view of religious believers as "self-originating sources of moral claims."[89] As early as
the Jehovah's Witnesses cases it was unclear when the Court was actually
invoking the Free-Exercise Clause, and often religion seems merely to be
subsumed under freedom of expression,[90] as in the "equal access" cases
involving religious groups in public schools. (It has been argued that religion need not be defined, because almost all issues of religious freedom
can be treated as freedom of expression.)[91]

But the assumption that religion is intended to be wholly private cannot
account for the Religion Clauses themselves, whose special place in the
Constitution implies that religion has a public role.[92] The Framers obviously intended to protect freedom of religion itself, not merely religion as
an expression of personal choice.[93]

Religious believers ordinarily do not "choose," for example, the day of
the week they deem holy but accept it as a divine ordinance, and in earlier
times, the Court did not treat religion as a subjective spiritual experience.[94] More recently, however, in the various sabbath cases and the conscientious-objector cases the major emphasis was placed on individual
conscience, rights to be respected primarily because they were personally
chosen.[95] In *Goldman, Smith, Lyng,* and other free-exercise cases under
the Rehnquist Court the idea of religious duty seemed to be slighted.[96]

The fundamental fallacy of defining religion as private is that such an
understanding itself restricts religious freedom, since most religions teach
that belief must have public manifestations and must guide people in all
aspects of their lives. Beliefs are never merely private and personal but are
expressed in a community.[97] Thus excluding religion from public discourse makes it impossible for believers to express their beliefs ade-
quately.[98] They are required to develop "bifurcated minds" in which their
deepest beliefs have nothing to do with their public lives.[99]

Although the nineteenth-century Court recognized religious liberty primarily in terms of organized groups, the Court after 1940 tended to regard religious belief as important only as the personal choice of individuals,[100] so that in a sense religious groups enjoy rights only through the
rights of their members.[101] But full religious liberty requires the recognition of religious groups as well as of individuals,[102] and one manifestation
of the decline of respect for this liberty is the modern tendency to see
religion as primarily individual rather than communal, thereby greatly
diminishing its social impact.[103]

The pattern has been traced to an underlying conflict between alternative American traditions—the republican legacy of communitarianism

and the liberal tradition of individualism, with the republican tradition cherishing religion as the basis of personal character.[104] Although churches sometimes win legal and constitutional battles, they do so merely as "interest groups," not as religious bodies as such.[105] In particular the Warren Court has been credited with exalting democratic individualism by deligitimizing social relations that do not flow from individual choice.[106] Liberalism tends to destroy "socially constructed hierarchies"[107] and to promote an atomistic conception of the self that recognizes no authority higher than the self,[108] an outlook that has been attributed to a "Lockean individualism" in which all social bonds, including religion, are contractural only.[109]

An adequate respect for religious freedom would protect the rights of groups even to the point of acknowledging their right to function as "independent power bases." But the modern Court forces believers to make an artificial separation between themselves and their faith,[110] to "remake themselves" before they can join in the public discussion,[111] to posit a distinction between "religious" and "secular" that many people do not make in their own minds.[112]

Basing religious liberty solely on personal beliefs also provides no basis for determining which beliefs are to be honored and which not,[113] leading inevitably to charges of discrimination.

Since 1947 the Court has periodically scolded the citizens for failing to grasp what the Court considers the benign fact that religion is a "citadel of privacy." But such a position precisely establishes a particular view of religion that, like all establishments, discriminates against those who fail to conform.

RELIGION AS IRRATIONAL

If the Court is called upon to rule in matters of "religion," it must obviously be able to define that phenomenon, and through most of its history, it acted simply upon the commonsense definition of the term—an organized body of people believing in supernatural (almost always Christian) powers.

Expounding on natural law, Story identified "the prime duty of man" as ascertaining the will of God and following it.[114] Relative to conscientious objection, Holmes in the *Schwimmer* case (1929) described pacifists as people who took literally the Sermon on the Mount, and in the *MacIntosh* case (1931), Justice Sutherland spoke of the "the duty of obedience to the will of God," then bluntly told the plaintiff that he had misunderstood the divine will. In the same case, Hughes spoke of "supreme allegiance to the will of God" and of duties "superior to any arising from a purely human source." In the *Hamilton* case (1934), Cardozo referred to pacifists as "martyrs to principle," and in *Barnette*, Jackson argued the unfairness of requiring children to engage in an action they believed would make them liable to damnation. The Court rejected the Mormons' definition of their own faith and instead employed what it regarded as an objective definition of religion that excluded polygamy.

In the *Murdoch* case (1943), Reed argued that charitable institutions like orphanages were not religious in nature, an opinion echoed by Roberts in the *Follett* case the same year, both opinions part of a failing effort to maintain some objective definition of religion. (Reed also thought that collecting money in connection with religion "destroyed its sacred character.")

When the polygamy issue was revived in 1946, the Court was again confronted with a situation in which it felt called upon to curtail religious liberty. Douglas, who wrote the anti-polygamy decision in *Cleveland*, insisted both on and off the bench that the teaching about polygamy by dissident Mormons was a mere cloak for immorality. Ignoring the strictures about sincerity of belief laid down by the Court in *Ballard*, he asserted that "a 'religious' rite which violates the standards of Christian ethics and morality is not in the true sense, in the constitutional sense, included within 'religion,' the free exercise of which is guaranteed by the Bill of Rights."[115] Douglas's dilemma was that of the entire Court, but his attempt to avoid the dilemma by charging polygamists with insincerity merely served to expose the confused state of the question.

Beginning already in the *Ballard* case the Court had moved toward a "functional" definition of the kind employed by social scientists, an approach that in principle precludes any firm definition,[116] as Brennan observed in the *Amos* case (1987). The Court's new solicitude for religious liberty not only encompassed action as well as belief, it dictated as broad a definition of religion as possible, and in *Ballard* it came close to actually forbidding any definition, because a definition might exclude some of those claiming the term "religion" for themselves.[117]

The problem of defining religion seems insuperable under the Establishment Clause, since any definition would constitute an "establishment," although Madison himself, in his *Memorandum*, made authoritative pronouncements about the nature of religion,[118] with apparently no sense of irony as to whether these definitions themselves constituted religious "establishment."

The dilemma of definition has been avoided by a liberal theorist who describes religion as "a universal, diverse, and powerful human creation"[119] and:

> . . . a human cultural creation that cannot be confined to a particular religion, philosophy, or practice. It is the obligation of government

to resist any religious expression that reifies a particular interpretation of what religion is.[120]

During the Court's search for a new definition of religion, Frankfurter in the *Gobitis* case spoke of it as "ultimate mystery," Rutledge in the *Everson* case referred to it as "a feeling towards the ultimate issues of existence," and Frankfurter in the *Burstyn* case (1955) cited the philosopher William James's map of "the varieties of religious experience," which had "unascertainable bounds." Thus religion came to be seen as irrational—rooted in highly subjective perceptions of reality and incapable of being supported by evidence.[121]

Frankfurter asserted this in *Gobitis* and *Barnette*, and Rutledge set up a conflict between "progressing scientific discovery and . . . the established institutions of religion and politics." Reason alone, he thought, could not answer all questions, but "faith is more felt than thought,"[122] an assumption that soon became a consistent theme in the Court's jurisprudence.

No member of the Court embraced the teachings of the Jehovah's Witnesses, whom they perhaps regarded as obstreperous nuisances, but the justices could sympathize with the Witnesses as courageous adherents to principle. The *Ballard* case, however, brought forward a religious group for which there could be little respect and who were probably frauds (Jackson, even as he overturned their prosecution, exclaimed "I smell humbug" and hoped that few people would be attracted to the movement). Jackson located the value of the religion solely in whatever irrational, even illusory, emotional satisfaction it might give its adherents. Thus beginning with *Ballard* the Court began to move toward a definition of religion as a highly subjective phenomenon with no objective criteria of credibility. Chief Justice Stone dissented, making, for one of the last times in the Court's history, the argument that objective criteria did exist and that the I Am Movement was fraudulent, a position Douglas would take in the polygamy cases two years later but a position that most of the Court was in the process of abandoning.

The roots of the assumption about the irrationality of religion can perhaps be found in the personal histories of the majority of justices who during the 1940s fashioned the modern jurisprudence of the Religion Clauses. In 1947, for probably the first time in its history, the Court was composed of a majority who were alienated from the religions of their youth, men who had come to believe that the faiths in which they had been raised were to some extent false and even pernicious.

Black and Rutledge were former fundamentalist Baptists who had moved toward Unitarianism, as Douglas had moved away from fundamentalist Presbyterianism. Both Black and Douglas regarded active church members as "hypocrites" who used religion for bad purposes.

Frankfurter had abandoned the synagogue while an adolescent, unable to accept the beliefs of his elders. (Although often considered a "strict constructionist" who thought courts should defer to legislatures, in reality he usually voted against religious interests, often overturning legislative actions under the Establishment Clause.) Jackson had been raised in a family that despised the emotional religiosity of their neighbors. Murphy was a pious Catholic who nonetheless feared that his church had too much power, and Burton had become a Unitarian as a respectable way of expressing his religious doubts. (Ironically, Reed, the only member of the Court to question the new separationism, appears to have belonged to no church.) The Court in the 1940s for the first time manifested a "secular mind."[123]

The premodern Court was hardly a bastion of religious orthodoxy, as Bradley, Shiras, Holmes, Taft, Sutherland, Brandeis, Cardozo, and Hughes showed. But, as Bradley's rather cynical dichotomy between private belief and public profession illustrated, the justices' personal doubts seldom influenced their willingness to support religion, so that the *Pierce* and *Cochran* decisions, for example, were unanimous.

The fact that the justices probably had little personal respect for the Witnesses' beliefs, and none at all for the I Am Movement, reinforced their disrespect, causing them to perceive the religions that came before them as eccentric, marginal, virtually incomprehensible and incredible faiths, possessing in exaggerated form the errors of those creeds that most of the justices had rejected in their own lives.

In a way, the assumption that all religions are at root irrational has favored marginal groups, leading to a special solicitude for idiosyncratic beliefs that liberal justices, conscious of their own lack of sympathy for such beliefs, are determined to protect. Thus it also follows that the stronger the religious passion, the stronger the claim made on society's tolerance, since sincerity alone matters.[124]

But just as the reduction of religion to free expression cannot explain why the Religion Clauses were enacted in the first place, so also the primacy of place that religion enjoys in the Bill of Rights can scarcely be understood without a coherent definition of the phenomenon.[125] But the new definition enacted in *Seeger* is both too broad and too narrow—not every religion necessarily has to do with "ultimate concern," and for some people ultimate concerns have nothing to do with religion.[126] In addition, the Court's resolve to extend the benefits of religious liberty as widely as possible precludes any real definition.[127] Thus the Court must accept every proffered definition as legitimate.

But the very subjectivity of the definitions means that not all religions can make claims on public policy.[128] The Court now regards the Free Exercise Clause as a general protection of the claims of individual conscience against the state, but such rights are not absolute, and the Court has found no satisfactory principle for determining when they should prevail. From the liberal side also it has been argued that immunities from general laws ought not to be granted on religious grounds alone but solely on "principles of justice."[129]

An unusual attempt to solve the problem of definition was Powell's assertion, during deliberations in the *Bob Jones* case, that "Bob Jones is primarily a secular institution,"[130] a claim that the university itself did not make but that presumably was intended to acquit the Court of the charge that it was infringing on the university's religious liberty.

The *Smith* case, upholding the dismissal of state employees for the ritual use of a prohibited drug, had potentially far-reaching implications, since it seemed to deny that the government had an obligation to grant exemptions to religious bodies for purposes of worship, as had been done with alcohol from 1919 to 1933. While the polygamy cases outlawed personal behavior that Mormons claimed was required by their beliefs, *Smith* was the only case in which the Court recognized the authority of the government to place restrictions even on acts of worship. The decision partly reversed the Court's earlier stance, beginning with the *Sherbert* case, of accommodation to the conscientious demands of religion.[131]

The conundrum of definition was crucial to the case, as a majority of the Court deliberately prescinded from the argument that peyote was "central" to Indian religion, on the grounds that such an inquiry into the nature of belief was improper, while the minority argued that a judgment about "centrality" was essential and unavoidable.

The limit was also reached in the *Lyng* case, where Brennan reminded his brethren that the meaning of religion was broader than conventional believers might think. But his reminder was irrelevant, because the Court did not deny that the Indians held genuinely religious beliefs; it merely found that such beliefs did not override property rights or the general welfare as determined by public officials.

Brennan's dissent marked the first time the Court was asked to incorporate a possibly alien worldview into its understanding of the Constitution, to rethink radically not only the scope of religious liberty but fundamental assumptions about property as well. While the Indians sought merely the accommodation of their own beliefs, such accommodation, Brennan pointed out, embodied a challenge to Western culture's entire traditional way of thinking.

But here the sovereignty of personal belief, beyond objective scrutiny, clashed with broader social needs and could not be accommodated. The legal and constitutional difficulties posed by Brennan's argument were endless, since thousands of sites all over the country are sacred to various religions, whoever may own them, and to honor all those claims would require overriding property rights in a sweeping way. Hence the Court again reached the limits of its tolerance—personal beliefs cannot be protected if they require fundamental changes in law and public policy.

The incoherence of the modern jurisprudence of the Religion Clauses is the inescapable result of the Court's positing of religion as essentially irrational, since this "establishes" a particular understanding that perhaps a majority of citizens do not share. Some separationists insist that believers refrain from offering religious reasons for their positions and stipulate that believers can legitimately participate in public discussion only to the degree that they propose "accessible" secular (or "public") reasons.[132] A modified version of that position holds that, while believers may propose religious reasons for affirming the dignity of human beings, they must propose plausible secular reasons for any public policy that seeks to define what is necessary for human well-being, especially if such policies restrain personal conduct in some way.[133] Believers have also been urged to offer accessible secular reasons for their positions as a manifestation of respect for nonbelievers,[134] a position that appears to assume that religious arguments are inherently more divisive or disrespectful than secular arguments might be.[135]

The demand that believers present arguments that are accessible is both unexceptionable and unimportant, because those who offer no argument except religious dogma will scarcely prevail in the public square. Believers have a right to advance explicitly religious arguments on behalf of their positions, but they are unlikely to persuade their fellow citizens unless those arguments are in some way "accessible" to nonbelievers. In fact believers rarely offer arguments that are solely religious; most of the time they think that their positions are also persuasive on rational grounds.[136] (The Jehovah's Witnesses originally presented theological arguments in court, until they understood that such appeals would have no effect. Thereafter they translated their arguments into constitutional and legal terms.)[137]

Obviously the Court cannot undertake to evaluate claims about objective religious truth. But the reality of religion can be perceived even by nonbelievers, in terms of its affects on the lives of believers and on society.[138] The motivation for public positions is often mixed, so that the distinction between "religious" and "secular" is unreal and arbitrary in many cases.[139] On many issues, for example, abortion, "public reasons" are themselves in dispute and are not completely accessible to contending parties, nor is it evident how allegedly public reasons can nullify positions taken by a majority of the citizens.[140]

However, the distinction between religious and secular reasons or motives is often difficult to make and may seem artificial to believers,[141] and an insistence on "shared reasons" may favor nonbelievers, who can offer controversial secular arguments, while believers are barred from offering equally controversial religious arguments.[142] In terms of the transcendent nature of religion, it is perhaps important that believers in fact offer "non-public" ("prophetic")reasons for certain policies, for the good of society itself.[143] The requirement that believers not only offer secular arguments but also have secular motives for their positions[144] comes close to disenfranchising them completely and is potentially totalitarian, dictating inquires into people's personal beliefs.

The requirement of accessibility of argument is full of difficulties as it applies to establishment issues and fails completely with regard to free exercise, as the Court itself recognized in rejecting that criterion beginning with the Jehovah's Witnesses and *Ballard* cases, where the justices were far from being able to share the plaintiffs' creeds, yet still upheld their pleas.

The *Lukumi Babalu* case was decided on relatively narrow constitutional grounds—a municipal ordinance forbidding animal sacrifice was explicitly aimed at a particular church and was not generally applicable. Since the law was declared unconstitutional, the church did not have to be granted an exemption. But religious exemptions assume that extending the liberty of some citizens does no social harm to others, while many people would condemn animal sacrifice as a brutal practice intolerable in a humane society. It is a practice that is not "accessible" on any basis other than the beliefs of its practitioners.

The *Lyng* case presented this difficulty in an even more fundamental way. Indian tribes sought to prevent public access to lands they did not own but considered sacred. Many liberals thought the decision unjust. Yet the Indians' claim was, once again, based solely on their own beliefs and was "inaccessible" to those who did not share those beliefs.

Liberal agnosticism about meaning has led to a situation in which the state cannot respect beliefs as such but only the fact that certain people adhere to them,[145] but this makes the criterion of accessibility impossible, since accessibility requires the ability to evaluate the intrinsic merits of a belief.

If in a liberal society no one may claim moral insights not available to others, or may anyone in power claim to be morally superior to others,[146] these strictures scarcely apply only to religious believers. (The warning against those in power considering themselves morally superior to their fellow citizens seemed to apply, for example, to Black himself, who thought church-goers were moral weaklings in need of a crutch.)

A continued emphasis on religion as irrational tends therefore to restrict religious liberty, based on the often unexamined fear that religion is a dangerous phenomenon that needs to be controlled.

RELIGION AS INDOCTRINATION

Although unstated at the time, the flag-salute cases implicitly raised the issue of children being "indoctrinated" by their parents, as Frankfurter, for one, thought they were. (He praised his own parents because "they let me alone, almost completely.")[147]

In the seminal *McCollum* case the plaintiff, while ostensibly asking merely that the public schools be neutral between belief and unbelief, was herself a passionate atheist who charged that religion was truly the "opiate of the masses," in Karl Marx's words, and a "virus" injected into the minds of innocent children.[148] In ruling in her favor the Court did not of course endorse her claim, but, contrary to the principles of Legal Realism, it dealt with the matter as an abstract constitutional question, without scrutinizing the plaintiff's actual agenda. In the *Tilton* case, involving public aid to religious colleges and universities, one of the plaintiffs thought that religious instruction deformed young minds in the same way that the traditional practice of binding deformed the feet of Chinese women.[149]

Thus from the beginning of the modern constitutional era cases involving religious education have raised the question whether it can even be considered education at all or is merely the use of manipulative methods to inculcate irrational beliefs in impressionable children. Presumably the original separationist majority of 1947–48, each of whom had rejected much of the faith in which he had been raised, themselves tended to see religious education as mere "indoctrination," and over time, the Court developed a jurisprudence based on this assumption, consistently holding that younger students in religious schools are being indoctrinated or are in danger of such, while students at the higher level are independent enough to withstand such efforts. As White pointed out in the *Aguilar* case, the claims about such indoctrination have been asserted in various cases without proof.

But if children are susceptible to indoctrination, in the sense of being vulnerable to the inculcation of beliefs that they cannot critically evaluate, such indoctrination is likely to occur in any school, on almost any subject. Arguably, no education is even possible without some "authoritarian" determination of its purpose, for example, forming good citizens,[150] yet seldom has any member of the Court expressed a fear concerning public schools.[151] (The American Civil Liberties Union interprets the Constitution as guaranteeing students and teachers broad liberties of expression in the classroom, except for religious messages.)[152]

Fear of indoctrination encompasses not only the official activities of the schools but the possible affects that students might have on one another. Mrs. McCollum argued that her son was ostracized by his peers for choosing not to receive religious instruction, and the *McCollum* decision has been interpreted as forbidding any educational program that might "operate to compel the young and impressionable to orient to religion," even if no coercion is involved.[153] The ACLU holds that prayer in the classroom is forbidden in part because it exposes nonparticipants to ridicule, but on the other hand, students are not entitled to be excused from reading books that they find religiously offensive,[154] presumably because the former involves "indoctrination," while the latter is "education." Courts have generally upheld disciplinary action against students and teachers accused of "intruding" religion into the classroom, action they would probably not uphold if it involved controversial expression of other kinds.[155]

Separationists usually insist that religious instruction belongs in homes and churches, but among other things, this ignores the reality of dysfunctional families, whose inadequacies in the care of their children are assumed in other contexts by public agencies.[156] In fact schools would not be necessary at all if parents were fully competent to educate their children. (It was precisely this issue that Webster raised in the *Girard* case, arguing that orphan boys raised in a school devoid of religious instruction would inevitably grow up as nonbelievers.)[157] In reality the strict separationist position rests on the stark assumption, seldom candidly acknowledged, that religious education of any kind is not a good thing,[158] that even as imparted by parents it is a possible violation of the liberty of children.[159]

The *Pierce* decision, with McReynolds's ringing declaration "the child is not the creature of the state," was the charter of parental rights. But the majority position in *Gobitis*, passionately reaffirmed by Frankfurter in *Barnette*, made the claim—logical, given certain premises—that the religious beliefs of parents must be subordinated to public policy in matters of education.

Thus, according to one liberal theorist, the very right to conduct religious schools, as guaranteed in *Pierce*, is a violation of the liberty of children, so that it is doubtful whether such schools should be permitted at all, and, if they are, they must be closely monitored by government agencies to ensure that they do not impart "reactionary" and "oppressive" beliefs to children.[160] To this end he offers cautious support for "vouchers," precisely as a means of imposing government control on private schools.[161]

The *Yoder* decision has been criticized as violating children's rights, the decision tolerable only because its impact is marginal,[162] and the argument of the *Yoder* majority was paradoxical in that it seemed to imply that if few Amish children chose to leave their community, their apparent contentedness could be taken as evidence of undue parental influence.

Douglas's lone dissent in that case raised an issue that has never been faced by the Court but has radical implications—the meaning of familial authority. Compulsory schooling, itself dating only from the mid–nine-teenth century, is inherently a weakening of that authority, since it does not even allow parents to choose whether they wish their children to attend school. Douglas seemed to argue that parents have no right to "impose" their religion on their children, and he raised issues that have never been faced by the Court but that have radical implications, arguing that parental influence is an intolerable violation of a child's own rights of conscience.

CONCLUSION

THE UNITED STATES was the first liberal state, in that it rested on the twin concepts of self-government and personal liberty, of which separation of church and state was a corollary.

One account holds that the nation was from the beginning intended as a secular regime, without public religious presence.[1] Thus John Locke, the single greatest intellectual influence on the Founding Fathers, is said to have intended the principle of toleration to exclude religion from significant public effect.[2]

Contradicting this understanding is most of the history of the country until after World War II, more than a century and a half when the importance of religion in public life was largely taken for granted. In an alternative account Locke is understood as attempting not to weaken religion but simply to promote a tolerant Christianity, and by adopting his view, the Founders were able to construct a Christian model of a republic. The originality of Locke's position lay in the idea that government should not concern itself with the religious ends of society. He wanted to secure religion on a firm basis, free of the danger of being corrupted by political power,[3] his skepticism not philosophical or religious in nature but relative only to the political order.[4]

Thus the Founders, according to the second view, envisioned a secular government but a Christian society,[5] religion regarded as essential for inculcating in citizens those virtues that alone make self-government possible.[6] While the spirit of the Constitution and the spirit of Puritanism perhaps ought not to have coexisted, in reality they did throughout the history of the nation.[7]

Through most of that history the Court merely assumed that religion was to be encouraged as a positive social benefit. The *Holy Trinity* decision was the most sweeping in making that affirmation, and in the *Berea* case (1908), the first Justice Harlan could assert, as though it were axiomatic, that religion was "an institution given by the almighty for beneficial purposes."

But the fact that Harlan was a lone voice in defending the rights of a religious college also betrays the fact that the Court usually evaluated religious claims in terms of whether they contributed to the welfare of society. Thus in the *Beatty* case, Story deemed it appropriate that a church retain its parish cemetery, despite a defective title, because of the respect due to the dead. The *Dartmouth* decision implied that religious education was beneficial, while the polygamy cases reached the opposite conclusion about Mormon practices, and the *Speer* case (1905) held that religious groups were not "sectarian" if they performed useful social services. *Pierce* reaffirmed the public benefits of private education, but the conscientious-objector cases around 1930 found certain beliefs harmful to the welfare of the nation.

Although the United States was from the beginning the most liberal regime in the world, its commitment to liberty was never absolute, especially with regard to religion, as the polygamy cases and the conscientious-objector cases dramatized. Thomas Cooley was merely stating the obvious when he wrote that religious groups enjoyed complete liberty "except insofar as is necessary to protect the civil rights of others and to preserve public order."[8]

The Jehovah's Witnesses decisions were revolutionary in part because they went beyond that historic standard, recognizing for the first time the right of religious believers to be exempt from laws and public policies considered beneficial to society. Frankfurter fought a rear-guard action against this concession, as did Jackson in the *Kedroff* case (1952), where he dismissed the Russian Orthodox Church as a mere agent of the Soviet government, hence as inimical to American interests. The principle did not entirely die and was again invoked in the *Bob Jones* case (1983), where the Court upheld the denial of a tax exemption to a religiously affiliated university, because the university espoused certain kinds of racial segregation.[9]

But even as the Court after 1940 was granting believers exemptions from general laws and public policies, it was also, under the Establishment Clause, moving away from the assumption that religion was beneficial to society, to the point where the majority began to question even indirect assistance that religion might recieve from government.[10] In the *Sherbert* case Justice Stewart, although reiterating his general disagreement with separationism, argued that the Court's modern precedents logically dictated that officially mandated respect for sabbatarian beliefs was an unconstitutional promotion of religion. Chief Justice Burger in *Nyquist* (1971) and Justice Marshall in *Mueller* (1983) argued against public aid to religious education on the grounds that such aid might serve as an "inducement" to religious belief, and Justice O'Connor in *Allegheny* (1986) warned against an "endorsement" of religion, fears that the premodern Court would probably have found incomprehensible. (In *Nyquist*, Justice White revived the once commonplace argument that the religious practices that the Court held in suspicion served a beneficial social purpose.)

The *Flast* decision (1968) identified religion as a uniquely dangerous phenomenon, as the Court departed from precedent by granting taxpayers the right to sue under the Establishment Clause even if they themselves had not been directly harmed. This vigilance reached an almost absurd point in the *Larkin* case (1982), where the Court found a constitutional violation in the fact that a church had a discretionary voice in deciding whether a neighboring restaurant could be granted a liquor license, the fact that the Court even accepted the case indicating the extremity of its vigilance against religious "intrusions" into public life.

The *Walz* case raised this issue in an especially acute way, since presumably government could "subsidize" religion through tax exemptions only if religion were viewed as beneficial to society. The exemptions were justified partly by noting that all churches perform various kinds of social services—sponsoring Boy Scout troops or operating soup kitchens, for example—but it left open the question whether socially "useless" religion merits a tax exemption (for example, monasteries of strictly cloistered nuns or monks who eschew all contact with the outside world). In his majority opinion Burger had to rely heavily on historical precedent, precisely because the decision did not fit easily with modern separationist jurisprudence.[11] (Granting churches tax exemptions serves no clearly discernible "secular purpose," as Burger in his Lemon Test insisted was necessary.)[12] The *Marsh* case was decided on similar grounds and for a similar reason—the practice of formal prayers in legislative assemblies logically rests on the belief that prayers are in some way beneficial, a point that the dissenters clearly grasped and rejected.

Historically the moral basis for American democracy was civil religion combined with natural law, as epitomized in Story's assertion that the primary duty of man is to "ascertain the will of God and follow it."[13] Cooley argued that laws against blasphemy and sabbath violations were not necessarily dependant on religious belief but merely prohibited practices that undermined the moral basis of society, which happened to be Christianity.[14]

The concept of natural law has been proposed as underlying the Constitution itself,[15] the legitimacy of the law based on religion,[16] even as religion was also thought to support law by forming the character of the citizens.[17] Until well into the twentieth century these concepts held considerable sway in American jurisprudence.[18] Although the Court seldom formally decided cases on this basis, it often assumed it as the foundation of positive law.

In condemning Mormon polygamy, for example, the Court thought of itself as merely enforcing a broad moral consensus, thus as not in any way violating religious liberty. There was an almost universal agreement that religion was the basis of the civil order, and polygamy challenged that assumption precisely in the fact that the condemned practice was justified by religion, Mormons insisting that it was their opponents who had misin-

terpreted the scripture and the divine will. The Court condemned polygamy as a perversion of true religion, basing its decision on traditional
Christian (or, as Chief Justice Waite said, Protestant) morality.[19]

But Legal Realism took natural law as its special target, considering it
both untenable and a cloak for unacknowledged interests and prejudices.[20] Justice Black, although he rejected Legal Realism, led a revolt
against the entire concept of natural law, which he thought circumvented
the actual text of the Constitution.[21]

After World War I, there occurred a "Second Disestablishment" of religion in the United States, the first being the various states' formal disestablishment of their churches during the fifty years following the Revolution,
the second the abandonment in law of the moral authority of Christianity
as well.[22] The highly symbolic *Scopes* trial of 1925, involving the legal
prohibition on the teaching of evolution in the public schools, helped
effect an intellectual separation of law from religion.[23]

The Court's separationist position after World War II can be seen as
the constitutional enactment of the Second Disestablishment, as many of
the country's intellectual and political elite came to believe that the absolute claims of religion were intolerable within a liberal society.[24] Whether
or not directly traceable to his influence, the Second Disestablishment was
in many ways an application of the thought of John Dewey, America's
most influential philosopher, who rejected traditional religious belief as
both incredible and socially damaging and proposed a humanistic "religion" that he considered appropriate for democracy.[25] Dewey's pragmatism allowed him to dispense with the question of original intent, dismissing the Framers as outmoded and entitled to no enduring authority.[26] But
totalitarianism at the time of World War II inspired a renewed search for
a concept of law transcending the will of the lawgiver,[27] the *Barnette* decision perhaps its first expression.[28]

In reality liberal justices seem often to invoke some concept of natural
law, even if they do not call it that.[29] Murphy, for example, seemed to
believe that both the Constitution and the policies of the New Deal were
a direct application of higher moral and religious principles,[30] and Douglas in the *Gilette* case (1971) passionately invoked "the welfare of a single
human soul" as a basis for constitutional decisions. Racial and sexual
equality, abortion, and numerous other rights recognized by the modern
Court seem to rest on an appeal to moral principles higher than the law
itself, and sometimes in opposition to existing laws, as the Court attempts
to recall the citizens to "deeper values" based on an implied concept of
natural rights.[31] (The Warren Court especially has been characterized as
offering sweeping judgments without much regard for carefully reasoned
legal arguments.)[32] Not uncommonly, liberal theorists formally espouse a
view of law as conventional, even as the substance of their arguments

implies an objective morality beyond mere consensus.[33] Not all believers in natural law are conservatives,[34] while some of the leading conservatives on the Court, notably Chief Justice Rehnquist and Justice Scalia, can be seen as legal positivists.[35]

Although liberalism's most influential contemporary theorist disputes it,[36] some liberals recognize that a concept of law divorced from all considerations of morality leaves little reason for respecting the law.[37] Religion is in fact one of the sources of the moral beliefs on which modern liberalism itself is based,[38] supporting claims of natural rights but also setting limits on claims that would otherwise be restricted only by self-interest.[39] But much of modern liberalism denies that religion is necessarily supportive of public morality[40] and claims that the Religion Clauses were actually intended to prevent any official promotion of virtue.[41] Liberal separationism fails to recognize the pervasiveness of religion in American life, the influence it has over almost all aspects of society,[42] and the Court itself assumes a common secular culture whose very existence is doubtful,[43] since in some ways American society is made up of a variety of religious groups, with relatively few people belonging to none of them. Some liberal theorists express a preference for a society of fragmented meanings, as an alternative to any consensus that might have religion at its heart.[44]

Perhaps beginning with *Roe v. Wade* (1973), the decision that announced a constitutional right to abortion, there has occurred a "Third Disestablishment," which is the separation of law from traditional moral principles, a result that perhaps flowed inevitably from the Second Disestablishment, since moral principles once thought of as common to all are now seen as merely "sectarian."[45] Liberal Protestantism, which in the nineteenth century sought to replace piety by morality, by the 1960s found that there was no longer an accepted moral consensus. Like religion, morality had come to be regarded as essentially irrational.[46]

On this basis the social influence of conservative churches can be restricted, in part because there is to be no right to inhibit, on religious grounds, whatever subjective conceptions of the good life individuals might have.[47] Official government neutrality in practice becomes an "ideology of nonorthodoxy," and churches that advocate absolute moral standards are considered dangerous, religion not considered to have any role in maintaining personal liberty.[48]

But without an accepted moral basis, justification for the Court's own authority remains unclear. Attempts to ground jurisprudence on "the ethos of the nation"[49] or on the authority of "the people's will"[50] flounder on the obvious fact that at certain times in history this ethos has gone directly against the demands of liberal constitutionalism,[51] as was probably the case at the time of the desegregation decisions of the 1950s and has consistently been the case with the Establishment Clause decisions since 1947. Thus the abandonment both of civil religion and of natural law has left the Court bereft of fundamental principles, confused as to the proper role of religion in public life.

The term "liberalism" in modern American politics refers both to an agreement to abide by constitutional principles that provide access to all citizens ("political" liberalism) and to an ideological act of faith in a particular concept of a free and open society ("comprehensive" or "transformative" liberalism).[52] Traditional liberalism denied that it was comprehensive, insisting that it took no position on ultimate questions of meaning, but merely sought to maintain the democratic regime in the midst of "deep disagreements," holding it together by means of an "overlapping consensus" of various groups. Thus to disallow religious claims in the liberal regime implies nothing about the truth of the claims themselves.[53]

Belief in religious absolutes has been reconciled with the Religion Clauses by positing the latter as "articles of peace" rather than "articles of faith." No one is obliged to accept relativist assumptions but merely must agree to respect the Constitution for the sake of civil harmony.[54] In support of this view is the claim that the Constitution was never intended to embody some "grand value," abstract principles, or "superhuman qualities."[55]

From the standpoint of dogmatic religion, the liberal state has been criticized as inherently hostile to all claims of absolute truth, not equally open to all beliefs, thus unable to fulfill its promise of full religious liberty, since it cannot extend genuine toleration to those who believe that their religion is the true faith and who act accordingly.[56] However, such limits are inherent in all political regimes, not unique to modern democracy. Those who believe that their own religion is the true faith have more opportunity to act on that belief in a democratic society than in a society that identifies a rival faith as true, and historically the state's embrace of a particular faith has almost always led to restrictions on that faith in the state's own interest.

From the other side, in rejecting religious absolutism, Frankfurter in *Gobitis* also claimed that dogmatic religion was incompatible with democracy, insisting that Jehovah's Witnesses could enjoy freedom only by recognizing that such freedom was based on a relativistic view of all faiths, with none making absolute claims on its members. But in *Barnette* the Court as a whole seemingly rejected that contention.[57]

With the abandonment of both civil religion and natural law, a liberal understanding of the Constitution becomes itself the only authoritative text, immune to fundamental criticism;[58] liberal political processes themselves a kind of absolute;[59] and the Court a sacred entity, the arbiter of national conscience, guarding against the errors of both citizens and legislators.[60] According to an influential theory, the Constitution is "aspirational," in the sense that it embodies the deeper truths on which the polity is based, truths that can be gradually drawn out by the courts as a way of recalling the nation to its true self.[61]

The Court's way of dealing with polygamy—dissolving the Mormon church until it submitted to national policy—was the supreme instance of unchallenged judicial authority, seldom questioned because of the Mormons' intense unpopularity.[62] The *Bob Jones* decision was also not widely criticized, because the national consensus in favor of racial equality made the college's policies indefensible. But the long-term implications of that decision are potentially profound, precisely because of the power of consensus to restrict liberty.

In the *Jones* case the Court in effect treated a particular religious group as "heretics who disrupt social harmony by disavowing a major tenet of the American creed."[63] Following that decision it would be possible to argue that any number of tax-exempt groups act in certain ways contrary to "public policy," a finding that could lead precisely to sanctions against unpopular groups, something about which the Court has long been vigilant. While the Court was deliberating the case, Justice Brennan stated the issue forthrightly:

> I have long believed that the exercise of choices grounded on religious belief should not be penalized except in the face of the most powerful governmental interests. There are, however, virtually no governmental interests *more* compelling than the cause of racial justice.[64]

The *Jones* decision, rendered at the time that the Equal Rights Amendment, affirming complete legal and social equality between genders, was under consideration, raised the question whether, if that amendment were enacted, tax exemptions could be denied to churches that did not ordain women as clergy or to educational institutions reserved for a single sex.

How far this principle might extend is uncertain, but one liberal theorist goes so far as to argue that "society" may override commitments that individuals have to religious groups "which seriously restrain their members' capacities and opportunities for reflective, independent choice."[65] According to this claim, the stability of the liberal polity depends on even private beliefs being liberalized, "illiberal" private associations being denied public influence[66] because their beliefs can be a danger to liberal values.[67]

Comprehensive liberalism then serves as "a permanently educative order" that seeks to preserve the cohesiveness of the liberal regime.[68] The coercive power of government can be used for that purpose, since the use of such power against illiberal churches promotes greater freedom.[69] As happened in the nineteenth century with the Mormons, the liberal state uses its power to remake religious groups in accordance with the requirements of society.[70] In the late nineteenth century the Court on a number of occasions upheld arrangements whereby people who joined religious communities surrendered their right to own property. But according to modern liberal theory, such agreements probably should have been invalidated on the grounds that citizens do not have the right to reject liberal values.

The premodern Court could be accused of insufficient concern for the Religion Clauses, seldom finding either a violation of free exercise or an act of establishment. On the whole it was perhaps more solicitous of free exercise, in that it protected the corporate identities of churches and allowed them wide influence in public life.[71]

But the fact that Frankfurter was a minority of one in the *Barnette* case obscured the Court's acceptance of his demand that believers relativize their beliefs in order to enjoy liberty. Following World War II the Court in effect offered believers a bargain, with only Frankfurter and Rutledge disclosing its terms from the beginning. Since 1940 the scope of personal religious liberty has expanded immensely, even as the public role of religion has been steadily constricted. As Rutledge warned in *Everson*, believers who wish to enjoy liberty must forgo the possibility of bringing their beliefs to bear in the public square, must accept the Court's view of religion as essentially private.

For the first time, the Religion Clauses were brought into tension with one another, the Establishment Clause becoming a major barrier to full religious freedom, the Court lacking any coherent theory of how the two clauses could be harmonized,[72] its inability to recognize the historical importance of "de facto establishment" (civil religion) having the effect of rendering the Religion Clauses incoherent.[73]

As in other issues pertaining to the Religion Clauses, the Court's approach seems to be in flux at the beginning of the twenty-first century, with a series of close decisions—*Witters, Zobrest, Agostini, Mitchell, Zelman*—recognizing that religious persons and institutions have a right to share, without discrimination, in the benefits of the welfare state.

But, barring a permanent reorientation of its jurisprudence, the modern Court sees religious liberty as a conditional freedom only, not merely in the obvious sense that society cannot tolerate everything done in the name of religion but in the sense that believers may claim freedom for themselves only to the extent that they adhere to the separationist understanding of the Establishment Clause, now made into an orthodoxy. While the Establishment Clause is often treated as absolute, the Free-Exercise Clause is not.[74] The state makes certain claims that are inviolable, while the claims of religion are not.[75] In discussions prior to the *McCollum* decision, Frankfurter asserted bluntly, "In this country, the *church* is *subordinate* to the state."[76]

In *Everson*, Rutledge announced, with no constitutional warrant, that the "price of religious freedom is double," in that the same Constitution that guaranteed freedom to the believer also forbade any attempt by the government to alleviate the financial burdens of religion. There would necessarily be hardships for those who forwent attending "the common schools," he warned, and those who exercised religious freedom most fully would necessarily pay the highest price.

In making this assertion, Rutledge, who, as the son of a Baptist minister, was presumably quite familiar with the Bible, made a telling error, referring to the Apostle Paul's freedom as having been purchased at a great price, when in fact Paul claimed that freedom as his birthright.[77] For Rutledge, religious liberty was not a birthright but was bestowed by society conditionally.

The growth of the welfare state has had a further privatizing and debilitating affect on religion, both by taking upon itself many of the social responsibilities that the churches once discharged and by extending the state's influence into more and more areas of life, even as religion is excluded from the territory it once occupied.[78] While Franklin Roosevelt probably in no way intended the New Deal to spawn a revolutionary understanding of the Religion Clauses, it was perhaps not altogether coincidental that the Court that legitimized the New Deal under the Constitution also effected that revolution.

The Equal Protection Clause of the Fourteenth Amendment seems to require that religious groups have a right to share in the benefits offered to others,[79] and the very pervasiveness of the welfare state in modern life makes it an injustice to deny to religious groups benefits available to others.[80] However, what the Free-Exercise Clause guarantees, the Lemon Test, with its requirement of a "secular purpose," undermined,[81] and in doing so the Court placed the welfare state in opposition to religious groups.[82]

The controversy over public support of social programs carried out by charitable religious organizations ("charitable choice" or "faith-based communities") again brings into focus the question whether religion can be considered beneficial to society.[83]

A common objection to such arrangements, first formulated by Madison himself, is that the rights of taxpayers are violated if they are required to fund the activities of religious groups not their own.[84] But whatever validity this principle may have had in the 1770s, it is discriminatory under the conditions of modern politics, because all morally aware citizens can find numerous publicly funded activities to which they object. Taxpayers who want none of their money used to support religious education have no stronger claim than, for example, pacifists who oppose military expenditures or people who object to the perceived ideological bias of grants made to the arts and humanities.

The larger objection to such support—that it places the authority of the government behind religion[85]—is subject to the same counterclaim. Government appears to "endorse" all kinds of controversial things,[86] so that the argument inevitably turns on the assumption that religion is simply not a socially beneficial activity.

Aid to "faith-based communities" is also opposed by separationists because they fear that, besides providing social services, religious agencies might proselytize their clients,[87] a fear that goes to the heart of the issue. If, for example, the experience of religious conversion has a transformative affect on troubled (and troubling) members of society—alcoholics, derelicts, criminals—then proselytization appears to achieve good for everyone, harm to no one.[88] Prohibiting such proselytizing, while placing no such restrictions on secular institutions, restricts free expression, in a discriminatory way, as a condition of receiving a public benefit.[89] Excluding religious organizations from such programs denies to churches benefits that the government makes available to secular groups and implies that religion has no important relevance to social problems.[90]

The Court's test inquiring whether certain programs or organizations are "pervasively sectarian" itself violates the Lemon Test, in that it requires "excessive entanglement." It imposes a religious test on the recipients of government assistance, and in seeking to identify "pervasively sectarian" elements, it makes a kind of theological judgment, one that is likely to discriminate against conventional forms of religions and benefit unfamiliar forms.[91]

The liberal state excludes churches from any direct participation in the formation of public policy,[92] the modern Court's interpretation of the Establishment Clause requiring not only separation of church and state but separation of religion from politics.[93] The *McRae* (1980), *Bowen* (1985), and *Romer* (1996) cases, each turning on the formulation of public policy in areas of personal behavior, questioned the right of churches to have any influence on public policy. In the first two, the Court seemed to uphold that right, but in *Romer* it rejected it.

The modern welfare state requires an essentially benign view of government, to the point where one liberal Protestant theorist insists that churches have nothing at all to fear from the state and should simply accept its decrees,[94] while another insists that the churches have no right to separate themselves from the welfare state and should not be given exemptions from any of its requirements.[95] Thus an allegedly benign state, by its own understanding of the Religion Clauses, decides what is good for religion, even if this judgment does not coincide with what the churches think is good for themselves.[96]

Separationists also insist that in resisting separationism, believers fail to understand their own interests. As with other kinds of public assistance, religious agencies receiving public subsidies might find their autonomy threatened by governmental scrutiny.[97] That danger, however, is not unique to religious institutions and is merely a possibility that all groups must guard against through the democratic process.

The liberal concept of individual freedom tends to create an atmosphere in which religion is merely tolerated to the degree that it is deemed harmless,[98] as in the *Lynch* decision, which found Christian symbols to be props in a civic celebration, partly included to stimulate commerce,[99] or in Brennan's finding in the *Marsh* case—that the words of President Lincoln's second Inaugural Address and the prayer "God save this honorable Court" have lost their original meaning.

The liberal regime sometimes tolerates public references to a vague and remote God, but believers are required to privatize and trivialize their religion as mere "heritage" or "tradition," its public role made to fit with the existing agenda[100] and tolerated only to the point where it makes strong demands on its adherents.[101] Rather than fostering a genuine pluralism, the liberal state strips religions of their specificity.[102]

Thus, according to some liberal theorists, religious liberty does not rest on respect for religious beliefs as such but for "rational and reasonable capacities of persons themselves to originate, exercise, express, and change theories of life and how to live it well," on respect for "human moral powers."[103] In this view, despite the actual words of the Religion Clauses, the Constitution, instead of protecting religion, ought to protect "conscience."[104]

It is, however, itself a violation of religious liberty to force believers to accept an alien understanding of their faith, to act as though that faith does not rest on transcendent realities, that it is private only and makes no comprehensive claims.[105] (Paradoxically, many modern separationists assert that position as an absolute, even as they espouse relativism in other areas of moral and political life.)[106]

In the *Hamilton* case (1934), Hughes was the first justice in the history of the Court to acknowledge the fundamental dilemma of religious liberty, a dilemma the Court slid past in both the polygamy and conscientious-objection cases—the fact that most religions teach that the laws of God supersede those of men and that the conflict cannot be reconciled within the political system itself. Cardozo at the same time recognized the same dilemma but reached the opposite conclusion from Hughes. Whereas the chief justice dissented in *Hamilton*, voting to respect the consciences of the objectors, Cardozo noted that the individual conscience might simply be in error and that government could not formulate policy on that basis.

One of religion's most important tasks is precisely that of questioning state policies on moral grounds,[107] so that the welfare of society itself requires that churches survive as an independent moral force.[108] Now, however, the state makes itself the ultimate arbiter of conscience, which is treated as secular and individual, morality as relative,[109] the churches as mere private associations.[110]

It is, however, also inadequate to consider the social benefits of religion as moral only. Even when the Court permits religious participation in the benefits of the welfare state, it sometimes ignores the churches' own stated purposes and redefines their activities as secular in nature,[111] as in the *Bowen* case (1986), upholding public funding of a sex-education program emphasizing chastity,[112] or the *Bob Jones* case, where religion was treated merely as a kind of "charity."[113]

Religion's highest social benefit is not whatever services it may provide, or the virtues it cultivates in citizens, but its answers to the perennial question of the meaning of life, its offering a sense of hope and fulfill-ment,[114] facilitating the exploration of the meaning of existence.[115] Thus, paradoxically, the "secular purpose" of religion is in fact otherworldly, and it best fulfills its purpose when it reminds people of a higher reality.[116] It is in this broadest sense that religion is part of the common good and should be respected by government.[117]

But it is this most fundamental religious purpose—articulating the meaning of existence—that is finally at the root of religion's tension with liberalism.[118] The liberal state as such is unable to comprehend or relate to religion in this ultimate sense, so that religion remains a mysterious phenomenon, nonbelievers unable to understand believers' need to ex-press their faith outside the confines of home and church.[119] Deep faith is both incomprehensible and threatening to the liberal order,[120] which therefore diminishes religion to fit the liberal framework, the state deny-ing to believers their uniqueness.[121] Religion is not treated as real, in the way that believers regard it as real,[122] and the irreducible mysteriousness of religion leads the Court to define it as irrational, private, and divisive.

It is also sometimes redefined in secular ways that serve the liberal state, as Warren did when he cited the Apostle Paul's definition of faith—"the substance of things hoped for, the evidence of things unseen"—then con-strued it to mean the hope that Americans would be able to preserve their liberties for their children.[123] Although Warren's definition had no consti-tutional status, it reflected the fact that the modern Court can scarcely relate to any understanding of religion as the worship of higher powers in the universe. (Often members of the Court, like Warren, seem not even to understand traditional religious doctrines, and if they do show understanding, as Brennan did in *Lynch*, it is only in order to argue that such doctrines cannot be allowed any public influence.)

Thus the modern state tends to subjugate institutions intermediate between itself and the citizens,[124] so that organized religion is steadily stripped of its influence in people's lives,[125] the very "neutrality" of liberal government giving it a power denied other institutions. The churches enjoy freedom of expression, but at the same time separationism tends to guarantee that they will not prevail.[126]

In a sense, both church and state compete to offer citizens authoritative guidance,[127] so that a comprehensive religious liberty would invite religious challenges to the state's own authority.[128] Religion is by its nature absolute, refusing to be treated merely as one voice among many, but it is treated politically as though it were relative,[129] so that there can be no "redemptive communities" that seek to transform society[130] and the liberal state recognizes no religious principles relevant to public life. Thus in their capacity as citizens, believers are required to put aside their sense of God's will.[131]

If the liberal polity demands some kind of consensus,[132] then religious groups may be forced to prove that their existence is beneficial to the community,[133] and if no "deep conflicts" are permissible in the liberal state, authoritarian methods may be necessary to restrain them.[134] Ostensibly building on the Framers' fear of "factions," liberals exclude ultimate questions from the public square by curtailing serious philosophical reasoning, in effect claiming that common liberal positions transcend the merely self-interested positions of particular groups.[135] All discussion must then take place within a certain restricted range of disagreement,[136] the liberal state suspicious of passion and commitment and tolerant in inverse proportion to the seriousness of what is at stake.[137]

According to one liberal reading of Locke and the Framers, the Constitution itself intended to remove religion and morality from the public sphere, in the expectation that citizens would then be content to pursue merely material goals.[138] Religion addresses "comprehensive" human purposes, and politics "immediate" purposes, so that politics attempts to remove deep issues from public debate,[139] making the "highest things" merely ephemeral.[140]

Religion is not allowed to offer final answers to public questions, because to do so would be to "establish" particular answers. The liberal regime must then be constituted by the questions themselves, not by any proffered answers.[141] Government cannot even recognize "spiritual interests" and cannot accommodate such interests in its policies, for example, in education.[142] Religion is reluctantly tolerated without regard for its intrinsic worth,[143] so that the Court in *Walz* could not justify tax exemptions for churches simply by declaring that religion as such is beneficial to society.

Since most religions proclaim divine power as sovereign over the state itself, no political regime in history has ever allowed full freedom of religion. Religion does not define its own boundaries and cannot exist on a basis of equality with the state.[144] The liberal state is by no means distinctive in this regard; in fact it permits a wider range of freedoms than any other kind of regime. But a state that claims authority from God also lays itself open to divine judgment, a paradoxical situation that led to the overthrow of the English monarchy in the 1640s and contributed to its overthrow in America in the 1770s. If, on the other hand, the liberal regime is the source of its own legitimacy, there can be no appeal beyond itself, which inescapably raises the question whether the modern liberal state can fulfill its promise fully to respect religious liberty.

The test of its ability to tolerate what it considers intolerant is part of the larger test whether the liberal state can function nonideologically, providing maximum freedom for contending viewpoints, or whether it is itself an ideology that demands adherence (comprehensive liberalism). The *Everson* and *McCollum* decisions announced the emergence of liberalism as an ideology. In *Barnette*, solicitude for Jehovah's Witnesses did not require that all schoolchildren cease saluting the flag, but in *McCollum* solicitude for secular-minded students required that no religious instruction be given within school walls.[145] While Frankfurter was consistent in his suspicion of religion, the other liberals on the Court seemingly reversed themselves between 1943 and 1947, moving from unusual solicitude for religion to inhibiting it in the public sphere. What motivated the transition was the fact that the issues raised in 1947–48 seemed to threaten the secular hegemony in education, in a way the Jehovah's Witnesses, a marginal group readily granted an exemption, did not.

Thus not only is prayer in the public schools declared unconstitutional, its advocates are told that the issue itself is a "distraction" that should not even be discussed,[146] a claim that Burger sought to give constitutional weight in his *Lemon* decision. Believers are expected to engage in "ecumenical politics," in which they accept the relativity of their own faiths for the sake of social peace,[147] and churches must engage in "reflective self-criticism" as a condition of participation in public life.[148] (The requirement of reflective self-criticism would of course benefit society if all citizens engaged in it, but once again the demand is made only of religion.)

Paradoxically, instead of modern liberalism's tolerating the widest possible divergence of views, a commitment to comprehensive liberalism itself becomes a test of orthodoxy that churches are expected to meet.[149] Some liberal thinkers see traditional religion as almost inherently inimical to democracy and wish the Establishment Clause to be used to prevent its negative affects on society.[150]

Allegedly the Constitution is neutral, not only among all religions but between religion and irreligion.[151] But the very possibility of this neutrality is open to question, as some liberals admit.[152] Failure to accept religions in their own terms is already a violation of neutrality.[153] A "neutral" approach to religion in reality may not satisfy the claims of neutrality, because a phenomenon cannot be fully understood without entering sympathetically into its inner meaning.[154]

The Court has devised a tripartite scheme for classifying phenomena—religious, nonreligious, antireligious—with the Constitution taken to forbid government support for the first and third but not for the second. But where particular policies fall within this classification is often precisely the focus of the controversy.[155] Separationists define neutrality as government's avoiding the promotion of either religion or antireligion, while many religious people doubt that "nonreligion" is neutral. The fear that churches will impose their religion on society is not matched by an equal fear that the schools may impose secularity,[156] and the banning of religion from public life rests on the dubious assumption that government endorses what it does not exclude.[157] Separating "religious" from "secular" elements in education, for example, already involves a kind of entanglement and can be used to suppress the free expression of religion.[158]

An influential "postmodern" theorist readily admits that liberalism does not achieve its promised neutrality, that it has become an ideology making use of the rhetoric of neutrality. But he ridicules believers for invoking liberal principles on their own behalf, arguing that they should not expect to benefit from liberalism's promises but ought to oppose it.[159] Another liberal theorist bluntly argues that government cannot be neutral toward those who deny the principle of neutrality itself.[160] A commitment to liberalism itself is even called a kind of "ethnocentrism," justified on the grounds that it is preferable to other kinds of group identity.[161]

Another liberal theorist urges "the right sort of liberal partisanship in all spheres of life" and argues that certain religious believers (notably Catholics) can legitimately be excluded from various areas of public life, such as serving as judges. Such exclusion, he predicts, will cause believers to find their faiths less credible, and he justifies tolerating them merely on the grounds that such toleration can create an environment in which it might be possible to wean them away from their beliefs.[162]

If the Religion Clauses are thus considered "articles of faith," society must of necessity discourage belief in ultimate truths, because such beliefs tend to foster intolerance. The Religion Clauses are then interpreted in a "secular fundamentalist" way—as timeless and absolute principles—

similar to the religiously fundamentalist way of approaching the Bible,[163] a kind of secular sectarianism.[164]

The liberal state now requires that the Religion Clauses be accepted precisely as "articles of faith," that citizens believe in religious pluralism as a positive good.[165] But this requirement seems itself to be a religious test, of the kind prohibited by Article VI of the Constitution.[166] An undisclosed part of the bargain the Court offered believers in 1947–48 was not only that they would have to abandon any public role for their faith, but that they would also have to act as though their beliefs are merely relative,[167] an interpretation of the Free-Exercise Clause that protects religion while at the same time implying that its teachings are incredible.[168] In minimizing the role of religion in the public sphere, modern liberalism also renders it more difficult to live it in private,[169] and some liberals acknowledge that religious beliefs are indeed threatened by the liberal order.[170]

Thus the cultural value of having a diversity of religious schools may be outweighed by the virtues of "enlightenment,"[171] and according to one liberal theory, the Establishment Clause actually establishes a culture from which there can be no legitimate dissent, religion tolerated "insofar as it is consistent with the establishment of the secular moral order." Candidly, this theory admits that "the Religion Clauses enable the government to endorse a culture of liberal democracy that will predictably clash over many issues with religious subcultures," so that believers "must pay for the secular army which engineers the truce among them."[172] Adherence to "particularistic theological notions" is then said to be contrary to the "universal theology of the Republic."[173] For example, opponents of the theory of evolution are accused of being in violation of the spirit of the Constitution, which itself is said to have been "shaped by an argument honoring Galileo's defense of empirical rationality against the abuses of Bible interpretation," the state obligated to encourage "scientific rationality."[174]

Thus not only are churches to be made to conform to law and public policy, liberal values are required to be internalized by those who wish to have a legitimate place in society. They must be capable of conceiving themselves as citizens apart from any particular social group to which they belong,[175] and the secular arguments they employ in support of their positions (for example, on abortion) cannot be considered legitimate unless nonbelievers accept them as persuasive.[176] Secularists are given final authority to determine whether religious arguments even deserve to be heard.

Religious groups should not even be allowed to "inject" their own views of gender roles into public discussions, according to one account,[177] the concept of religious liberty itself rejected as "patriarchal," because it allegedly means something different for women than for men, and government must therefore deny tax exemptions and other kinds of assistance to all churches that manifest "sexist" attitudes.[178] By the same argument

a Catholic bishop who threatens religious sanctions against dissident church members is guilty of "a religiously based threat to the prerogatives of democratic citizenship," which is true also of religious opposition to homosexual marriages or abortion.[179]

The constraints to be placed on illiberal churches go beyond matters of church and state and reach into the areas of belief, so that, for example, churches can be allowed to exclude women from the ranks of the clergy only so long as this does not "impede the functioning of the civil public order."[180] Those religions are pronounced "historically naive" that do not participate in ecumenical dialogue, and full freedom is to be extended to those religions that have a "dynamic" concept of God.[181] The right to participate in public life is used as an instrument for pressuring conservative religions to change their beliefs, as liberal kinds of religion are in effect "established."[182]

Even in offering a defense of religion, some liberals do so only on the basis of liberal orthodoxy—that at its best religion supports causes like feminism,[183] or by finding that Rev. Martin Luther King Jr., for example, passed the liberal test, while conservative religious groups are "divisive."[184] Some religious issues (opposition to abortion) are deemed legitimate, others (opposition to homosexuality) illegitimate,[185] final judgment reserved to "progressive" believers. Greater participation in politics by religiously conservative Jews is questioned on the grounds that it would not "have the capacity to move American politics in a more progressive direction."[186]

Logically, the liberal state must therefore discriminate among religious groups on the basis of how liberal each may be, so that some can be accommodated in the public sphere but others cannot.[187] According to some liberal theorists, religion can only enjoy constitutional liberties if it undergoes a basic transformation to make itself more "rational" or "self-critical,"[188] a condition not required for the enjoyment of other guaranteed rights. Religious groups need not be granted "equal access" to public facilities because "only evangelical Protestants" require this. Since most other groups do not emphasize either public prayer or proselytization,[189] they are granted a preferred status because of their "moderation."

While such claims do not enjoy constitutional standing, they have been endorsed by individual members of the Court. Justice Goldberg, for example, dismissed the charge that government is hostile to religion by noting that public officials welcome the support of "socially minded churches and synagogues."[190] Murphy thought the policies of the New Deal were a practical application of Christianity and therefore did not regard those policies as a violation of the Establishment Clause, as logically he should have done.

Douglas in particular frequently distinguished "good" from "bad" religion, regarding "sectarian" religion as an obstacle to "progress"[191] and, quoting a Unitarian sermon, telling believers that the essential message of all religions is to "heal the world's miseries." He characterized the Bible as promoting "a diversity of ideas" and "dissident views."[192] In Douglas's mind, while clergy in general were to be held in suspicion, as "aligned with the Establishment," certain clergy were to be admired and heeded.[193]

Douglas's view of religion also permitted him to make constitutional claims about internal church matters, for example, that a Catholic bishop who admonished his flock about the moral issues in an election was violating the Establishment Clause. In the name of "the entire First Amendment community" Douglas congratulated a Catholic priest who had been disciplined for rejecting certain church teachings.[194]

Douglas came close to imposing an ideological test on churches when, in dissenting in the *Allen* and *Tilton* cases, he distinguished "true" and "false" interpretations of history—the Crusades, the Spanish Inquisition, the Protestant Reformation, the government of Francisco Franco, and other issues on which, for Douglas, there were correct and incorrect positions, with Catholic schools suspected of being on the wrong side. (Denial of public aid to religious schools, on the grounds that they involve religious indoctrination, is perhaps a unique case of aid being denied on the basis of intellectual content, something that the Bill of Rights is ordinarily thought to prohibit.)[195]

Ostensibly the primary political argument against strong religious beliefs is that they threaten civic peace, so that the Constitution is said to decree "a secular liberal democracy in a way that is intended to minimize religious tension."[196] However, the secular argument against religion in public life ignores the ways in which secular beliefs can also be divisive and intolerant,[197] and it excludes even religious groups that agree to participate in the liberal process. Paradoxically, the liberal state is urged to force the intolerant to be tolerant, with government serving as "a divine instrument" for depriving groups of weapons to use against one another.[198] If traditional religion is thought to be more "repressive" than atheism, it would then be appropriate to reverse the historic roles of the two, granting atheism a special place in the polity and restricting religion.[199]

Beginning with Jefferson himself there has always existed a "low road" of invoking high constitutional principle on behalf of specific religious agenda: Jefferson's maneuvers at the University of Virginia to exclude Calvinists in favor of theological liberals; Madison's desire to prohibit churches from owning any significant amount of property, in order to limit their influence; the attempt to use state power to liberalize Dartmouth College; Horace Mann's promotion of "common schools" as a way of strengthening liberal Protestantism. The *McDaniel* decision

(1977) was a very late nullification of an Enlightenment-era law excluding clergy from public office.

A test of liberalism's commitment to liberty should be precisely whether or not it can "tolerate the intolerant"—those who make absolute claims for their beliefs.[200] Toleration should not require philosophical skepticism, merely a commitment to political liberty,[201] a test that most modern religious groups would pass. If a religion baldly demands that government restrict other faiths, it has no possibility of success, and the issue is trivial. (However, one liberal theorist argues that the Free-Exercise Clause permits religious oppression in allowing the dominant Christian religion even to proselytize among non-Christians).[202]

But if any commitment to a dogmatic creed signifies intolerance, quarantining dogmatism would require potentially totalitarian inquiries into people's private beliefs. As with the larger problem of divisiveness, the condemnation of religious intolerance also fails to explain why secular, overtly political, kinds of intolerance should not be subject to the same restrictions. It is, to say the least, paradoxical to restrict a religion because it is deemed insufficiently supportive of democracy.[203] Although separationists never note the connection, restraining the liberty of some religious believers because they are illiberal is exactly comparable to restraining the political expression of those who might use it to subvert the democratic order.

Inevitably much of this conflict is focused on education, where most of the battles over the Establishment Clause take place, and it is sharpest in two areas—sex education and the teaching of evolution.

Compulsory school attendance preempts most of students' available hours in their formative years,[204] an issue already raised by Webster in the *Girard* case, where he pointed out that orphan boys raised in a completely nonreligious environment were likely to grow up as nonbelievers.[205] Although religious schools predated public schools, they are now treated as a deviation from the normative pattern,[206] the general Protestant acquiescence in public education being a crucial stage in this development.[207]

The *Pierce* decision was a significant barrier to excessive state power.[208] But, despite McReynolds's assertion in that case that "the child is not the creature of the state," public schools are often treated as though they alone provide a proper education for democracy.[209] Following Dewey's philosophy in general terms, this has sometimes led to a quasi-religious veneration for democracy, especially as incarnated in the schools, to which traditional religion is seen as a rival. (Frankfurter perhaps carried this veneration to its furthest point. In a note to his brethren during the *Barnette* case, he testified that once he had shed his traditional religious loyalties, American citizenship had become for him a kind of religious substitute.)[210]

The anti-Catholicism of the *Everson* plaintiffs and the militant atheism of the *McCollum* plaintiff were instances of such agenda at the very beginning of modern separationism, and the unsuccessful plaintiff in the *Tilton* case, attempting to deny public aid to religious colleges and universities, was a militant "freethinker" who thought serious damage was done to students in religious schools, akin to the damage done to the limbs of Chinese women by the custom of foot-binding.[211] The *Jaffree* plaintiff, in the case that forbade an authorized "moment of silence" in public schools, was an atheist who remembered his mother as a "religious hypocrite" and wanted his children to be free of all religious influence.[212]

Leo Pfeffer, the most successful separationist attorney ever to plead before the Court, and himself the architect of much of modern separationist jurisprudence,[213] was candid about his agenda. In the late 1950s he celebrated the "triumph of secular humanism," which he thought had transformed Protestantism into a "this-worldly" religion but to which some churches, notably the Catholic Church, were still resistant, a fact that made that church a dangerous institution. Pfeffer expressed particular concern that, while Catholics accepted democracy as a political system, they had not adopted it in matters of religion.[214] Catholic schools were said to be academically inferior, authoritarian, and guilty of "weakening democratic brotherhood."[215]

But Pfeffer regretted, for strategic reasons, that in the *Torcaso* case Black had listed Secular Humanism as a religion,[216] and a few years later Pfeffer began using the term "deism" instead of "Secular Humanism." He saw deism as inevitably triumphing in all the churches, with Catholics belatedly following the pattern, and took satisfaction in the fact that Catholic schools were declining because "Catholics in increasing numbers are tasting the fruits of humanistic deism and finding that they like it."[217] Pfeffer, like some other liberals, thought that American democracy was incompatible with traditional religious belief and that the Establishment Clause was precisely designed to force believers into conformity with the spirit of liberal democracy.

The state is not neutral between public and nonpublic education and, according to one liberal theorist, should promote the former "to foster the development of an integrated national (or state) policy," to "break down social barriers," and to "promote citizenship."[218] The public schools become in effect the church of the American public faith,[219] through which the liberal state exercises its "meaning creating power." Increasingly, liberal theorists admit that there is no such thing as "value neutral" education but nonetheless hold that the state need not be concerned that its educational system might violate the rights of religious believers.[220]

If public education is considered normative for society, and if religious instruction has no place in it, society is in effect deciding that religion is irrelevant to contemporary life.[221] Religious critics of the public schools understand this, and it is this that has led to the sharpest conflicts.

> School censors, and those who do battle with them, do nothing more than the common ideology of schooling has taught them to do. They take seriously the message, imbedded in one hundred years of of compulsory, universal, publicly funded schooling: that public education is the great cohesive force of a democratic society.

Parents' desire for more control over their children's education is thus transformed into "a political war over public orthodoxy,"[222] with believers insisting that religious freedom implies the right to religious education.[223]

The issue was raised in starkest form in the flag-salute cases, where Frankfurter made the bold argument that national unity required a uniform national system of education excluding religious "deviance." In effect he tried to sacralize the public schools, and, although he was unsuccessful on that occasion, the *McCollum* decision went on to treat them as the seedbed of civic unity.[224] Although *Pierce* seemed to have disposed of the question, Frankfurter's passionate argument for the unifying function of the schools, later echoed even by justices who did not accept his *Barnette* opinion, logically implied that private schools ought not to exist at all.[225]

Secularists consider themselves to have triumphed in the Enlightenment, so that recognizing the authenticity of religion would require returning to the churches territory previously taken from them. Liberalism, because of the Enlightenment, cannot cherish religion and cannot require "reason" to justify itself in more ultimate terms.[226] The liberal state's avoidance of ultimate questions is said to be for the purpose of fostering "a religion and an ethics that validate the highest-order moral powers of rationality and reasonableness of a free people," which is in turn declared to be "the only kind of religion suitable for a democracy."[227]

On the assumption that religion is essentially irrational, it would indeed be appropriate to exclude it from an educational process supposedly designed to encourage students' ability to think critically, and some liberals, contrary to what most believers hold, regard faith and reason as mutually exclusive ways of approaching reality, necessarily in conflict with each other.[228] Only religiously held beliefs are treated as irrational.[229]

However, the phenomenon of "postmodernism" now undermines the Enlightenment's very faith in critical reason,[230] an action that arguably revalidates ideas the Enlightenment had declared untenable, including religious faith,[231] making it invalid for nonbelievers to posit a simple divergence between "rational" and "irrational" arguments.[232]

Postmodernist theory logically must question the tenability of any uni-
fied educational purpose and seems to require a plurality of systems precisely as a way of ensuring social diversity.[233] But in the *Epperson* and
Edwards cases, the Court, in order to protect public education from religious "incursion," was forced in effect to assert that biological evolution
is a "fact," presumably immune to challenge,[234] even though there is no
constitutional authority, or intellectual competence, for the Court to decide questions of science.[235]

Black himself, complaining of the "pallid defense" that the state of
Arkansas offered in the *Epperson* case,[236] raised the question in a direct
way, wondering how the Court had competence to pass on scientific questions and pointing out that the Court usually held that the motives of
legislators were not relevant to the constitutionality of a law. He also
speculated that Arkansas could legitimately have forbidden the teaching
of evolution simply because of the "divisiveness" doctrine. In his majority
opinion Justice Fortas merely assumed the religious roots of the Arkansas
statute, cited no evidence of such motivation, and omitted from his opinion a statement by legislators offering secular reasons for the law.[237]

The *Edwards* decision was even more problematic, in that the nullified
state law did not prohibit any teaching but merely mandated that "creationism" be given equal time in the public schools. The plaintiffs were
unable to show that the disputed laws violated anyone's religious
liberty.[238]

The fact that these cases were decided by reference to the Establishment
Clause reveals that the Court did not see itself as adjudicating merely a
disagreement over scientific pedagogy but precisely a dispute over fundamental beliefs in which the beliefs of one side were officially established
and those of the other excluded. Perhaps unique in a First Amendment
case, the Court decided the issue essentially on the grounds that one side
in the dispute possessed the truth, while the other was in error.[239] By treating evolution as a fact, the Court also departed from liberal respect for
conscience, in that the authority of science was protected from whatever
conscientious doubts individuals might have about it.[240]

Reacting to the historically Protestant character of the public schools,
the modern Court succeeded, not in making them neutral, but in making
them predominantly secular.[241] The Court since 1948 has had no way of
even considering complaints by parents that the public schools are a
threat to their children's faith,[242] even though the *McCollum* decision took
seriously the complaint that nonbelieving children were being treated un-
fairly. There, the rights of the atheist plaintiff were respected, while those
of religious parents were ignored. The *Yoder* case was a major triumph
for parental rights, but the fact that it applied only to a small and marginal
group made its wider relevance doubtful.

As the majority opinion in *Yoder* was being drafted, Stewart objected to the claim that the Constitution protected parental "rights," and Brennan modified the decision to refer merely to their "interests."[243] In dissenting in the case, Douglas got to the heart of the matter by asking if parents had the right to "impose" their beliefs on their children, and whether on the contrary the state did not have an obligation to expose children to the opportunities of "the new and amazing world of diversity which we have today." (Douglas believed that 90 percent of people were not even fit to be parents.)[244] Logically this left it at best an open question whether parents posses the right to determine their children's religion.

"Comprehensive" liberalism claims that citizenship requires the fostering of habits of "moral freedom" and "critical thinking," for which the public schools are the principal agencies.[245] It is not the duty of state, according to this argument, to "relieve the tensions and perplexities to which a good education may give rise,"[246] an unexceptionable principle in itself, except that it seems to apply only to those "perplexities" that religious believers experience, while nonbelievers are protected from unwanted confrontations with religion. In disallowing religious exercises in public schools, the Court has frequently cited the discomfort such exercises cause some students, but it has never addressed the discomfort religious students feel in programs that affront their beliefs.[247]

Indeed some liberals argue that believers should not even be exempted from participating in public-school programs that may "confront" their beliefs.[248] The American Civil Liberties Union holds that, while it is permissible to grant exemptions from, for example, controversial sex-education programs, the school is under no obligation to respect such conscientious scruples.[249]

Often the public schools have a double standard with regard to student intellectual freedom—a broad one for expression in general, a very narrow one for religious expression (for example, forbidding students to write essays on Jesus Christ, while allowing essays on reincarnation and spiritualism).[250] In some public schools, students have been forbidden to speak or write on religious subjects,[251] and public-school textbooks frequently neglect or distort religion's role in society, to the point of even seeming overtly hostile to it.[252] As White pointed out in the *Aguilar* case, the Court has never seriously concerned itself with whether public-school teachers act in neutral ways, and in his *Edwards* dissent, Scalia asked whether secular education could not itself be thought to "indoctrinate" students.

Comprehensive liberalism leads to the conclusion that the *Pierce* decision was fundamentally in error and that there is no right to religious education at all, especially in conjunction with the "repressive" beliefs of parents. One liberal theorist expresses the hope that education will divest young people of "rigid" principles and concedes that religious conservatives can be tolerated because they are a disappearing breed and toleration may be an effective way of drawing them into the broader liberal consensus.[253] In the most extreme version of this, all religious education inculcates "reactionary and repressive" values in children, and for the good of the child, the state is obligated either to prohibit such schools completely or to monitor them closely, possibly using government "vouchers" as instruments for that purpose. To the same end the state must also closely monitor even those parents who choose to educate their children at home.[254]

The issue thus turns inevitably on the question of parental authority, of the very nature of the family, and one of the most sensitive public issues of the coming decades is likely to be whether the family possesses an authority that precedes that of the state, so that the state may not impinge on parents' efforts to raise their children in a particular faith.[255] The thrust of recent liberal theory has been precisely in the direction of "liberating" children from parental influence, with the state possessing an authority, its source unspecified, to decide which values are appropriate for a democratic society.

The issue ostensibly raised in the *Yoder* case was the rights of children, a formulation that obscured the fact that in practice the only alternative to parental authority is the authority of the state. No evidence was presented that Amish children wished to attend a public high school, and, had *Yoder* been decided differently, it would have marked the triumph of the rights not of children but of government bureaucracy.

In its extreme form, liberal theory asserts, almost casually, that parental choice in education might be "inconsistent with the state's aims," a formulation in which parental rights are subordinated even to those of teachers and in which advocacy on behalf of "children" blends imperceptibly into the aims of the state,[256] children defined as "future citizens" whose educations are therefore too important to be left entirely to parents.[257]

This liberal approach to education ignores the inherently coercive nature of all education, at least at the level of younger children. Those who regard education as designed to encourage critical thought overlook the fact that, in perhaps most cases, children accept without question ideas proposed by constituted authorities such as teachers,[258] and, where children's beliefs do diverge from those of their parents (for example, concerning drug use), the children's beliefs may well be harmful to their own interests. The principal fallacy in the concept of "children's rights" is the fact that most children probably do not hold deep beliefs contrary to those of their parents, and it is therefore left to state officials to determine what an "enlightened" child ought to believe, with no reason to assume that such officials are wiser than parents.

This concept of "children's rights," as with the evolution issue, inevitably seeks to enforce intellectual orthodoxy, with public agencies in effect determining that certain beliefs are true and others false and pernicious. Those who urge that the schools assume the primary responsibility for forming children's attitudes are proponents of comprehensive liberalism, according to which, ironically, certain beliefs are enforced by the state in the name of freedom, for example, in the demand that all forms of education inculcate feminism and permissive attitudes toward sexual behavior and that religions that fail to do so are dangerous to the public welfare and subject to state regulation.[259]

Although the Court has stopped well short of adopting such a a position, it is a position that is potentially compatible with the Court's tortured inability, because of its understanding of the Establishment Clause, to affirm the positive social benefits of religion. Contrary to the assumption that religion is incompatible with a free society, religious believers tend to be active and conscientious citizens,[260] and religion can actually strengthen democratic values by grounding them in the citizens' deepest beliefs, a task that a secular public education cannot fulfill.[261] Religious discourse can serve as a basis for common discussion and provide moral insights.[262] It is thus inappropriate for schools to seek to relativize their students' faith, and they ought to respect parents' wishes to include religion in their children's educations.[263]

At its heart, comprehensive liberalism assumes that education must foster fundamental habits of intellectual questioning, of doubt directed at the student's own inherited beliefs.[264] Closely related is the insistence that all education foster "respect for diversity," although in principle a pluralistic society should be allowed to require merely that different groups recognize one another's existence and understand one another's beliefs.[265]

But even a leading proponent of comprehensive liberalism acknowledges that democratic education should not assume that only one kind of public identity is legitimate, even that of the critical inquirer.[266] A properly political liberalism ought not to instruct students definitively in the proper use of their freedom[267] or, as the *Barnette* decision recognized, impose a single set of values through the schools.[268]

Genuine liberalism ought in principle to tolerate even the "unexamined life,"[269] whereas education for "diversity" is yet another ironic enforcement of orthodoxy in the name of freedom, a pedagogical formulation that inherently tends to undermine the legitimacy of religious faith.[270] While comprehensive liberalism assumes that the danger of religious education is that children will become fanatics, in fact the dominant cultural spirit may threaten the opposite—lack of all real conviction.[271] The intelligibility of particular views requires not detached academic exposition but "serious advocacy,"[272] and presenting religious ideas in a detached fashion may have the effect of relativizing them in the minds of students.[273]

The most sensitive area of conflict is probably sexual morality, as it enters the curricula of the public schools. Thus a program promoting sexual abstinence can be challenged as unconstitutional on the grounds that it arises from theistic beliefs, while a program encouraging sexual experimentation is justified on the grounds that it is not religious in nature. In such conflicts, under the present rules, theists are slated always to lose, which a leading postmodernist theorist insists is entirely appropriate.[274]

There is also bitter controversy over public subsidies to the arts, some of the works subsidized being denounced as immoral, indecent, and insulting to religion. The controversy closely parallels that over religion, involving as it does the use of taxes to finance things that some taxpayers find profoundly offensive, since the arts, like religion, embody fundamental values some of which are in conflict with one another.

For some liberals, therefore, the Free-Exercise Clause has itself become problematic, the liberty the Bill of Rights guarantees to religion now to be extended to all beliefs,[275] toleration separated from the value of that which is tolerated.[276] Even the modern Court's definition of religion as "ultimate concern" then becomes overly narrow.[277]

Thus, according to one theorist, religion should enjoy no more liberty than any other matter of conscience, full protection extended only to views that are "unpopular," many of which are secular.[278] Another theorist argues that the Free-Exercise Clause should protect only minority faiths, not the majority Christianity.[279]

But this nullifies the Free-Exercise Clause, which would be redundant if religious freedom were merely a form of free expression.[280] A subjective and personal definition of religion does not explain the Clause, which otherwise could have been cast merely in terms of freedom of conscience.[281] The very existence of the Free-Exercise Clause implies a special place for religion in public life.[282] The Bill of Rights was not "agnostic" about religious liberty, which it forthrightly favored; it was agnostic about the meaning of "establishment."[283] But the modern Court, beginning in 1947, elevated the Establishment Clause to an importance it did not previously have, at a time when religious liberty was also being expanded, although the latter often occurred under the rubric of free expression rather than of freedom of religion as such.[284]

The Religion Clauses were traditionally reconciled on the assumption that the Establishment Clause was intended to serve as a protection for free exercise,[285] but the modern Court has often not even attempted to reconcile them. The priority of the two clauses has been reversed, with the Court now much more vigilant about establishment than about free exercise. Not only is the Establishment Clause no longer thought to exist

to guard religious liberty, it places restrictions on it[286] by excluding religion from public education and from the formation of public policy.[287] (Frankfurter, the most rigid of separationists, was so devoted to the Establishment Clause that he could only with difficulty affirm religious liberty at all.)

Thus the Establishment Clause is said to impose unique disabilities on religion,[288] and one theorist argues that the government does not violate the Establishment Clause as long as its actions are intended to inhibit religion rather than to favor it.[289] Religion is claimed to enjoy less protection than other forms of free expression, the Establishment Clause necessarily requiring that religion be treated "asymmetrically" from other freedoms,[290] so that "entanglement" between government and religion is a good thing for the purpose of restraining religion.[291] The liberal society is urged to admit frankly its uncompromisable hostility to certain kinds of dogmatic religion, so that religious freedom should be interpreted narrowly, restricted by the Establishment Clause.[292] Thus one liberal theorist would prohibit believers from trying to enact "restrictive" laws on the grounds that such laws are incompatible with liberal democracy, which is the best form of government.[293] The Court's nullification of the Religious Freedom Restoration Act has been justified on the grounds that the law gave religion a privileged place with respect to nonreligion,[294] and a liberal theorist postulates that religious liberty sometimes undermines other freedoms and thus should always be subordinated to those freedoms (for example, there can be no right to speak against the use of contraceptives).[295]

However, another theorist acknowledges that the Establishment Clause does not actually restrict religion in this way and instead proposes that separationists bypass the Constitution by appealing to the Civil Rights Act of 1964, so that legal action for personal liability can be brought against both school officials and parents accused of violating the rights of others by "intruding" religion into the public schools, even as religious believers themselves are denied any legal basis to complain of discrimination against their own beliefs.[296]

Liberalism has moved toward becoming a secular orthodoxy that places believers in the situation where a minimal understanding of religious liberty excludes them from full participation in public life. As Burger claimed in the Lemon case, the Court then has the task of removing religious issues from debate, of imposing restraints on religious believers as a condition of their entering the public sphere. Inevitably, such an attitude to religion justifies overt discrimination, as in the claim that religious believers lack the necessary commitment to the Constitution to qualify to serve on the Court,[297] despite the Constitution's explicit prohibition of any religious test for public office (Article VI).

Under an increasingly common liberal view of the Free-Exercise Clause, any "sincerely held ideology" qualifies for special protection.[298] If true, this raises the question whether there is any meaningful distinction between religion and nonreligion for purposes of free expression,[299] so that the protection of the Free-Exercise Clause should be extended, for example, to those who believe in the mystical power of narcotics,[300] and that religion should enjoy no more protection than business corporations.[301] The Constitution is said to respect not religion as such but "individual understanding of the world."[302]

If this is so, then the state's attempt, through public schools, to persuade students of the truth of certain secular beliefs should be treated no differently from its endorsement of religious beliefs[303] so that schools may not promote, for example, the ideas of John Dewey, Karl Marx, or John Maynard Keynes, any more than they may promote Chrisitanity, and a constitutional doctrine must be developed to prevent schools from fostering "narrowly partisan ideologies."[304]

The implications of this have been evaded by treating the two Religion Clauses as embodying different meanings of the term. In *McCollum*, Rutledge insisted that the meaning was the same in both clauses. But a distinction between the two was turned into a constitutional principle by a leading liberal theorist, who proposed that if a reasonable argument could be made that a particular belief constituted a religion, that belief was entitled to the protection of the Free-Exercise Clause, while, if a reasonable argument could be made against that claim, the belief in question would not be subject to the Establishment Clause.[305] This bifurcated distinction has been used to argue that some forms of religion may be supported by the government, because they have a secular purpose,[306] or by arguing that secular humanism is not credal but merely "a language of translation and discussion."[307]

But this dual definition obviously gives nontheistic ideologies a competitive advantage.[308] If religion were taken to mean the same in both the Religion Clauses, it would restrain government from promoting secular values.[309] If Justice Clark's definition of religion as "ultimate concern" were taken as adequate, it would both permit government support of certain beliefs now ordinarily considered religious and prohibit support of certain beliefs now generally considered secular.[310]

The cultural phenomenon called New Age is at present a major ground of conflict, with no clear constitutional guidelines. A teacher who advocated overtly religious beliefs would violate the Establishment Clause, but at present there appears to be no obstacle to a teacher's sympathetic presentation of beliefs about magic, witchcraft, myths, reincarnation, and other things that traditional believers find harmful to their children.

In broadening its definition of religion in the 1960s, the Court could have laid a basis for resolving continuing conflicts by redefining the issue not as between religion and nonreligion, in the conventional sense, but as between competing ideologies or worldviews. If "religion" includes beliefs not necessarily theistic in nature, not recognized as such in common parlance, it seems to follow that those beliefs fall under both the Religion Clauses. John Dewey insisted that "humanism" was itself a religion, indeed a religion superior to traditional kinds.[311] Already in the *Schempp* case, Clark warned of the potential danger of establishing a "religion of secularism," although he denied that the Court was doing so, while in the *Torcaso* case, Douglas actually urged that the Court recognize "humanism" as a religion.[312] Following logically from the Court's expanded definition of religion, separationism might itself be expanded to forbid not merely the "intrusion" of religion into public education but the "intrusion" of any ideology, secular or religious, that is offensive to some of the citizens.

But the definition of religion has been expanded without regard for its affects on the issue of establishment,[313] and the modern interpretation of the Establishment Clause partly inhibits religious freedom because the clause has no secular equivalent. Thus, without constitutional restraint, the government may "endorse" all kinds of controversial positions, all of which make at least some of the citizens feel "excluded," a situation in which religious beliefs are automatically handicapped.[314]

A possible resolution of the dilemma is to see separation as governing the relationship between religion and government, accommodation the relationship between religion and culture. Thus government may not conduct itself according to overtly religious principles but may act according to principles that are compatible with religion.[315] However, it is precisely the "culture wars"—the points at which culture affects public policy—that are the locus of the problem.[316]

The Framers obviously intended to protect nonbelievers, in the sense that no one could be required by law to accept any religious doctrine or practice. Beyond that, however, they did not intend the Free-Exercise Clause to protect religion and secular beliefs equally. But liberalism now promises not only religious liberty but the liberation of people from the constraints of their inherited faiths,[317] and in the *McGowan* case, Douglas proclaimed a constitutionally guaranteed "freedom from religion." The Court has greatly expanded the rights of nonbelievers, to the point where in some ways freedom of religion has come to mean, most importantly, freedom to reject religious claims.[318]

This idea has now come to dominate much of liberal thought, to the point where the affirmation of religious liberty in the traditional sense causes misgivings, lest it have the affect of strengthening a cultural phenomenon that some liberals consider unhealthy, even if merely promoted

privately. Thus it is now mainly secularists who espouse an absolute separationist position.

Liberalism emphasizes rights so strongly that it overlooks the question
of the goods that individuals should pursue in their lives, political rights
being taken as prior to the good itself. Liberal thought cannot conceive
of persons belonging to communities bound by moral ties that are antecedent to choice,[319] an attitude that inevitably sees strong religious groups
as dangerous. Contemporary liberalism seems bifurcated, in that it is obsessed with "rights talk," even as it treats certain rights, especially those
having to do with religion, as though they were merely conferred by the
state.[320]

The ultimate issue is whether citizens possess natural rights, which the
Constitution merely promises to respect, or whether rights are conditionally bestowed by the state. Traditionally, the first position has largely been
taken for granted,[321] so that morality precedes politics,[322] and if it is assumed that public issues are formed outside the sphere of politics, within
the larger culture,[323] it seems to follow that the state merely serves as a
kind of referee among values that antecede, and are superior to, politics.
Thus, to take what is now the most sensitive instance, parents have the
primary right to educate their children, which they only partially cede to
the state.

The deepest threat to constitutionally guaranteed liberty is now posed
by the postmodernist phenomenon of "deconstruction," in its claim that
texts have no clear, stable meanings, thus making it problematical
whether such texts can serve as enduring guarantors of liberties. One influential theorist argues that legal texts do not posses that stability and
that they depend on "interpretive authority and power." Thus "the Constitution . . . is not a repository of meaning; rather, its meaning is always
being conferred on it by . . . political and institutional forces."[324]

A related theory denies that there are philosophical foundations for
human rights, insisting that a respect for rights is primarily a matter of
"sentiment." Rights are best secured not by rational argument but by attempts to make available to everyone a sense of "security and sympathy"
in their own states of life. This in turn implies that human beings are far
more "malleable" than was thought in earlier times, and they can be transformed by "manipulating sentiments," by "sentimental education."[325]

The same theorist judges that the highest achievements of humanity are
incompatible with traditional forms of religion,[326] and this position would
seem to justify a radical reinterpretation of the Free-Exercise Clause, as
well as the systematic use of education to wean people away from religion
in the name of human progress. The loss of a sense of "security and sympathy" is precisely what motivates many conservative combatants in the

"culture wars," but liberalism now extends its solicitude only to favored social groups.

Absent any accepted theory of the ultimate basis either of rights or of the authority of the state itself, absent either an overtly religious foundation for politics or an accepted theory of natural law, the state in practice cannot help but treat rights as conferred by itself. Citizens then have no higher authority to which they can appeal, precisely the bargain that Rutledge offered in 1948 when he misread the Bible in asserting that personal religious liberty could be enjoyed only if believers agreed to restrictions on their rights as citizens.

Under the modern theory of separationism, the Declaration of Independence itself cannot be affirmed as true by any public authority, because of its religious (even if deistic) foundation, and must be treated merely as an important historical document.[327] The test that now faces the liberal polity is whether its embrace of secularization has gone so far that citizens must now abandon the claim that they have been endowed by their Creator with certain inalienable rights.

NOTES

NOTES TO CHAPTER ONE

1. 9 *Cranch* 42, at 46–48.
2. *Reynolds* (98 US 145), at 163.
3. Ibid., at 163–64.
4. Ibid., at 164.
5. Ibid., at 165.
6. *Late Corporation* (136 US 1), at 49–50.
7. 143 US 457, at 465–71.
8. 310 US 586, at 594.
9. *Murdock* (319 US 105).
10. Ibid., at 122–26.
11. *Barnette* (319 US 624), at 646.
12. Ibid., at 652–53.
13. Ibid., at 649–50.
14. *Ballard* (322 US 78), at 87.
15. 330 US 1, at 8–10.
16. Ibid., at 11–13. Jefferson's "Bill for Establishing Religious Freedom" is in *The Papers of Thomas Jefferson*, ed. Julian P. Boyd (Princeton, N.J., 1950), II, 545–46.
17. 330 US 1, at 13–14.
18. Ibid., at 14.
19. Ibid., at 18–28.
20. Ibid., at 31–32.
21. Ibid., at 31–38. Madison's *Memorial and Remonstrance against Religious Assessments* is in *The Papers of James Madison*, ed. William T. Hutchison and William M.E. Rachal (Chicago, 1962), VIII, 298–304.
22. 330 US 1, at 38–40.
23. Ibid., at 40–42.
24. Ibid., at 53–55.
25. 333 US 203.
26. Ibid., at 213, 231. For a discussion of the evolving use of the "wall" metaphor, see Daniel Dreisbach, *Thomas Jefferson and the Wall of Separation between Church and State* (New York, 2000), 55–70, 83–106.
27. 333 US 203, at 238.
28. Ibid., at 244–48.
29. *Burstyn* (347 US 495), at 518.
30. *Torcaso* (366 US 488) at 490.
31. *McGowan* (366 US 420), at 430.
32. Ibid., at 437–39.
33. Ibid., at 465–66.
34. Ibid., at 494–95.
35. Ibid., at 561–81.

36. 370 *US* 421, at 429–30.
37. Ibid., at 432–33.
38. Ibid., at 436.
39. Ibid., at 444.
40. Ibid., at 445–50.
41. Ibid., at 445–46.
42. 374 *US* 203, at 213–14.
43. Ibid., at 233–34.
44. Ibid., at 234–37.
45. Ibid., at 237–41.
46. Ibid., at 254–55.
47. Ibid., at 256–57.
48. Ibid., at 259–60.
49. Ibid., at 294–95.
50. Ibid., at 309–10.
51. *Seeger* (380 *US* 163).
52. *Flast* (392 *US* 83).
53. Ibid., at 103.
54. Ibid., at 126–30.
55. 397 *US* 664.
56. Ibid., at 668.
57. Ibid., at 680–81.
58. Ibid., at 682–85.
59. Ibid., at 684–85, fn. 5.
60. Ibid., at 704–706, 710–15.
61. 403 *US* 602.
62. Ibid., at 634.
63. Ibid., at 645–47.
64. 403 *US* 672, at 696–97.
65. *Lemon v. Kurtzman*, II (411 *US* 192), at 209–12.
66. *Yoder* (406 *US* 205), at 225.
67. *Nyquist* (413 *US* 756), at 760–61.
68. *Wolman* (444 *US* 646), at 263.
69. *McDaniel* (435 *US* 618).
70. Ibid., at 621–24.
71. Ibid., at 637.
72. *Thomas v. Review Board* (450 *US* 707), at 720–21.
73. *Valley Forge* (454 *US* 464), at 501–504, 513.
74. *Larkin* (459 *US* 116), at 122–23.
75. 463 *US* 783, at 786–90.
76. Ibid., at 791–92.
77. Ibid., at 807–808.
78. Ibid., at 814–15.
79. Ibid., at 816–17.
80. *Mueller v. Allen* (463 *US* 388), at 399–400.
81. 465 *US* 668, at 674–76.
82. Ibid., at 720–24.
83. 472 *US* 38, at 80–81.

84. Ibid., at 92.
85. Ibid., at 93–94.
86. Ibid., at 94–98.
87. Ibid., at 98–100.
88. Ibid., at 100.
89. Ibid., at 101–104.
90. Ibid., at 104–106.
91. Ibid., at 106–107.
92. Ibid., at 113–14.
93. *Allegheny* (492 US 573), at 589–90.
94. *Employment Division* (494 US 872), at 902.
95. *Weisman* (505 US 577).
96. Ibid., at 590.
97. Ibid., at 612.
98. Ibid., at 612–14.
99. Ibid., at 616–24.
100. Ibid., at 626.
101. Ibid., at 633–45.
102. *Lamb's Chapel* (508 US 384).
103. *Kiryas Joel* (512 US 687), at 732.
104. 515 US 819, at 852.
105. Ibid., at 854–55.
106. Ibid., at 862.
107. Ibid., at 856.
108. Ibid., at 857.
109. Ibid., at 859, 862.
110. Ibid., at 869.
111. Ibid., at 873.
112. Ibid., at 872–73.
113. *Capitol Square* (515 US 753), at 797, 813–14.
114. 521 US 507, at 658.
115. Ibid., at 659–63.
116. Ibid., at 664–66.
117. Ibid., at 661.
118. Ibid., at 663.
119. Ibid., at 650–51.
120. Ibid., at 651–52.
121. Ibid., at 653.
122. Ibid., at 653.
123. *Santa Fe* (530 US 290), at 320.
124. *Mitchell v. Helms* (530 US 793), at 871–72, 906.
125. *Zelman* (122 S.Ct. 2460), at 2499.

NOTES TO CHAPTER TWO

1. H. J. Eckenrode, *Separation of Church and State in Virginia* (New York, 1971 [originally 1910]); Thomas E. Buckley, *Church and State in Revolutionary*

Virginia, 1776–1787 (Charlottesville, Va., 1977), 38–70; Thomas J. Curry, *Farewell to Christendom* (New York, 2001), 39–40; Leonard Levy, *The Establishment Clause: Religion and the First Amendment* (New York, 1986), 51–60; Edwin S. Gaustad, *Sworn on the Altar of God, a Religious Biography of Thomas Jefferson* (Grand Rapids, Mich., 1996), 54–56; Mark A. Beliles, in Garrett Ward Sheldon and Daniel L. Dreisbach (eds.), *Political Culture in Jefferson's Virginia* (Lanham, Md., 2000), 27–50; Dreisbach, in ibid., 135–66, 189–218.

2. Eckenrode, *Separation*, 74–105; Buckley, *Church-State*, 71–143; Gaustad, *Neither King nor Prelate: Religion and the New Nation, 1776–1826* (Grand Rapids, Mich., 1993), 37–40; Buckley, in Merrill D. Peterson (ed.), *The Virginia Statute for Religious Freedom* (New York, 1988), 116–18, 121, 123; Dreisbach, *Real Threat or Mere Shadow?: Religious Liberty and the First Amendment* (Westchester, Ill., 1987), 135–45; Michael Corbett, *Politics and Religion in the United States* (New York, 1999).

3. Philip Hamburger, *Separation of Church and State* (Cambridge, Mass., 2002), 10, 58–59, 63; Steven D. Smith, *Getting over Equality: A Critical Diagnosis of Religious Freedom in America* (New York, 2002), 16.

4. Rodney R. Smith, *School Prayer and the Constitution* (Wilmington, Del., 1987), 47–49, 53–54; Gaustad, *Faith of Our Fathers: Religion and the New Nation* (San Francisco, 1987), 142–49; Levy, *Establishment*, 102–109; Smith, *Getting*, 14.

5. Text in Phlip Kurland and Ralph Lerner (eds.), *The Founders' Constitution* (Chicago, 1987), V, 82–84. See Gerard V. Bradley, *Church-State Relationships in America* (New York, 1987), 39.

6. Curry, *The First Freedom: Church and State in America to the Passage of the First Amendment* (New York, 1986), 209–11, 217, and *Farewell*, 15, 58, 60, 110, 125; Bradley, *Church-State*, 13.

7. Text in Kurland, *Founders*, V, 84–85.

8. Gaustad, *Faith*, 149–51, and in Jerald C. Brauer (ed.), *The Lively Experiment* (Macon, Ga., 1987), 85–104; Buckley, *Church-State*, 144–72, and in Peterson, *Virginia Statute*, 82–86.

9. David Little, in Russell E. Richey and Donald G. Jones (eds.), *Civil Religion in American Life* (New York, 1974), 189–99.

10. Rhys Isaac, in Peterson, *Virginia Statute*, 163.

11. Robert L. Cord, *Separation of Church and State: Historical Fact and Current Fiction* (New York, 1982), 33–34; Gaustad, *Faith*, 51–52, and *Neither*, 51; Robert S. Alley, *School Prayer: The Court, the Congress, and the First Amendment* (Buffalo, 1994), 19–58.

12. Leo Pfeffer, in Peterson, *Virginia Statute*, 293–94;

13. Cord, *Separation*, 23, 40; James M. O'Neil, *Religion and Education in the Constitution* (New York, 1949), 87–107; Donald L. Drakeman, in Sheldon and Dreisbach, *Political Culture*, 219–34; Dreisbach, *Real*, 103–22.

14. Dreisbach, *Real*, 117–24; Dreisbach, in Luis E. Lugo (ed.), *Religion, Public Life, and the American Polity* (Knoxville, Tenn., 1994), 80–92; Dreisbach, *Jefferson and Wall*, 58–59; Dreisbach, in Sheldon and Dreisbach, *Political Culture*, 189–218; The "Levitical Law" referred to the Book of Leviticus in the Bible.

15. Smith, *School Prayer*, 98; O'Neil, *Religion*, 66–86; Cord, in Sheldon and Dreisbach, *Religion and Culture*.

16. Dreisbach, *Jefferson and Wall*, 60, 63, 68; Cord, in Sheldon and Dreisbach, *Political Culture*, 167–88.

17. Dreisbach, *Jefferson and Wall*, 57.

18. Joseph F. Costanzo, *Thomas Jefferson, Religious Education, and Public Law* (Atlanta, 1959), 72–73, 179.

19. Cord, *Separation*, 41–45; Dreisbach, *Real*, 127–29; James H. Hutson, *Religion and the Founding of the American Republic* (Washington, 1998), 58; David P. Currie, *The Constitution in Congress . . . 1789–91* (Chicago, 1994), 207; Bernard W. Sheehan, *Seeds of Extinction: Jeffersonian Philanthropy and the American Indian* (Chapel Hill, N.C., 1973), 120, 126–28.

20. Dreisbach, *Real*, 130; *Jefferson and Wall*, 29–32, 56.

21. Robert M. Healey (ed.), *Thomas Jefferson on Religion and and Public Education* (Hamden, Conn., 1962), 216–20.

22. Charles B. Sanford, *The Religious Life of Thomas Jefferson* (Charlottesville, Va., 1984), 1–6, 85–99, and in Sheldon and Dreisbach, *Political Culture*, 61–92; Daniel H. Boorstin, *The Lost World of Thomas Jefferson* (Boston, 1948), 29–54; John Eidsmoe, Arnold Burron, and Dean Turner, *Christianity and the Constitution* (Grand Rapids, Mich., 1987), 215–46; Henry F. May, *The Enlightenment in America* (New York, 1976), 287–302; Costanzo, *Jefferson*, 143.

23. Sanford, *Religion*, 6–13; Boorstin, *Lost*, 151–66; Jean M. Yarbrough, in Gary L. McDowell, *Reason and Republicanism: Thomas Jefferson's Legacy of Liberty* (Lanham, Md., 1997), 290–93; Healey, *Jefferson and Education*, 109, 113; Gaustad, *Faith*, 97–108; Gaustad, *Sworn*, 16–41, 111–21, 132–40, 145–46, 182–200; Gaustad, *Neither*, 98–107; Rockne McCarthy, James W. Skillen, and William A. Harper, *Disestablishment a Second Time* (Grand Rapids, Mich., 1982), 15–29; Allen Jayne, *Jefferson's Declaration of Independence* (Lexington, Ky., 1989), 18, 34, 39, 81–85, 165–66; Ronald Hoffman and Peter J. Albert, *Religion in a Revolutionary Age* (Charlottesville, Va., 1994), 290–307.

24. Sanford, *Religion*, 25–26, 48–54, 59, 61, 83, 101, 106, 111–12, 120, 145; Costanzo, *Jefferson*, 59–63; Hamburger, *Separation*, 147–50; Dreisbach, *Jefferson and Wall*, 28–29; Boorstin, *Lost*, 160–62; Isaac Kramnick and R. Lawrence Moore, *The Godless Constitution* (New York, 1996), 88–100; Gaustad, *Neither*, 48; Gaustad, *Faith*, 45–49; Gaustad, *Sworn*, 200–207; McCarthy, *Disestablishment*, 27–29; Jayne, *Declaration*, 37–38, 99–103, 107, 141, 143–44, 149, 172; Robert K. Faullkner, in McDowell, *Reason*, 41.

25. Hamburger, *Separation*, 82; Sanford, *Religion*, 62, 83, 90, 97; Healey, *Jefferson and Education*, 95, 105, 115–27.

26. Jayne, *Declaration*, 160–61.

27. Little, in Richey, *Civil Religion*, 185–89.

28. McCarthy, *Disestablishment*, 28, 32, 35, 43. For the argument that Jefferson had a respectful view of religious diversity, see Sheldon, in Sheldon and Dreisbach, *Political Culture*, 93–106.

29. Gaustad, *Sworn*, 166; Gaustad, *Neither*, 49; Leonard Baker, *John Marshall* (New York, 1974), 651–52.

30. Healey, *Jefferson and Education*, 211; Gaustad, *Neither*, 47.

31. Healey, *Jefferson and Education*, 170, 176, 207–208, 216–26, 230, 233, 235, 237, 240; Gaustad, *Neither*, 48; John G. West, *The Politics of Revelation and Reason* (Lawrence, Kans., 1996), 62–65.

32. Jayne, *Declaration*, 106.

33. Hamburger, *Separation*, 5, 161.

34. Healey, *Jefferson and Education*, 242–44, 257; Garry Wills, *Under God: Religion and American Politics* (New York, 1990), 363, 369.

35. Martin Marty, in Peterson, *Virginia Statute*, 19.

36. Ralph L. Ketcham, in Robert S. Alley (ed.), *James Madison on Religious Liberty* (Buffalo, 1985), 175–92; Lance Banning, in Peterson, *Virginia Statute*, 109–10; William Lee Miller, *The Business of May Next: James Madison and the Founding* (Charlottesville, Va., 1992), 105–106; West, *Politics*, 67–73; Richard K. Mathews, *If Men Were Angels: James Madison and the Heartless Empire of Reason* (Lawrence, Kans., 1995), 32–42. For the influence of Calvinism on Madison, see Sheldon, *The Political Philosophy of James Madison* (Baltimore, 2001), and Mary-Elaine Swanson, in Sheldon and Dreisbach, *Political Culture*, 119–32.

37. West, *Politics*, 67–73; Ketcham, *Made for Posterity: The Enduring Philosophy of the Constitution* (Lawrence, Kans., 1993), 95; Smith, *School Prayer*, 41, and *Getting*, 20–21; Matthews, *Men-Angels*, 54–55.

38. Gaustad, *Faith*, 52; Gaustad, *Neither*, 53.

39. Hamburger, *Separation*, 100, 102, 105.

40. Ibid., 10, 58–59, 63, 67–68, 74, 84–85, 93–94, 165–78.

41. Gary Rosen, *American Compact: James Madison and the Problem of the Founding* (Lawrence, Kans., 1999), 20–25; Robert N. Bellah, *The Broken Covenant: Civil Religion in Time of Trial* (New York, 1970), 173–74.

42. Bradley, *Church-State*, 123–24; Stephen B. Presser, *Recapturing the Constitution: Race, Religion, and Abortion Reconsidered* (Washington, 1994), 45, 59–61; Stephen V. Monsma, *Positive Neutrality: Letting Religious Freedom Ring* (Westport, Conn., 1993), 86–93, 96–97; David Little, in Peterson, *Virginia Statute*, 238–51; Hutson, *Religion*, 84; West, *Politics*, 17–73; Matthews, *Men-Angels*, 34; Graham Walker, in Gary L. Gregg II (ed.), *Vital Remnants: America's Founding and the Western Tradition* (Wilmington, Del., 1999), 102–29; Little, in ibid., 185–99.

43. George A. Kelly, *Politics and Religious Consciousness in America* (New Brunswick, N.J., 1984), 53, 55, 217; Leo Paul S. de Alvarez, in Sarah B. Thurow (ed.), *Constitutionalism in America* (Lanham, Md., 1988), III, 255–76; Michael Novak, *On Two Wings: Humble Faith and Common Sense at the Time of the American Founding* (San Francisco, 2001), 62; Hamburger, *Separation*, 67–68; Corbett, *Politics*, 62–70.

44. Costanzo, *Jefferson*, 116; Michael P. Zuchert, in Robert A. Licht (ed.), *The Framers and Fundamental Rights* (Washington, 1991), 142.

45. Smith, *School Prayer*, 57–58, and *Getting*, 15.

46. Gaustad, *Faith*, 57.

47. Sanford, *Religion*, 102–105, 111, 123, 131, 181–201; Gaustad, *Sworn*, 123–31; Boorstin, *Lost*, 156–57.

48. Hamburger, *Separation*, 155–59; Dreisbach, *Jefferson and Wall*, 25–54; Healey, *Jefferson and Education*, 130–31; Smith, *School Prayer*, 61–62; Hutson,

Religion, 93; Michael S. Ariens and Robert A. Destro (eds.), *Religious Liberty in a Pluralistic Society* (Durham, N.C., 1996), 92–96.

49. Hamburger, *Separation*, 159; Dreisbach, *Jefferson and Wall*, 44–47.

50. Hamburger, *Separation*, 144, 162–63; Dreisbach, *Jefferson and Wall*, 52.

51. Hamburger, *Separation*, 6, 79, 81, 83–84, 112–19, 120–21, 126, 130–32, 150; Dreisbach, *Jefferson and Wall*, 18–21.

52. Hamburger, *Separation*, 162, 181; Dreisbach, *Jefferson and Wall*, 21–23.

53. Text in Kurland, *Founders*, V, 103–105. See also Cord, *Separation*, 30–32; Gaustad, *Faith*, 53–55; Levy, *Establishment*, 98–102; Dreisbach, *Threat*, 152–56; T. Jeremy Gunn, *A Standard for Repair: The Establishment Clause, Equality, and Natural Rights* (New York, 1992), 177–83, 196.

54. Cushina Strout, *The New Heavens and the New Earth: Political Religion in America* (New York, 1973), 97.

55. Dreisbach, *Real*, 99–111, and in Sheldon and Dreisbach, *Political Culture*, 155; Curry, *Farewell*, 52, 112, 125.

56. Michael Kammen, *A Machine That Would Go of Itself: The Constitution in American Culture* (New York, 1986), 74, 81.

57. Smith, *School Prayer*, 63.

58. Mark Anthony DeWolfe Howe, *The Garden and the Wilderness: Religion and Government in American Constitutional History* (Chicago, 1965), 6–9, 17–19, 31; Timothy L. Hall, *Separating Church and State: Roger Williams and Religious Liberty* (Urbana, Ill., 1998); Bradley, *Church-State*, 27–30; John Witte, *Religion and the American Constitutional Experiment* (Boulder, Colo., 2000), 25–26; Stephen M. Feldman, *Please Don't Wish Me a Merry Christmas: A Critical History of the Separation of Church and State* (New York, 1997), 157; Hamburger, *Separation*, 38–52.

59. Eckenrode, *Separation*, 74–76, 85, 94–95; Hutson, *Religion*, 67–74, 76; Bradley, *Church-State*, 38–40; Gaustad, *Neither*, 39.

60. West, *Politics*, 39.

61. Derek Davis, *Religion and the Continental Congress, 1784–1789* (New York, 2000), 39–51, 59–60, 65–68; Richard E. Morgan, *The Supreme Court and Religion* (New York, 1972), 21–24.

62. Novak, *Two Wings*, 6–7.

63. Davis, *Religion*, 95–112; Hutson, *Religion*, 49–55; Witte, *Religion*, 57–59.

64. Cord, *Separation*, 24.

65. Anson Phelps Stokes, *Church and State in the United States* (New York, 1950), I, 292–357, 447–517; Chester J. Antieau, Arthur R. Downey, and Edward C. Roberts, *Freedom from Federal Establishment: The Formation and Early History of the First Amendment Religion Clauses* (Milwaukee, 1964), 189–203; Eidsmoe, *Christianity;* May, *Enlightenment*, 72, 96–97, 121–22. 126–31, 223–51, 252–86; M.E. Bradford, *Founding Fathers* (Lawrence, Kans., 1994); Ellis Sandoz, *A Government of Law: Political Theory, Religion, and the Americcn Founding* (Baton Rouge, La., 1990), 125–62, 178–99; M. Stanton Evans, *The Theme Is Freedom: Religion, Politics, and the American Tradition* (Washington, 1994), 272–74; John M. Murrin, in Mark A. Noll (ed.), *Religion and American Politics form the Colonial Period to the 1980s* (New York, 1990), 31; West, *Politics*, 17–73; Eidsmoe, in H. Wayne House (ed.), *Christianity and American Law* (Grand

Rapids, Mich., 1998), 84–98; Gaustad, *Neither*, 59–67, 77, 88–96; Sidney Mead, *The Old Religion in the Brave New World* (Berkeley, Calif., 1977), 79, 82–84; For the argument that the Founders were not themselves religious and did not intend to establish genuine religious freedom see Kenneth R. Craycraft, *The American Myth of Religious Freedom* (Dallas, 1999).

66. Novak, *Two Wings*, 127–58; Stephen A. Marini, in Hoffman, *Religion*, 189, 191.

67. Davis, *Religion*, 17–20; Cord, *Separation*, 5–12, 26; Stokes, *Church and State*, I, 518–64; Gunn, *Standard*, 39–67; Drakeman, *Church-State Constitutional Issues* (New York, 1991), 51–80; Dreisbach, *Real*, 55–66; Evans, *Theme*, 275–85; Witte, *Religion*, 64–75, 78; Bradley, *Church-State*, 72–78, 85–95; Miller, *May Next*, 245–49, 251–59; Ariens, *Religious Liberty*, 74–91.

68. Winfred E. A. Bernhard, *Fisher Ames, Federalist and Statesman, 1758–1809* (Chapel Hill, N.C., 1965), 330–31.

69. Davis, *Religion*, 16, 21; Antieau, *Freedom*, 123–58; Jean Yarbrough, in Michael A. Gillespie and Michael Lienesch (eds.), *Ratifying the Constitution* (Lawrence, Kans., 1989), 237–42.

70. Davis, *Religion*, 21, 35; Steven Smith, *Foreordained Failure: The Quest for a Constitutional Principle of Religious Freedom* (New York, 1995), 17–18, 25–26, 28–30, 33–35, 39, 47; Drakeman, *Church-State*, 95–128; Peter J. Ferrara, *Religion and the Constitution, a Reappraisal* (Washington, 1983), 19–27; Dreisbach, *Real*, 83–87; Bradley, *Church-State*, 79–80, 95–96; Feldman, *Please*, 167; Marini, in Hoffman, *Religion*, 188–89; Gaustad, in ibid., 225; Akhil Reed Amar, *The Bill of Rights: Creation and Reconstruction* (New Haven, Conn., 1998) 33–35, 41, 43; Saul Cornell, *The Other Founders: Anti-Federalism and the Dissenting Tradition in America, 1789–1828* (Chapel Hill, N.C., 199), 57, 94, 101–102.

71. Stokes, *Church and State*, I, 404–46; Antieau, *Freedom*, 30–61; Davis, *Religion*, 25–34, 36; Bradley, *Church-State*, 42–55; Hamburger, *Separation*, 89–91; Edward R. Norman, *The Conscience of the State in North America* (London, 1968), 79–84; Gunn, *Standard*, 69–96; Drakeman, *Church-State*, 81–94; Dreisbach, *Real*, 77–82; Feldman, *Please*, 154; Morton Borden, *Jews, Turks, and Infidels* (Chapel Hill, N.C., 1984), 18–19, 28–50; Witte, *Religion* 47–54, 88–100; Gaustad, *Neither*, 112–15; Ariens, and Destro, *Liberty*, 46–71; Hamburger, *Separation*, 89. Curry argues that none of the states in 1789 had an "establishment" of religion in the full sense (*Farewell*, 28, 36, 39, 41–43, 128–30).

72. Davis, *Religion*, 73–91; Cord, *Separation*, 23, 27–29; Antieau, *Freedom*, 159–88; Bradley, *Church-State*, 97–100; Ferrara, *Religion*, 27–32; Dreisbach, *Real*, 66–75; Stephen Botein, in Richard Beeman, Botein, and Edward Carter III (eds.), *Beyond Confederation: Origins of the Constitution and American National Identity* (Chapel Hill, N.C., 1987), 322–23; Kelly, *Politics*, 53–55, 217; Currie, *Constitution*, 12–13, 243; Witte, *Religion*, 34–39, 76; Novak, *Two Wings*, 13–24, 29–47.

73. Davis, *Religion*, 137–44; Hutson, *Religion*, 50.

74. Davis, *Religion*, 146–48; Hutson, *Religion*, 56.

75. Davis, *Religion*, 168–72; Bradley, *Church-State*, 101; Gaustad, *Sworn*, 78–80; Hutson, *Religion*, 57–58; Gaustad, in Hoffman, *Religion*, 232–33; Currie,

Constitution, 104; Witte, *Religion*, 60; Richard J. Gabel, *Public Funds for Church and Private Schools* (Washington, 1937), 174–76.

76. Dreisbach, *Jefferson and Wall*, 45.

77. Davis, *Religion*, 90; Eidsmoe, *Christianity*, 117; Morgan, *Supreme Court*, 28; Gaustad, *Sworn*, 95–96, and *Neither*, 181–82; Hutson, *Religion*, 78–81; Kelly, *Politics*, 53–55.

78. Howe, *Garden*, 11; Feldman, *Please*, 168; Curry, *Farewell*, 53; Corbett, *Politics*, 154–58.

79. Curry (*Farewell*, 52) treats official manifestations of religion in the early Republic as failures to realize that the Constitution had definitively rejected the idea of "Christendom." However, his argument is an anachronistic reading back into the Constitution certain modern positions, notably the decrees of the Second Vatican Council of the Catholic Church.

80. May, *Enlightenment*, 304; Monsma, *Positive*, 120–26; West, *Politics*, 82–114.

81. Gaustad, *Faith*, 120–32.

82. May, *Enlightenment*, 335.

83. Perry Miller, *The Legal Mind in America: From Independence to the Civil War* (Ithaca, N.Y., 1962), 66; Borden, *Jews*, 31. For the blasphemy laws, see Levy, *Treason against God: History of the Offense of Blasphemy* (New York, 1981) and *Blasphemy, a Verbal Offense Against the Sacred from Moses to Salman Rushdie* (New York, 1993).

84. Kramnick and Moore, *Godless*, 28, 31; Murrin, in Noll, *Religion*, 33–34; Harry S. Stout, in ibid,, 62–74; Robert Handy, *Undermined Establishment: Church-State Relations in America, 1880–1920* (Princeton, N.J., 1991), 27–28, 60–62; Miller, *May Next*, 107.

85. For example, Timothy Dwight, president of Yale College (Stephen E. Berk, *Calvinism versus Democracy: Timothy Dwight and the Origins of American Evangelical Orthodoxy* [Hamden, Conn., 1974]). See also Gaustad, in James Wood (ed.), *The First Freedom: Religion and the Bill of Rights* (Waco, Tex., 1993), 41–44.

86. Mead, *Old*, 95.

87. Hutson, *Religion*, 76–77; Bradley, *Church-State*, 74; A. James Reichley, in Charles Dunn (ed.), *Religion in American Politics* (Washington, 1989), 3.

88. Dreisbach (ed.), *Religion and Politics in the Early Republic: Jasper Adams and the Church-State Debate* (Lexington, Ky., 1996), 39–104.

89. Ibid., 113–14.

90. Ibid., 115–17. Emphasis in original.

91. Ibid., 118–20.

92. Gordon, *Mormon Question*, 74, 79.

93. Ibid., 91.

94. Hamburger, *Separation*, 291; Borden, *Jews*, 58, 69, 74; Naomi W. Cohen, *Jews in Christian America: The Pursuit of Religious Equality* (New York, 1992), 66–70; Botein, in Beeman, *Beyond*, 329–30; Joseph Blau (ed.), *Cornerstones of Religious Freedom in America* (New York, 1964), 210–32; Handy, *Undermined*, 25–27; Ward McAfee, *Religion and Reconstruction: The Public School and the Politics of the 1870s* (Albany, N.Y., 1998), 51–52.

95. Borden, *Jews*, 71; Cohen, *Jews*, 70.

96. Brewer, *The United States, a Christian Nation* (Smyrna, Ga., 1996 [original edition 1905]); Cohen, *Jews*, 101; Dunn, *Religion*, xiii.

97. Schwartz, *Common Law*, 134, 141–42.

98. Ibid., 61–62; Dreisbach, *Adams*, 115–16; James R. Stoner, in McDowell, *Reason*, 110–12, and in Gregg, *Vital Remnants*, 175–78.

99. Russell Kirk, *Rights and Duties: Reflections on Our Conervative Constitution* (Dallas, 1997), 145–46.

100. Miller, *Legal*, 201–202.

101. Borden, *Jews*, 77–78; Smith, *School Prayer*, 110; John H. Laubach, *School Prayers: Congress, the Courts, and the Public* (Washington, 1969), 22; Eidsmoe, *Christianity*, 124; Cohen, *Jews*, 36.

102. Borden, *Jews*, 79–94.

103. Hutson, *Religion*, 84–91.

104. West, *Politics*, 153–59; Hamburger, *Separation*, 200–201; John F. Wilson (ed.), *Church and State in American History* (Boston, 1965), 100–103.

105. West, *Politics*, 137–53; Leland Winfield Meyer, *The Life and Times of Colonel Richard Johnson of Kentucky* (New York, 1932), 256–61.

106. Meyer, *Johnson*, 380–84. The college was the forerunner of the modern George Washington University.

107. Nathan O. Hatch, *The Democratization of American Christianity* (New Haven, Conn., 1989), 100, 162–92.

108. Howe, *Garden*, 26, 30; Allen C. Guelzo, *Abraham Lincoln, Redeemer President* (Grand Rapids, Mich., 2000), 57, 60–62; Hamburger, *Separation*, 185.

109. Miller, *Legal*, 38; Guelzo, *Lincoln*, 62.

110. Eldon Eisenach, *The Next Religious Establishment* (Lanham, Md., 2000), 45.

111. Hamburger, *Separation*, 265.

112. West, *Politics*, 166.

113. Jonathan D. Sarna, *Religion and the State in the American Jewish Experience* (Notre Dame, Ind., 1997), 103, 112–23, 134–37, 140–48, 167–71, 175–79; Feldman, *Please*, 191–92, 201; Borden, *Jews*, 37–40, 58, 71–74, 103; Cohen, *Jews*, 48–50, 58–64, 66–70, 72–79, 100–108; Hamburger, *Separation*, 391–96.

114. Paul F. Prucha, *American Indian Policy in the Formative Years* (Lincoln, Nebr., 1962), 214–22; Handy, *Undermined*, 45–47; Gabel, *Public Funds*, 178, 303–304, 521–22; William G. McLoughlin, *Cherokees and Missionaries, 1789–1839* (New Haven, Conn., 1984), 2–4; R. Pierce Beaver, *Church, State, and the American Indian* (St. Louis, 1966), 53–58, 63–78.

115. Robert F. Berkhofer, *Salvation and the Savage, an Analysis of Protestant Missions and the American Indian Response, 1787–1862* (Lexington, Ky., 1965), 31–35, 44–69.

116. West, *Politics*, 189, 211; McLoughlin, *Cherokees*, 239–64, 308; Beaver, *Church*, 97–98, 112–13.

117. Prucha, *American Indian Policy in Crisis: Christian Reformers and the Indians, 1865–1900* (Norman, Okla., 1976), 31, 35–46, 53–55; Prucha, *The Churches and the Indian Schools, 1888–1912* (Lincoln, Nebr., 1979), 2–8; Henry E. Fritz, *The Movement for Indian Assimilation, 1860–1890* (Philadelphia,

1963), 73–79; Loring B. Priest, *Uncle Sam's Stepchildren: The Reformation of United States Indian Policy, 1865–1887* (Lincoln, Nebr., 1942), 28–41; Beaver, *Church*, 124–26, 132–51.

118. Prucha, *Crisis*, 53, 56, 62, 304; Fritz, *Movement*, 87, 102–107, 152–54, 178; Donald L. Kinzer, *An Episode of Anti-Catholicism: The American Protective Association* (Seattle, 1964), 74–79, 135–38, 205–207; Peter J. Rahill, *The Catholic Indian Missions and Grant's Peace Policy, 1870–1884* (Washington, 1953); Gabel, *Public Funds*, 527–32; Beaver, *Church*, 151, 158–63.

119. Prucha, *Crisis*, 301; Prucha, *Churches*, 26, 29–30; Kinzer, *Episode*, 74–79, 135–38, 205–207; Beaver, *Church*, 164.

120. Prucha, *Crisis*, 402; Prucha, *Churches*, 24–25, 31, 35; Beaver, *Church*, 165–67.

121. Prucha, *Churches*, 46, 58, 85–116, 149–60.

122. Ibid., 161–62, 165–68, 187, 190–93, 197, 203.

123. Charles L. Glenn, *The Myth of the Common School* (Amherst, Ma., 1988), 140–44; Robert S. Michaelson, *Piety in the Public Schools* (New York, 1970), 71–78.

124. Glenn, *Myth*, 143–41, 146–56, 172–78; Laubach, *School Prayers*, 25–26; Blau, *Cornerstones*, 160–204; McAfee, *Religion*, 9; Norman, *Conscience*, 137–43; James W. Fraser, *Between Church and State: Religion and Public Education in a Multicultural America* (New York, 1999), 24–31.

125. Lloyd P. Jorgenson, *The State and the Non-Public Schools, 1825–1925* (Columbia, Mo., 1987), 37; Michaelson, *Piety*, 78.

126. Glenn, *Myth*, 179–204, 217–19.

127. Ibid., 143, 146–56, 172–78; Michaelson, *Piety*, 81–82, 116–22, 133; Sidney E. Mead, *The Lively Experiment: The Shaping of Christianity in America* (New York, 1963), 67–68; McAfee, *Religion*, 39–40; Bradley, *Church-State*, 125–29; Fraser, *Between*, 32–43.

128. Glenn, *Myth*, 84; Jorgenson, *State*, 69–110; Hamburger, *Separation*, 202, 211–19.

129. Hamburger, *Separation*, 65, 223, 235, 288.

130. Jorgenson, *State*, 111–35, 144–215; Edward J. Power, *Religion and the Public Schools in Nineteenth-Century America: The Contribution of Orestes A. Brownson* (New York, 1996); Richard Shaw, *Dagger John: The Life and Unquiet Times of Archbishop John Hughes of New York* (New York, 1977), 139–202; Handy, *Undermined*, 36–44; Michaelson, *Piety*, 85–89; McAfee, *Religion*, 60–61, 65, 188; Laubach, *School Prayer*, 26–29; Diane Ravitch, *The Great School Wars* (New York, 1974), 27–99; Fraser, *Between*, 49–65.

131. Cohen, *Jews*, 79–87.

132. Michaelson, *Piety*, 83–84, 89–96; McAfee, *Religion*, 27–28, 31–32; Wilson, *Church-State*, 121–26; Charles Fairman, *Reconstruction and Reunion, 1864–88* (New York, 1971), I, 1310–18; Fraser, *Between*, 110.

133. Michaelson, *Piety*, 96, 100–101; McAfee, *Religion*, 34; Hampton L. Carson, *The History of the Supreme Court of the United States* (Philadelphia, 1902), II, 482–83.

134. Handy, *Undermined*, 160.

135. Gabel, *Public Funds*, 523; McAfee, *Religion*, 192; Hamburger, *Separation*, 322.

136. Kinzer, *Episode*, 7–10; Hamburger, *Separation*, 324–25; Jefferson Powell, *The Moral Tradition of American Constitutionalism* (Durham, N.C., 1993), 131; Gabel, *Public Funds*, 524; McAfee, *Religion*, 210; Carl J. Zollman, *American Church Law* (St. Paul, Minn., 1933), 75–76; Laubach, *School Prayer*, 29–30; Fraser, *Between*, 106–108.

137. McAfee, *Religion*, 198, 204; Hamburger, *Separation*, 326.

138. McAfee, *Religion*, 51.

139. Ibid., 194–95.

140. Ibid., 5–7, 163, 167.

141. Ibid., 7, 27, 29, 161, 175; Bradley, *Church-State*, 17.

142. McAfee, *Religion*, 192–94.

143. Ibid., 76, 113; Mark W. Summers, *Rum, Romanism, and Rebellion* (Chapel Hill, N.C., 2000).

144. McAfee, *Religion*, 4, 32, 179; Bradley, *Church-State*, 10.

145. McAfee, *Religion*, 192.

146. Ibid., 57–58, 213.

147. Hamburger, *Separation*, 223–29.

148. McAfee, *Religion*, 200; Zollman, *Church Law*, 9, 77.

149. Gabel, *Public Funds*, 177, 179, 302–303, 514–21. For a survey of state decisions, see Thomas Cooley, *Treatise on the Constitutional Limitations Which Rest upon the Legislative Power of the States* (Boston, 1927 [originally 1880]), II, 970–74.

150. Amar, *Bill*, 175–86, 254–57, 284; Bradley, *Church-State*, 10; Howe, *Garden*, 101.

151. *Democracy in America*, tr. Henry Reeve, ed. Phillips Bradley (New York, 1953 [originally 1833]), I, 300–14.

152. Schaff, *America, a Sketch of Its Political, Social, and Religious Character* (Cambridge, Mass., 1961 [originally 1854]), 76–77.

153. Baird, *Religion in the United States of America* (Glasgow, 1844), 253, 261–67, 386–411.

154. Bryce, *The American Commonwealth* (London, 1891), II, 576–77.

155. Story, *Commentaries on the Constitution of the United States*, ed. Ronald D. Rotunda and John E. Nowack (Durham N.C., 1987 [originally 1833]), 690–91.

156. Ibid., 698–99.

157. Ibid., 699.

158. Morgan, *Court*, 36, 40.

159. *Commentaries*, 700–702.

160. Ibid., 702–703. Emphasis added.

161. Cooley, *The General Principles of Constitutional Law* (Boston, 1898), 224–25.

162. Ibid., 225; *Constitutional Limitations*, II, 975–76.

163. *Constitutional Law*, 225.

164. Ibid., 226–27.

165. Ibid., 227; *Constitutional Limitations*, 977–78.

166. *Constitutional Limitations*, 981.

167. *Constitutional Law*, 227.

168. *Constitutional Limitations*, 974–75.

169. Ibid., 975.

170. Ibid., 960–61.

171. Bellah, in Richey (ed.), *Civil Religion*, 21–44, 255–70; Bellah and Philip E. Hammond, *Varieties of Civil Religion* (San Francisco, 1980), 11–14. For a critique of the concept, see: Mead, Wilson, and Marty, in Richey, *Civil Religion*, 45–75, 115–56, and Henry Warner Bowden, in Marty (ed.), *Modern American Religion* (Chicago, 1986), III, 16–26; Wilson, *Public*, 23–66, 19–42. Eisenach (*Disestablishment*, 53–55) rejects the term "civil religion" and proposes "national political theology" instead.

172. Eisenach, *Disestablishment*, 59.

173. Bellah, *Broken*, 176–77; Bellah, *Beyond*, 168, 176; Hammond, in Bellah and Hammond, *Varieties*, 41–42, 69, 71.

174. Hammond (with William A. Cole), in Marty, *Modern*, III, 3–15; Wilson, *Public*, 7, 18.

175. Kelly, *Politics*, 215–16, 219.

176. Guelzo, *Lincoln*, 19–20, 36–38, 49–50, 80–81, 116–19, 152–60, 313, 318–29, 342, 417–19, 441–46, 461–63; Lucas E. Morel, *Lincoln's Sacred Effort: Defining Religion's Role in American Self-Government* (Lanham, Md., 2002).

177. Hamburger, *Separation*, 293–321; Kinzer, *Episode*, 11; Eugene F. Klug, in Albert G. Huegli (ed.), *Church and State under God* (St. Louis, 1964), 371–73; Kramnick and Moore, *Godless*, 110–30.

178. Botein, in Beeman, *Beyond*, 328; Norman, *Conscience*, 77.

179. Hamburger, *Separation*, 331–37.

180. Marvin Frankel, *Faith and Freedom: Religious Liberty in America* (New York, 1994), 57.

NOTES TO CHAPTER THREE

1. 2 *Howard* 125, at 131.

2. Ibid., at 163. In 1834 an anti-Catholic mob destroyed a convent at Charlestown near Boston (Nancy Lusignan Schultz, *Fire and Roses: The Burning of the Charlestown Convent, 1834* [New York, 2000]).

3. Ray Billington, *The Protestant Crusade* (New York, 1938), 220–37.

4. 2 *Howard* 125, at 174.

5. Ibid., at 197–98.

6. Gerald T. Dunne, *Justice Joseph Story and the Rise of the Supreme Court* (New York, 1970), 331.

7. 13 *Wallace* 679, at 735.

8. *Davis v. Beason* (1890) (133 *US* 333), at 342–43.

9. 310 *US* 586, at 592.

10. 310 *US* 296, at 310.

11. 319 *US* 624, at 641.

12. Ibid., at 653–54.

13. *Prince* (321 *US* 158), at 175–76.

14. *Ballard* (322 US 78).

15. Ibid., at 86–87.

16. Ibid., at 95.

17. 330 *US* 1, at 8–16.

18. Ibid., at 23, 27.

19. Ibid., at 53–54.

20. Ibid., at 69.

21. 333 *US* 203, at 213–14.

22. Ibid., at 214–32. The concluding line was from Robert Frost's poem "Mending Wall."

23. 333 *US* 203, at 235.

24. Ibid., at 236.

25. 343 *US* 306, at 319.

26. *Torcaso* (367 US 488), at 490.

27. *McGowan* (366 US 420), at 460–66.

28. 370 *US* 421, at 425–33.

29. Ibid., at 437–43.

30. 374 *US* 203, at 213–14.

31. Ibid., at 238–42, 270–76.

32. *Epperson* (393 US 97), at 106–107.

33. *Board of Education v. Allen* (392 US 236).

34. Ibid., at 251–52.

35. Ibid., at 254.

36. Ibid., at 256.

37. Ibid., at 258–62.

38. 397 *US* 664.

39. Ibid., at 672.

40. Ibid., at 689.

41. Ibid., at 711–14.

42. *Tilton* (403 US 672), at 695–97.

43. 403 *US* 602, at 613.

44. Ibid., at 622–23.

45. Ibid., at 627–41.

46. *Yoder* (406 US 205).

47. Ibid., at 223–24.

48. Ibid., at 241–48.

49. *Nyquist* (413 US 756), at 794.

50. *Meek* (421 US 349), at 374.

51. *Roemer* (426 US 736), at 771.

52. *Wolman* (433 US 229), at 258.

53. *Hardison* (432 US 63), at 96–97.

54. *McDaniel* (435 US 618), at 640–42.

55. *Valley Forge* (454 US 464), at 499–504.

56. Ibid., at 514–15. Powell cited Fortas's opinion in the *Flast* case (392 US 83).

57. *Larkin* (459 US 116), at 126.

58. Ibid., at 128. One of the most infamous religious atrocities in European history occurred on the feast of St. Bartholomew, August 24, 1572, when by prear-

rangement, and with the complicity of the royal government, Catholics in Paris and other French cities massacred several thousand Protestants (Henri Nogueres, *The Massacre of St. Bartholomew* [New York, 1962]).

59. *Bob Jones* (461 US 574), at 609.

60. *Marsh* (463 US 783), at 805.

61. Ibid., at 823.

62. 445 US 668, at 684.

63. Ibid., at 689.

64. Ibid., at 718–25.

65. *County of Allegheny* (492 US 573), at 589.

66. Ibid., at 629, 634.

67. Ibid., at 645.

68. Ibid., at 651.

69. Ibid., at 655, 664, 670–73.

70. Ibid., at 677–78. In George Orwell's novel *1984*, a totalitarian government manipulates language, using words in ways almost opposite to their meanings, in order to control its people.

71. 472 US 381.

72. *Aguilar* (473 US 402).

73. *Grand Rapids* (473 US 373).

74. *Bowen v. Kendrick* (487 US 589), at 617.

75. Ibid., at 639–42.

76. *Lyng* (485 US 439), at 452. *Federalist*, X, cited by O'Connor, was probably written by Madison. It did not discuss religion as such but the general subject of "factions" (*The Federalist*, ed. Jacob E. Cooke [Middletown, Conn., 1977], 56–65).

77. *Lee v. Weisman* (505 US 577), at 617.

78. Ibid., at 607.

79. Ibid., at 638.

80. 515 US 819.

81. *Capitol Square* (515 US 753), at 813–14.

82. Ibid., at 797–98, 811.

83. Ibid., at 799.

84. *Agostini* (521 US 203), at 229.

85. *Santa Fe* (530 US 290), at 319.

86. *Mitchell v. Helms* (530 US 793), at 872.

87. *Zelman* (536 US 639), at 685.

88. Ibid., at 687.

89. Ibid., at 725.

90. 98 US 145, at 162–66.

91. *Davis v. Beason* (133 US 333), at 342–44.

92. *Jacobellis v. Ohio* (378 US 184), at 197.

93. 4 *Wheaton* 518, at 634.

94. *McIntosh* (283 US 605), at 632–33.

95. *Gobitis* (310 US 586), at 593.

96. *Barnette* (319 US 624).

97. Ibid., at 658.

98. *Murdock* (319 US 105), at 131–32.
99. *Follett* (321 US 573), at 582–83.
100. 330 *US* 1, at 45.
101. Ibid., at 57–58.
102. 333 *US* 203, at 237–38.
103. *Zorach* (343 US 346).
104. *Burstyn* (1951) (347 US 495), at 537.
105. *Kedroff* (344 US 94), at 131.
106. *First Unitarian* (357 US 545), at 548.
107. *McGowan* (366 US 420), at 461–62.
108. Ibid., at 466.
109. *Schempp* (374 US 203), at 225.
110. *Torcaso* (367 US 488), at 495, fn. 11.
111. 380 *US* 163.
112. Ibid., at 165.
113. Ibid., at 167–69.
114. Ibid., at 174.
115. Ibid., at 175.
116. Ibid., at 176.
117. Ibid., at 180–81. Clark cited Tillich's *Systematic Theology* (New York, 1948) and Robinson's *Honest to God* (Philadelphia, 1963).
118. 380 *US* 163, at 182.
119. Ibid., at 182–83. Clark cited the Second Vatican Council's "Decree on Non-Christian Religions," officially titled *Nostrae Aetate* ("Our Age") (Austin Flannery, O.P. [ed.] *Vatican Council II: The Conciliar and Post-Conciliar Documents* [Northport, N.Y., 1975], 738–42). He also cited a book by an officer of the Ethical Culture Society, David Saville Muzzey—*Ethics As a Religion* (New York, 1967).
120. 380 *US* 163, at 186–87.
121. Ibid., at 188–92.
122. 398 *US* 333.
123. Ibid., at 344–67.
124. *Gilette* (401 US 437), at 464–66.
125. 406 *US* 205, at 215–16.
126. Ibid., at 248–49.
127. *Christian Echoes* (404 US 561), at 563.
128. *Wolman* (433 US 229), at 264.
129. *Thomas* (450 US 707), at 715.
130. *Larsen* (456 US 228), at 267–72.
131. *Lynch* (465 US 668) and *County of Allegheny* (492 US 573).
132. *Allegheny* (465 US 668), at 693.
133. Ibid., at 708–709.
134. Ibid., at 715–17. "Deism" is the term ordinarily used for the "religion of reason" common in the eighteenth-century Enlightenment, which held that the existence of a Supreme Being who created the universe could be known from reason but that such a being revealed nothing of itself beyond the scope of reason and that all traditional religions were therefore illusory (Paul Hazard, *European*

Thought in the Eighteenth Century [Cleveland, 1963], 44–73, 113–29; Herbert M. Morais, *Deism in Eighteenth-Century America* [New York, 1960]).

135. *Amos* (483 US 327).
136. Ibid., at 335–37.
137. Ibid., at 343–44.
138. *Lyng* (485 US 439), at 460–67.
139. *Employment Division* (494 US 872).
140. *Frazee* (489 US 829), at 833–34.
141. *Weisman* (505 US 577).
142. *Lukumi Babalu* (508 US 217).
143. *McIntosh* (283 US 605).
144. Ibid., at 624.
145. Ibid., at 633–34.
146. *Hamilton* (293 US 345), at 268.
147. *Gobitis* (310 US 586), at 593–95.
148. *Barnette* (319 US 624).
149. Ibid., at 643–44.
150. Ibid., at 651.
151. 322 US 78.
152. Ibid., at 86.
153. Ibid., at 89–90.
154. Ibid., at 93–94. See James, *The Will to Believe and Other Essays in Popular Philosophy*, ed. Frederick H. Burkhardt, et al. (Cambridge, Mass., 1979).
155. 322 US 78, at 94–95.
156. *Engel* (370 US 421).
157. Ibid., at 432.
158. Ibid., at 442–43.
159. *Schempp* (374 US 203), at 226.
160. *Sherbert* (374 US 398), at 412.
161. 374 US 203, at 313.
162. *Walz* (397 US 664), at 711.
163. *Lemon* (403 US 602), at 625.
164. Ibid., at 630–31.
165. 406 US 205, at 215–16.
166. Ibid., at 243.
167. *Weisman* (505 US 577).
168. Ibid., at 589.
169. Ibid., at 645.
170. *Prince* (321 US 158), at 165.
171. 330 US 1, at 45, 57–58.
172. *Kedroff* (344 US 94), at 131.
173. *Serbian Orthodox Diocese* (426 US 696), at 714–15.
174. *Thomas* (450 US 707), at 714.
175. 465 US 668.
176. Ibid., at 685.
177. Ibid., at 690.
178. Ibid., at 699–701.

179. Ibid., at 726–27.

180. *County of Allegheny* (492 US 573).

181. Ibid., at 678.

182. *515 US 753*.

183. *Lyng* (485 US 439).

184. Ibid., at 451–53.

185. Ibid., at 460–67, 473.

186. *330 US 1*, at 23–24.

187. *333 US 203*, at 213, 217.

188. *343 US 346*, at 316, 318–19.

189. Ibid., at 323.

190. Ibid., at 324–25.

191. *Webster's Third New International Dictionary* (Springfield, Mass., 1968).

192. *403 US 602*, at 613–14, 616–17.

193. Douglas, *Anatomy*, 24.

194. *403 US 602*, at 666–68.

195. *Tilton* (403 US 672).

196. Ibid., at 686–87.

197. Ibid., at 694.

198. *Roemer* (426 US 736).

199. Ibid., at 773–75.

200. *Yoder* (406 US 205), at 241–48.

201. *Meek* (421 US 349).

202. Ibid., at 371.

203. Ibid., at 392. Rehnquist called the majority's opinion "an *ex cathedra* pronouncement," probably a jibe at what he considered their dogmatism, since the term "ex cathedra" ("from the throne") is used for solemn pronouncements by the pope (*New Catholic Encyclopedia* [New York, 1967], V, 699).

204. *Aguilar* (473 US 402) and *Grand Rapids* (487 US 589).

205. *Wolman* (433 US 229), at 244.

206. Ibid., at 260.

207. *Stone* (449 US 39).

208. *Marsh* (463 US 783).

209. *Grand Rapids* (487 US 589).

210. *Edwards* (482 US 578), at 627.

211. *Westside Schools* (496 US 226), at 275.

212. *Weisman* (505 US 577).

213. Ibid., at 593–97.

214. Ibid., at 639.

215. *Zobrest* (509 US l), at 18–19.

216. *Kiryas Joel* (512 US 687).

217. Ibid., at 711.

218. Ibid., at 749.

219. *Zelman* (122 S.Ct. 460).

NOTES TO CHAPTER FOUR

1. The statistics are compiled from the complete list of Court members and their religions in Lee Epstein, Jeffrey A. Segel, Harold J. Spaeth, and Thomas G. Walker (eds.), *The Supreme Court Compendium: Data, Decisions, and Development* (Washington, 1994), 193–205. See also John R. Schmidhauser, in Kermit Hall (ed.), *The Judiciary in American Life: Major Historical Interpretations* (New York, 1987), 541; Albert P. Blaustein and Roy M. Mersky, *The First One Hundred Justices* (Hamden, Conn., 1978), 24.

2. Roger Finke, *The Churching of America, 1776–1990: Winners and Losers in Our Religious Economy* (New Brunswick, N.J., 1992), 55; Gaustad, *Historical Atlas of Religion in America* (New York, 1976), 52–53.

3. Albert Beveridge, *The Life of John Marshall* (Boston, 1919), IV, 69–71, 589; Leonard Baker, *John Marshall, a Life in the Law* (New York, 1974), 82, 751–52; Robert K. Faulkner, *The Jurisprudence of John Marshall* (Princeton, N.J., 1968), 35, 37, 139; Jean E. Smith, *John Marshall, Definer of a Nation* (New York, 1996), 12, 36, 406.

4. Faulkner, *Marshall*, 9, 10, 37, 137–38.

5. Ibid., 140; Baker, *Marshall*, 95.

6. Thomas C. Shevory, *John Marshall's Law: Interpretation, Ideology, Interest* (Westport, Conn., 1994), 43–44; Robert F. Newmeyer, *John Marshall and the Heroic Age of the Supreme Court* (Baton Rouge, La., 2001), 83–85.

7. James McClellan, *Joseph Story and the American Constitution* (Norman, Okla., 1971), 21; Dunne, *Story*, 48, 193, 420; R. Kent Newmyer, *Supreme Court Justice Joseph Story, Statesman of the Old Republic* (Chapel Hill, N.C., 1985), 13, 18.

8. McClellan, *Story*, 49, 119–21, 127, 136–42, 313–24; Newmyer, *Story*, 28–29, 180.

9. McClellan, *Story*, 65–74, 313–24.

10. Charles Haine, *The Role of the Supreme Court in American Government and Politics* (Berkeley, Calif., 1944), I, 412.

11. Ibid., 131.

12. Dunne, *Story*, 419–20.

13. Francis P. Weisenberger, *The Life of John McLean, a Politician on the United States Supreme Court* (Columbus, Ohio, 1937), 7.

14. Ibid., 44–45, 223–24.

15. Ibid., 77, 143–44.

16. Ibid., 175–79.

17. Bernard C. Steiner, *Life of Roger Brooke Taney, Chief Justice of the United States Supreme Court* (Baltimore, 1922), 44–47; Frank Otto Gatell, in Leon Friedman and Fred L. Israel (eds.), *The Justices of the United States Supreme Court, 1789–1969* (New York, 1969), I, 636.

18. Epstein, *Compendium*, 195.

19. Clare Cushman (ed.), *The Supreme Court Justices: Illustrated Biographies, 1789–1993* (Washington, 1993), 151; Gatell, in Friedman, *Justices*, II, 873.

20. Robert Saunders Jr., *John Archibald Campbell, Southern Moderate* (Tuscaloosa, Ala., 1997), 8; Henry G. O'Connor, *John Archibald Campbell, Associate Justice of the United States* (New York, 1971), 279–80, 287.

21. Epstein, *Compendium*, 193–205; Schmidhauser, in Hall, *Judiciary*, 541.

22. Charles W. McCurdy amd Philip J. Bergman, in Bergman, Owen M. Fiss, and McCurdy, *The Fields of the Law* (San Francisco, 1986), 6, 21; Robert McCloskey, in Friedman, *Justices*, II, 1069; Borden, *Jews*, 125.

23. Charles Fairman, *Mr. Justice Miller and the Supreme Court, 1862–1890* (Cambridge, Mass., 1939), 14; William Gillette, in Friedman, *Justices*, II, 1013.

24. C. Peter Magrath, *Morrison R. Waite: The Triumph of Character* (New York, 1963), 25, 306; Bruce R. Trimble, *Chief Justice Waite, Defender of the Public Interest* (Princeton, N.J., 1938), 18.

25. Trimble, *Waite*, 244.

26. Stanley I. Cutter, in Friedman, *Justices*, II, 1153–55, 1161; Melvin I. Urofsky, *The Supreme Court Justices, a Biographical Dictionary* (New York, 1994), 445; Carson, *History*, I, 461, 464; McAfee, *Religion and Reconstruction*, 51–52.

27. Strong, *Two Lectures on the Relations of Civil Law to Church Polity, Discipline, and Property* (New York, 1897), 55–59, 87–88, 98–99. The lectures were given at Union Theological Seminary (New York City) during 1874–75.

28. Ibid., 36.

29. Carson, *History*, II, 482–83; Urofsky, *Dictionary*, 315; McAfee, *Religion*, 31–35; Louis Filler, in Friedman, *Justices*, II, 1352–53.

30. Willard R. King, *Melville Weston Fuller, Chief Justice of the United States, 1888–1910* (Chicago, 1967), 12–13.

31. Ibid., 69–70; Guelzo, *For the Union of Evangelical Christendom: The Irony of Reformed Episcopalianism* (University Park, Pa., 1994), 70–71; Irving Schiffman, in Friedman, *Justices*, II, 1475–76; Carson, (*History*, II, 536) erroneously places Fuller on the opposite side in the dispute.

32. Bradley, *Miscellaneous Writings of the Late Hon. Joseph P. Bradley*, ed. Charles Bradley (Newark, 1902), 1, 365, 368, 370, 379–80; Friedman, in Friedman, *Justices*, II, 1199–1200.

33. Bradley, *Writings*, 369, 401–403, 422, 425–26.

34. Ibid., 402, 427–31, 433–35.

35. Ibid., 404–405.

36. Ibid., 404–407.

37. Ibid., 357–59.

38. Ibid., 407–20.

39. Epstein classifies him as a Unitarian (*Compendium*, 196), while Cushman (*Justices*, 234) has him an active Episcopalian.

40. James B. Murphy, *Lucius Q.C. Lamar, Pragmatic Patriot* (Baton Rouge, La., 1973), 8–11, 82–83; Cushman, *Justices*, 242; Arnold M. Paul, in Friedman, *Justices*, II, 143.

41. George Shiras III, *Justice George Shiras Jr. of Pittsburgh, Associate Justice of the Supreme Court, 1892–1903* (Pittsburgh, 1953), 20–21, 38–40, 207–10; Paul, in Friedman, *Justices*, II, 1578; Epstein, *Compendium*, 206.

42. Shiras, *Shiras*, 38–40.

43. Michael J. Brodhead, *David J. Brewer, the Life of a Supreme Court Justice, 1837–1910* (Carbondale, Ill., 1994), 1–3, 128–30, 179–80; Paul, in Friedman, *Justices*, I, 1515, 1520.

44. Brewer, *The United States, a Christian Nation* (Smyrna, Ga., 1996 [originally 1905]).

45. Tinsley E. Yarbrough, *Judicial Enigma: The First Justice Harlan* (New York, 1995), 209–10; Loren P. Beth, *John Marshall Harlan, the Last Whig Justice* (Lexington, Ky., 1992), 37, 149, 171, 187; Linda Przybyszewski, *The Republic according to John Marshall Harlan* (Chapel Hill, N.C., 1999), 47–48, 53, 55, 57; Filler, in Friedman, *Justices*, II, 1293.

46. Beth, *Harlan*, 149–50, 187.

47. Przybyszewski, *Republic*, 57–58.

48. Yarbrough, *Harlan*, 72–75; Beth, *Harlan*, 84–86; Przybyszewski, *Republic*, 54; Floyd B. Clark, *The Constitutional Theories of Justice Harlan* (Baltimore, 1915).

49. Epstein classifies him as a Lutheran (*Compendium*, 196), but James F. Watts Jr. calls him a Methodist (Friedman, *Justices*, III, 1775). The uncertainty may derive from the fact that Day's father's given name was Luther.

50. Epstein, *Compendium*, 201.

51. Ibid., 193–205.

52. Marie C. Klinkhamer, *Edward Douglass White, Chief Justice of the United States* (Washington, 1943), 1–3, 11–13, 23–25, 39–41, 52, 94, 241; Robert B. Highsaw, *Edward Douglass White, Defender of the Conservative Faith* (Baton Rouge, La., 1981), 17–18; Watts, in Friedman, *Justices*, III, 1635.

53. Matthew McDevitt, *Joseph McKenna, Associate Justice of the United States* (New York, 1974 [originally 1945]); Urofsky, *Dictionary*, 289; Watts, in Friedman, *Justices*, III, 1720, 1722, 1725; Cortez A.M. Ewing, *The Justices of the Supreme Court, 1789–1937* (Minneapolis, 1938), 27; Margaret Leech, *In the Days of McKinley* (New York, 1959), 621.

54. Philippa Sturm, *Louis D. Brandeis, Justice for the People* (Cambridge, Mass., 1984), 9–10, 224–90, 442; Lewis J. Paper, *Brandeis* (Englewood Cliffs, N.J., 1983), 200.

55. Thomas Karfunkel and Thomas W. Ryley, *The Jewish Seat: Anti-Semitism and the Appointment of Jews to the Supreme Court* (Hickville, N.Y., 1978), 44–58; Paper, *Brandeis*, 201; John A. Maltese, *The Selling of Supreme Court Nominees* (Balimore, 1995), 49–51; Alpheus T. Mason, *William Howard Taft, Chief Justice* (Lanham, Md., 1983), 72–74.

56. James E. Bond, *I Dissent: The Legacy of Justice James Clark McReynolds* (Fairfax, Va., 1992), 5, 24, 112, 116, 120, 126; Urofsky, *Dictionary*, 326; David Burner, in Friedman, *Justices*, III, 2024–25, 2033.

57. Bond, *McReynolds*, 128.

58. Ross, *Forging*, 190–93.

59. David J. Danelski, *A Supreme Court Justice Is Appointed* (New York, 1964), 43–44, 52, 56.

60. Ibid., 44, 56–63, 68, 74–75, 91–92, 195.

61. Ibid., 4–5, 19; Francis J. Brown, *The Social and Economic Philosophy of Pierce Butler* (Washington, 1945), 1, 4, 104.

62. White, *Holmes*, 404.

63. Danelski, *Appointed*, 189; Brown, *Butler*, 76. The sterilization case was *Buck v. Bell* (274 US 200).

64. Albert W. Alschuler, *Law without Values: The Life, Work, and Legacy of Justice Holmes* (Chicago, 2000), 20; White, *Holmes*, 23, 73–74; 481–82; Liva Baker, *The Justice from Beacon Hill: The Life and Times of Oliver Wendell Holmes* (New York, 1991), 57, 67, 75–77, 222, 623, 643.

65. Alschuler, *Law without Values*, 16.

66. Ibid., 26; White, *Holmes*, 448; Baker, *Justice*, 622–23.

67. Joel F. Paschal, *Justice Sutherland, a Man Against the State* (Princeton, N.J., 1951), 3, 5–6, 8, 23–25, 49–52.

68. Ibid., 52–53. Epstein classifies Sutherland as an Episcopalian (*Compendium*, 202).

69. Hughes, *The Autobiographical Notes of Charles Evans Hughes*, ed. Danelski, and Joseph E. Tulchin (Cambridge, Mass., 1973), 3, 10, 25, 27, 40, 112; Merlo J. Pusey, *Charles Evans Hughes* (New York , 1951), I, 1, 14, 25–26, 34, 56–57, 110–11.

70. Pusey, *Hughes*, I, 111–13.

71. Hughes, *Autobiography*, 25, 112–13; Pusey, *Hughes*, 1, 111–13; II, 621.

72. Pusey, *Hughes*, II, 729.

73. Epstein, *Compendium*, 201.

74. George S. Hellman, *Benjamin N. Cardozo, American Judge* (New York, 1940), 163–64, 166–67, 170; Andrew L. Kaufman, *Cardozo* (Cambridge, Mass., 1998), 23–24, 69–70, 87, 175–77, 189–90, 487, 578; Karfunkel and Ryley, *Jewish Seat*, 85–86.

75. Mason, *Taft*, 170.

76. Epstein, *Compendium*, 202.

77. Ibid., 193–205. See also Schmidhauser, *Judges*, 64–65, and Blaustein, *First Hundred*, 24. For church membership, see Finke, *Churching*, 248, and Gaustad, *Historical Atlas*, 53, 111–12, 169.

78. William E. Leuchtenberg, *The Supreme Court Reborn: The Constitutional Revolution in the Age of Roosevelt* (New York, 1995).

79. Black, *Mr. Justice and Mrs. Black: The Memoirs of Hugo L. Black and Elizabeth Black* (New York, 1986), 21, 32; Roger K. Newman, *Hugo Black, a Biography* (New York, 1994), 67–68.

80. Hugo Black Jr., *My Father, a Remembrance* (New York, 1975), 11, 13, 24, 172–74; Newman, *Black*, 521.

81. Black, *Father*, 175–76.

82. Black, *Memoirs*, 70; Dunne, *Hugo Black and the Judicial Revolution* (New York, 1977), 71–75; Black, *Father*, 104; Maltese, *Selling*, 101–104. Hamburger (*Separation*, 422–34) points out that Black's ties to the Klan were much deeper than he admitted.

83. Black, *Father*, 104.

84. Virginia V. Hamilton, *Hugo Black, the Alabama Years* (Baton Rouge, La., 1972), 70–93; Newman, *Black*, 87; Black, *Father*, 52.

85. Newman, *Black*, 104, 137; Hamilton, *Black*, 150–59.

86. Hamburger, *Separation*, 462–70.

87. Epstein lists him merely as "Protestant" (*Compendium*, 201).

88. Frankfurter, *Felix Frankfurter Reminisces* (Westport, Conn., 1978 [originally 1960]), 289–91.

89. Maltese, *Selling*, 104–107; Karfunkel and Ryley, *Jewish Seat*, 93–96.

90. Douglas, *Go East, Young Man: The Early Years* (New York, 1974), 6, 13–16, 18, 21, 60–62; James F. Simon, *Independent Journey* (New York, 1973), 1–2.

91. Douglas, *Go East*, 110; Simon, *Independent*, 44–46.

92. Douglas, *An Almanac of Liberty* (Garden City, N.Y., 1954), 172, 184, 366.

93. Douglas, *Go East*, 14–15, 110–11, 226; Douglas, *Holocaust or Hemispheric Co-Op: Cross Currents in Latin America* (New York, 1971), 71, 103–108, 112–14, 147.

94. Douglas, *A Living Bill of Rights* (Garden City, N.Y., 1961), 69.

95. Douglas, *Correspondence: Selections*, ed. Urofsky (Bethesda, Md., 1987). The priest was Charles Curran of the Catholic University of America (Washington).

96. Douglas, *Go East*, 114, 203–205, 433.

97. Douglas, *Letters*, 425–26.

98. Richard D. Lunt, *The High Ministry of Government: The Political Career of Frank Murphy* (Detroit, 1965), 23, 89; J. Woodfoorde Howard, *Mr. Justice Murphy, a Political Biography* (Princeton, N.J., 1968), 4, 57, 66–67, 72, 81, 450; Sidney Fine, *Frank Murphy* (Ann Arbor, Mich., 1975–84), 1, 11–12, 200; II, 31–32, 286.

99. Fine, *Murphy*, I, 199, 212, 435, 454; II, 238, 506–507, 511–12; Howard, *Murphy*, 168–69, 253.

100. Fine, *Murphy*, I, 255, 438, 448, 451; II, 203, 220–22, 234; III, 212; Lunt, *Ministry*, 125–26, 135.

101. Fine, *Murphy*, II, 287; III, 10, 198; Lunt, *Ministry*, 16, 21; Howard, *Murphy*, 6, 15, 33, 202, 405, 443, 445.

102. Fine, *Murphy*, I, 228, 512; II, 30–14, 83; III, 221, 230–33; Lunt, *Ministry*, 200; Howard, *Murphy*, 353.

103. Fine, *Murphy*, I, 451; III, 12; Harold Norris (ed.), *Mr. Justice Murphy and the Bill of Rights* (Dobbs, Ferry, N.Y., 1965); Howard, *Murphy*, 160.

104. Jeffrey D. Hockett, *New Deal Justice: The Constitutional Jurisprudence of Hugo Black, Felix Frankfurter, and Robert H. Jackson* (Lanham, Md., 1966), 217–18.

105. Epstein, *Compendium*, 198.

106. Fowler V. Harper, *Justice Rutledge and the Bright Constellation* (Indianapolis, 1965), 4, 336; Israel, in Friedman, *Justices*, IV, 2593. Epstein classifies Rutledge as a Unitarian (*Compendium*, 201).

107. Rutledge, *A Declaration of Legal Faith* (Lawrence, Kans., 1947), 4, 6–10, 18.

108. Howard, *Murphy*, 251, 288. Murphy's papers appear to give by far the fullest picture of the Court's deliberations in the Jehovah's Witnesses cases.

109. Peters, *Judging*, 51.

110. Ibid., 52, 55, 65–66; Howard, *Murphy*, 250, 287–88; Fine, *Murphy*, III, 186–87.

111. H. N. Hirsch, *The Engima of Felix Frankfurter* (New York, 1981), 169.

112. Howard, *Murphy*, 296, 299, 343–44, 348; Fine, *Murphy*, III, 183–87, 372–89, 430–35. Since Christianity came to Ireland in the fifth century, Murphy's surmise of only eight hundred years is puzzling.

113. Fine, *Murphy*, III, 385.

114. Ibid., III, 378; Howard, *Murphy*, 297–98.

115. Epstein, *Compendium*, 194; Howard, *Murphy*, 452.

116. Howard, *Murphy*, 448–50; Fine, *Murphy*, III, 567–71.

117. Newman, *Black*, 361–65.

118. Howard, *Murphy*, 451–52; Fine, *Murphy*, III, 571–75; Frankfurter, *From the Diaries of Felix Frankfurter*, ed Joseph P. Lash (New York, 1975), 344.

119. David Yaloff, *Pursuit of Justices: Presidential Politics and the Selection of Supreme Court Nominees* (Chicago, 1999), 34–37; Richard Kirkendall, in Friedman, *Justices*, IV, 2667; Epstein, *Compendium*, 195, 200. Epstein cassifies Minton merely as "Protestant."

120. Yaloff, *Pursuit*, 54–59; Kim E. Eisler, *A Justice for All: William J. Brennan and the Decisions Which Transformed America* (New York, 1993), 89; E. Joshua Rosenkranz and Bernard Schwartz (eds.), *Reason and Passion: Justice Brennan's Enduring Influence* (New York, 1997), 81.

121. R. Hunter Clark, *Justice Brennan, the Great Conciliator* (New York, 1990), 109–11.

122. Dickson, *Court in Conference*, 411.

123. Schwartz, *Super Chief: Earl Warren and His Supreme Court* (New York, 1983), 442; John D. Weaver, *Warren: The Man, the Court, the Era* (Boston, 1967), 168; Ed Cray, *Chief Justice, a Biography of Earl Warren* (New York, 1997), 62, 38. Warren himself merely reported that he attended a Methodist church as a boy (*The Memoirs of Earl Warren* [Garden City, N.Y, 1970], 17).

124. Warren, *Memoirs*, 122–23; Warren, *Public Papers* (New York, 1959), 14–18, 74–75, 97–100.

125. Yarbrough, *John Marshall Harlan, the Great Dissenter on the Warren Court* (New York, 1992), 335.

126. Epstein, *Compendium*, 202.

127. Dennis J. Hutchinson, *The Man Who Once Was Whizzer White* (New York, 1998), 23, 197, 324. Epstein classifies White as an Episcopalian (*Compendium*, 204).

128. *Rocky Mountain News*, April 21, 2002, 1A.

129. Urofsky, *Dictionary*, 169.

130. Yaloff, *Pursuit*, 104, 118; Epstein, *Compendium*, 194.

131. Juan Williams, *Thurgood Marshall, American Revolutionary* (New York, 1998) 37, 310; Mark V. Tushnet, *Making Constitutional Law: Thurgood Marshall and the Supreme Court, 1961–1991* (New York, 1997), 180, 223, 278, 289.

132. Black, *Memoirs*, 95; Newman, *Black*, 4, 365.

133. Warren, *A Republic, If You Can Keep It* (New York, 1972), 116–19; Warren, *Memoirs*, 316.

134. Schwartz, *Super Chief*, 467.

135. Goldberg, *The Defense of Freedom: Public Papers of Arthur J. Goldberg*, ed. Daniel P. Moynihan (New York, 1966), 49, 57–59.

136. Epstein, *Compendium*, 194, 200, 201, 202. See fn. 47.

137. Yaloff, *Pursuit*, 128. The proposed candidate was Dallin Oaks, then president of Brigham Young University.

138. Richard A. Brisbin, *Justice Antonin Scalia and the Conservative Revival* (Baltimore, 1997); Christopher E. Smith and David A. Schulz, *The Jurisprudential Vision of Justice Antonin Scalia* (Lanham, Md., 1996).

139. Epstein, *Compendium*, 198; Urofsky, *Dictionary*, 277; *Eight Men and a Lady: Profiles of the Justices of the Supreme Court* (Bethesda, Md., 1990), 275, 284.

140. Urofsky, *Dictionary*, 526–27; Scott D. Gerber, *First Principles: The Jurisprudence of Clarence Thomas* (New York, 1999), 11–12.

141. Mark Zimmerman, "Justice Describes Return 'Home' to Catholic Faith," *Catholic Standard* (Washington), Apr. 22, 1999, 1, 13.

142. Edward Lazarus, *Closed Chambers: The First Eyewitness Account of the Epic Struggles inside the Supreme Court* (New York, 1998), 332; Simon, *The Center Holds: The Power Struggle inside the Rehnquist Court* (New York, 1995), 245.

143. Stevens, *The Bill of Rights, a Century of Progress* (Chicago, 1992), 19–20. Published also in Geoffrey Stone, Richard A. Epstein, and Cass R. Sunstein (eds.), *The Bill of Rights and the Modern State* (Chicago, 192), 29–32.

144. O'Connor and H. Alan Day, *Lazy B: Growing up on a Cattle Ranch in the American Southwest* (New York, 2002), 142, 286; Epstein, *Compendium*, 202.

145. *Eight Men*, 232–34.

146. Scalia, *A Matter of Interpretation: Federal Courts and the Law* (Princeton, N.J., 1997).

147. Scalia, "God's Justice and Ours," *First Things*, 123 (May, 2002), 17–21.

148. Ibid., 126 (October 2002), 8–18.

149. Breyer's daughter reported him to be an observant Jew (Chloe Breyer, *The Close: A Young Woman's First Year at Seminary* [New York, 2000], xiii).

NOTES TO CHAPTER FIVE

1. For the range of positions in the debate, see Rakove (ed.), *Interpreting the Constitution: The Debate over Original Intent* (Boston, 1990). For further views, see: Scalia, *Matter*, with replies by Lawrence Tribe and Ronald Dworkin; Bork, *Tempting*, 143–85; Mark V. Tushnet, *Red, White, and Blue: A Critical Analysis of Constitutional Law* (Cambridge, Mass., 1988), 35–68, 168–72; Michael Perry, *Morality, Politics, and Law* (New York, 1988), 128–65, and *The Constitution in the Courts* (New York, 1994), 9–58; John Hart Ely, *Democracy and Distrust: A Theory of Judicial Review* (Cambridge, Mass., 1980); Stanford Levinson, *Constitutional Fate* (Princeton, N.J., 1988); David Richards, *Toleration and the Constitution* (New York, 1986), 34–41, and *Foundations of American Constitutionalism* (New York, 1989), 3–15; Derek Davis, *Original Intent: Chief Justice Rehnquist and the Course of American Church-State Relations* (Buffalo, 1991); Levy, *Original Intent and the Framers' Constitution* (New York, 1988); Earl M. Maltz, *Rethinking Constitutional Law* (Lawrence, Kans., 1994); Schwartz, *New Right*, 7–35; Ronald B. Flowers, in Brauer, *Lively*, 161–84; Christopher Wolfe, *How to Read the Constitution: Originalism* (Lanham, Md., 1996).

2. Warren, *Republic*, 117.

3. Howe, *Garden*, 15, 154; Yehudah Mirsky, in Murphy, *Bill of Rights*, II, 163.

4. Howe, *Garden;* Corwin, *A Constitution of Powers in a Secular State* (Charlottesville, Va., 1951), 109–16, and in Murphy, *Religious Freedom*, I, 345–64. For other criticisms of the Court's understanding of original intent and religion, see: John Courtney Murray, in McCloskey, *Essays*, 317–41; Joseph H. Brady, *Confusion Twice Confounded: The First Amendment and the Supreme Court* (South Orange, N.J., 1954); Cushing Strout, in Peterson and Vaughan, *Virginia Statute*, 219; Levy, *Judgments: Essays on American Constitutional History* (Chicago, 1972), 77–78; Cord, *Separation*, 117–28, and in Murphy, *Religious Freedom*, I, 307–19; Rodney R. Smith, *School Prayer and the Constitution* (Wilmington, Del., 1987); Dreisbach, *Real Threat*.

5. Bobbitt, *Constitutional Fate*, 30–31; Levy, *Judgments*, 77.

6. Kalman, *Realism at Yale*, 9, 43.

7. Douglas, *The Court Years, 1939–1975* (New York), 8.

8. Irving Brant, in Harper, *Rutledge*, xii.

9. Rutledge, *Declaration*, 16–17.

10. Levy, *The Supreme Court under Earl Warren* (New York, 1972), 9, and *Establishment Clause*, 164.

11. Goldberg, *Equal Justice: The Warren Era of the Supreme Court* (New York, 1971), 25–26.

12. Tushnet, *Red*, 65.

13. For a variety of views, see: Paul G. Kauper, *Religion and the Constitution* (Baton Rouge, La., 1964), 55–56; Tushnet, *Red*, 253; Howe, *Garden*, 138, and in William Lee Miller (ed.), *Religion in a Free Society* (New York, 1958), 55; Arlin M. Adams, and Charles J. Emmerich, *A Nation Dedicated to Religious Liberty* (Philadelphia, 1990), 48; Levy, *The Establishment Clause* (New York, 1986), 167, and *Judgments: Essays on American Constitutional History* (Chicago, 1972), 77; McCloskey, in Paul Murphy (ed.), *The Bill of Rights: Religious Freedom: Separation and Free Exercise* (New York, 1990), II, 89.

14. Howe, *Garden*, 138, 140; Corwin, *Constitution of Powers*, 114; Lawrence Tribe, *On Reading*, 249, 253; Michael W. McConnell, in Stone, Epstein, and Sunstein, *Bill of Rights*, 118, 158; Christopher F. Mooney, *Boundaries Dimly Perceived: Law, Religion, Education and the Common Good* (Notre Dame, Ind., 1990), 75; Douglas Laycock, in Kelley, *Government Intervention*, 46; Franklin I. Gamwell, *The Meaning of Religious Freedom* (Albany, N.Y., 1995), 162. For the argument that the Establishment Clause should not be restricted by the Free-Exercise Clause, see: Sadurski, *Moral Pluralism*, 170; Kurland, in Sadurski, *Law and Religion*, 111; Tushnet, in ibid., 212; Rogers M. Smith, in Monsma, *Equal Treatment*, 181; Leo Pfeffer, in Murphy, *Bill*, I, 203.

15. Amar, *The Bill of Rights* (New Haven, Conn., 1998), 33–34, and in Ronald Hoffman and Peter J. Albert (eds.), *The Bill of Rights* (Charlottesville, Va., 1997), 312–14; Peter J. Ferrara, *Religion and the Constitution* (Washington, 1983), 40–41.

16. Howe, *Garden*, 72–85, 101–102, 172; David Lowenthal, *No Liberty, No License: The Forgotten Logic of the First Amendment* (Dallas, 1997), 232.

17. For a sustained critique of the Court's 1947–48 use of precedent, see Brady, *Confusion*, 50–126. For example, Rutledge dismissed the *Bradfield* decision as a

distortion and erroneously claimed that in *Quick Bear* the Court held that direct payments of public funds to religious schools was unconstitutional. He cited President Grant's proposal for a constitutional amendment banning such aid, omitting the obvious fact that Grant did not believe that the Fourteenth Amendment already served that purpose, as Rutledge claimed it did. In the justices' deliberations before reaching a final decision, Chief Justice Fred M. Vinson invoked the *Cochran* precedent, but Frankfurter replied that "since then much has changed" (Dickson, *Court in Conference*, 400).

18. Bradley, *Strange Career*, 2; Berns, *First Amendment*, 50; Jonathan Weis, in Sadurski, *Law and Religion*, 88; William Gorman, in Dallin Oaks (ed.), *The Wall between Church and State* (Chicago, 1963), 48; Sadurski, *Moral Pluralism*, 189; Smith, *Foreordained Failure*, 63; Howe, *Garden*, 165, and in Miller, *Religion and Free Society*, 60; Rakove, *Original Meanings: Politics and Ideas in the Making of the Constitution* (New York, 1996), 312; Monsma, *Positive Neutrality*, 52; Jelen, in Segers and Jelen, *Wall*, 42; Kauper, *Religion*, 43; Schwartz, *Warren Court*, 107–108, 114; Murray, in McCloskey, *Essays*, 329; Adams and Emmerich, *Nation Dedicated*, 170, 80. Kurland argues that government should not take account of religion, either positively or negatively, in formulating public policy (*Church, State, and the Supreme Court* [Chicago, 1961]; *Church and State* [Chicago, 1975]; *Religion and Law*). For a critique of Kurland's position, see Jesse H. Choper, *Securing Religious Liberty* (Chicago, 1995), 21–24, and in Murphy, *Bill of Rights*, I, 159, Alan Wolfe, in ibid., 247–57; Kauper, *Religion*, 16. For a defense of Kurland's position see Weber, in Dunn, *Religion in Politics*, 30–32.

19. Douglas, *Bible and Schools*, 4.

20. Gedicks and Hendrix, *Choosing*, 3–4; Smith, *Liberalism*, 19, 21; Gamwell, *Meaning*, 8; Berns, *Taking*, 164, 170, 180; and in Muncy, *End of Democracy*, I, 71; Tushnet, *Red*, 262, and in Marty, *Modern*, III, 317; Mead, *Nation*, 93; Evans, *Interpreting*, 32; Sullivan, *Paying*, 159.

21. Jeffrey James Poelvoorde, in Goldwin, *How Does Constitution Work?*, 150–51.

22. Wolfe, *How to Read*, 171.

23. Ibid., 171.

24. Milner S. Ball, in Witte and Alexander, *Weightier Matters*, 308.

25. Carl Esbeck, in Derek Davis and Barry Hankins (eds.), *Welfare Reform and Faith-Based Organizations* (Waco, Tex., 1990), 184–85.

26. Stevens, in Stone, Epstein, and Sunstein, *Bill of Rights*, 29. There is no evidence that the Framers were mindful of the hanging of witches in colonial times.

27. Ronald F. Thiemann, *Religion in Public Life* (Washington, 1996), 97.

28. M. James Perton, *Apocalypse Delayed: The Story of the Jehovah's Witnesses* (Toronto, 1985), 127, 136, 143; Peters, *Judging*, 1–8, 17, 33–35, 72–163, 180, 210–11, 217; Michael Kent Curtis (ed.), *The Constitution and the Flag* (New York, 1993), I, 281.

29. Dickson, *ourt in Conference*, 405. Frankfurter's reference was to *The American Commonwealth* (London, 1891), by the English nobleman James Bryce. However, Frankfurter completely misconstrued Bryce, who actually wrote that the American system depended on the acceptance of Christianity as the common religion (*AC*, II, 576–77).

30. Dickson, *Court in Conference*, 424.

31. Michael Wolstertorff, in Theodore R. Sizer (ed.), *Religion and Public Education* (Washington, 1982), 10–12; Berns, *First Amendment*, 71; Frederick M. Gedicks and Roger Hendrix, *Choosing the Dream: The Future of Religion in American Public Life* (New York, 1991), 4, and Gedicks, *The Rhetoric of Church and State* (Durham, N.C., 1995), 40; Steven D. Smith, *Getting over Equality, a Critical Diagnosis of Religious Freedom in America* (New York, 2001), 81; Stanford Levinson, in Soterios A. Barber and Robert M. George (eds.), *Constitutional Politics* (Princeton, N.J., 2001), 207.

32. Glendon A. Schubert, *The Constitutional Polity* (Boston, 1970), 167–73; Laubach, *Schoool Prayers*, 147–154; Donald E. Boles, *The Bible, Religion, and the Schools* (Ames, Iowa, 1961); Robert Sidorksi (ed.), *Prayer in the Public Schools* (New York, 1993), I, 411–73; William M. Beaney and Edward S. Beiser, in Theodore L. Becker and Malcolm M. Feeley (eds.), *The Impact of Supreme Court Decisions* (New York, 1973), 22–36; Alley, *School Prayer*, 107–214; Smith, *School Prayer*, 265–84; Charles E. Rice, *The Supreme Court and Public Prayer* (New York, 1964), 149–57; Monsma, *Positive Neutrality*, 2.

33. Ackerman, *We the People*, II. In formulating his thesis, Ackerman does not mention the religion cases.

34. Goldberg, *Equal Justice*, 8.

35. Hamburger, *Separation*, 10, 235–40, 449.

36. Daryl R. Fair, in Formacola and Morken, *Everson*, 3–7; Hamburger, *Separation*, 454–63; Michaelson, *Piety*, 170–81.

37. Hambuger, *Separation*, 477; Ivers, *Build a Wall*, 82, 120.

38. Newman, *Black*, 364; Hamburger, *Separation*, 469.

39. Hugo Black Jr., *My Father*, 104; Dunne, *Black*, 268–69; Newman, *Black*, 521. Blanshard's works included *American Freedom and Catholic Power* (Boston, 1949) and *Communism, Democracy, and Catholic Power* (Boston, 1951). For the Masonic presence on the Court, see Hamburger, *Separation*, 451.

40. Schwartz, *New Right*, 54.

41. Cooper, *Battles*, 132.

42. Howard, *Murphy*, 449.

43. Dickson, *Court in Conference*, 401–402. Rutledge's reference to textbooks was presumably to the *Cochran* decision. The Court paid minimal attention to that case in its *Everson* decision, and Rutledge's comment indicates that he thought *Cochran* had been wrongly decided.

44. Douglas, *Bible and Schools*, 61.

45. Douglas, *Letters*, 113. Wiececk refers to "the scarcely concealed anti-Catholicism of Black and Douglas" (*Libery under Law*, 173). Lucius Powe Jr. says that both were "classic mid-century liberals who found anti-Catholicism an acceptable and respectible prejudice," and refers to "their thorough-going, long-standing anti-Catholicism" (*The Warren Court and American Politics* [Cambridge, Mass., 2000], 190, 368). Referring to the members of the Warren Court, Tushnet says that "Others represented traditional anti-Catholic views about religion and politics." (*Warren Court*, 20).

46. Harold E. Fey, in Oaks, *Wall*, 38. Fey was editor of *The Christian Century*, the leading liberal Protestant journal in the country. Stephen Carter argues that given the anti-Catholic history of the issue, the Court should hesitate to use the Establishment Clause to deny Catholic schools public aid (*The Dissent of the Governed, a Meditation on Law, Religion, and Loyalty* [Cambridge, Mass., 1998], 129).

47. Howard, *Murphy*, 449–50; Fine, *Murphy*, III, 569; Simon, *The Antagonists: Hugo Black Felix Frankfurter, and Civil Liberties in Modern America* (New York), 181; Frankfurter, *Diaries*, 344.

48. Fine, *Murphy*, III, 574.

49. Dickson, *Court in Conference*, 416.

50. Ibid., 423.

51. Sarna and Dalin, *Jewish Experience*, 251.

52. Hamburger, *Separation*, 470–72; Ivers, *Build Wall*, 26.

53. Alley, *School Prayer*, 97.

54. Esbeck, in Kelley, *Government Intervention*, 41–42.

55. Ivers, *Build Wall*, 190, 209.

56. Ivers, *Build*, 152, 177; Cohen, *Jews*, 177, 182–84; Jacob J. Petuchowski, in Dalin (ed.), *American Jews and the Separationist Faith* (Washington, 1993), 101; Sarna, *Religion*, 215, 266. For the argument that the Religion Clauses are discriminatory against Jews, see Feldman, *Please Don't* and *Law and Religion*, 261–65.

57. Tushnet, *Red*, 262; Thiemann, *Religion*, 88; Carter, *In God's Name: The Wrongs and Rights of Religion in Politics* (New York, 2000), 93, 97–115, 184; Timothy P. Jackson, in Paul J. Weithman (ed.), *Religion and Liberalism* (Notre Dame, Ind., 1997), 209; Perry, *Religion in Politics*, 59.

58. Evans, *Interpreting*, 187; Weber and Gilbert, *Private Churches*, 124, 126.

59. Wolfe, in Murphy, *Bill*, I, 268; Arthur Cohen, in Miller, *Religion*, 47.

60. Curry, *Farewell*, 56.

61. McConnell, in Stephen Macedo and Yael Tamir (eds.), *Moral and Political Education* (New York, 2002), 114.

62. Alexander Bickel, *The Supreme Court and the Idea of Progress* (New York, 1970), 124.

63. Sunstein, *The Plural Constitution* (Cambridge, Mass., 1993), 308. See also Pfeffer, *Creeds*, 79. For the argument that religious schools should either not be tolerated or should be subjected to close governmental supervision, see James G. Dwyer, *Religious Schools versus Children's Rights* (Ithaca, N.Y., 1998).

64. Dwyer, *Religious Schools*, 98.

65. Dickson, *Court in Conference*, 417.

66. McConnell, in Stone, Epstein, and Sunstein, *Bill of Rights*, 165; Choper, *Securing*, 29.

67. Tushnet, in Sadurski, *Law*, 216.

68. Webster, *Papers*, XI, 161.

69. Greenawalt, *Conviction*, 159; Perry, *Religion in Politics*, (New York, 1997), 45, 53.

70. John Rawls, *Political Liberalism* (New York, 1993), xxviii.

71. For example, one secular critic warns that "the Religious Right" threatens violence to its opponents (Frank S. Ravitch *School Prayer and Discrimination* [Boston, 1999], 80), without citing dangers from the other side. For a well-known example of violence directed at believers see James W. Fraser, *Between Church and State* (New York, 1999), 207–208.

72. Carter, *Dissent*, 66.

73. Philip L. Quinn, in Weithman, *Religion and Liberalism*, 177; Carter, *God's Name*, 73.

74. Jelen, in Seeger and Jelen, *Wall*, 3. 26. See also Audi, in Weithman, *Religion and Liberalism*, 63.

75. John Murray Cuddihy, *No Offense: Civil Religion and Protestant Taste* (New York, 1978).

76. Carter, in McConnell, Robert G. Cochrane Jr., and Angela C. Carmela (eds.), *Christian Perspectives on Legal Thought* (New Haven, Conn., 2002), 40.

77. Smith, *Getting Over*, 78.

78. For a variety of views, see: Rice, *Supreme Court*, 124; "The Williamsburg Charter," in James Davison Hunter and Os Guiness (eds.), *Articles of Faith, Articles of Peace: The Religious Liberty Clause and the American Public Philosophy* (Washington, 1990), 58–60; Sheffer, *God and Caesar*, 13; Richards, *Toleration*, 142; Tushnet, in Marty, *Modern*, III, 234, and *Red*, 276; Philip E. Johnson, in Sadurski, *Law and Religion*, 189; Tushnet, in ibid., 241; Witte, *Religion*, 239; Gedicks, *Rhetoric*, 75; Levinson, in Barber and George, *Constitutional Politics*, 213–14; Smith, *Getting Over*, 66–67, 81, 116.

79. Smith, *Foreordained*, 112, 114, 116; Sullivan, *Paying*, 159.

80. Irving Kristol, in Licht and Goldwin, *Spirit*, 85; Tushnet, in Marty, *Modern*, III, 318; Gamwell, *Meaning*, 70.

81. Douglas, *Almanac*, 115.

82. Warren, *A Republic, If You Can Keep It* (New York, 1972), 119.

83. Powe, *Warren Court*, 258.

84. McConnell, in Stone, Epstein, and Sunstein, *Bill of Rights*, 120; Thiemann, *Religion*, 96; Harold Berman, in Hunter and Guiness, *Articles*, 51.

85. Gorman, in Oaks, *Wall*, 47; McConnell, in Stone, Epstein, and Sunstein, *Bill of Rights*, 125, 172; Sandel, in Hunter and Guiness, *Articles*, 89–90; Evans, *Interpreting*, 21, 24–25, 39. Choper argues that full religious exemptions should only be given to those who fear the eternal consequences of their actions (*Securing*, 75–81). For a critique of that position, see Berns, *Taking the Constitution Seriously* (New York, 1987), 319.

86. Lowenthal, *No Liberty*, 201; Tushnet, *Red*, 265, and in Marty, *Modern*, III, 310; Monsma, *Equal Treatment*, 193; Ball, in Witte and Alexander, *Weightier Matters*, 310; Sadurski, *Moral Pluralism*, 192; Evans, *Interpreting*, 120.

87. During preliminary deliberations, Warren proposed that the *Torcaso* decision had defined "religion" as including all religions and that requiring belief in a "Supreme Being" would be discriminatory. Douglas insisted that the "right" of conscientious objection should not depend on belief in God. Clark proposed that the phrase "Supreme Being does not mean a God, but includes all religious beliefs," and several other justices agreed (Dickson, *Court in Conference*, 134–36).

88. Seeger, in Peter H. Irons, *The Courage of Their Convictions* (New York, 1988), 169–75.

89. Miton R. Konvitz, *Religious Liberty and Conscience* (New York, 1968), 99; Craycraft, *American Myth*, 41; Richards, *Toleration*, 136, 140; Tushnet, *Red*, 264, and in Marty, *Modern*, III, 305; Ball, in Witte and Alexander, *Weightier Matters*, 309; Gorman, in Oaks, *Wall*, 47; Sandel, in Hunter and Guiness, *Articles*, 89; Mansfield, *Constitutional Soul*, 218.

90. Tushnet, *Red*, 249, 264; Winifrd F. Sullivan, *Paying the Words Extra: Religious Discourse in the Supreme Court* (Cambridge, Mass., 1994), 115; Louis B. Boudin, in Curtis, *Flag Salute*, 228; Derek Davis, in Wood, *The Role of Religion in the Making of Public Policy* (Waco, Tex., 1991), 111; Carter, *The Culture of Disbelief* (New York, 1993), 130.

91. Choper, *Securing*, 64.

92. Tushnet, in Sadurski, *Law and Religion*, 238.

93. Sandel, in Hunter and Guiness, *Articles*, 87.

94. Stanley Fish, in Feldman, *Law and Religion*, 446.

95. Hadley Arkes, *First Things, an Inquiry into the First Principles of Morals and Justice* (Princeton, N.J., 1986), 180–90; Sandel, in Hunter and Guiness, *Articles*, 85–86; J. Judd Owen, *Religion and the Demise of Liberal Rationalism* (Chicago, 2001), 138.

96. Evans, *Interpreting*, 201; Wunder, *Retained*, 196–97; Martin L. Loesch, in Wunder (ed.), *Native American Cultural and Religious Freedom* (New York, 1996), 58–64; Stephen McAndrew, in ibid., 225–50; Rashelle Perry, in ibid., 335–52.

97. Thiemann, *Religion*, 132; Monsma, *Positive*, 65; McCarthy, Skillen, and Harper, *Disestablishment*, 95; Murray, *We Hold*, 21, 53; Bradley, in Robert P. Hunt and Kenneth L. Grasso (eds.), *John Courtney Murray and the American Civil Conversation* (Grand Rapids, Mich., 1992), 187; Carter, *Culture*, 134; Gamwell, *Meaning*, 70; Jelen, *To Serve God and Mammon: Church-State Relations in American Politics* (Boulder, Colo., 2000), 124–25. For the argument that the Constitution intended religion to be wholly private, see: Tushnet, *Red*, 266, and in Sadurski, *Law*, 229; Berns, in *End of Democracy?* 77.

98. Gedicks and Hendrix, *Chooosing*, 92.

99. Rawls, *Liberalism*, 32; Mead, *Old Religion*, 82, and *Lively Experiment*, 65.

100. McConnell, in Stone, Epstein, and Sunstein, *Bill of Rights*, 172; Michael Sandel, in Hunter and Guiness, *Articles*, 86; Davis, in Davis and Wood (eds.), *The Role of Government in Monitoring and Regulating Religion in Public Life* (Waco, Tex., 1993), 113; Fish, *The Trouble with Principle* (Cambridge, Mass., 1990), 41; Christopher L. Eisgruber and Lawrence G. Sager, in Feldman, *Law and Religion*, 205–206.

101. Evans, *Interpreting*, 126; Mary Ann Glendon, *Rights Talk* (New York, 1991), 67, and in Terry Eastland (ed.), *Religious Liberty in the Supreme Court* (Washington, 1993), 477; Craycraft, *American Myth*, 57; Ball, in Witte and Alexander, *Weightier Matters*, 309; Gedicks, *Rhetoric*, 52–59; Richard John Neuhaus, *The Naked Public Square: Religion and Democracy in America* (Grand Rapids, Mich., 1984), 136; Daniel J. Elazar, in Licht (ed.), *Old Rights and New* (Washington, 1993), 45; Sandel, in Hunter and Guiness, *Articles*, 89. For the argument

that the Framers did not intend to recognize group religious rights, see Clinton, *God and Man*, 161, 167.

102. Tribe, in Kelley, *Government Intervention*, 32; Gedicks and Hendrix, *Choosing*, 149.

103. Carter, *Dissent*, 20, 29. Evans, *Interpreting*, 6, 126, 180; Thiemann, *Religion*, 100, 132, 134; Glendon, *Rights Talk*, 67; Monsma, *Positive*, 198; Neuhaus, *Naked*, 136; Kelley, *Government Intervention*, 42, 5; Sadurski, *Moral Pluralism*, 194; Gedicks, *Rhetoric*, 4; Tushnet, in Marty, *Modern*, III, 321. Evans points out that communal religion need not be "conservative" in its agenda but includes, for example, religious movements for social change (*Interpreting*, 5).

104. Tushnet, *Red*, 23, 34, 186, and in Sadurski, *Law*, 233–34; Robin West, in Tushnet, *Making*, 42.

105. Gedicks and Hendrix, *Choosing*, 16, and Gedicks, *Rhetoric*, 21; Carter, *Dissent*, 19.

106. Tushnet, *Warren Court*, 126.

107. Robin West, in Tushnet, *Constitutional Law*, 44.

108. Carter, in McConnell, *Christian Perspectives*, 46.

109. Murray, *We Hold*, 306; Sandel, in Hunter and Guiness, *Articles*, 76.

110. Carter, *Culture*, 134, 141–42, 169, and *Dissent*, 62; Neuhaus, *Naked*, 142.

111. Carter, *Dissent*, 30, 48.

112. Evans, *Interpreting*, 114.

113. Arkes, *First Things*, 190.

114. McClellan, *Story*, 313–24.

115. Douglas, *An Almanac of Liberty* (Garden City, N.Y., 1954), 301. See also Douglas, *The Right of the People*, 140–41, and *The Anatomy of Liberty* (New York, 1963), 27.

116. Hunter and Guiness, *Articles*, 58–60; Sheffer, *God and Caesar*, 13; Richards, *Toleration*, 142.

117. Jonathan Weiss, in Sadurski, *Law*, 78.

118. Craycraft, *American Myth*, 83.

119. Sullivan, *Paying*, 181.

120. Sullivan, in Feldman, *Law and Religion*, 50. Sullivan offered her formula as one the Court might properly have adopted in the *Lynch* case.

121. Carter, in Sadurski, *Law*, 252, and *Choosing Dream*, 27. For a candid argument that religion is essentially irrational, see Abraham, in Goldwin and Kaufman, *How Does the Constitution Protect Religious Freedom?* 15.

122. Rutledge, *Declaration*, 4–5.

123. Howe, *Garden*, 109.

124. Berns, *First Amendment*, 78–79.

125. Adams and Emmerich, *Nation Dedicated*, 91.

126. Choper, *Securing*, 68–75; and in Sadurski, *Law*, 351–52; Evans, *Interpreting*, 58–61; Richard A. Posner, *Overcoming Law* (Cambridge, Mass., 1990), 183–84; Steven D. Smith, in Smith, Pierre Schlag, and Paul F. Campos, *Against the Law* (Durham, N.C., 1996), 184; Lowenthal, *No Liberty*, 236.

127. Evans, *Interpreting*, 73.

128. Marc Galanter, in Murphy, *Bill of Rights*, I, 413–15; McCloskey, in ibid., 137; Sullivan, *Paying*, 181; Weiss, in Sadurski, *Law*, 78.

129. Daniel A. Dombrowski, *Rawls and Religion: The Case for Political Liberalism* (Albany, N.Y., 2001), 137–38.

130. Dickson, *Court in Conference*, 421.

131. Smith, *Getting Beyond*, 104.

132. Audi, in Feldman, *Law and Religion*, 78–79; Dombrowski, *Rawls*, 108, 117.

133. Perry, in ibid., 125, and *Religion in Politics*, 66.

134. Weithman, in Weithman, *Religion and Liberalism*, 5–8.

135. Perry, *Religion in Politics*, 50, 65.

136. Greenawalt, *Religious Convictions and Public Reasons* (New York, 1995); Perry, *Religion in Politics*, 69–70.

137. Richard Danzig, in Curtis, *Flag Salute*, I, 245–47.

138. Gedicks and Hendrix, *Choosing*, 99, 106–107, 112; Thiemann, *Religion*, 154; Weiss, in Sadurski, *Law*, 82; Perry, *Religion in Politics*, 81.

139. Kent Greenawalt, *Religious Convictions and Political Choice* (New York, 1988), 253; Ben Clements, in Sadurski, *Law*, 317.

140. Perry, *Religion in Politics*, 57–59.

141. Perry, *Love and Power: The Role of Religion and Morality in American Politics* (New York, 1991), 14; in Feldman, *Law and Religion*, 129; and *Religion in Politics*, 34, 77; Evans, *Interpreting*, 114.

142. Perry, *Love*, 14, 20.

143. Perry, *Religion in Politics*, 61.

144. Abner S. Greene, in Feldman, *Law and Religion*, 231–32; Audi, in Sadurski, *Law*, 29–66. See the critique of this position by Dean M. Kelley, in Wood and Davis, *Role*, 201.

145. Fish, *Trouble*, 41.

146. Ackerman, *Social Justice*, 10, 11.

147. Danzig, in Curtis, *Constitution and Flag*, 270–73.

148. Vashti C. McCollum, *One Woman's Fight* (Boston, 1961); Gregg Ivers, *To Build a Wall: American Jews and the Separation of Church and State* (Charlottesville, Va., 1995), 79; Cohen, *Jews*, 141. The Jewish groups supporting her case dissociated themselves from McCollum's claims about religion.

149. Frank Sorauf, *The Wall of Separation: The Constitutional Politics of Church and State* (Minneapolis, 1976), 135. As in *McCollum*, some of the supporting Jewish groups found the principal plaintiffs something of an embarrassment—"fairly bigoted—with loud mouths" (Ivers, *Build Wall*, 175).

150. Fish, *Trouble*, 155, 158.

151. Manning, *Law*, 173.

152. Price, *Rights of Students*, 11, 14–15, 18, 31; Rubin, *Rights of Teachers*, 117–27.

153. Choper, *Securing*, 141, and in Murphy, *Bill*, I, 86, 88, 146.

154. Barry Lynn, *The Rights of Religious Liberty* (Carbondale, Ill., 1995), 11, 16, 20, 24.

155. Warren A. Nord, *Religion and American Education* (Chapel Hill, N.C., 1995), 266–69, 271–74, 279.

156. Goldberg, *Reconstructing*, 118.

157. Glenn, *Common*, 191.

158. Eugene F. Provenzo Jr., *Religious Fundamentalism and American Education* (Albany, N.Y., 1990), 93–94; Dwyer, *Vouchers within Reason: A Child-Centered Approach to Education Reform* (Ithaca, N.Y., 2002), 171–74. For a critique, see Philip F. Johnson, in Sadurski, *Law*, 189, and McConnell, in Macedo, *Moral and Political*, 116–17.

159. Richards, *Toleration*, 157; Ackerman, *Social Justice*, 149; Dwyer, *Vouchers*, and *Religious Schools*.

160. Dwyer, *Religious Schools*.

161. Dwyer, *Vouchers*.

162. Tribe, *Constitutional Law* (1988), 1258; Sadurski, *Moral Pluralism*, 192.

NOTES TO CONCLUSION

1. Powell, *Moral Tradition*, 276; Macedo, The *New Right versus the Constitution* (Washington, 1987), 58; Mead, *Old Religion*, 79–95, and *Lively Experiment*, 35–44; Soterios Barber, *On What the Constitution Means* (Baltimore, 1984), 135–36; Berns, in Muncy and J. Budziszewski (eds.), *The End of Democracy*, II (Dallas, 1999), 97. For an extended argument to that effect, from a "conservative" standpoint, see Craycraft, *American Myth*.

2. Rogers M. Smith, *Liberalism and American Constitutional Law in a Free Society* (Cambridge, Mass., 1990), 19–21, 31–38, 50–52; Craycraft, *American Myth*, 36–66; Berns, *Taking*, 164; Bellah, *Varieties*, 35–36.

3. Richards, *Toleration*, 94, 118, and in Sadurski, *Law*, 128.

4. Richards, *Foundations*, 30–31, 184, and in Sadurski, *Law*, 132–33.

5. Willmoore Kendall, *The Basic Symbols of the American Political Tradition* (Baton Rouge, La., 1976), 73.

6. Murray, *We Hold*, 36–37; Harvey Mansfield, in Goldwin, *How Does Constitution Work?*, 1–14; Poelvoorde, in ibid., 151; Alvarez and Richard M. Battistori, in Thurow, *Constitutionalism*, III, 255–95. See the counterargument by Wayne Ambler, in ibid., 296–305.

7. Harry S. Stout, in Noll, *Religion and Politics*, 73.

8. Cooley, *Constitutional Limits*, II, 960–61.

9. For a critique of the decision, arguing that it permitted a misuse of the power of the Internal Revenue Service, see Lief H. Carter, *Contemporary Constitutional Lawmaking* (New York, 1985), 144–45.

10. McConnell, in Stone, Epstein, and Sunstein, *Bill of Rights*, 151, 155.

11. Wolfe, *Rise*, 316.

12. Kurland, in Francis Graham Lee (ed.), *Neither Conservative nor Liberal: The Burger Court on Civil Rights and Liberties* (Malabar, Fla., 1983), 74–75.

13. Story, "Natural Law," in McClellan, *Story*, 313.

14. Cooley, *Constitutional Limits*, II, 976–77, 986.

15. Murray, *We Hold*, 41; Arkes, *Beyond*, 64; Smith, in Smith, Schlag, and Campos, *Against Law*, 100, 180. Ely, on the other hand, argues that natural law played little role in the Constitution and was employed only vaguely and contradictorily in later disputes, such as that over slavery (*Democracy and Distrust*, 49–51).

16. Harold Berman, *The Interaction of Law and Religion* (Atlanta, 1993).

17. Smith, *Foreordained Failure*, 101–102.

18. Herget, *Jurisprudence*, 228–61; Robert M. George, *The Clash of Orthodoxies* (Wilmington, Del, 2001), 67–83; Feldman, *Legal Thought*, 55, 673–75; Ketcham, *Framed*, 116–17; Franck, *Imperial*, 161; Wiceck, *Lost*, 36; Shavory, *Marshall's Law*, 123.

19. Gordon, *Mormon Question*, 11, 22–23, 38, 66, 69–74, 79, 91, 126, 135, 138–40, 222, 228.

20. Herget, *Jurisprudence*, 147–227; Feldman, *Legal Thought*, 106–17; Kalman, *Realism at Yale*, and *The Strange Career of Legal Realism* (New Haven, Conn., 1996).

21. Arkes, *The Return of George Sutherland* (Princeton, N.J., 1994), 26–27.

22. Purcell, *Crisis;* Monsma, *Positive*, 126; Ronald Kahn, *The Supreme Court and Constitutional Theory, 1953–1993* (Lawrence, Kans., 1994), 69.

23. Schwartz, *Main Currents*, 437–42.

24. Larry Cata' Backer, in Feldman, *Law and Religion*, 450.

25. Purcell, *Crisis*, 206; Kahn, *Supreme Court*, 70.

26. Gary J. Jacobsohn, *The Supreme Court and the Decline of Constitutional Aspiration* (Totowa, N.J., 1986), 184; Steven C. Rockefeller, *John Dewey: Religious Faith and Democratic Humanism* (New York, 1991).

27. White, *Patterns*, 132. The most ambitious attempt to revive natural law was Murray, *We Hold*. For recent natural-law arguments see especially the works of Robert M. George: *Natural Law Theories* (New York, 1992); *Natural Law, Liberalism, and Morality* (New York, 1996); *The Autonomy of Law* (New York, 1996); *In Defense of Natural Law* (New York, 1999); *Making Men Moral* (New York, 1993); and *Clash*. See also Clinton, *God and Man*, 221; Smith, in Smith, Schlag, and Campos, *Against Law*, 107; Arkes, *Beyond;* Brian Stiltner, *Religion and the Common Good* (Lanham, Md., 1999), 89–90.

28. Maltz, *Rethinking*, 116.

29. Smith, *Constitution*, 98.

30. Howard, *Murphy*, 443.

31. Tushnet, *Red*, 149; Arkes, *Sutherland*, 28, 282–83; Feldman, *Legal Thought*, 148–50, 193; Greenawalt, *Private Consciences*, 82; Elazar, in Licht, *Old Rights*, 45; Smith, in Smith, Schlag, and Campos, *Against Law*, 188; Sadurski, *Moral Pluralism*, 21; Jacobsohn, *Supreme Court*, 184; Brisbin, *Scalia*, 79.

32. White, *Patterns*, 150–53.

33. Steven D. Smith, *The Constitution and the Pride of Reason* (New York, 1998), 98, 112; Feldman, *Legal Thought*, 148–50; Greenawalt, *Private Consciences*, 82; Tushnet, *Red*, 137; Arkes, *Beyond*, 13.

34. Robin West, in Tushnet, *Constitutional Law*, 73; Bork, *Tempting*, 6; Arkes, in Austin Sarat and Thomas R. Kearns (eds.), *Legal Rights* (Ann Arbor, Mich., 1996), 202.

35. Arkes, *Beyond*, 14–16, and *Sutherland*, 28; Harry V. Jaffa, *Original Intent and the Framers of the Constitution* (Washington, 1994); Brisbin, *Scalia*, 333.

36. Rawls, *Liberalism*, xxvii–viii.

37. Levinson, *Constitutional Faith*, 74, 88; Smith, *Liberalism*, 91.

38. Charles F. Taylor, in Hunter and Guiness, *Articles*, 108; Novak, *Two Wings*, 59; John Tomasi, in Macedo and Yael Tamir (eds.) *Moral and Political Education* (New York, 2002), 194, 198–202.

39. Poelvoorde, in Goldwin, *How Does Constitution Work?* 325.

40. Jelen, in Seger and Jelen, *Wall*, 11; Dwyer, *Vouchers*, 225.

41. Graham Walker, in Gary L. Gregg, *Vital Remnants: America's Founding and the Western Tradition* (Wilmington, Del., 1999), 102–103.

42. John F. Wilson, in Dunn, *Religion*, 88; Smith, *Getting*, 68.

43. McCarthy, Skillen, and Harper, *Disestablishment*, 92.

44. Evans, *Interpreting*, 13.

45. Mooney, *Boundaries*, 82; Canavan, *Pluralism*, 21; Bork, in Muncy, *End*, I, 121–23.

46. Bork, in Muncy, *End*, I, 182, 184.

47. Sadurski, *Moral Pluralism*, 200.

48. Gedicks and Hendrix, *Choosing*, 88, 90.

49. Bobbitt, *Constitutional Fate*, 94.

50. Rawls, *Liberalism*, 231.

51. Tushnet, *Red*, 137, 149.

52. Rawls, *Liberalism*, xxviii.

53. Ibid., xxvii–viii, 138, 140; Daniel A. Dombrowski, *Rawls and Religion* (Albany, N.Y., 2001), 89, 110; Galston, *Liberal Purposes*, 80; Tomasi, in Macedo and Tamir, *Moral and Political*, 207.

54. The seminal argument is Murray, *We Hold*. Craycraft suggests that Murray was being "ironic" and did not himself believe that the American regime was benign, as he claimed (*American Myth*, 104). Bradley argues that Murray underestimated the degree to which Protestantism underlay the Religion Clauses, thus making their status as "articles of peace" problematic (Hunt and Grasso, *Murray*, 190–94).

55. Smith, *Constitution and Pride*, 77–79; Smith, in Smith, Schlag, and Campos, *Against Law*, 178; Tushnet, *Red*, 25.

56. Craycraft, *American Myth*, 100.

57. Ketcham, *Framed*, 116.

58. Gamwell, *Meaning*, 193; Taylor, in Hunter and Guiness, *Articles*, 109; Neuhaus, *Naked*, 157; Lowenthal, *No Liberty*, 250; Campos, in Smith, Schlag, and Campos, *Against Law*, 135, 159; Evans, *Interpreting*, 86; Wolfe, *How to Read*, 97, 326.

59. Hammond, in Bellah, *Varieties*, 160.

60. Francis Canavan, *The Pluralism Game: Pluralism, Liberalism, and the Moral Conscience* (Lanham, Md., 1995), 40. For a sustained critique of the Court's power, see the essays in Muncy, *End*, I and II. For a candid argument that a "progressive" Court should assume much of the responsibility for government, because of the failures of both the citizens and the legislators, see Arthur S. Miller, *Towards Increased Judicial Activism* (Westport, Conn., 1982).

61. Ackerman, *We People*; Macedo, *Liberal Virtues* (New York, 1990), 34, 37.

62. Firmage, *Zion*, 259.

63. Michael E. Smith, in Marty, *Modern*, II, 237. Reportedly Justice O'Connor said, during the Court's conference over the *Jones* case, "I argue that compelling public policy overcomes the First Amendment," and the other justices agreed (Bernard Schwartz, *The Ascent of Pragmatism* [Reading, Mass., 1990], 208).

64. Dickson, *Court in Conference*, 419.

65. Smith, *Liberalism*, 232.

66. Macedo, *Liberal Virtues*, 54–55.

67. Sadurski, *Moral Pluralism*, 189.

68. Macedo in Barber, *Constitutional Politics*, 167. Macedo refers to the liberal regime as "our *political* order" (emphasis in original), implying that liberals have a proprietary claim that others do not.

69. Ibid., 170.

70. Carter, *Dissent*, 56.

71. For a brief survey of religious involvement in public life throughout American history see Kelley, in Wood, *Role*, 159–67.

72. Tushnet, *Red*, 249.

73. Howe, *Garden*, 15.

74. Scott S. Idelman, in Feldman, *Law and Religion*, 178.

75. Carter, *God's Name*, 168–69.

76. Dickson, *Court in Conference*, 403 (emphasis in original).

77. *Acts of the Apostles* (Authorized Version), 22, verse 28: "And the chief captain answered, 'With a great sum obtained I this freedom.' And Paul said, 'But I was born free.' " Rutledge's error was repeated by Abraham, in Goldwin and Kaufman, *How Does the Constitution Protect Religious Freedom?* 39.

78. Berman, in Hunter and Guiness, *Articles*, 49–50; Adams and Emmerich, *Nation Dedicated*, 48; Galanter, in Murphy, *Bill of Rights*, I, 416; Carl H. Esbeck, in Monsma and J. Christopher Soper (eds.), *Equal Treatment of Religion in a Pluualistic Society* (Grand Rapids, Mich., 1998), 13–14; Levenson, in Barber, *Constitutional Politics*, 201–203.

79. Weber, in Dunn, *Religion and Politics*, 29; Carter, *Culture*, 200; Witte, *Religion*, 237; Destro, in Monsma and Soper, *Equal*, 121.

80. Levenson, in Barber, *Constitutional Politics*, 203, 209.

81. Weber, *Private Churches*, 140, 143; McConnell, in Stone, *Bill of Rights*, 128, 185; Choper, *Securing*, 41; Presser, *Recapturing*, 227; Monsma, *When Sacred and Secular Mix: Religious Non-Profit Organizations and Public Money* (Lanham, Md., 1998); McConnell, in Eugene W. Hickok (ed.), *The Bill of Rights* (Charlottesville Va., 1991), 64; Witte, *Religion and Constitution*, 237.

82. McConnell, in Stone, *Bill of Rights*, 134; Monsma, *Positive*, 39; Esbeck, in Monsma and Soper, *Equal Treatment*, 13.

83. E. J. Dionne and Ming Hsu Chen (eds.), *Sacred Places, Civic Purposes: Should Government Aid Faith-Based Charity?* (Washington, 2001); Davis and Hankins, *Welfare Reform*; Glenn, *The Ambiguous Embrace: Government and Faith-Based Schools and Social Agencies* (Princeton, N.J., 2000).

84. Melissa Rogers, in Dionne and Chen, *Sacred Places*, 137–42; Julie A. Segal in Davis and Hankins, *Welfare Reform*, 12–23.

85. Davis, in Davis and Hankins, *Welfare Reform*, 285–90.

86. McConnell, in Stone, Epstein, and Sunstein, *Bill of Rights*, 165.

87. Alan Brownstein, in Davis and Hankins, *Welfare Reform*, 223, 227, 241.

88. James Q. Wilson, in Dionne and Chen, *Sacred Places*, 160–70; Stanley Carlson-Thies, in Davis and Hankins, *Welfare Reform*, 114–18.

89. Brownstein, in Davis and Hankins, *Welfare Reform*, 241–44.

90. Ronald J. Sider and Heidi Rolland Unruh, in ibid., 132–33.

91. Esbeck, in Davis and Hankins, *Welfare Reform*, 175–85; Sider and Unruh, in ibid., 198.

92. Tushnet, *Red*, 272–73, and in Marty, *Modern*, III, 320; Neuhaus, in Muncy, *End of Democracy*, I, 5, 6; Bork, in ibid., 10–17.

93. Monsma, *Positive*, 32.

94. William Lee Miller, in Kelley, *Government Interaction*, 41–49.

95. Kathleen M. Sullivan, in Stone, *Bill of Rights*, 221.

96. Murray, in McCloskey, *Essays*, 327.

97. Rogers, in Davis and Hankins, *Welfare Reform*, 63–78.

98. Ibid., 249, 257, 266.

99. Weber, *Equal Separation*, 81; Monsma, in ibid., 181; Ball, in Witte and Alexander, *Weightier Matters*, 309; Sullivan, *Paying*, 126, 129, 131, 135; Adams and Emmerich, *Nation Dedicated*, 127.

100. Gedicks and Hendrix, *Choosing*, 71–73, 75, 88.

101. Owen, *Religion and Rationalism*, 141.

102. Monsma, *Positive*, 196; Evans, *Interpreting*, 13, 180; Campos, in Campos, Schlag, and Smith, *Against Law*, 200; Carter, *Culture*, 230.

103. Richards, *Toleration*, 136, 140.

104. Hammond, *With Liberty for All* (Louisville, 1998), 54.

105. Gamwell, *Meaning*, 65, 67, 70–71.

106. Jacobsohn, *Supreme Court*, 163.

107. Carter, *Culture*, 37; Gedicks and Hendrix, *Choosing*, 143, 148, 154; Perry, *Religion and Politics*, 59.

108. Carter, *Culture*, 29, 134.

109. Canavan, *Pluralist Game*, 40; Wolfe, *Essays*, 123–26; Greenawalt, *Private Consciences*, 204.

110. Murray, *We Hold*, 53.

111. Michael E. Smith, in Marty, *Modern*, III, 280.

112. Monsma, *Positive*, 43.

113. Neuhaus, *Naked*, 159.

114. Dean M. Kelley, *Why Churches Should Not Pay Taxes* (New York, 1977), and in Weber, *Equal Separation*, 33–38; Perry, *Love*, 73.

115. George, *Making*, 220.

116. Peter Berger, in Hunter and Guiness, *Articles*, 117.

117. George, *Defense*, 125–38; Mansfield, *Constitutional Soul*, 218, and in Goodwin, *How Does Constitution Work?* 14.

118. Evans, *Interpreting*, 40; J.G.A. Pocock, in Peterson and Vaughan, *Virginia Statute*, 71.

119. Wolfe, *Essays*, 95.

120. Carter, in McConnell, *Christian Perspectives*, 43.

121. Tushnet, *Red*, 273.

122. Carter, in McConnell, *Christian Perspectives*, 51.

123. Warren, *Memoirs*, 74–75.

124. Tushnet, *Red*, 270; West, in Tushnet, *Constitutional Law*, 44; Adams and Emmerich, *Nation Dedicated*, 50; Berns, *First Amendment*, 26; Carter, *Contemporary*, 144–46.

125. Monsma, *Positive*, 46; Mansfield, *America's Constitutional Soul* (Baton Rouge, La., 1991), 114.

126. Esbeck, in Kelley, *Government Intervention*, 54.

127. Drakeman, *Church-State*, 111.

128. Idelman, in Feldman, *Law and Religion*, 187.

129. Bradley, in Hunt and Grasso, *Murray*, 187–88; Arthur Cohen, in Miller, *Religion and Free Society*, 43; Backer, in Feldman, *Law and Religion*, 453.

130. Evans, *Interpreting*, 239, 241–42.

131. J. Judd Owen, *Religion and the Demise of Liberal Rationalism* (Chicago, 2001), 117–19.

132. Gamwell, *Meaning*, 177; Everett, *Religion*, 142.

133. Dwyer, *Religious Schools*, 98.

134. Campos, in Smith, Schlag, and Campos, *Against Law*, 200.

135. Thiemann, *Religion*, 96–97.

136. Macedo, *Liberal Virtues*, 64.

137. Stanley Fish, *There's No Such Thing as Free Speech* (New York, 1994), 217, 297.

138. Berns, *Taking*, 177; Mead, *Lively Experiment*, 65.

139. Gamwell, *Meaning*, 36; Rawls, *Liberalism*, xxvii, xxviii, 4, 151; Bellah and Hammond, *Varieties*, 126; Murray, *We Hold*, 53, 73; Jacobsohn, *Supreme Court*, 184.

140. Posner, *Overcoming*, 12.

141. Gamwell, *Meaning*, 40.

142. Dwyer, *Religious Schools*, 82, 143.

143. Smith, *Getting Over*, 7.

144. Backer, in Feldman, *Law and Religion*, 425, 430.

145. Goldberg, *Reconsecrating*, 51–52.

146. Kramnick and Moore, *Godless*, 165.

147. Perry, *Love*, 138.

148. Ibid., 100; Gamwell, *Meaning*, 41.

149. George, *Clash*, 51–57; Gorman, in Oaks, *Wall*, 50.

150. Amy Gutmann and Dennis Thompson, *Democracy and Disagreement* (Cambridge, Mass., 1996), 66; Wilbur Edel, *Defenders of the Faith: Religion and Politics from the Pilgrim Fathers to Ronald Reagan* (New York, 1987); Marvin Frankel, *Faith and Freedom: Religious Liberty in America* (New York, 1994), 12–15, 20, 37, 44, 99, 117–18. Frankel calls religion "the last refuge of scoundrels."

151. Gamwell, *Meaning*, 154.

152. Fish, *No Such Thing*, Gutmann, in Macedo and Tamir, *Moral and Political*, 37; Peter de Marneffe, in ibid., 223–25; Owen, *Religion and Rationalism*, 132–33; Galston, *Liberal Purposes*, 293, 299; Smith, *Getting*, 57, 105, 159; Thiemann, in Feldman, *Law and Religion*, 359–61; Fish, in ibid., 406; Sider and Unruh, in Davids, *Welfare Reform*, 116; Stiltner, *Religion*, 73; Macedo, *Liberal Virtues*, 260; Hitchcock, in Sadurski, *Law and Religion*, 155–73.

153. Smith, *Foreordained*, 94.

154. Gleason, in Marty, *Modern*, III, 403.

155. Smith, *Foreordained*, 85; Esbeck, in Monsma and Soper, *Equal*, 13; Wolstertorff, in Sizer, *Religion*, 8–9; Smith, *Foreordained*, 85; Gail Menel, in Murphy, *Bill of Rights*, II, 119.

156. Carter, *Culture*, 145; Wolfe, *Essays*, 74–75.

157. Laycock, in Sikorski, *Prayer*, III, 175.

158. Ibid., 186–87; Tribe, *American Constitutional Law* (1988), 1211.

159. Fish, *Trouble*, 38–42, 156, 167, 172, 178, 185, 189, 192–202; *No Such Thing*, 137; and in Feldman, *Law and Religion*, 387 394, 404–406. See also Smith, *Getting Beyond*, 159.

160. Sadurski, *Moral Pluralism*, 189, 198.

161. Owen, *Religion and Rationalism*, 77–78. Owen attributes this position to Richard Rorty.

162. Macedo, in Barber, *Constitutional Politics*, 176–80, 183–84. See also Dombrowski, *Rawls*, 111.

163. Daniel O. Conkle, in Feldman, *Law and Religion*, 320–21.

164. Perry, *Religion and Politics*, 48.

165. Sullivan, *Paying*, 153; Dombrowski, *Rawls*, 9.

166. Murray, *We Hold*, 12, 52.

167. Ibid., 85.

168. Gamwell, *Meaning*, 74–75; Lowenthal, *No Liberty*, 200; Smith, *Getting Over*, 153.

169. Carter, in McConnell, *Christian Perspectives*, 51.

170. Gutmann and Thompson, *Democracy*, 374.

171. Galanter, in Murphy, *Bill of Rights*, I, 435,

172. Sullivan, in Stone, *Bill of Rights*, 198–99, 213–14, 221.

173. Mead, *Nation*, 69–70.

174. Ibid., 153.

175. Macedo, *Liberal Virtues*, 55–56. For a similar argument, from the opposite ideological side, see Craycraft, *American Myth*, 25, 84.

176. Macedo, *Liberal Virtues*, 136–38.

177. Ibid., 221.

178. Mary E. Becker, in Stone, *Bill of Rights*, 459–86. Becker claims that since she does not advocate direct government regulation of churches, her approach is "exceedingly moderate."

179. Jelen, in Segers and Jelen, *Wall*, 31, 38. In ostensibly defending the public role of religion, Segers claims that opposition to abortion manifests a "weak and tenuous commitment to the First Amendment" on the part of Catholics (106).

180. Sullivan, in Stone, *Bill of Rights*, 220.

181. Perry, in Feldman, *Law and Religion*, 118, 131. Perry attributes the requirement of a "dynamic" concept of God to the Jesuit theologian David Hollenbach. Perry justifies his own defense of religion on the grounds that he is a "thoroughly Vatican II Catholic" (*Law and Religion*, 7).

182. As, for example, in the suggestion that participation in a democratic society has the affect of making church structures themselves more democratic (Dombrowski, *Rawls*, 112.)

183. Perry, *Morality*, 183. See also Dombrowski, *Rawls*, 112.

184. Kramnick and Moore, *Godless*, 160.

185. Perry, *Law and Religion*, 70, 85, 99.

186. Mark A. Graber, in Feldman, *Law and Religion*, 281, 286. Graber criticizes Feldman's claims about anti-Jewish discrimination in American society, on the grounds that such concerns distract Jews from progressive causes.

187. Sullivan, *Paying*, 153–56, 166; Sadurski, *Moral Pluralism*, 169.

188. Smith, in Monsma, *Equal Treatment*, 190; Gamwell, *Meaning*, 41; Frank S. Ravitch, *School Prayer and Discrimination* (Boston, 1999), 77.

189. Ruth Teitel, in Sikorski, *Prayer*, III, 290–92.

190. Goldberg, *Defense*, 59.

191. Douglas, *Bible and Schools*, 40.

192. Douglas, *Almanac*, 172, 366.

193. Douglas, *Go East*, 13–16, and *Holocaust*, 71, 103–108, 112–14, 147.

194. Douglas, *Living*, 69, and *Correspondence*, 154.

195. McConnell, in Stone, *Bill of Rights*, 133; Destro, in Monsma, *Equal Treatment*, 121.

196. Sunstein, *Partial Constitution*, 307. See also Christopher L. Eisgruber and Lawrence G. Sager, in Feldman, *Law and Religion*, 212; Graber, in ibid., 282; Nancy L. Rosenbaum, in Macedo, *Moral and Religious*, 158, 166.

197. Perry, *Religion and Politics*, 49–50.

198. Mead, *Nation*, 93, 96–97; Evans, *Interpreting*, 239.

199. Richards, *Foundations*, 186.

200. Richards, *Toleration*, 96, 136; Gedicks, *Rhetoric*, 13; Dombrowski, *Rawls*, 130.

201. Richards, *Foundations*, 184.

202. Feldman, *Please Don't*.

203. Gorman, in Oaks, *Wall Between*, 49.

204. James Hurst, *Law and Social Process in United States History* (Ann Arbor, Mich., 1960), 229; Wolfe, *Essays*, 79.

205. Webster, *Papers*, XI, 143.

206. McCarthy, Skillen, and Harper, *Disestablishment*, 99, 104.

207. Mead, *Lively Experiment*, 66.

208. Levinson, in Barber, *Constitutional Politics*, 200.

209. McCarthy, Skillen, and Harper, *Disestablishment*, 51.

210. Hirsch, *Enigma*, 169.

211. Sorauf, *Wall*, 135.

212. Irons, *Courage*, 368.

213. Ivers, *Build Wall*.

214. Pfeffer, *Creeds*, 5, 13–14, 23, 29–31, 34, 35–42, 50–53, 79–80, 112–32.

215. Ibid., 79.

216. Pfeffer, in White and Zimmerman, *Unsettled*, 81–82.

217. Pfeffer, *God, Caesar, and the Constitution* (Boston, 1975), 8–13, 18, 47–49, 88, 231, 237–40, 253.

218. Sunstein, *Partial Constitution*, 308.

219. Wilson, *Public Religion*, 127; Semonche, *Keeping Faith*, 329; Amar, in Hoffman and Albert, *Bill of Rights*, 317.

220. Fish, *No Such Thing*, 136; Gutmann and Thompson, *Democracy*, 66–67; Macedo, in Barber, *Constitutional Politics*, 171, 176, 185; Evans, *Interpreting*, 86. See also Owen, *Religion and Rationalism*, 143.

221. Gedicks and Hendrix, *Choosing*, 14.

222. Stephen Arons, *Compelling Belief: The Culture of American Schooling* (New York, 1983), 27–28. See also Fraser, *Between Church and State*, 156–82; McConnell, in Macedo, *Moral and Political Education*, 119.

223. Carter, *In God's Name*, 77.

224. McConnell, in Macedo, *Moral*, 105; Murray, in McCloskey, *Essays*, 337; Peter Riga, in Murphy, *Bill of Rights*, I, 223.

225. Bickel, *Court and Progress*, 124.

226. Fish, *No Such Thing*, 135.

227. Richards, *Toleration*, 252.

228. Tushnet, in Sadurski, *Law*, 253–54.

229. Gedicks and Hendrix, *Choosing*, 27.

230. Gamwell, *Meaning*, 101, 120–27; Gedicks, *Rhetoric*, 32. For a discussion of various intellectual reactions to postmodernism, see Owen, *Religion and Rationalism*.

231. Owen, *Religion and Rationalism*, 13–14, 65, 135–38.

232. Rorty, *Philosophy and Social Hope* (New York, 1999), 172.

233. Levinson, in Barber, *Constutional Politics*, 200; McConnell, in Macedo, *Moral*, 124; Robert Booth Fowler, in Formicola and Morken, *Everson*, 167–85.

234. Gedicks, *Rhetoric*, 32–34; Smith, *Getting Beyond*, 117.

235. Carter, *Culture*, 169; *God's Name*, 286; and in Sadurski, *Law and Religion*, 250.

236. Susan Epperson, the plaintiff in the case, believed that the assistant attorney general who represented the state oof Arkansas was embarrassed by the case and did not pursue it vigorously (Irons, *Courage*, 228). See also Larson, *Trial and Error*, 98–108, 115.

237. Larson, *Trial and Error*, 114–16, 198; Smith, *Getting Beyond*, 117. Larson speculates that Fortas, who was raised in Memphis, was especially influenced by his memories of the Scopes trial.

238. Choper, *Securing*, 145.

239. William Cohen and David Danelski, *Constitutional Law: Civil Liberty and Individual Rights* (Westbury, N.Y., 1994), 692. For the argument that government may not make policy on the assumption that particular ideas, religious or nonreligious, are true, see Perry, *Religion and Politics*, 33.

240. Carter, in Sadurski, *Law and Religion*, 256. Dwyer (*Vouchers*, 200) argues bluntly that the schools must practice "viewpoint discrimination," in order to exclude religious influences, and Ravitch (*School Prayer*, 184) that schools may restrict free speech for the same reason.

241. McConnell, in Monsma, *Equal Treatment*, 32.

242. Wolfe, *Essays*, 90.

243. Schwartz, *Ascent*, 205–206.

244. Douglas, *Go East*, 249.

245. Gutmann and Thompson, *Democracy*, 67–68; Gutmann, in Macedo, *Moral and Political*, 25, 44.

246. Richards *Toleration*, 154.

247. Tushnet, in Sadurski, *Law*, 260.

248. Evans, *Interpreting*, 239.

249. Lynn, *Right of Religious Liberty*, 24. See also Pfeffer, in Ronald C. White Jr. and Albright F. Zimmerman (eds.), *An Unsettled Arena: Religion and the Bill of Rights* (Grand Rapids, Mich., 1990), 86.

250. Ferrara, *Religion*, 1–4; McConnell, in Monsma, *Equal Treatment*, 38–40; Glenn, in ibid., 78–85; Nord, *Religion and Education*, 271–79. In most such cases lower courts upheld the schools' exclusion of religion.

251. Nord, *Religion*, 266–69, 271–74, 279. Fraser, *Between*, 205–10; Ravitch, *School Prayer*, 86–87, 238. Ravitch argues that only religiously conservative students are divisive and dismisses claims that they are the objects of discrimination.

252. Nord, *Religion*, 138–91.

253. Macedo, in Barber, *Constitutional Politics*, 183–86.

254. Dwyer's *Religious Schools* and *Vouchers* are sustained arguments to this effect.

255. Carter, *Dissent*, 31.

256. Dwyer, Vouchers, 43, 65, 96, 193, 229. For less extreme versions of this argument, see Gutmann and Thompson, *Democracy*, 67; Gutmann, in Macedo, *Moral and Political*, 25–38; Harry Brighouse, in ibid., 271; Bob Reich, in ibid., 286, 289, 299–304; Rosenbaum, in ibid., 158, 166–67.

257. Gutmann and Thompson, *Democracy*, 374.

258. Arons, *Compelling Belief*, 57.

259. Becker, in Stone, *Bill of Rights*, 459–86; Ravitch, *School Prayer*, 86–87; Brighouse, in Macedo, *Moral and Religious*, 252, 254, 265; Eisgruber and Sager, in Feldman, *Law and Religion*, 214; Provenzo, *Fundamentalism*; Dwyer, *Religious Schools* and *Vouchers*.

260. McConnell, in Macedo, *Moral and Political*, 126.

261. Ibid., 122; Stiltner, *Religion*, 76, 83; Galston, *Liberal Purposes*, 281; Perry, *Religion and Politics*, 68.

262. Perry, *Religion and Politics*, 48.

263. McConnell, in Macedo, *Moral and Religious*, 100.

264. Gutmann and Thompson, *Democracy*, 67–68.

265. Brighouse, in Macedo, *Moral and Religious*, 268.

266. Gutmann, in Macedo, *Moral and Political*, 50.

267. John Tomasi, in ibid., 207, 209, 211–12.

268. Levinson, in Barber, *Constitutional Politics*, 208–209; McConnell, in Macedo, *Moral and Political*, 97.

269. Galston, *Liberal Purposes*, 254; Marneffe, in Macedo, *Moral and Political*, 223, 243.

270. Dombrowski, *Rawls*, 108.

271. Galston, *Liberal Purposes*, 255.

272. Brighouse, in Macedo, *Moral and Religious*, 262–63.

273. Choper, *Securing*, 105; Nord, *Religion*, 306–16.

274. Fish, *No Such Thing*, 137–38.

275. Weber, *Equal Separation*, 40; Sadurski, *Moral Pluralism*, 193.

276. Stiltner, *Religion*, 74.

277. Ivers, in Monsma, *Equal Treatment*, 193.

278. Smith, in ibid., 181.

279. Feldman, *Please Don't*, 375.

280. Tushnet, in Marty, *Modern*, III, 305.

281. Sadurski, *Moral Pluralism*, 173; Backer, in Feldmam, *Law and Religion*, 440, 446.

282. Howe, *Garden*, 156, 164; William Bentley Ball, in Sizer, *Religion*, 148; Goldberg, *Reconstructing*, 118.

283. Amar, *Bill of Rights*, 34.

284. Monsma, *Positive Neutralitiy*, 23.

285. Choper, *Securing*, 97.

286. Sunstein, *Partial Constitution*, 307. Ravitch argues candidly that the free exercise of religion ought to be restricted (*School Prayer*, 186).

287. Carter in Sadurski, *Law and Religion*, 251.

288. Sunstein, *Partial Constitution*, 307.

289. Dwyer, *Religious Schools*, 180.

290. Sullivan, in Stone, *Bill of Rights*, 200, 206, 213.

291. Dwyer, *Vouchers*, 144.

292. Macedo, *Liberal Virtues*, 74–75, 166; Jelen, in Segers and Jelen, *Wall*, 41–42.

293. Audi, in Weithman, *Religion*, 64.

294. Semonche, *Keeping the Faith: A Cultural History of the U.S. Supreme Court* (Lanham, Md., 1998), 350.

295. Martha Nussbaum, in Weithman, *Religion and Liberalism*, 93–124. Nussbaum primarily discusses non-Western societies, but she seems to intend her arguments to apply to Western democracies as well.

296. Ravitch, *School Prayer*, 89, 91, 103, 122, 131, 147–53, 170–71, 173–79, 199.

297. Macedo, in Barber, *Constitutional Politics*, 184. See also the remarks about Anthony Kennedy by Joel D. Joseph (*Eight Men*, 275, 284–87); about Scalia by Smith and Schultz (*Vision of Scalia*, 210); and about Thomas by Smith and Schultz (*Justice Antonin Scalia and the Supreme Court's Conservative Moment* [Westport, Conn., 1993], 126–27). Smith and Schultz particularly objected to a published photograph of Thomas and his wife reading the Bible together.

298. Choper, *Securing*, 116.

299. Tushnet, in Marty, *Modern*, III, 304.

300. Konvitz, *Religious Liberty*, 67.

301. Kramnick and Moore, *Godless*, 15.

302. Eisgruber and Sager, in Feldman, *Law and Religion*, 200–205. See also Greene, in ibid., 229.

303. Choper, *Securing*, 105.

304. Choper, in Sadurski, *Law and Religion*, 368.

305. Richards, *Toleration*, 145; Tribe, *American Constitutional Law* (1978), 826–28. Tribe retracted the position in the 1988 edition of his book (1186).

306. Sadurski, *Moral Pluralism*, 18.

307. Hammond, *With Liberty*, 83–84.

308. Ball, in Wood and Davis, *Role of Government*, 148; Johnson, in Sadurski, *Law and Religion*, 193; Choper, in ibid., 361.

309. McConnell, in Stone, *Bill of Rights*, 173.

310. Johnson, in Sadurski, *Law and Religion*, 193; Tushnet, in ibid., 318.

311. Rockefeller, *Dewey*, 265–68, 445–90.

312. For a discussion of humanism as a religion, see McCarthy, *Society, State, and Schools* (Grand Rapids, Mich., 1981), 112–34.

313. John Saxton, in Bernard Schwartz (ed.), *The Warren Court* (New York, 1996), 114.

314. Choper, *Securing*, 106; Reichley, in Dunn, *Religion*, 9.

315. Noll, *Religion and Politics*, 89.

316. For an extended discussion of the issue, see George, *Clash*.

317. Tushnet, *Red*, 6.

318. Murray, *We Hold*, 53; Esbeck, in Davis, *Welfare Reform*, 101.

319. Sandel, in Hunter and Guiness, *Articles*, 76.

320. Dwyer (*Vouchers*, 65) holds that whatever authority parents possess is itself conferred by the state.

321. Arkes, *Beyond*, 81.

322. Perry, *Love*, 87.

323. Tushnet, *Red*, 271.

324. Fish, *Doing What Comes Naturally* (Durham, N.C., 1989), 98, 133, 139, 320, 356.

325. Rorty, *Truth and Progress* (Cambridge, England, 1991), 170, 172, 175–76, 180–81.

326. Ibid., 196, 199.

327. Murray, *We Hold*, 28; Lowenthal, *No Liberty*, 185; Rice, *Supreme Court*, 78–79; Wolfe, *Essays*, 79.

BIBLIOGRAPHY

Primary

Ariens, Michael S., and Robert A. Destro (eds.), *Religious Liberty in a Pluralistic Society* (Durham, N.C., 1996).

Baird, Robert, *Religion in the United States of America; or, an Account of the Origins, Progress, Relations to the State, and Present Condition of the Evangelical Churches in the United States, with Notice of Unevangelical Denominations* (Glasgow, 1844).

Black, Hugo L., *Mr. Justice and Mrs. Black: The Memoirs of Hugo L. Black and Elizabeth Black* (New York, 1986).

Black, Hugo L. Jr., *My Father, a Remembrance* (New York, 1975).

Blanshard, Paul, *American Freedom and Catholic Power* (Boston, 1949).

———, *Communism, Democracy and Catholic Power* (Boston, 1951).

———, *Religion and the Schools: The Great Controversy* (Boston, 1963).

Bradley, Joseph P., *Miscellaneous Writings of the Late Hon. Joseph P. Bradley*, ed. Charles Bradley (Newark, 1902).

Brennan, William J., *An Affair with Freedom: A Collection of His Opinions and Speeches Drawn from His First Decade As a United States Supreme Court Justice*, ed. Stephen J. Friedman (New York, 1967).

Brewer, David J., *The United States, a Christian Nation* (Smyrna, Ga., 1996 [original edition 1905]).

Bryce, James, *The American Commonwealth* (London, 1891), two volumes.

Cooley, Thomas M., *The General Principles of Constitutional Law in the United States of America* (Boston, 1898).

———, *Treatise on the Constitutional Limitations Which Rest upon the Legislative Power of the States of the American Union* (Boston, 1927), two volumes.

Dickson, Del (ed.), *The Supreme Court in Conference (1940–1985)* (New York, 2001).

Doerr, Edd, and Albert J. Menendez (eds.), *Religious Liberty and State Constitutions* (Buffalo, 1993).

Douglas, William O., *An Almanac of Liberty* (Garden City, N.Y., 1954).

———, *The Anatomy of Liberty: The Rights of Man without Force* (New York, 1963).

———, *The Bible and the Schools* (Boston, 1966).

———, *The Douglas Letters: Selected from the Private Papers of Justice William O. Douglas*, ed. Melvin I. Urofsky (Bethesda, Md., 1987).

———, *The Douglas Opinions*, ed. Vern Countryman (New York, 1978).

———, *Go East, Young Man: The Early Years* (New York, 1974).

———, *Holocaust or Hemispheric Co-Op: Cross Currents in Latin America* (New York, 1971).

———, *A Living Bill of Rights* (Garden City, N.Y., 1971).

Dreisbach, Daniel L.(ed.), *Religion and Politics in the Early Republic: Jasper Adams and the Church-State Debate* (Lexington, Ky., 1996).

Fellman, David (ed.), *The Supreme Court and Education* (New York, 1969).

Fisher, William W. III, Morton J. Horwitz, and Thomas Reed (eds.), *American Legal Realism* (New York, 1993).

Frankfurter, Felix, *Felix Frankfurter Reminisces* (New York, 1994).

———, *From the Diaries of Felix Frankfurter*, ed. Joseph P. Lash (New York, 1975).

Friedman, Leon, and Fred L. Israel (eds.), *The Justices of the United States Supreme Court, 1789–1969: Their Lives and Major Opinions* (New York, 1969), five volumes.

Goldberg, Arthur J., *The Defense of Freedom: Public Papers of Arthur J. Goldberg*, ed. Daniel Patrick Moynihan (New York, 1966).

———, *Equal Justice: The Warren Era of the Supreme Court* (New York, 1971).

———, *The Evolving Constitution: Essays on the Bill of Rights and the U.S. Supreme Court*, ed. Norman Dorsen (Middletown, Conn., 1986).

Hughes, Charles Evans, *The Autobiographical Notes of Charles Evans Hughes*, ed. David J. Danelski and Joseph E. Tulchin (Cambridge, Mass., 1973).

Irons, Peter (ed.), *The Courage of Their Convictions* (New York, 1988).

Jackson, Robert H., *Dispassionate Justice: A Synthesis of the Judicial Opinions of Robert H. Jackson*, ed. Glendon A. Schubert (Indianapolis, 1969).

Jefferson, Thomas, *Jefferson on Religion and Public Education*, ed. Robert M. Healey (Hamden, Conn., 1962).

Kurland, Philip, and Ralph Lerner (eds.), *The Founders' Constitution* (Chicago, 1987), five volumes.

Lowell, C. Stanley, *Embattled Wall: Americans United, an Idea and a Man* (Washington, 1966).

———, *The Great Church-State Fraud* (Washington, 1973).

Madison, James, *James Madison on Religious Liberty*, ed. Robert S. Alley (Buffalo, 1985).

Marshall, John, *An Autobiographical Sketch by John Marshall, Written at the Request of Joseph Story* (Ann Arbor, Mich., 1937).

McCollum, Vashti C., *One Woman's Fight* (Boston, 1961).

Miller, Samuel Freeman, *Lectures on the Constitution of the United States* (Littleton, Colo., 1980 [original edition 1881]).

Murray, William J., *Let Us Pray, a Plea for Prayer in Our Schools* (New York, 1995).

———, *My Life without God* (Nashville, 1982).

Noonan, John T. Jr., and Edward McGlynn Gaffney Jr. (eds.), *Religious Freedom: History, Cases, and Other Materials on the Interaction of Religion and Government* (New York, 2001).

O'Connor, Sandra Day, and H. Alan Day, *Lazy B: Growing up on a Cattle Ranch in the American Southwest* (New York, 2002).

O'Hair, Madalyn Murray, *Freedom under Siege: The Impact of Organized Religion on Your Liberty and Your Pocketbook* (Los Angeles, 1974).

Pfeffer, Leo, *Church, State, and Freedom* (Boston, 1953).

———, *Creeds in Competiton: A Creative Force in American Culture* (New York, 1958).

———, *God, Caesar, and the Constitution: The Court As Referee of Church-State Confrontation* (Boston, 1975).

———, *The Liberties of an American: The Supreme Court Speaks* (Boston, 1956).

———, *Religion, State, and the Burger Court* (Buffalo, 1984).

———, *Religious Freedom* (Skokie, Ill., 1977).

———, *This Honorable Court: A History of the United States Supreme Court* (Boston, 1965).

Rutledge, Wiley, *A Declaration of Legal Faith* (Lawrence, Kans., 1947).

Scalia, Antonin, *A Matter of Interpretation: Federal Courts and the Law, an Essay* (Princeton, N.J., 1997).

Schaff, Philip, *America, a Sketch of Its Political, Social, and Religious Character* (Cambridge, Mass., 1961 [originally 1854]).

Schwartz, Bernard (ed.), *Roots of the Bill of Rights* (New York, 1980), five volumes.

Stevens, John Paul, *The Bill of Rights, a Century of Progress* (Chicago, 1992).

Story, Joseph, *Commentaries on the Constitution of the United States*, ed. Ronald D. Rotunda and John E. Nowack (Durham, N.C., 1987 [originally 1833]).

Strong, William, *Two Lectures on the Relations of Civil Law to Church Polity, Discipline, and Property* (New York, 1897).

Thomas, Clarence, *Confronting the Future: Selections from the Senate Confirmation Hearings and Prior Speeches* (Washington, 1992).

Tocqueville, Alexis de, *Democracy in America*, tr. Henry Reeve, ed. Phillips Bradley (New York, 1953), two volumes.

Veit, Helen E., Kenneth R. Bowling, and Charlene Bangs Bickford (eds.), *Creating the Bill of Rights: The Documentary Record from the First Federal Congress* (Baltimore, 1991).

Warren, Earl, *The Memoirs of Earl Warren* (Garden City, N.Y., 1977).

———, *Public Papers* (New York, 1959).

———, *A Republic, If You Can Keep It* (New York, 1972).

Secondary

Abraham, Henry J., *Freedom and the Court: Civil Rights and Liberties in the United States* (New York, 1977).

———, *Justices and Presidents: A Political History of Appointments to the Supreme Court* (New York, 1992).

Ackerman, Bruce A., *Social Justice in the Liberal State* (New Haven, Conn., 1980).

———, *We The People* (Cambridge, Mass., 1991), two volumes.

Adams, Arlin M., and Charles J. Emmerich, *A Nation Dedicated to Religious Liberty: The Constitutional Heritage of the Religion Clauses* (Philadelphia, 1990).

Agresto, John, *The Supreme Court and Constitutional Democracy* (Ithaca, N.Y., 1984).

Alexander, Thomas S., *Mormonism in Transition: The History of the Latter-Day Saints, 1890–1930* (Urbana, Ill., 1996).

Allen, David S., and Robert Jensen (eds.), *Freeing the First Amendment: Critical Perspectives on Freedom of Expression* (New York, 1995).

Alley, Robert S., *School Prayer: The Court, the Congress, and the First Amendment* (Buffalo, 1994).

Alschuler, Albert W., *Law without Values: The Life, Work, and Legacy of Justice Holmes* (Chicago, 2000).

Amar, Akhil Reed, *For the People: What the Constitution Really Says about Your Rights* (New York, 1998).

———, *The Bill of Rights: Creation and Reconstruction* (New Haven, Conn., 1998).

Anastalpo, George, *The Amendments to the Constitution: A Commentary* (Baltimore, 1995).

———, *The Constitutionalist: Notes on the First Amendment* (Dallas, 1971).

Antieau, Chester J., *Commentary on the Constitution of the United States* (Buffalo, 1960).

———, *The Higher Law Origins of Modern Constitutional Law* (Buffalo, 1994).

———, *The Rights of Our Fathers* (Vienna, Va., 1968).

Antieau, Chester J., Arthur T. Downey, and Edward C. Roberts, *Freedom from Federal Establishment: Formation and Early History of the First Amendment Religion Clauses* (Milwaukee, 1964).

Arkes, Hadley, *Beyond the Constitution* (Princeton, N.J., 1990).

———, *First Things: An Inquiry into the First Principles of Morals and Justice* (Princeton, N.J., 1986).

———, *The Return of George Sutherland: Restoring the Jurisprudence of Natural Rights* (Princeton, N.J., 1994).

Arons, Stephen, *Compelling Belief: The Culture of American Schooling* (New York, 1983).

Auerbach, Jerold S., *Rabbis and Lawyers: The Journey from Torah to Constitution* (Bloomington, Ind., 1990).

Baker, Leonard, *Back to Back: The Duel between FDR and the Supreme Court* (New York, 1967).

———, *John Marshall, a Life in the Law* (New York, 1974).

Baker, Liva, *The Justice from Beacon Hill: The Life and Times of Oliver Wendell Holmes* (New York, 1991).

Ball, Howard, *A Defiant Life: Thurgood Marshall and the Persistence of Racism in America* (New York, 1999).

———, *Hugo L. Black, Cold Steel Warrior* (New York, 1996).

———, *Judicial Craftsmanship or Fiat?: Direct Overturn by the United States Supreme Court* (Westport, Conn., 1978).

———, *The Vision and the Dream of Justice Hugo L. Black: An Examination of a Judicical Philosophy* (Tuscaloosa, Ala., 1975).

Ball, Milner S., *Lying down Together: Law, Metaphor, and Theology* (Madison, Wis., 1985).

———, *The Praise of American Law: A Theological, Humanistic View of the Legal Process* (Athens, Ga., 1981).

———, *The Word and the Law* (Chicago, 1993).

Ball, Terence, and J.G.A. Pocock, *Conceptual Change and the Constitution* (Lawrence, Kans., 1988).

Ball, William Bentley (ed.), *In Search of a National Morality: A Manifesto for Evangelicals and Catholics* (San Francisco, 1992).

Barber, Sotirios A., *The Constitution of Judicial Power* (Baltimore, 1993).

———, *On What the Constitution Means* (Baltimore, 1984).

Barber, Sotirios A., and Robert P. George (eds.), *Constitutional Politics: Essays on Constitution Making, Maintenance, and Change* (Princeton, N.J., 2001).

Barlow, J. Jackson, Leonard W. Levy, and Ken Masugi (eds.), *The American Founding: Essays on the Formation of the Constitution* (New York, 1988).

Barr, David L., and Nicholas Piediscalzi (eds.), *The Bible in American Education: From Sourcebook to Textbook* (Philadelphia, 1982).

Baxter, Maurice G., *Daniel Webster and the Supreme Court* (Amherst, Mass., 1966).

Beaver, R. Pierce, *Church, State, and the American Indian: Two and Half Centuries of Partnership in Missions between Protestant Churches and Government* (St. Louis, 1966).

Becker, Theodore L., and Malcolm M. Feeley (eds.), *The Impact of Supreme Court Decisions* (New York, 1973).

Beeman, Richard, Stephen Botein, and Edward Carter II (eds.), *Beyond Confederation: Origins of the Constitution and American National Identity* (Chapel Hill, N.C., 1987).

Bellah, Robert N., *Beyond Belief: Essays on Religion in a Post-Traditional World* (New York, 1970).

———, *The Broken Covenant: American Civil Religion in Time of Trial* (New York, 1970).

Bellah, Robert N., and Philip E. Hammond, *Varieties of Civil Religion* (San Francisco, 1980).

Bellah, Robert N., and Frederick E. Greenspahn (eds.), *Uncivil Religion: Interreligious Hostility in America* (New York, 1987).

Belz, Herman, *A Living Constitution or Fundamental Law?: American Constitutionalism in Historical Perspective* (Lanham, Md., 1998).

Bennett, John Coleman, *Christians and the State* (New York, 1958).

Berger, Raoul, *The Fourteenth Amendment and the Bill of Rights* (Norman, Okla., 1989).

———, *Government by Judiciary: The Transformation of the Fourteenth Amendment* (Cambridge, Mass., 1977).

Bergman, Philip J., Owen M. Fiss, and Charles W. McCurdy, *The Fields of the Law: Essays* (San Francisco, 1986).

Berk, Stephen E., *Calvinism versus Democracy: Timothy Dwight and the Origins of American Evangelical Orthodoxy* (Hamden, Conn., 1974).

Berkhofer, Robert F., *Salvation and the Savage: An Analysis of Protestant Missions and the American Indian Response, 1787–1862* (Lexington, Ky., 1965).

Berman, Harold J., *Faith and Order: The Reconciliation of Law and Religion* (Atlanta, 1993).

———, *The Interaction of Law and Religion* (Nashville, 1974).

Bernhard, Winfred E. A., *Fisher Ames, Federalist and Statesman, 1758–1809* (Chapel Hill, N.C., 1965).

Berns, Walter, *The First Amendment and the Future of American Democracy* (New York, 1976).

———, *Freedom, Virtue, and the First Amendment* (Baton Rouge, La., 1957).

———, *Taking the Constitution Seriously* (New York, 1987).

Berry, Mary Frances, *Stability, Security, and Continuity: Mr. Justice Burton and Decision-Making in the Supreme Court, 1945–1958* (Westport, Conn., 1978).

Beth, Loren P., *The American Theory of Church and State* (Gainesville, Fla., 1958).

———, *John Marshall Harlan, the Last Whig Justice* (Lexington, Ky., 1992).

Beveridge, Albert J., *The Life of John Marshall* (Boston, 1916–19), four volumes.

Bickel, Alexander, *The Morality of Consent* (New Haven, Conn., 1975).

———, *Politics and the Warren Court* (New York, 1965).

———, *The Supreme Court and the Idea of Progress* (New York, 1970).

Biskupic, Joan, and Elder Witt, *The Supreme Court and the Powers of American Government* (Washington, 1997).

Black, Charles L., *The People and the Courts: Judicial Review and Democracy* (New York, 1960).

———, *Perspectives on Constitutional Law* (Engelwood Cliffs, N.J., 1963).

Blasi, Vincent (ed.), *The Burger Court, the Counter-Revolution That Wasn't* (New Haven, Conn., 1983).

——— (ed.), *Law and Liberalism in the 1980s* (New York, 1991).

Blaustein, Albert P., and Roy M. Mersky, *The First One Hundred Justices: Statistical Studies of the Supreme Court of the United States* (Hamden, Conn., 1978).

Bloomfield, Maxwell H., *Peaceful Revolution: Constitutional Change and American Culture from Progressivism to the New Deal* (Cambridge, Mass., 2001).

Bobbitt, Philip, *Constitutional Fate: Theory of the Constitution* (New York, 1982).

———, *Constitutional Interpretation* (Cambridge, Mass., 1991).

Boles, Donald E. *The Bible, Religion, and the Public Schools* (Ames, Ia., 1961).

———, *Mr. Justice Rehnquist, Judicial Activist* (Ames, Ia., 1987).

Bond, James E., *I Dissent: The Legacy of Justice James Clark McReynolds* (Fairfax, Va., 1992).

Boorstin, Daniel H., *The Lost World of Thomas Jefferson* (Boston, 1948).

Borden, Morton, *Jews, Turks, and Infidels* (Chapel Hill, N.C., 1984).

Bork, Robert H., *Slouching towards Gomorrah: Modern Liberalism and American Decline* (New York, 1996).

———, *The Tempting of America: The Political Seduction of the Law* (New York, 1990).

Bradford, M. E., *Original Intentions: The Making and Ratification of the United States Constitution* (Athens, Ga., 1993).

Bradley, Gerard V., *Church-State Relationships in America* (New York, 1987).

Brady, Joseph H., *Confusion Twice Confounded: The First Amendment and the Supreme Court, an Historical Study* (South Orange, N.J., 1954).

Brassham, Gregory, *Original Intent and the Constitution, a Philosophical Study* (Lanham Md., 1992).

Brauer, Jerald C. (ed.), *The Lively Experiment Continued* (Macon, Ga., 1987).

—— (ed.), *Religion and the American Revolution* (Philadelphia, 1976).

Brigham, John, *Civil Liberties and American Democracy* (Washington, 1984).

——, *Constitutional Language, an Interpretation of Judicial Decision* (Westport, Conn., 1979).

——, *The Constitution of Interest: Beyond the Politics of Rights* (New York, 1996).

——, *The Cult of the Court* (Philadelphia, 1987).

Brisbin, Richard A., *Justice Antonin Scalia and the Conservative Revival* (Baltimore, 1997).

Brodhead, Michael J., *David J. Brewer: The Life of a Supreme Court Justice, 1837–1910* (Carbondale, Ill., 1994).

Brown, Francis J., *The Social and Economic Philosophy of Pierce Butler* (Washington, 1945).

Bryson, Joseph E., and Samuel H. Houston Jr., *The Supreme Court and Public Funds for Religious Schools: The Burger Years, 1969–1986* (Jefferson, N.C., 1990).

Buckley, Thomas E., *Church and State in Revolutionary Virginia, 1776–1787* (Charlottesville, Va., 1977).

Burt, Robert, *The Constitution in Conflict* (Cambridge, Mass., 1992).

——, *Two Jewish Justices: Outcasts in the Promised Land* (Berkeley, Calif., 1988).

Burton, David H., *Taft, Holmes, and the 1920s Court: An Appraisal* (Madison, N.J., 1998).

Butts, R. Freeman, *The American Tradition in Religion and Education* (Boston, 1950).

Buzzard, Lynn R. (ed.), *Freedom and Faith: The Impact of Law on Religious Liberty* (Elgin, Ill., 1982).

Buzzard, Lynn R., and Samuel Ericsson, *The Battle for Religious Liberty* (Elgin, Ill., 1982).

Cahn, Edmund N., *Supreme Court and Supreme Law* (Bloomington, Ind., 1954).

Campos, Paul F., Pierre Schlag, and Steven D. Smith, *Against the Law* (Durham, N.C., 1996).

Canavan, Francis, *The Pluralism Game: Pluralism, Liberalism, and the Moral Conscience* (Lanham, Md., 1995).

Carey, George W., *In Defense of the Constitution* (Indianapolis, 1995).

Carey, George W., and James V. Schall (eds.), *Essays on Christianity and Political Philosophy* (Lanham, Md., 1984).

Carson, Hampton L., *The History of the Supreme Court of the United States, with Biographies of All the Chief and Associate Justices* (Philadelphia, 1902), two volumes.

Carter, Lief H., *Contemporary Constitutional Law Making: The Supreme Court and the Art of Politics* (New York, 1985).

—— *Reason in Law* (Boston, 1984).

Carter, Stephen L., *The Culture of Disbelief: How American Law and Politics Trivialize Religious Devotion* (New York, 1993).

Carter, Stephen L. *The Dissent of the Governed: A Meditation on Law, Religion, and Loyalty* (Cambridge, Mass., 1998).

———, *In God's Name: The Wrongs and Rights of Religion in Politics* (New York, 2000).

Casper, Jonathan D., *The Politics of Civil Liberties* (New York, 1972).

Choper, Jesse H. *Securing Religious Liberty: Principles for Judicial Interpretation of the Religion Clauses* (Chicago, 1995).

———, (ed.), *The Supreme Court and Its Justices* (Chicago, 1987).

Chroust, Anton-Herman, *The Rise of the Legal Profession in America* (Norman, Okla., 1965), two volumes.

Clark, Floyd B., *The Constitutional Doctrines of Justice Harlan* (Baltimore, 1915).

Clark, Henry B., II (ed.), *Freedom of Religion in America: Historical Roots, Philosophical Concepts, and Contemporary Problems* (Los Angeles, 1982).

Clark, R. Hunter, *Justice Brennan, the Great Conciliator* (New York, 1990).

Clinton, Robert Lowry, *God and Man in the Law: The Foundations of Anglo-American Constitutionalism* (Lawrence, Kans., 1997).

Cobb, Sanford, *The Rise of Religious Liberty in America* (New York, 1902).

Cochrane, Claude E., *Religion in Public and Private Life* (New York, 1990).

Cohen, Jeremy, *Congress Shall Make No Law: Oliver Wendell Holmes, the First Amendment, and Judicial Decision-Making* (Ames, Ia., 1989).

Cohen, Naomi W., *Jews in Christian America: The Pursuit of Religious Equality* (New York, 1992).

Cohen, William, and David Danelski, *Constitutional Law: Civil Liberty and Individual Rights* (Westbury, N.Y., 1994).

Commager, Henry Steele, *The Empire of Reason: How Europe Imagined and America Realized the Enlightenment* (Garden City, N.Y., 1977).

Cookson, Peter W., *School Choice: The Struggle for the Soul of American Education* (New Haven, Conn., 1940).

Cooper, Philip J., *Battles on the Bench: Conflict inside the Supreme Court* (Lawrence, Kans., 1995).

Corbett, Michael, *Politics and Religion in the United States* (New York, 1999).

Cord, Robert L., *Separation of Church and State* (Milwaukee, 1985).

———, *Separation of Church and State: Historical Fact and Current Fiction* (New York, 1982).

Cornell, Saul, *The Other Founders: Anti-Federalism and the Dissenting Tradition in America, 1789–1828* (Chapel Hill, N.C., 1999).

Cortner, Richard C., *The Supreme Court and the Second Bill of Rights: The Fourteenth Amendment and the Nationalization of Civil Liberties* (Madison, Wis., 1981).

Corwin, Edward S., *A Constitution of Powers in a Secular State* (Charlottesvile, Va., 1951).

———, *Constitutional Revolution Ltd.* (Claremont, Calif., 1941).

———, *Corwin on the Constitution*, ed. Richard Loss (Ithaca, N.Y., 1981–88), three volumes.

———, *Courts over Constitution: A Study of Judicial Review As an Instrument of Popular Government* (Princeton, N.J., 1938).

————, The "Higher Law" Background of American Constitutional Law (Ithaca, N.Y., 1955).

Costanzo, Joseph F., This Nation under God: Church, State, and Schools in America (New York, 1964).

————, Thomas Jefferson, Religious Education, and Public Law (Atlanta, 1959).

Cox, Archibald, Civil Rights, the Constitution, and the Courts (Cambridge, Mass., 1967).

Cray, Ed, Chief Justice, a Biography of Earl Warren (New York, 1997).

Craycraft, Kenneth R., The American Myth of Religious Freedom (Dallas, 1999).

Cromartie, Michael (ed.), Ceasar's Coin: Christians and the Limits of Government (Grand Rapids, Mich., 1996).

Cuddihy, John Murray, No Offense: Civil Religion and Protestant Taste (New York, 1978).

Currie, David P., The Constitution in Congress: The First Congress, 1789–1791 (Chicago, 1994).

————, The Constitution in the Supreme Court: The First Hundred Years, 1789–1888 (Chicago, 1985).

Curry, Thomas J., Farewell to Christendom: The Future of Church and State in America (Nww York, 2001).

————, The First Freedom: Church and State in America to the Passage of the First Amendment (New York, 1986).

Cushman, Barry, Rethinking the New Deal Court: The Structure of a Constitutional Revolution (New York, 1998).

Cushman, Clare (ed.), The Supreme Court Justices: Illustrated Biographies, 1789–1993 (Washington, 1993).

Dalin, David G. (ed.), American Jews and the Separationist Faith: The New Debate on Religion in Public Life (Washington, 1993).

Danelski, David (ed.), Rights, Liberties, and Ideals: The Contribution of Milton Konvitz (Littleton, Colo., 1983).

————, A Supreme Court Justice Is Appointed (New York, 1964).

Dargo, George, Roots of the Republic: New Perspectives on Early American Constitutionalism (New York, 1974).

Davis, Derek, Original Intent: Chief Justice Rehnquist and the Course of American Church-State Relations (Buffalo, 1991).

————, Religion and the Continental Congress, 1774–1789 (New York, 2000).

Davis, Derek and Barry Hankins (eds.), Welfare Reform and Faith-Based Organizations (Waco, Tex., 1999).

Davis, Michael D., Thurgood Marshall: Warrior at the Bar, Rebel on the Bench (Secaucus, N.J., 1992).

Davis, Sue, Justice Rehnquist and the Constitution (Princeton, N.J., 1989).

Dennis, Everette E., Donald M. Gilmor, and David L. Grey (eds.), Justice Hugo Black and the First Amendment: "No Law Means No Law" (Ames, Ia., 1978).

Dietze, Gottfried (ed.), Essays on the Constitition, a Commemorative Volume in Honor of Alpheus T. Mason (Englewood, Cliffs, N.J., 1964).

Dionne, E. J. Jr., and Ming Hsu Chen (eds.), Sacred Places, Civic Purposes: Should Government Help Faith-Based Charity? (Washington, 2001).

Dombrowski, Daniel A., *Rawls and Religion: The Case for Political Liberalism* (Albany, N.Y., 2001).

Donohue, William A., *The Politics of the American Civil Liberties Union* (New Brunswick, N.J., 1985).

———, *The Twilight of Liberty: The Legacy of the ACLU* (New Brunswick, N.J., 1984).

Drakeman, Donald J., *Church-State Constitutional Issues: Making Sense of the Establishment Clause* (New York, 1991).

Dreisbach, Daniel L., *Real Threat or Mere Shadow?: Religious Liberty and the First Amendment* (Westchester, Ill., 1987).

———, *Thomas Jefferson and the Wall of Separation between Church and State* (New York, 2002).

Drinan, Robert F., *Religion, the Court and Public Policy* (New York, 1963).

Dunham, Allison, and Philip B. Kurland (eds.), *Mr. Justice* (Chicago, 1956).

Dunn, Charles (ed.), *Religion in American Politics* (Washington, 1989).

Dunne, Gerald T. Jr., *Hugo Black and the Judicial Revolution* (New York, 1977).

———, *Justice Joseph Story and the Rise of the Supreme Court* (New York, 1970).

Duxbury, Neil, *Patterns of American Jurisprudence* (New York, 1995).

Dworkin, Ronald M., *Freedom's Law: A Moral Reading of the American Constitution* (Cambridge, Mass., 1996).

———, *Law's Empire* (Cambridge, Mass., 1986).

———, *A Matter of Principle* (Cambridge, Mass., 1985).

———, *Taking Rights Seriously* (Cambridge, Mass., 1977).

Dwyer, James G., *Religious Schools v. Children's Rights* (Ithaca, N.Y., 1998).

———, *Vouchers within Reason: A Child-Centered Approach to Education Reform* (Ithaca, N.Y., 2002).

Eckenrode, H. J., *Separation of Church and State in Virginia: A Study in the Development of the Revolution* (New York, 1971 [originally 1910]).

Edel, Wilbur, *Defenders of the Faith: Religion and Politics from the Pilgrim Fathers to Ronald Reagan* (New York, 1987).

Eidelberg, Paul, *A Discourse on Statesmanship: The Design and Transformation of the American Polity* (Urbana, Ill., 1974).

———, *The Philosophy of the American Constitution, a Reinterpretation of the Intentions of the Founding Fathers* (New York, 1968).

Eidsmoe, John, Arnold Burron, and Dean Turner, *Christianity and the Constitution: The Faith of Our Founding Fathers* (Grand Rapids, Mich., 1987).

———, *Classrooms in Crisis: Parents' Rights and the Public Schools* (Denver, 1986).

———, *God and Caesar: Biblical Faith and Political Action* (Westchester, Ill., 1984).

Eight Men and a Lady, Profiles of the Justices of the Supreme Court (Bethesda, Md., 1990).

Eisenach, Eldon, *The Next Religious Establishment: National Identity and Political Theology in Post-Protestant America* (Lanham, Md., 2000).

Eisler, Kim E., *A Justice for All: William J. Brennan and the Decisions That Transformed America* (New York, 1993).

Ely, James A., *The Chief Justiceship of Melville W. Fuller, 1888–1910* (Columbia, S.C., 1995).

Ely, John Hart, *Democracy and Distrust, a Theory of Judicial Review* (Cambridge, Mass., 1980).

———, *On Constitutional Ground* (Princeton, N.J., 1996).

Emerson, Thomas I., *Toward a General Theory of the First Amendment* (New York, 1966).

Emerson, Thomas I., David Haber, and Norman Dorsen (eds.), *Political and Civil Rights in the United States, a Collection of Legal and Related Material* (Boston, 1967).

Epps, Garrett, *To an Unknown God: Religious Freedom on Trial* (New York, 2001).

Epstein, Lee, *Conservatives in Court* (Knoxville, Tenn., 1985).

Epstein, Lee, and Jack Knight, *The Choices Justices Make* (Washington, 1998).

Epstein, Lee, Jeffrey A. Segel, Harold J. Spaeth, and Thomas G. Walker (eds.), *The Supreme Court Compendium: Data, Decisions, and Development* (Washington, 1994), 195.

Esbeck Carl H. (ed.), *The Regulation of Religious Organizations as Recipients of Governmental Assistance* (Washington, 1996).

———, *Religious Beliefs, Human Rights and the Moral Foundations of Western Democracy* (Columbia, Mo., 1986).

Evans, Bette Novit, *Interpreting the Free Exercise of Religion: The Constitution and American Pluralism* (Chapel Hill, N.C., 1997).

Evans, M. Stanton, *The Theme Is Freedom: Religion, Politics, and the American Tradition* (Washington, 1994).

Everett, William J., *God's Federal Republic: Reconstructing Our Governing Symbols* (New York, 1988).

——— *Religion, Federalism, and the Struggle for Public Life* (New York, 1997).

Ewing, Cortez A. M., *The Justices of the Supreme Court, 1789–1937, a Study of Their Qualifications* (Minneapolis, 1938).

Faille, Christopher C., *The Decline and Fall of the Supreme Court: Living Out the Nightmare of the Federalists* (Westport, Conn., 1995).

Fairman, Charles, *American Constitutional Decisions* (New York, 1948).

———, *Mr. Justice Miller and the Supreme Court, 1862–1890* (Cambridge, Mass., 1939).

———, *Reconstruction and Reunion, 1864–88* (New York, 1971), two volumes.

Farber, Daniel A., *Beyond All Reason: The Radical Assault on Truth in American Law* (New York, 1997).

———, *The First Amendment* (New York, 1998).

Farber, Daniel A., and Suzanna Sherry, *A History of the American Constitution* (St. Paul, Minn., 1990).

Faulkner, Robert K., *The Jurisprudence of John Marshall* (Princeton, N.J., 1968).

Feldman, Stephen M., *American Legal Thought from Premodernism to Postmodernism, an Intellectual Voyage* (New York, 2000).

——— (ed.), *Law and Religion, a Critical Anthology* (New York, 2000).

———, *Please Don't Wish Me a Merry Christmas: A Critical History of the Separation of Church and State* (New York, 1997).

Fellman, David, *The Limits of Freedom* (New Brunswick, N.J., 1959).

———, *Religion in American Public Law* (Boston, 1965).

Fenwick, Lynda Beck, *Should the Children Pray?: A Historical, Judicial, and Political Examination of Public School Prayer* (Waco, Tex, 1989).

Ferrara, Peter J. *Religion and the Constitution, a Reappraisal* (Washington, 1983).

Fine, Sidney, *Frank Murphy* (Ann Arbor, Mich., 1975–84), three volumes.

Finke, Roger, *The Churching of America, 1776–1990: Winners and Losers in Our Religious Economy* (New Brunswick, N.J., 1992).

Firmage, Edwin B., *Zion in the Courts, a Legal History of the Church of Jesus Christ of Latter Day Saints, 1830–1900* (Urbana, Ill., 1988).

Fish, Stanley E., *Doing What Comes Naturally* (Durham, N.C., 1989).

——, *There's No Such Thing As Free Speech and It's a Good Thing, Too* (New York, 1990).

——, *The Trouble with Principle* (Cambridge, Mass., 1999).

Fisher, Louis, *Constitutional Dialogue: Interpretation As Political Process* (Princeton, N.J., 1988).

Fisher, Louis, and Neal Evans, *Political Dynamics of Constitutional Law* (St. Paul, Minn., 1996).

Flanders, Henry, *The Lives and Times of the Chief Justices of the Supreme Court* (New York, 1875), two volumes.

Fleming, Donald, and Bernard Bailyn (eds.), *Law in American History* (Boston, 1971).

Flowers, Ronald B., *The Godless Court: Supreme Court Decisions on Church-State Relationships* (Louisville, 1994).

Formicola, Jo Renee, and Hubert Morken (eds.), *Everson Revisited: Education and Law at the Crossroads* (Lanham, Md., 1997).

Forte, David F., *Natural Law and Contemporary Public Policy* (Washington, 1998).

Franck, Matthew J., *Against the Imperial Judiciary: The Supreme Court versus the Sovereignty of the People* (Lawrence, Kans., 1996).

Frank, Jerome, *Fate and Freedom: A Philosophy for Free Americans* (New York, 1945).

Frankel, Marvin, *Faith and Freedom: Religious Liberty in America* (New York, 1994).

Fraser, James W., *Between Church and State: Religion and Public Education in a Multicultural America* (New York, 1999).

Freund, Paul A., and Robert Ulich, *Religion and the Public Schools* (Cambridge, Mass., 1965).

Freyer, Tony (ed.), *Justice Hugo Black and Modern America* (Tuscaloosa, Ala., 1990).

Friedelbaum, Stanley H., *The Rehnquist Court: In Pursuit of Judicial Conservatism* (Westport, Conn., 1994).

Fritz, Henry E., *The Movement for Indian Assimilation, 1860–1890* (Phliladelphia, 1963).

Fuller, Lon L., *The Morality of Law* (New Haven, Conn., 1969).

Funston, Richard, *Constitutional Counter-Revolution?: The Warren Court and the Burger Court—Judicial Policy-Making in Modern America* (Cambridge, Mass., 1977).

———, *Judicial Crises: The Supreme Court in a Changing America* (Cambridge, Mass., 1977).

Furer, Howard B., *The Fuller Court, 1888–1910* (Port Washington, N.Y., 1986).

Gaddy, Barbara R., *School Wars: Resolving Our Conflicts over Religion and Values* (San Francisco, 1996).

Gaffney, Edward McGlynn (ed.), *Private Schools and Public Schools: Policy Alternatives for the Eighties* (Notre Dame, Ind., 1981).

Galston, William A., *Liberal Purposes: Goods, Virtues, and Diversity in the Liberal State* (New York, 1991).

Galub, Arthur, *The Burger Court, 1968–1984* (Millwood, N.Y., 1986).

Gamwell, Franklin I., *The Meaning of Religious Freedom: Modern Politics and the Democratic Revolution* (Albany, N.Y., 1995).

Garvey, Gerald, *Constitutional Bricolage* (Princeton, N.J., 1971).

Gaustad, Edwin S., *Faith of Our Fathers: Religion and the New Nation* (San Francisco, 1987).

———, *Neither King nor Prelate: Religion and the New Nation, 1776–1826* (Grand Rapids, Mich., 1993).

———, *Sworn on the Altar of God, a Religious Biography of Thomas Jefferson* (Grand Rapids, Mich., 1996).

Gedicks, Frederick M., *The Rhetoric of Church and State* (Durham, N.C., 1995).

Gedicks, Frederick M., and Roger Hendrix, *Choosing the Dream: The Future of Religion in American Public Life* (New York, 1991).

Gelfand, Lavinia, *The Freedom of Religion in America* (Minneapolis, 1969).

George Robert M. (ed.), *The Autonomy of Law: Essays on Legal Positivism* (New York, 1996.

———, *The Clash of Orthodoxies: Law, Religion, and Morality in Crisis* (Wilmington, Del., 2001).

———, *In Defense of Natural Law* (New York, 1999).

———, *Making Men Moral: Civil Liberties and Publc Morality* (New York, 1993).

——— (ed.), *Natural Law, Liberalism, and Morality: Contemporary Essays* (New York, 1996).

——— (ed.), *Natural Law Theories: Contemporary Essays* (New York, 1992).

Gerber, Scott D., *First Principles: The Jurisprudence of Clarence Thomas* (New York, 1997).

———, *To Secure These Rights: The Declaration of Independence and Constitutional Interpretation* (New York, 1995).

Gillespie, Michael A., and Michael Lienesch (eds.), *Ratifying the Constitution* (Lawrence, Kans., 1989).

Gilman, Howard, *The Constitution Besieged: The Rise and Demise of the Lochner Era Police Powers Jurisprudence* (Durham, N.C., 1993).

Glendon, Mary Ann, *Rights Talk: The Impoverishment of Political Discourse* (New York, 1991).

Glenn, Charles L., *The Ambiguous Embrace: Government and Faith-Based Schools and Social Agencies* (Princeton, N.J., 2000).

———*The Myth of the Common School* (Amherst, Mass., 1988).

Goldberg, George, *Reconsecrating America* (Grand Rapids, Mich., 1984).

Goldman, Roger L., *Justice William J. Brennan Jr.: Freedom First* (New York, 1994).

———, *Thurgood Marshall, Justice for All* (New York, 1992).

Goldwin, Robert A., *Why Blacks, Women, and Jews Are Not Mentioned in the Constitution, and Other Unorthodox Views* (Washington, 1990).

Goldwin, Robert A., and Art Kaufman (eds.), *How Does the Constitution Protect Religious Freedom?* (Washington, 1987).

Goldwin, Robert A., and William A. Schambra (eds.), *The Constitution and the Quest for Justice* (Washington, 1989).

——— (eds.), *Constitutional Controversies* (Washington, 1987).

——— (eds.), *How Does the Constitution Secure Rights?* (Washington, 1985).

Gordon, Sarah Barringer, *The Mormon Question: Polygamy and Constitutional Conflict in Nineteenth-Century America* (Chapel Hill, N.C., 2002).

Grasso, Kenneth L., Gerard V. Bradley, and Robert P. Hunt (eds.), *Catholicism, Liberalism, and Communitarianism: The Catholic Intellectual Tradition and the Moral Foundations of Democracy* (Lanham, Md., 1995).

Greenawalt, Kent, *Conflict of Law and Morality* (New York, 1987).

———, *Law and Objectivity* (New York, 1992).

———, *Private Conscience and Public Reasons* (New York, 1995).

———, *Religious Convictions and Political Choice* (New York, 1988).

Gregg, Gary L. II (ed.), *Vital Remnants: America's Founding and the Western Tradition* (Wilmington, Del., 1999).

Guelzo, Allen C., *Abraham Lincoln, Redeemer President* (Grand Rapids, Mich., 2000).

Guliuzza, Frank III, *Over the Wall: Protecting Religious Expression in the Public Square* (Albany, N.Y., 2000).

Gunn, T. Jeremy, *A Standard for Repair: The Establishment Clause, Equality, and Natural Rights* (New York, 1992).

Gutmann, Amy, and Denis Thompson, *Democracy and Disagreement* (Cambridge, Mass., 1996).

Haines, Charles G., *The Revival of Natural Law Concepts: A Study of the Establishment and of the Interpretation of the Limits on Legislation, with Special Reference to the Development of Certain Phases of American Constitutional Law* (Buffalo, 1978 [originally 1930]).

———, *The Role of the Supreme Court in American Government and Politics* (Berkeley, Calif., 1944–57), two volumes.

Hall, Kermit L. (ed.), *By and for the People: Constitutional Rights in American History* (Arlington Heights, Ill., 1991).

——— (ed.), *Civil Liberties in American History: Major Historical Interpretations* (New York, 1987).

——— (ed.), *The Judiciary in American Life: Major Historical Interpretations* (New York, 1987).

——— (ed.), *Main Themes in American Constitutional and Legal History: Major Historical Essays* (New York, 1987).

——— (ed.), *The Oxford Guide to United States Supreme Court Decisions* (New York, 1999).

———— (ed.), *The Supreme Court and Judicial Review in ' American History* (Washington, 1985).

Hall, Kermit L., James W. Ely Jr., Joel B. Grossman, and William M. Wiecek (eds.), *The Oxford Companion to the Supreme Court of the United States* (New York, 1992).

Hall, Timothy L., *Separating Church and State: Roger Williams and Religious Liberty* (Urbana, Ill., 1998).

Hamburger, Philip, *Separation of Church and State* (Cambridge, Mass., 2002).

Hamilton, Virginia V. (ed.), *Hugo Black and the Bill of Rights* (University, Ala., 1978).

————, *Hugo Black: The Alabama Years* (Baton Rouge, La., 1972).

Hammond, Philip E., *With Liberty for All: Freedom of Religion in the United States* (Louisville, 1998).

Handy, Robert T., *The Protestant Quest for a Christian America, 1830–1930* (Philadelphia, 1967).

————, *Undermined Establishment: Church-State Relations in America, 1880– 1920* (Princeton, N.J., 1991).

Harper, Fowler V., *Justice Rutledge and the Bright Constellation* (Indianapolis, 1965).

Harris, William F. II, *The Interpretable Constitution* (Baltimore, 1993).

Hatch, Nathan O., *The Democratization of American Christianity* (New Haven, Conn., 1989).

Hellman, George S., *Benjamin N. Cardozo, American Judge* (New York, 1940).

Hendel, Samuel, *Charles Evans Hughes and the Supreme Court* (New York, 1951).

Herberg, Will, *Protestant, Catholic, Jew, an Essay in Religious Sociology* (Garden City, N.Y., 1955).

Hickok, Eugene W. (ed.,), *The Bill of Rights: Original Meaning and Current Understanding* (Charlottesvile, Va., 1991).

Hickok, Eugene W., and Gary L. McDowell, *Justice versus Law: Court and Politics in American Society* (New York, 1993).

Hickok, Eugene W., Gary L. McDowell, and Philip J. Costopoulos (eds.), *Our Peculiar Society: The Constitution and Limited Government* (Lanham, Md., 1993).

Highsaw, Robert B., *Edward Douglass White, Defender of the Conservative Faith* (Baton Rouge, La., 1981).

Hirsch, H. N., *The Enigma of Felix Frankfurter* (New York, 1981).

————, *A Theory of Liberty: The Constitution and Minorities* (New York, 1992).

Hobson, Charles F., *The Great Chief Justice: John Marshall and the Rule of Law* (Lawrence, Kans., 1996).

Hockett, Jeffrey D., *New Deal Justice: The Constitutional Jurisprudence of Hugo Black, Felix Frankurter, and Robert H. Jackson* (Lanham, Md., 1996).

Hoffman, Ronald, and Peter J. Albert (eds.), *The Bill of Rights: Government Proscribed* (Charlottesville, Va., 1997).

Hoffman, Ronald, and Peter J. Albert, *Religion in a Revolutionary Age* (Charlottesville, Va., 1994).

Hook, Sidney, *Religion in a Free Society* (Lincoln, Nebr., 1967).

Hooker, Clifford P. (ed.), *The Courts and Education* (Chicago, 1978).

Horowitz, Donald L., *The Courts and Social Policy* (Washington, 1977).

Horwitz, Morton J., *The Transformation of American Law, 1780–1860* (Cambridge, Mass., 1977).

House, H. Wayne (ed.), *The Christian and American Law* (Grand Rapids, Mich., 1998).

Howard, J. Woodford, *Mr. Justice Murphy, a Political Biography* (Princeton, N.J., 1968).

Howe, Mark Antony DeWolfe, *The Garden and the Wilderness: Religion and the Government in American Constitutional History* (Chicago, 1965).

Huegli, Albert G.(ed.), *Church and State under God* (St. Louis, 1964).

Hunt, Robert P., and Kenneth L. Grasso (eds.), *John Courtney and the American Civil Conversation* (Grand Rapids, Mich., 1992).

Hunter, James Davison, and Os Guiness (eds.), *Articles of Faith, Articles of Peace: The Religious Liberty Clause and the American Public Philosophy* (Washington, 1990).

Hurst, James W., *The Growth of American Law: The Law Makers* (Boston, 1950).

———, *Law and the Conditions of Freedom in the Nineteenth Century United States* (Madison, Wis., 1956).

———, *Law and Social Order in the United States* (Ithaca, N.Y., 1977).

———, *Law and Social Process in United States History* (Ann Arbor, Mich., 1960).

Hutchinson, Dennis J., *The Man Who Once Was Whizzer White* (New York, 1998).

Hutson, James H., *Religion and the Founding of the American Republic* (Washington, 1998).

Hyman, Harold M., and William M. Wiecek, *Equal Justice under Law: Constitutional Development, 1835–1875* (New York, 1982).

Irons, Peter H., *Brennan versus Rehnquist: The Battle for the Constitution* (New York, 1994).

Ivers, Gregg, *Lowering the Wall: Religion and the Supreme Court in the 1980s* (New York, 1991).

———, *Redefining the First Freedom: The Supreme Court and the Consolidation of State Power* (New Brunswick, N.J., 1993).

———, *To Build a Wall: American Jews and the Separation of Church and State* (Charlottesville, Va., 1995).

Jacobsohn, Gary J., *Pragmatism, Statesmanship, and the Supreme Court* (Ithaca, N.Y., 1977).

———, *The Supreme Court and the Decline of Constitutional Aspiration* (Totowa, N.J., 1986).

Jaffa, Harry V., *Original Intent and the Framers of the Constitution: A Disputed Question* (Washington, 1994).

Jayne, Allen, *Jefferson's Declaration of Independence: Origins, Philosophy, and Theology* (Lexington, Ky., 1989).

Jeffries, John C., *Justice Lewis F. Powell Jr.* (New York, 1994).

Jelen, Ted G., *Public Attitudes toward Church and State* (Armonk, N.Y., 1995).

———, *To Serve God and Mammon: Church-State Relations in American Politics* (Boulder, Colo., 2000).

Johnson, F. Ernest (ed.), *American Education and Religion: The Problem of Religion in the Schools* (Port Washington, N.Y., 1969).

Johnson, Herbert A., *The Chief Justiceship of John Marshall, 1801–1835* (Columbia, S.C., 1997).

Johnson, John W., *American Legal Culture, 1908–1940* (Westport, Conn., 1981).

Johnson, Stephen D., and Joseph B. Tamney (eds.), *The Political Role of Religion in the United States* (Boulder, Colo., 1986).

Kahn, Ronald, *The Supreme Court and Constitutional Theory, 1953–1993* (Lawrence, Kans., 1994).

Kairys, David, *With Liberty and Justice: A Critique of the Conservative Supreme Court* (New York, 1993).

Kalman, Laura, *Legal Realism at Yale, 1927–1960* (Chapel Hill, N.C., 1986).

———, *The Strange Career of Legal Realism* (New Haven, Conn., 1996).

Kammen, Michael G. (ed.), *Contested Values: Democray and Diversity in American Culture* (New York, 1995).

———, *A Machine That Would Go of Itself: The Constitution in American Culture* (New York, 1986).

———, *Sovereignty and Liberty: Constitutional Discourse in American Culture* (Madison, Wis., 1989).

———, *Spheres of Liberty: Changing Perceptions of Liberty in American Culture* (Madison, Wis., 1986.

Karfunkel, Thomas, and Thomas W. Ryley, *The Jewish Seat: Anti-Semitism and the Appointment of Jews to the Supreme Court* (Hicksville, N.Y., 1978).

Katz, Wilbur G., *Religion and American Constitutions* (Evanston, Ill., 1964).

Kaufman, Andrew L., *Cardozo* (Cambridge, Mass., 1998).

Kauper, Paul G., *Religion and the Constitution* (Baton Rouge, La., 1964).

———, *Uncivil Liberties and the Constitution* (Ann Arbor, Mich., 1962).

Kelley, Dean M. (ed.), *Government Intervention in Religious Affairs* (New York, 1986).

——— (ed.), *The Uneasy Boundary: Church and State* (Philadelphia, 1979).

———, *Why Churches Should Not Pay Taxes* (New York, 1977).

Kelly, Alfred H., *Foundations of Freedom in the American Constitution* (New York, 1958).

Kelly, Alfred H., and Winfred A. Harbison, *The American Constitution* (New York, 1983).

Kelly, George A., *Politics and Religious Consciousness in America* (New Brunswick, N.J., 1984).

Kendall, Willmoore, *The Basic Symbols of the American Political Tradition* (Baton Rouge, La., 1970).

Kens, Paul, *Justice Stephen Field: Shaping Liberty from the Gold Rush to the Gilded Age* (Lawrence, Kans., 1997).

Ketcham, Ralph L., *Made for Posterity: The Enduring Philosophy of the Constitution* (Lawrence, Kans., 1993).

Keynes, Edward, *The Court v. Congress: Prayer, Busing, and Abortion* (Durham, N.C., 1989).

Keynes, Edward, *Undecided: The Twilight Zone of Constitutional Power* (University Park, Pa., 1982).

King, Willard L., *Melville Weston Fuller, Chief Justice of the United States, 1888–1910* (Chicago, 1967).

Kinzer, Donald L., *An Episode of Anti-Catholicism: The American Protective Association* (Seattle, 1964).

Kirk, Russell, *Rights and Duties, Reflections on Our Conservative Constitution* (Dallas, 1997).

Klinkhamer, Marie C., *Edward Douglass White, Chief Justice of the United States* (Washington, 1943).

Kommers, Donald, and Michael J. Wahoske (eds.), *Freedom and Education: Pierce v. Society of Sisters Reconsidered* (Notre Dame, Ind., 1978).

Konvitz, Milton R., *Expanding Liberties: Freedom's Gains in Postwar America* (New York, 1966).

———, *Fundamental Liberties of a Free People: Religion, Speech, Press, Assembly* (Ithaca, N.Y., 1957).

———, *Religious Liberty and Conscience: A Constitutional Inquiry* (New York, 1968).

Kramnick, Isaac, and R. Lawrence Moore, *The Godless Constitution: The Case against Religious Correctness* (New York, 1996).

Kurland, Philip B., *Church and State: The Supreme Court and the First Amendment* (Chicago, 1975).

———, *Mr. Justice Frankfurter and the Constitution* (Chicago, 1971).

———, *Of Church, State, and the Supreme Court* (Chicago, 1961).

———, *Religion and the Law of Church and State and the Supreme Court* (Chicago, 1962).

La Follette, Marcel C. (ed.), *Creationism, Science, and the Law: The Arkansas Case* (Cambridge, Mass., 1983).

Lacey, Michael J., and Knud Haakonssen (eds.), *A Culture of Rights: The Bill of Rights in Philosophy, Politics, and Law—1791 and 1991* (Washington, 1991).

Lader, Lawrence, *Politics, Power, and the Church: The Catholic Crisis and the Challenge to American Pluralism* (New York, 1987).

Lamb, Charles M., and Stephen C. Halpern (eds.), *The Burger Court: Political and Judicial Profiles* (Urbana, Ill., 1991).

Lamb, Charles M., and Stephen C. Halpern (eds.), *Supreme Court Activism and Restraint* (Lexington, Mass., 1982).

Larson, Edward J. (ed.), *Trial and Error: The American Controversy over Creation and Evolution* (New York, 1985).

Laubach, John H., *School Prayers: Congress, the Courts, and the Public* (Washington, 1969).

Lazarus, Edward, *Closed Chambers: The First Eyewitness Account of the Epic Struggles inside the Supreme Court* (New York, 1998).

Leahy, James E., *The First Amendment, 1791–1991: Two Hundred Years of Freedom* (Jefferson, N.C., 1991).

———, *Freedom Fighters of the United States Supreme Court: Nine Who Championed Individual Liberty* (Jefferson, N.C., 1996).

——, *Liberty, Justice, Equality: How These Constitutional Guarantees Have Been Shaped by the United States Supreme Court* (Jefferson, N .C., 1992).

Lee, Francis Graham (ed.), *All Imaginable Liberty: The Religious Liberty Clauses of the First Amendment* (Lanham, Md., 1995).

—— (ed.), *Neither Conservative Nor Liberal: The Burger Court on Civil Rights and Liberties* (Malabar, Fla.,1983).

Leonard, Charles A., *A Search for a Judicial Philosophy: Mr. Justice Roberts and the Constitutional Revolution of 1937* (Port Washington, N.Y., 1971).

Leuchtenberg, William E., *The Supreme Court Reborn: The Constitutional Revolution in the Age of Roosevelt* (New York, 1995).

Levinson, Stanford, *Constitutional Faith* (Princeton, N.J., 1988).

Levy, Leonard W., *Blasphemy, a Verbal Offense against the Sacred from Moses to Salman Rushdie* (New York, 1993).

——, *Constitutional Opinions: Essays on the Bill of Rights* (New York, 1986).

—— (ed.), *Encyclopedia of the American Constitution* (New York, 1988), four volumes.

—— (ed.), *Essays on the Making of the Constitution* (New York, 1969).

——, *The Establishment Clause: Religion and the First Amendment* (New York, 1986).

——, *Judgments: Essays on American Constitutional History* (Chicago, 1972).

—— (ed.), *Judicial Review and the Supreme Court: Selected Essays* (New York, 1967).

——, *Original Intent and the Framers' Constitution* (New York, 1988).

——, *Origins of the Bill of Rights* (New Haven, Conn., 1999).

——, *Seasoned Judgments: The American Constitution, Rights, and History* (New Brunswick, N.J., 1995).

——, *The Supreme Court under Earl Warren* (New York, 1972).

——, *Treason against God: A History of the Offense of Blasphemy* (New York, 1981).

Levy, Leonard W., and Dennis J. Mahoney (eds.), *The Framing and Ratification of the Constitution* (New York, 1987).

Lewis, Frederick P., *The Context of Judicial Activism: The Endurance of the Warren Court Legacy in a Conservative Age* (Lanham, Md., 1998).

——, *The Nationalization of Liberty* (Lanham, Md., 1990).

Licht, Robert A., *The Framers and Fundamental Rights* (Washington, 1991).

——, *Is the Supreme Court the Guardian of the Constitution?* (Washington, 1993).

—— (ed.), *Old Rights and New* (Washington, 1993).

Licht, Robert A., and Robert A. Goldwin (eds.), *The Spirit of the Constitution: Five Conversations* (Washington, 1990).

Lienesch, Michael, *The New Order of the Ages: Time, the Constitution, and the Making of Modern American Political Thought* (Princeton, N.J., 1988).

Littell, Franklin H., *From State Church to Pluralism: A Protestant Interpretation of Religion in American History* (Garden City, N.Y., 1962).

—— (ed.), *Religious Liberty in the Cross Fire of Creeds* (Philadelphia, 1978).

Long, Carolyn N., *Religious Freedom and Indian Rights: The Case of Oregon v. Smith* (Lawrence, Kans., 2000).

Love, Thomas T., *John Courtney Murray and Contemporary Church-State The-ory* (Garden City, N.Y., 1965).

Lowenthal, David, *No Liberty for License: The Forgotten Logic of the First Amendment* (Dallas, 1997).

Lugo, Luis E. (ed.), *Religion, Public Life, and American Polity* (Knoxville, Tenn., 1994).

Lunt, Richard D., *The High Ministry of Government: The Political Career of Frank Murphy* (Detroit, 1965).

Lusky, Louis, *By What Right?: A Commentary on the Supreme Court's Power to Revise the Constitution* (Charlottesville, Va., 1975).

———, *Our Nine Tribunes: The Supreme Court in Modern America* (Westport, Conn., 1993).

Lutz, Donald S., *The Progress of American Constitutionalism* (Baton Rouge, La., (1988).

Lutz, Donald S., and Jack D. Warren, *A Covenanted People: The Religious Tradi-tion and the Origins of American Constitutional Law* (Providence, R.I., 1987).

Lynn, Barry, *The Right of Religious Liberty: A Basic ACLU Guide to Religious Rights* (Carbondale, Ill., 1995).

Lytle, Clifford M., *The Warren Court and Its Critics* (Tucson, Ariz., 1968).

Macedo, Stephen, *Diversity and Distrust: Civic Education in a Multicultural De-mocracy* (Cambridge, Mass., 2000).

———, *Liberal Virtues: Citizenship, Virtue, and Community in Liberal Constitu-tonalism* (New York, 1990).

———, *The New Right v. the Constitution* (Washington, 1987).

Macedo, Stephen, and Yael Tamir (eds.), *Moral and Political Education* (New York, 2002).

Maddox, Robert L., *Separation of Church and State: Guarantor of Religious Free-dom* (New York, 1987).

Magee, James J., *Justice Black, Absolutist on the Court* (Charlottesville, Va., 1980).

Magrath, C. Peter, *Morrison R. Waite, the Triumph of Character* (New York, 1963).

Maltese, John A., *The Selling of Supreme Court Nominees* (Baltimore, 1995).

Maltz, Earl M., *The Chief Justiceship of Warren Burger, 1969–1986* (Columbia, S.C., 2000).

———, *Civil Rights, the Constitution, and Congress, 1863–1869* (Lawrence, Kans., 1990).

———, *Rethinking Constitutional Law: Originalism, Interventionism, and the Politics of Judicial Review* (Lawrence, Kans., 1994).

Mansfield Harvey C., *America's Constitutional Soul* (Baton Rouge, La., 1991).

Marion, David E., *The Jurisprudence of Justice William J. Brennan Jr.: The Law And Politics of "Libertarian Dignity"* (Lanham, Md., 1997).

Marnell, William H., *The First Amendment: The History of Religious Freedom in the United States* (Garden City, N.Y., 1964).

Marty, Martin E. (ed.), *Civil Religion, Church and State* (Munich, N.Y., 1992).

———, *Modern American Religion* (Chicago, 1986), three volumes.

Marty, Martin E., and Jonathan Moore, *Education, Religion, and the Common Good* (San Franciso, 2000).

Mason, Alpheus T., *Harlan Fiske Stone, Pillar of the Law* (New York, 1956).

——, *The Supreme Court from Taft to Burger* (Baton Rouge, La., 1979).

——, *The Supreme Court from Taft to Warren* (New York, 1964).

——, *The Supreme Court in a Free Sociey* (New York, 1968).

——, *The Supreme Court, Palladium of Freedom* (Ann Arbor, Mich., 1962).

——, *The Supreme Court: Vehicle of Revealed Truth or Power Group?* (Boston, 1953).

——, *William Howard Taft, Chief Justice* (Lanham, Md., 1983).

Matthews, Richard K., *If Men Were Angels: James Madison and the Heartless Empire of Reason* (Lawrence, Kans., 1995).

Maveety, Nancy, *Justice Sandra Day O'Connor, Strategist on the Supreme Court* (Lanham, Md., 1996).

May, Henry F., *The Enlightenment in America* (New York, 1976).

Mayer, Donald N., *The Constitutional Thought of Thomas Jefferson* (Charlottesville, Va., 1994).

McAfee, Ward, *Religion and Reconstruction: The Public School and the Politics of the 1870s* (Albany, N.Y., 1998).

McBrien, Richard P., *Ceasar's Coin: Religion and Politics in America* (New York, 1987).

McCarthy, Rockne, *Society, State, and Schools, a Case for Structural and Confessional Pluralism* (Grand Rapids, Mich., 1981).

McCarthy, Rockne, and James W. Skillen (eds.), *Political Order and the Plural Structure of Society* (Atlanta, 1991).

McCarthy, Rockne, James W. Skillen, and William A. Harper, *Disestablishment a Second Time: Genuine Pluralism for American Schools* (Grand Rapids, Mich., 1982).

McClellan, James, *Joseph Story and the American Constitution, a Study in Political and Legal Thought* (Norman, Okla., 1971).

McCloskey, Robert G., *The American Supreme Court* (Chicago, 1994).

——, *Essays in Constitutional Law* (New York, 1957).

——, *The Modern Supreme Court* (Cambridge, Mass., 1972).

McConnell, Michael, Robert F. Cochran Jr., and Angela C. Carmela (eds.), *Christian Perspectives on Legal Thought* (New Haven, Conn., 2002).

McDevitt, Matthew, *Joseph McKenna, Associate Justice of the United States* (New York, 1974 [originally 1945]).

McDonald, Forrest M., *Novus Ordo Seclorum: The Intellectual Origins of the Constitution* (Lawrence, Kans., 1985).

McDowell, Gary L., *Curbing the Courts: The Constitution and the Limits of Judicial Power* (Baton Rouge, La., 1988).

——, *The Constitution and Contemporary Constitutional Theory* (Cumberland, Va., 1985).

McDowell, Gary L., and Ralph A. Russum (eds.), *The American Founding: Politics, Statesmanship, and the Constitution* (Port Washington, N.Y., 1981).

McDowell, Gary L., and Sharon L. Noble (eds.), *Reason and Republicanism: Thomas Jefferson's Legacy of Liberty* (Lanham, Md., 1997).

McElroy, Robert W., *The Search for an American Public Philosophy: The Contribution of John Courtney Murray* (New York, 1989).

McGarry, Daniel D., *Educational Freedom and the Case of Government Aid to Students in Independent Schools* (Milwaukee, 1966).

———, *Public Schools Teach Religion and Should Not Have a Monopoly: Secularism in American Public Education and the Unconstitutionality of Its Exclusive Governmental Support* (St. Louis, 1986).

McLean, Edward B. (ed.), *Derailing the Constitution: The Lost World of American Federalism* (Bryn Mawr, Pa., 1995).

McLean, Joseph E., *William Rufus Day, Supreme Court Justice from Ohio* (Baltimore, 1946).

McLoughlin, William G., *Cherokees and Missionaries, 1789–1839* (New Haven, Conn., 1984).

McMillen, Richard C.(ed.), *Education, Religion, and the Supreme Court* (Danville, Va., 1979).

———, *Religion in the Public Schools, an Introduction* (Macon, Ga., 1984).

Mead, Sidney E., *The Lively Experiment: The Shaping of Christianity in America* (New York, 1963).

———, *The Nation with the Soul of a Church* (New York, 1975).

———, *The Old Religion in the Brave New World* (Berkeley, Calif., 1977).

Melvin, Edward J., *The Founding Fathers, an Examination of Conscience* (Huntington, Ind., 1976).

———, *A Nation Built on God* (Huntington, Ind., 1975).

Mendelson, Wallace, *The American Constitution and the Judicial Process* (Homewood, Ill., 1980).

———, *The Constitution and the Supreme Court* (New York, 1965).

———, *Justices Black and Frankfurter: Conflict on the Court* (Chicago, 1961).

———, *Supreme Court Statecraft: The Rule of Law and Men* (Ames, Ia., 1985).

Menendez, Albert J., *The December Wars: Religious Symbols and Ceremonies in the Public Square* (Buffalo, 1993).

———, *School Prayer and Other Religious Issues in American Public Education, a Bibliography* (New York, 1980).

Menendez, Albert J., and Edd Doerr, *Religion and Public Education: Common Sense and the Law* (Long Beach, Calif., 1991).

Meyer, David N., *The Constitutional Thought of Thomas Jefferson* (Charlottesville, Va., 1994).

Michaelson, Robert S., *Piety in the Public Schools: Trends and Issues in the Relationship between Religion and the Public School in the United States* (New York, 1970).

Miller, Arthur S., *The Supreme Court and the Living Constitution* (Washington, 1968).

———, *Towards Increased Judicial Activisim: The Political Role of the Supreme Court* (Westport, Conn., 1982).

Miller, Charles A., *The Supreme Court and the Uses of History* (Cambridge, Mass., 1969).

Miller, Perry, *The Legal Mind in America, from Independence to the Civil War* (Ithaca, N.Y., 1962).

Miller, William Lee, *The Business of May Next: James Madison and the Founding* (Charlottesville, Va., 1992).

——, *The First Liberty: Religion and the American Republic* (New York, 1985).

—— (ed.), *Religion and the Free Society* (New York, 1958).

——, *Religion and the Public Good, a Bicentennial Forum* (Macon, Ga., 1988).

Monsma, Stephen V., *Positive Neutrality: Letting Religious Freedom Ring* (Westport, Conn., 1993).

——, *When Sacred and Secular Mix: Religious Non-Profit Organizations and and Public Money* (Lanham, Md., 1998).

Monsma, Stephen V., and J. Christopher Soper (eds.), *Equal Treatment of Religion in a Pluralistic Society* (Grand Rapids, Mich., 1998).

Mooney, Christopher F., *Boundaries Dimly Perceived: Law, Religion, Education and the Common Good* (Notre Dame, Ind., 1990).

——, *Religion and the American Dream: The Search for Freedom under God* (Philadelphia, 1977).

Morel, Lucas E., *Lincoln's Sacred Effort: Defining Religion's Role in American Self-Government* (Lanham, Md., 2002).

Morgan, Donald G., *Justice William Johnson, the First Dissenter: The Career and Constitutional Philosophy of a Jeffersonian Judge* (Columbia, S.C., 1954).

Morgan, Richard E., *The Politics of Religious Conflict: Church and State in America* (Washington, 1980).

——, *The Supreme Court and Religion* (New York, 1972).

Mulder, John M., and John F. Wilson (eds.), *Religion in American Life* (Englewood Cliffs, N.J., 1978).

Muncy, Mitchell S. (ed.), *The End of Democracy?: The Celebrated First Things Debate* (Dallas, 1997).

Muncy, Mitchell S., and J. Budziszewski (eds.), *The End of Democracy?, II: The Crisis of Democracy* (Dallas, 1999).

Murphy, James B., *L.Q.C. Lamar, Pragmatic Patriot* (Baton Rouge, La., 1973).

Murphy, Paul L. (ed.), *The Constitution in Crisis Times, 1918–1969* (New York, 1972).

——, *The Constitution in the Twentieth Century* (Washington, 1986).

——, *Religious Freedom: Separation and Free Exercise* (New York, 1990), two volumes.

——, *The Shaping of the First Amendment, 1791 to the Present* (New York, 1992).

Murphy, Paul L., and James Morton Smith (eds.), *Liberty and Justice* (New York, 1965, 1968), two volumes.

Murphy, Walter F., James E. Fleming, and William F. Harris II, *American Constitutional Interpretation* (Mineola, N.Y., 1986).

Murray, John Courtney, *Bridging the Sacred and the Secular: Selected Writings of John Courtney Murray*, ed. J. Leon Hooper (Washington, 1994).

——, *The Problem of Religious Freedom* (Westminster, Md., 1965).

——, *We Hold These Truths: Catholic Reflections on the American Proposition* (New York, 1960).

Nagel, Robert F., *Constitutional Culture: The Mentality and Consequences of Judicial Review* (Berkeley, Calif., 1989).

Nagel, Robert F., *Judicial Power and American Character: Censoring Ourselves in an Anxious Age* (New York, 1994).

Nelson, William E., *The Fourteenth Amendment: From Political Principle to Judicial Doctrine* (Cambridge, Mass., 1988).

Nelson, William E., and Robert C. Palmer, *Liberty and Community: Constitution and Rights in the Early American Republic* (New York, 1987).

Neuhaus, Richard J., *Christian Faith and Public Policy: Thinking and Acting in the Courage of Uncertainty* (Minneapolis, 1977).

———, *The Naked Public Square: Religion and Democracy in America* (Grand Rapids, Mich., 1984).

Newman, Roger K., *Hugo Black, a Biography* (New York, 1994).

Newmeyer, Robert F., *John Marshall and the Heroic Age of the Supreme Court* (Baton Rouge, La., 2001).

———, *Supreme Court Justice Joseph Story: A Statesman of the Old Republic* (Chapel Hill, N.C., 1985).

———, *The Supreme Court under Marshall and Taney* (Arlington Heights, Ill., 1968).

Nieman, Donald G. (ed.), *The Constitution, Law, and American Life: Critical Aspects of the Nineteenth-Century Experience* (Athens, Ga., 1992).

Noll, Mark A.(ed.), *Religion and American Politics from the Colonial Period to the 1980s* (New York, 1990).

Noonan, John T., *The Believers and the Powers That Are: Cases, History, and Other Data Bearing on the Relation of Religion and Government* (New York, 1987).

———, *Narrowing the Nation's Power: The Supreme Court Sides with the States* (Berkeley, Calif., 2002).

Nord, Warren A., *Religion and American Education: Rethinking a National Dilemma* (Chapel Hill, N.C., 1995).

Norman, Edward R., *The Conscience of the State in North America* (London, 1968).

Norris, Harold (ed.), *Mr. Justice Murphy and the Bill of Rights* (Dobbs Ferry, N.Y., 1965).

North, Arthur A., *The Supreme Court: Judicial Politics and Judicial Process* (New York, 1966).

Novak, Michael, *On Two Wings: Humble Faith and Common Sense at the Time of the American Founding* (San Francisco, 2001).

Novick, Sheldon M., *Honorable Justice: The Life of Oliver Wendell Holmes* (Boston, 1989).

O'Brien, David M., *Constitutional Law and Politics* (New York, 1991).

———, *Storm Center: The Supreme Court in American Politics* (New York, 1986).

O'Brien, Francis W., *Justice Reed and the First Amendment: The Religion Clauses* (Washington, 1958).

O'Brien, J. Stephen, and Richard B. Vacca, *The Supreme Court and the Religious-Education Controversy: Tightrope to Entanglement* (Durham, N.C., 1974).

O'Connor, Henry G., *John Archibald Campbell, Associate Justice of the United States Supreme Court* (New York, 1971).

O'Neill, James M., *Religion and Education in the Constitution* (New York, 1949).

Oaks, Dallin, *Trust Doctrine in Church Controversies* (Macon, Ga., 1984).

—— (ed.), *The Wall between Church and State* (Chicago, 1963).

Owen, J. Judd, *Religion and the Demise of Liberal Rationalism* (Chicago, 2001).

Palm, Daniel C. (ed.), *Faith and Free Government* (Lanham, Md., 1997).

Pangle, Thomas L., *The Spirit of Modern Republicanism: The Moral Vision of the American Founders and the Philosophy of Locke* (Chicago, 1988).

Paper, Lewis J., *Brandeis* (Englewood Cliffs, N.J., 1983).

Parrish, Michael E., *Felix Frankfurter and His Times* (New York, 1982).

Parsons, Wilfred, *The First Freedom: Considerations on Church and State in the United States* (New York, 1948).

Paschal, Joel F., *Justice Sutherland, a Man against the State* (Princeton, N.J., 1951).

Paul, Arnold M., *Conservative Crisis and the Rule of Law: The Attitude of Bar and Bench, 1887–1895* (Ithaca, N.Y., 1960).

Pavlischek, Keith J., *John Courtney Murray and the Dilemma of Religious Toleration* (Kirksville, Mo., 1994).

Pederson, Wlliam D., and Norman W. Provizer (eds.), *Great Justices of the Supreme Court: Ratings and Case Studies* (New York, 1993).

Pennock, Roland, and John W. Chapman (eds.), *Religion, Morality, and the Law* (New York, 1988).

Perry, H. W., *Deciding to Decide: Agenda Setting in the United States Supreme Court* (Cambridge, Mass., 1991).

Perry, Michaal J., *The Constitution in the Courts: Law or Politics?* (New York, 1994).

——, *Morality, Politics, and Law* (New York, 1988).

——, *Religion and Morality in American Politics* (New York, 1991).

——, *Religion in Politics: Constitutional and Moral Perspectives* (New York, 1997).

——, *We the People: The Fourteenth Amendment and the Supreme Court* (New York, 1999).

Peters, Shawn F., *Judging Jehovah's Witnesses: Religious Persecution and the Dawn of the Rights Revolution* (Lawrence, Kans., 2000).

Peterson, Merrill D., *The Virginia Statute for Religious Freedom: Its Evolution and Consequences in American History* (New York, 1988).

Pollack, Jack H., *Earl Warren, the Judge Who Changed America* (Englewood Cliffs, N.J., 1979).

Pollard, Joseph P., *Mr. Justice Cardozo, a Liberal Mind in Action* (Westport, Conn., 1970).

Posner, Richard A., *Overcoming Law* (Cambridge, Mass., 1997).

——, *The Problem of Jurisprudence* (Cambridge, Mass., 1990).

Powe, L. A. Scott, *The Warren Court and American Politics* (Cambridge, Mass., 2000).

Powell, Jefferson, *The Moral Tradition of American Constitutionalism: A Theological Interpretation* (Durham, N.C., 1993).

Powell, Thomas Reed, *Vagaries and Varieties in Constitutional Interpretation* (New York, 1956).

Power, Edward J., *Religion and the Public Schools in Nineteenth-Century America: The Contribution of Orestes A. Brownson* (New York, 1996).

Pratt, Walter F., *The Supreme Court under Edward Douglass White, 1910–1921* (Columbia, S.C., 1999).

Presser, Stephen B., *Recapturing the Constitution: Race, Religion, and Abortion Reconsidered* (Washington, 1994).

Price, Don K., *America's Unwritten Constitution: Science, Religion, and Political Responsibility* (Baton Rouge, La., 1983).

Priest, Loring B., *Uncle Sam's Stepchildren: The Reformation of United States Indian Policy, 1865–1887* (Lincoln, Nebr., 1942).

Pritchett, C. Herman, *The American Constitution* (New York, 1968).

———, *Constitutional Civil Liberties* (Englewood Cliffs, N.J., 1984).

———, *The Roosevelt Court: A Study in Constitutional Politics and Values, 1937–1947* (New York, 1948).

Provenzo, Eugene F. Jr., *Religious Fundamentalism and American Education* (Albany, N.Y., 1990).

Prucha, Francis Paul, *American Indian Policy in Crisis: Christian Reformers and the Indians, 1865–1900* (Norman, Okla., 1976).

———, *American Indian Policy in the Formative Years: The Indian Trade and Intercourse Acts, 1780–1834* (Lincoln, Nebr., 1962).

———, *The Churches and the Indian Schools, 1888–1912* (Lincoln, Nebr., 1979).

Przybyszewski, Linda. *The Republic according to John Marshall Harlan* (Chapel Hill, N.C., 1999).

Purcell, Edward A., *The Crisis of Democratic Theory: Scientific Naturalism and the Problem of Value* (Lexington, Ky., 1973).

Pusey, Merlo J., *Charles Evans Hughes* (New York, 1951), two volumes.

Rahill, Peter J., *The Catholic Indian Missions and Grant's Peace Policy, 1870–1884* (Washington, 1953).

Rakove, Jack (ed.), *Interpreting the Constitution: The Debate over Original Intent* (Boston, 1990).

———, *Original Meanings: Politics and Ideas in the Making of the Constitution* (New York, 1996).

Ravitch, Diane, *The Great School Wars: New York City, 1805–1873, a History of the Public Schools as a Battlefield of Social Change* (New York, 1974).

Ravitch, Frank S., *School Prayer and Discrimination: The Civil Rights of Religious Minorities and Dissenters* (Boston, 1999).

Rawls, John, *Political Liberalism* (New York, 1993).

———, *A Theory of Justice* (Cambridge, Mass., 1971).

Reichley, A. James, *Religion in American Public Life* (Washington, 1985).

Reid, John Philip, *The Concept of Liberty in the Age of the American Revolution* (Chicago, 1988).

———, *The Constitutional History of the American Revolution* (Madison, Wis., 1986–93), four volumes.

Rice, Arnold S., *The Warren Court, 1953–1969* (Millwood, N.Y., 1987).

Rice, Charles E., *Beyond Abortion: The Theory and Practice of the Secular State* (Chicago, 1978).

———, *The Supreme Court and Public Prayers: The Need for Restraint* (New York, 1964).

Richards, David A. J., *American Constitutionalism* (New York, 1989).

———, *Conscience and the Constitution: History, Theory, and Law of the Reconstuction Amendments* (Princton, N.J., 1993).

———, *Foundations of American Constitutionalism* (New York, 1989).

———, *The Moral Criticism of Law* (Encino, Calif., 1977).

———, *Toleration and the Constitution* (New York, 1986).

Richards, Robert D., *Freedom's Voice: The Uncertain Future of the First Amendment* (Washington, 1998).

———, *Uninhibited, Robust, and Wide Open: Mr. Justice Brennan's Legacy to the First Amendment* (Boone, N.C., 1994).

Richey, Russell E., and Donald G. Jones (eds.), *American Civil Religion* (New York, 1974).

Riemer, Neal, *James Madison: Creating the American Constitution* (Washington, 1986).

Robbins, Thomas, and Roland Robertson (eds.), *Church-State Relations: Tensions and Transitions* (New Brunswick, N.J., 1987).

Robbins, Thomas, William C. Shepherd, and James McBride (eds.), *Cults, Culture, and the Law: Perspectives on the New Religious Movements* (Chico, Calif., 1985).

Roberts, Ronald S., *Clarence Thomas and the Tough Love Crowd: Counterfeit Heroes and Unhappy Truths* (New York, 1995).

Rockefeller, Steven C., *John Dewey: Religious Faith and Democratic Humanism* (New York, 1991).

Rorty, Richard, *Consequences of Pragmatism* (Minneapolis, 1982).

———, *Objectivity, Relativism, and Truth* (New York, 1991).

———, *Philosophy and Social Hope* (New York, 1999).

———, *Truth and Progress* (Cambridge, England, 1998).

Rosen, Gary, *American Compact: James Madison and the Problem of Founding* (Lawrence, Kans., 1999).

Rosen, Paul L., *The Supreme Court and Social Science* (Urbana, Ill., 1972).

Rosenburg, Gerald N., *The Hollow Hope: Can Courts Bring about Social Change?* (Chicago, 1991).

Rosenkranz, E. Joshua, and Bernard Schwartz (eds.), *Reason and Passion: Justice Brennan's Enduring Influence* (New York, 1997).

Ross, William G., *Forging New Freedoms: Nativism, Education, and the Constitution, 1917–1927* (Lincoln, Nebr., 1994).

Rowan, Carl T., *Dream Makers, Dream Breakers: The World of Justice Thurgood Marshall* (Boston, 1993).

Rudko, Francis H., *Truman's Court, a Study in Judicial Restaint* (New York, 1988).

Rutland, Robert A., *The American Solution: The Origins of the U.S. Constitution* (Washington, 1987).

———, *The Birth of the Bill of Rights, 1776–1791* (Boston, 1983).

Sadurski, Wojciech (ed.), *Ethical Demensions of Legal Theory* (Atlanta, 1991).

——— (ed.), *Law and Religion* (New York, 1992).

Sadurski, Wojciech (ed.), *Moral Pluralism and Legal Neutrality* (Boston, 1990).

Sanders, Thomas G., *The Protestant Concept of Church and State: Historical Background and Approaches for the Future* (New York, 1964).

Sandoz, Ellis A., *Conceived in Liberty: American Individual Rights Today* (North Scituate, Mass., 1978).

———, *A Government of Law: Political Theory, Religion and the American Founding* (Baton Rouge, La., 1990).

———, *A Government of Laws* (Columbia, Mo., 2001).

Sanford, Charles B., *The Religious Life of Thomas Jefferson* (Charlottesville, Va., 1984).

Sarat, Austin, and Thomas R. Kearns (eds.), *Legal Rights: An Historical and Philosophical Perspective* (Ann Arbor, Mich., 1996).

———, *The Rhetoric of Law* (Ann Arbor, Mich, 1994).

Sarna, Jonathan D., *Religion and the State in the American Jewish Experience* (Notre Dame, Ind., 1997).

Saunders, Robert Jr., *John Archibald Campbell, Southern Moderate* (Tuscaloosa, Ala., 1997).

Savage, David G., *Turning Right: The Rehnquist Supreme Court* (New York, 1992).

Schmidhauser, John R., *Judges and Justices: The Federal Appellate Judiciary* (Boston, 1979).

Schubert, Glendon A., *The Constitutional Polity* (Boston, 1970).

Schultz, Jeffrey D., John G. West Jr., and Ian McLean (eds.), *Encyclopedia of Religion in American Politics* (Phoenix, 1999).

Schwartz, Bernard, *The Ascent of Pragmatism: The Burger Court in Action* (Reading, Mass., 1990).

———, *A Commentary on the Constitution of the United States* (New York, 1963–68), five volumes.

———, *Main Currents in American Legal Thought* (Durham N.C., 1993).

———, *The New Right and the Constitution: Turning Back the Legal Clock* (Boston, 1990).

———, *The Reins of Power, a Constitutional History of the United States* (London, 1963).

——— (ed.), *Roots of the Bill of Rights* (New York, 1980), five volumes.

———, *Super Chief: Earl Warren and His Supreme Court, a Judicial Biography* (New York, 1983).

———, *The Supreme Court: Constitutional Revolution in Retrospect* (New York, 1957).

——— (ed.), *The Warren Court, a Retrospective* (New York, 1996).

Schwartz, Herman (ed.), *The Burger Years: Rights and Wrongs in the Supreme Court, 1969–1986* (New York, 1987).

Segers, Mary C., and Ted G. Jelen, *A Wall of Separation: Debating the Public Role of Religion* (Lanham, Md., 1998).

Seidman, Louis M., *Remnants of Belief: Contemporary Constitutional Issues* (New York, 1996).

Semonche, John E., *Charting the Future: The Supreme Court Responds to a Changing Society, 1890–1920* (Westport, Conn., 1978).

————, *Keeping the Faith, a Cultural History of the U.S. Supreme Court* (Lanham, Md., 1998).

————, *Religion and Constitutional Government in the United States, a Historical Overview with Sources* (Carrboro, N.C., 1985).

Shannon, Christopher, *Conspicuous Criticism: Tradition, Individual, and Culture in American Social Thought* (Baltimore, 1996).

Sheehan, Bernard W., *Seeds of Extinction: Jeffersonian Philanthropy and the American Indian* (Chapel Hill, N.C., 1973).

Sheffer, Martin S., *God Versus Caesar: Belief, Worship, and Proselytization under the First Amendment* (Albany, N.Y., 1999).

Sheldon, Garrett Ward, and Daniel Dreisbach (eds.), *Religion and Political Culture in Jefferson's Virginia* (Lanham, Md., 2000).

Shepherd, William C., *To Secure the Blessings of Liberty: American Constitutional Law and the New Religious Movements* (New York, 1985).

Shevory, Thomas C., *John Marshall's Law: Interpretation, Ideology, and Interest* (Westport, Conn., 1994).

Shiras, George III, *Justice George Shiras Jr. of Pittsburgh, Associate Justice of the Supreme Court, 1892–1903, a Chronicle of His Family, Life, and Times* (Pittsburgh, 1953).

Sickels, Robert J., *John Paul Stevens and the Constitution: The Search for Balance* (University Park, Pa., 1988).

Siegel, Adrienne, *The Marshall Court, 1801–1835* (Millwood, N.Y., 1987).

Sikorski, Robert (ed.), *Prayer in the Public Schools and the Constitution, 1961–1992* (New York, 1993), three volumes.

Silverstein, Mark, *Constitutional Faiths: Felix Frankfurter, Hugo Black, and the Process of Judicial Decision-Making* (Ithaca, N.Y., 1984).

Simon, James F., *The Center Holds: The Power Struggle inside the Rehnquist Court* (New York, 1995).

————, *In His Own Image: The Supreme Court in Richard Nixon's America* (New York, 1973).

————, *Independent Justice: The Life of William O. Douglas* (New York, 1980).

Sizer, Theodore R. (ed.), *Religion and Public Education* (Washington, 1982).

Smidt, Corwin E. (ed.), *In God We Trust?: Religion and American Political Life* (Grand Rapids, Mich., 2001).

Smith, Christopher E., *Crucial Judicial Nominations and Political Change, the Impact of Clarence Thomas* (Westport, Conn., 1993).

————, *Justice Antonin Scalia and the Supreme Court's Conservative Moment* (Westport, Conn., 1993).

Smith, Christopher E., and David A. Schultz, *The Jurisprudential Vision of Justice Antonin Scalia* (Lanham, Md., 1996).

Smith, Elwyn A. (ed.), *The Religion of the Republic* (Philadelphia, 1971).

————, *Religious Liberty in the United States: The Development of Church-State Thought since the Revolutionary Era* (Philadelphia, 1972).

Smith, Jean Edward, *John Marshall, Definer of a Nation* (New York, 1996).

Smith, Rodney R., *School Prayer and the Constitution, a Case Study in Constitutional Interpretation* (Wilmington, Del., 1987).

Smith, Rogers M., *Liberalism and and American Constitutional Law in a Free Society* (Cambridge, Mass., 1990).

Smith, Steven D., *The Constitution and the Pride of Reason* (New York, 1998).

———, *Foreordained Failure: The Quest for a Constitutional Principle of Religious Freedom* (New York, 1995).

———, *Getting over Equality, a Critical Diagnosis of Religious Freedom in America* (New York, 2001).

Sorauf, Frank, *The Wall of Separation: The Constitutional Politics of Church and State* (Minneapolis, 1976).

Spicer, George W., *The Supreme Court and Fundamental Freedoms* (Chicago, 1970).

Stanmeyer, William A., *Clear and Present Danger: Church and State in Post-Christian America* (Ann Arbor, Mich., 1983).

Starr, Kenneth W., *First among Equals: The Supreme Court in American Life* (New York, 2002).

Stebene, David, *Arthur Goldberg, New Deal Liberal* (New York, 1996).

Steiner, Bernard C., *Life of Roger Brooke Taney, Chief Justice of the United States Supreme Court* (Baltimore, 1922).

Stiltner, Brian, *Religion and the Common Good: Catholic Contributions to Building a Liberal Society* (Lanham, Md., 1999).

Stites, Francis N., *John Marshall, Defender of the Constitution* (Boston, 1981).

———, *Private Interest and Public Good: The Dartmouth College Case* (Amherst, Mass., 1972).

Stone, Geoffrey, Richard A. Epstein, and Cass R. Sunstein (eds.), *The Bill of Rights and the Modern State* (Chicago, 1992).

Strong, Frank R. *Substantive Due Process: A Dichotomy of Sense and Nonsense* (Durham, N.C., 1986).

Strout, Cushing, *The New Heavens and the New Earth: Political Religion in America* (New York, 1973).

Sturm, Philippa, *Louis D. Brandeis, Justice for the People* (Cambridge, Mass., 1984).

Sullivan, Winifred F., *Paying the Words Extra: Religious Discourse in the Supreme Court of the United States* (Cambridge, Mass., 1994).

Sunstein, Cass R., *One Case at a Time: Judicial Minimalism on the Supreme Court* (Cambridge, Mass., 1999).

———, *The Partial Constitution* (Cambridge, Mass., 1993).

Swindler, William F., *The Constitution and Chief Justice Marshall* (New York, 1978).

———, *Court and Constitution in the Twentieth Century* (Indianpolis, 1969–74), three volumes.

Swomley, John M. Jr., *Religion, the State, and the Schools* (New York, 1968).

———, *Religious Liberty and the Secular State: The Constitutional Context* (Buffalo, 1987).

Thiemann, Ronald F., *Constructing a Public Theology: The Church in a Pluralistic Culture* (Louisville, 1991).

———, *Religion in Public Life, a Dilemma for Democracy* (Washington, 1996).

Thomas, Andrew Payton, *Clarence Thomas, a Biography* (San Franciso, 2001).

Thomas, Helen S., *Felix Frankfurter, Scholar on the Bench* (Baltimore, 1960).

Thurow, Sarah B., *Constitutionalism in America* (Lanham, Md., 1988), three volumes.

Tise, Larry E. *The American Counter-Revolution: Retreat from Liberty, 1783–1800* (Mechanicsburgh, Pa., 1998).

Torpey, William G., *Judicial Doctrines of Religious Rights in the United States* (New York, 1948).

Tribe, Laurence H., *American Constitutional Law* (Mineola, N.Y., 1978, 1988).

Trimble, Bruce R., *Chief Justice Waite, Defender of the Public Interest* (Princeton, N.J., 1938).

Tushnet, Mark V., *Making Constitutional Law: Thurgood Marshall and the Supreme Court, 1961–1991* (New York, 1997).

——, *Red, White, and Blue: A Critical Analysis of Constitutional Law* (Cambridge Mass., 1988).

——, *Taking the Constitution away from the Courts* (Princeton, N.J., 1999).

—— (ed.), *The Warren Court, an Historical and Political Perspective* (Charlottesville, Va., 1993).

Urofsky, Melvin I., *The Continuity of Change: The Supreme Court and Individual Liberties, 1953–1986* (Belmont, Calif., 1991).

——, *Division and Discord: The Supreme Court under Stone and Vinson, 1941–1953* (Columbia, S.C., 1997).

——, *Felix Frankurter: Judicial Restraint and Individual Liberties* (Boston, 1991).

——, *The Supreme Court Justices, a Biographical Dictionary* (New York, 1994).

Van Ee, Daun, *David Dudley Field and the Reconstruction of the Law* (New York, 1986).

Van Sickel, Robert W., *Not a Particularly Different Voice: The Jurisprudence of Sandra Day O'Connor* (New York, 1998).

Wald, Kenneth D., *Religion and Politics in the United States* (New York, 1987).

Weaver, John D., *Warren: The Man, the Court, the Era* (Boston, 1967).

Weber, Paul J. (ed.), *Equal Separation: Understanding the Religion Clauses of the First Amendment* (New York, 1990).

Weber, Paul J., and Dennis A. Gilbert, *Private Churches and Public Money: Church-Government Relations* (Westport, Conn., 1981).

Wechsler, Herbert, *The Nationalization of Civil Liberties and Civil Rights* (Austin, Tex., 1969).

Weisenberger, Francis P., *The Life of John McLean, a Politician on the United States Supreme Court* (Columbus, Ohio, 1937).

Weithman, Paul J. (ed.), *Religion and Contemporary Liberalism* (Notre Dame, Ind., 1997).

Wellington, Harry H., *Interpreting the Constitution: The Supreme Court and the Process of Adjudication* (New Haven, Conn., 1990).

West, John G., *The Politics of Revelation and Reason: Religion and Civic Life in the New Nation* (Lawrence, Kans., 1996).

West, Robin, *Progressive Constitutionalism: Reconstructing the Fourteenth Amendment* (Durham, N.C., 1994).

White, G. Edward, *The Constitution and the New Deal* (Cambridge, Mass., 2000).

———, *Earl Warren, a Public Life* (New York, 1982).

———, *Intervention and Detachment: Essays in Legal History and Jurisprudence* (New York, 1994).

———, *Justice Oliver Wendell Holmes: Law and Inner Self* (New York, 1993).

———, *The Marshall Court and Cultural Change, 1815–1835* (New York, 1991).

———, *Patterns of American Legal Thought* (Indianapolis, 1978).

White, Ronald C. Jr., and Albright G. Zimmerman (eds.,), *An Unsettled Arena: Religion and the Bill of Rights* (Grand Rapids, Mich., 1990).

Whitehead, John W., *The Separation Illusion: A Lawyer Examines the First Amendment* (Milford, Mich., 1977).

Whitehead, K. D., *Catholic Colleges and Federal Funding* (San Franciso, 1988).

Whittington, Keith E., *Constitutional Construction: Divided Powers and Constitutional Meaning* (Cambridge, Mass., 1999).

———, *Constitutional Interpretation: Textual Meaning, Original Intent, Judicial Review* (Lawrence, Kans., 1999).

Wiecek, William M., *Liberty under Law: The Supreme Court in American Life* (Baltimore, 1988).

———, *The Lost World of Classical Legal Thought: Law and Ideology in America, 1886–1937* (New York, 1998).

Williams, Charlotte, *Hugo L. Black, a Study in Judicial Process* (Baltimore, 1950).

Williams, Juan, *Thurgood Marshall: American Revolutionary* (New York, 1998).

Wills, Garry, *Under God: Religion and American Politics* (New York, 1990).

Wilson, John F., *Public Religion in American Culture* (Philadelphia, 1979).

Wilson, John F., and Donald Drakeman (eds.), *Church and State in American History: The Burden of Religious Pluralism* (Boston, 1987).

Witt, Elder, *A Different Justice: Reagan and the Supreme Court* (Washington, 1986).

———, *The Supreme Court and Individual Rights* (Washington, 1988).

Witte, John Jr., *Religion and the American Constitutional Experiment, an Essay on Essential Rights and Liberties* (Boulder, Colo., 2000).

Witte, John Jr., and Frank S. Alexander (eds.), *The Weightier Matters of the Law: Essays on Law and Religion, a Tribute to Harold J. Berman* (Atlanta, 1988).

Wohlgelernter, Maurice, *History, Religion, and American Democracy* (New Brunswick, N.J., 1993).

Wolf, Donald J., *Toward Consensus: Protestant and Catholic Interpretations of Church and State* (Garden City, N.Y., 1968).

Wolfe, Christopher, *Essays on Faith and Liberal Democracy* (Lanham, Md., 1987).

———, *How to Read the Constitution: Originalism, Constitutional Interpretation, and Judicial Power* (Lanham, Md., 1996).

———, *The Rise of Modern Judicial Review: From Constitutional Interpretation to Judge-Made Law* (New York, 1986).

Wood, James E. (ed.), *Ecumenical Perspectives on Church and State: Protestant, Catholic, and Jewish* (Waco, Tex., 1980).

—— (ed.), *The First Freedom: Religion and the Bill of Rights* (Waco, Tex., 1993).

—— (ed.), *Religion and the State: Essays in Honor of Leo Pfeffer* (Waco, Tex., 1985).

—— (ed.), *Religion, the State, and Education* (Waco, Tex., 1984).

—— (ed.), *The Role of Religion in the Making of Public Policy* (Waco, Tex., 1991).

Wood, James E. , and Derek Davis (eds.), *The Role of Government in Monitoring and Regulating Religion in Public Life* (Waco, Tex., 1993).

Woodward, Bob, and Scott Armstrong, *The Brethren* (New York, 1979).

Wright, Benjamin F., *American Intepretations of Natural Law, a Study in the History of Political Thought* (New York, 1931).

——, *The Growth of American Constitutional Law* (Chicago, 1967).

Wunder John R. (ed.), *Constitutionalism and Native Americans, 1903–1968* (New York, 1996).

—— (ed.), *Native American Cultural and Religious Freedoms* (New York, 1996).

——, *"Retained by the People": A History of American Indians and the Bill of Rights* (New York, 1994).

Wuthnow, Robert, *Christianity and Civil Society: The Contemporary Debate* (Valley Forge, Pa., 1996).

Yarbrough, Tinsley E., *John Marshall Harlan, the Great Dissenter of the Warren Court* (New York, 1992).

——, *Judicial Engima: The First Justice Harlan* (New York, 1995).

——, *Mr. Justice Black and His Critics* (Durham, N.C., 1988).

INDEX OF JUSTICES

INDEX OF JUSTICES

INDEX OF CASES

GENERAL INDEX

NEW FORUM BOOKS

New Forum Books makes available to general readers outstanding original inter-disciplinary scholarship with a special focus on the juncture of culture, law, and politics. New Forum Books is guided by the conviction that law and politics not only reflect culture but help to shape it. Authors include leading political scientists, sociologists, legal scholars, philosophers, theologians, historians, and economists writing for nonspecialist readers and scholars across a range of fields. Looking at questions such as political equality, the concept of rights, the problem of virtue in liberal politics, crime and punishment, population, poverty, economic development, and the international legal and political order, New Forum Books seeks to explain—not explain away—the difficult issues we face today.

Paul Edward Gottfried, *After Liberalism: Mass Democracy in the Managerial State*

Peter Berkowitz, *Virtue and the Making of Modern Liberalism*

John E. Coons and Patrick M. Brennan, *By Nature Equal: The Anatomy of a Western Insight*

David Novak, *Covenantal Rights: A Study in Jewish Political Theory*

Charles L. Glenn, *The Ambiguous Embrace: Government and Faith-Based Schools and Social Agencies*

Peter Bauer, *From Subsistence to Exchange and Other Essays*

Robert P. George, ed., *Great Cases in Constitutional Law*

Amitai Etzioni, *The Monochrome Society*

Daniel N. Robinson, *Praise and Blame: Moral Realism and Its Applications*

Timothy P. Jackson, *The Priority of Love: Christian Charity and Social Justice*

Jeffrey Stout, *Democracy and Tradition*

James Hitchcock, *The Supreme Court and Religion in American Life: Volume 1, The Odyssey of the Religion Clauses; Volume 2, From "Higher Law" to "Sectarian Scruples"*